Building Structures

The one-stop book for knowing everything important about building structures:

- follow the history of structural understanding
- grasp all the concepts of structural behaviour via step by step explanations
- apply the concepts to a simple building
- see how these concepts also apply to real buildings from Durham Cathedral to the Bank of China
- use the concepts to define the design process
- see how the concepts inform design choices
- understand how engineering and architecture have diverged and what effect this has had
- learn to do simple but relevant numerical calculations for actual structures
- enter the world of structural theory to see how modern techniques are applied

With over 400 pages and over 1000 user-friendly diagrams this book is a must for anyone who has to or would like to understand the fascinating world of structures.

Building Structures
From concepts to design

Second Edition

Malcolm Millais

Spon Press
Taylor & Francis Group

LONDON AND NEW YORK

First published 1997 by Spon Press

Reprinted 1997, 1999

Second edition published 2005
by Spon Press
2 Park Square, Milton Park, Abingdon, Oxon OX14 4RN

Simultaneously published in the USA and Canada
by Spon Press
270 Madison Ave, New York NY 10016

Transferred to Digital Printing 2006

Spon Press is an imprint of the Taylor & Francis Group, an informa business

© 1997 and 2005 Malcolm Millais

Typeset in Garamond and Arial by
Malcolm Millais
Printed and bound in Great Britain by
TJI Digital, Padstow, Cornwall

British Library Cataloguing in Publication Data
A catalogue record for this book is available from the British Library

Library of Congress Cataloging in Publication Data
Millais, Malcolm.
    Building Structures: from concepts to design/
    Malcolm Millais. – 2nd ed.
        p. cm.
    Includes bibliographical references and index.
    1. Buildings.   2. Structural design.   3. Structural analysis
(Engineering).   I. Title.
    TH845.M63 2004
    690–dc22   2004016690

ISBN 10: 0-415-33622-8 (cased)
ISBN 10: 0-415-33623-6 (limp)
ISBN 10: 0-203-42143-4 (ebook)

ISBN 13: 978-0-415-33622-2 (cased)
ISBN 13: 978-0-415-33623-9 (limp)
ISBN 13: 978-0-203-42143-7 (ebook)

This book is printed on paper from renewable sources

Contents

Preface to the Second Edition

It was only during the 19th century that the idea arose that the structure of a building could be seen as separate from the concept of the building itself. Nowadays the division between the architectural design of a building and the structural design is almost complete and this has led to numerous problems both large and small. This second edition aims, in various ways, to narrow this division with a consequent reduction in problems. Ideally everyone involved in the commissioning, design, construction, alteration and maintenance of buildings should have a mature understanding of the structural aspects; unfortunately this is not the current situation. The key to this is the conceptual understanding of structural behaviour and this remains the basic core of the book.

To enable readers to gain a wider understanding, new material has been added to the front of the book and at the back. At the front the **Introduction** has been altered and expanded to give a very brief history of the development of structural understanding. The new **Chapter 11**, **Structures and built form**, shows, with reference to numerous examples, how building form can be influenced by the choice of a structural system. It also deals with the effect of the difference between the technically based engineering perception of structures and the aesthetically based architectural one. The new **Chapter 12**, **A simple approach to calculations**, allows the reader to enter the technical world of engineering and shows how, using no more than simple arithmetic operations, understanding the concepts permits simple numerical calculations to be made. The penultimate section of this chapter give examples of how relevant calculations can easily be done for parts of some of the projects described earlier. The final **Chapter 13**, **The mathematical basis**, introduces the reader to the mathematical world of structures. This requires the rudiments of the differential calculus which are explained in detail. Then, using the concepts and the calculus, the mathematical formulation for columns, beams and frames is developed.

References have been added as required and appear at the end of each chapter. The reading list is shorter and annotated and an index has been added.

For their helpful comments and checking of parts of the new edition it is a pleasure to thank the following people; Bill Addis, Michael Barclay, Brian Bell, Prof. John Burland, Prof. Jacques Heyman, Sandra Leitão, Andrew MacKeith, Vera d'Almeida Ribeiro, Frank Simpson, Lucinda Smith, Stuart Smith, Prof. Derek Sugden, Tim Uden and Nick Weaver. The help given by the staff of the library of the Institution of Civil Engineers in London has been invaluable.

Caroline Mallinder, Helen Ibbotson, Michelle Green and Lucille Murby at Taylor & Francis Group have been continuously supportive.

The book design and the diagrams were done by the author.

Malcolm Millais 2005

Introduction

People are surrounded by natural and designed structures. They live in them, travel in them, eat with them, sleep on them, they contribute to almost every aspect of our lives. Indeed, humans, animals and plants are themselves structures. But few people give much thought to structures until they fail. Forks bend, glasses break, cars are wrecked in crashes, less often buildings and bridges collapse. These structural failures always cause inconvenience that may be minor, such as a broken glass, or major, involving loss of life and large financial cost such as the collapse of a bridge.

The horror of the attack on the World Trade Center towers on 11th September 2001 was not only the initial deliberate collision of large, fuel laden, passenger aircraft with the buildings but the subsequent dramatic collapse of both these enormous towers. These collapses, seen globally on television, caused not only great loss of life and enormous disruption to a major city but had a dramatic effect on the world political situation. The original designers had taken into account the possibility of an aircraft collision but not ones of the magnitude that actually occurred. So clearly it is important to know if structures are: **strong enough** and **stiff enough**.

For the designers of any structure, whether a fork or a bridge, there has to exist sufficient knowledge for them to feel confident that the proposed structure will be both strong enough and stiff enough under all reasonably foreseeable uses. There are also ancillary, but important requirements, such as whether the proposed structure is affordable or sufficiently durable.

These requirements seem perfectly reasonable but to satisfy them is not always so simple. Through the ages people have adopted various strategies to try and ensure that the structures they use are as safe as possible.

0.1   Pre-historic design

In pre-historical time people lived in small, more or less, self-contained groups. These groups would live as hunter-gatherers or perhaps herd animals. They would construct artefacts and shelters using natural materials and their designs, which would be typical for each group – see **Figs. 0.1** and **0.2** – were repeated endlessly. How these designs evolved is not known, nor how they were modified.

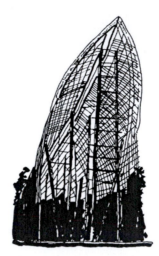

Fig. 0.1 Clubhouse structure in New Guinea

The origin of these designs is not known but they were built repetitively without any recorded form of instructions. Older members of the group would hand down their experience and often the construction process would be a group activity.

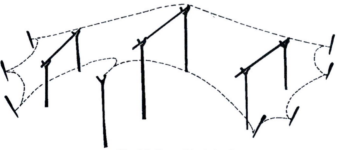

Fig. 0.2 Nomad tent structure

As the way of life of these groups was only changed temporarily by alterations in nature – such as droughts or storms – there was no need to make design changes, or to know how to make their structures stronger or stiffer.

0.2   Traditional design

With the discovery of agriculture in South West Asia in about 8000 BC the hunter-gatherers and nomads were gradually marginalised. The idea of cultivation meant that groups became geographically fixed; agricultural surpluses were produced needing storage and defence against other groups. The cultivators, due to the power they obtained from their productivity, became the dominant culture.

Fig. 0.3 Small granary in West Africa

This need for more permanent structures led to advances in building technology using mud, mud-dried bricks, and selected timber. But once cultivation became the way of life there was little further change for a long period. This meant that forms of building and the associated structures became fixed and thus traditional in each different area.

Fig. 0.4 Greek village

Traditional building was carried out by specially trained people who became craftsmen. With the rise of cities and powerful elites, new and different forms of building and structures were required. But as these new city buildings also developed over a long period, the result was again what became traditional building methods.

In terms of structures these traditional buildings could be of impressive dimensions – the seven-storey buildings in the Yemen or English barns for example. These buildings and structures were built by men without scientific knowledge or even the ability to read and write, yet they were practical, basing their work on experience. They left no evidence of what thought processes went into their designs and only (some of) the buildings remain. However as Bernard Rudofsky[1] has noted *"The beauty of this architecture has been dismissed as accidental but we should be able to recognise it is the result of rare good sense in the handling of practical problems"*.

Fig. 0.5 Post and truss building circa 1400 AD

As these agrarian societies expanded and became richer, some villages grew into bigger centres that became towns and then cities.[2] The cities grew out of the Neolithic villages and by 3500 BC sizeable cities existed in Mesopotamia, the Indus valley and on the Yellow and Nile rivers.

0.3   The effect of civilisation

Cities were a manifestation of **civilisations**, which is an evolving rather than static culture, and included new specialised groups such as ruling and religious elites and specially trained warriors as well as new forms of administrations and the levying of taxes. These developments meant that new types of buildings were required: temples, storehouses, castles and so on. Many of these buildings are well known such as the pyramids in Egypt, the Parthenon in Greece and the Coliseum in Rome amongst many others.

As the traditional methods no longer applied, new technology and design processes were required. What these design processes were is not known with any certainty, but there is no evidence that any sort of theory about the behaviour of structures was used before 1742.[3] As stone structures were almost always used for these monumental constructions, the predominant load was the weight of the structure itself. As the construction often took years, warning of impending structural failure would be given by the cracking and spalling of the work in progress allowing repairs to be made as part of the building process. However, structural failures did occur and some evidence still exists.

For example Snefru (reign 2613-2589 BC) was the first king of Egypt of the 4th dynasty. He began building a pyramid at Dashaur with a slope of 56°. As building progressed structural faults became apparent so the slope was changed abruptly to 43°, to allow the pyramid to be completed. He subsequently constructed a second pyramid, the Red pyramid, which had a slope of 43°. Both these pyramids still stand. The later and better-known pyramids at Giza have similar slopes to the Red pyramid.

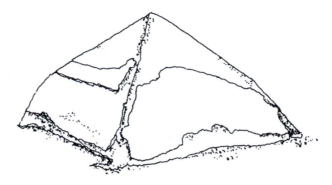

Fig. 0.6 'Bent' pyramid at Dashaur

Nearly four thousand years later a great church building programme took place in Northern Europe, the result of which included the Gothic cathedrals. Again it is hard to know exactly what structural design process was used, but the masons had to be experts in geometry to ensure that the whole masonry structure fitted together, especially the complex vaulting systems – *"it would perhaps be somewhat exaggerated to speak of the rationalism of medieval architects for this supposes an organisation of knowledge that was certainly lacking"*.[4] As the masons tried to glorify God with higher structures with bigger windows, problems with the slenderness of the masonry began to appear. The limit was passed with the cathedral of Saint-Pierre at Beauvais in Northern France. It was conceived as the largest and tallest cathedral to be built, but various parts collapsed during construction. The cathedral was never completed; only the choir and transept remain standing. Close inspection of the surviving structure reveals numerous cracks and repairs.

Fig. 0.7 Saint-Pierre at Beauvais

Many other famous large-scale buildings have suffered structural problems such as the St. Sophia in Istanbul, St. Peter's Basilica in Rome and St. Paul's cathedral in London. The fact that there were structural problems with many of these large buildings should not automatically lead to criticism of the designers who produced amazing structures that have basically stood the test of time.

0.4   The search for structural understanding

The generally accepted view nowadays is that the behaviour of physical phenomena can be explained by a rational scientific approach. This view is relatively recent, in the past magical explanations were used. However, magical explanations do not provide predictive information and this is what structural designers need.

The idea of logic and rational explanations began with the Greek philosophers Plato (428-348 BC) and Aristotle (384-322 BC) but it was another Greek, Archimedes (290/80-212/11 BC), who is considered the founder of theoretical mechanics. One of his nine treatises is called 'On the equilibrium of planes' which deals with centres of gravity (see **Section 3.2**) and the 'law of the lever' (see **Section 1.5**), though it is not totally clear whether this was his own work or copied from earlier unknown authors.

Fig. 0.8 Archimedes

No further attempts to understand theoretical mechanics are known to have been made until the work of the mysterious Jordanus Nemorarius. This was the name given in the Renaissance to the author of a 12th or 13th century mathematical manuscript. The equilibrium of a lever and the action of a weight on an inclined plane are discussed in this work. It is not surprising that Leonardo da Vinci (1452-1519) also tried to contribute to the understanding of structures.

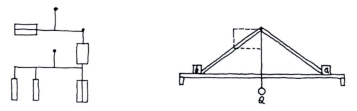

Fig. 0.9 Diagrams by Jordanus (Left) and Leonardo (Right)

The popular view of Leonardo da Vinci is that he was an artistic genius, which he was, and the inventor of everything, but his ambition was to be a recognised engineer and architect,[5] and it was by engineering that he earned his living. As an engineer and inventor he was no better than other contemporary engineers – Francesco di Giorgio for example [6] – and almost all of the technical drawings in his notebooks were copied from other sources.[7] However, Leonardo da Vinci was different in one aspect; in the late 1480s[8] he began to realise that there could be a physical understanding of the materials he used and this would inform and improve his engineering work. He made a number of tests on structures[9] and tried to draw conclusions from them. However, it is unclear whether these tests provided him with any useful quantitive information. His work was unpublished; his observations being recorded in his numerous notebooks, so other engineers were unable to profit from or to extend his work.

More than 100 years passed before further advances are recorded. Then two remarkable men Simon Stevin (1548-1620) and his better known contemporary Galileo Galilei (1564-1642) both investigated, amongst many other things, aspects of structural behaviour.

Fig. 0.10 Stevin (left) and Galileo (right)

Stevin correctly stated the triangle of forces (see **Chapter 12**) and Galileo tried to discover what happened inside a beam.

Fig. 0.11 Galileo's bending test

Although the findings of both Stevin and Galileo were published, they remained in the realm of research and were unused by the structural designers of the time.

The idea of elasticity, or springiness, of engineering materials, essential to the understanding of structural behaviour (see **Chapter 5**), was stated independently by Robert Hooke (1635-1703) and Edme Mariotte (1620-1684). Hooke came to the idea in 1660 but only published it in 1678 as *Ut tensio sic vis* (as the pull so the stretch), having previously published it, in 1676, in the form of an indecipherable anagram as *ceiiinosssttuv!* This is now known to all engineers as Hooke's Law. Mariotte, who published the result in 1680, also attempted to discover what happened inside a loaded beam though he did not arrive at the correct understanding. This had to wait for another sixty to a hundred years.

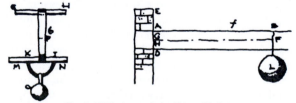

Fig. 0.12 Tests made by Edme Mariotte

The correct mathematical description of a beam needed the **differential calculus,** the most important tool in the mathematical theory of engineering. This was developed simultaneously and independently by Isaac Newton (1643-1727) and the German mathematician Gottfried Wilhelm Leibniz (1646-1716), however neither of them applied it to the theory of structures.

Fig. 0.13 Leibniz (left) and Newton (right)

The clarification of the mathematical theory of the beam was made by the brilliant Swiss mathematician Leonard Euler (1707-1783) whose principal interest was the behaviour of 'elastic curves'.[10]

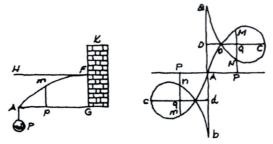

Fig. 0.14 Euler's elastic curves

The curves investigated by Euler were of little immediate use to the engineer as they took the forms shown in the diagram, though his work proved invaluable in the long run. A clearer explanation of beam behaviour was made by the French mathematician, physicist and military engineer Charles Augustin de Coulomb (1736-1806). In 1764 he was sent to Martinique, in the West Indies, where he spent nine years fortifying the island. During this time he also made numerous experiments and theoretical discoveries all of which were included in his famous paper written in 1776.[11] The conceptual explanations, given in **Section 3.4**, for the behaviour of a beam are due to his description.

So finally, towards the end of the 18th century, there existed a mathematical theory that described, and could be used to predict, the engineering behaviour of a simple beam. The understanding of shear stresses, see **Section 3.5**, came later, in 1858, with the clarification by WJM Rankine (1820-1872),[12] (the explanation of shear stresses in built-up sections (see **Section 4.3**, I beams for example) had to wait for the 1950s[13]). This had exercised some of the most brilliant minds over several centuries. Of course this lack of a predictive theory did not prevent thousands, probably millions, of beams being used in buildings all over the world. These were sized by experience, some local rule of thumb or perhaps just what came to hand, and probably most served their purpose. In 1826 the lecture notes of the mathematician and engineer CLM Navier (1785-1836) were published.[14] These were a summary of known structural theory together with original material. In these notes Navier formulated a general mathematical theory of elasticity which was the foundation of the modern approach.

0.5 The modern approach to structural design

The modern approach to the design of structures is to check any proposed design by making numerical calculations. These calculations are based on a mathematical theory that describes the physical behaviour of the system. Using known values such as the dimensions, the loads and the properties of the material to be used, a specific calculation can be made. The numerical result of this calculation indicates whether the proposed design will perform satisfactorily or not.

The **idea that numerical calculations** for a structure **could be made** is considered by several authors[15, 16] to have originated from the request, by pope Benedict XIV in 1742, from three mathematicians for a report on the reasons for the cracking of the dome of St. Peter's Basilica in Rome. According to H Straub [17] it *"must be considered as epoch-making in the history of civil engineering"*.

The **idea of training engineers** began in France with the founding, in 1671, of the Académie Royale d'Architecture that taught as much engineering as architecture. In 1672 the Corps du Génie (the French army engineering corps) was formed and in 1716 the Corps des Ponts et Chaussées. There were no textbooks so the professor of mathematics, B de Belidor (1693-1761), wrote several including the first one on engineering.[18] In 1747 the École des Ponts et Chaussées, the first ever engineering school, was founded to train military engineers. The first technical school in Britain was the Royal Military Academy, founded in 1741 at Woolwich. John Muller (1699-1784), the first director, wrote a textbook based on the work of Belidor.

As well as these events, the rapid acceleration of industrialisation, with the discovery of cheap ways to produce iron (see **Section 5.2**) and the introduction of steam power, first to factories and then to railways, required new types of structures to carry previously unimagined loads. Now, unlike massive stone structures, the new iron structures were light in comparison to the loads they had to carry and there was no time, or money, to see whether a new railway bridge would collapse when the train arrived.

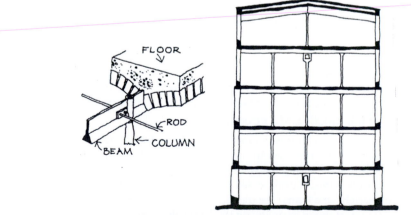

Fig. 0.15 Bage's mill 1796 detail and section

The 19th century was the century in which the modern approach emerged because a correct theory of structural behaviour had finally been discovered and there was a practical need to have predictive methods of calculating structures. Numerous mathematicians, physicists and engineers developed structural theory throughout the century;[19] however, actually applying the theory to specific projects was more difficult. Many tests were made to obtain correlations between theoretical predictions and actual behaviour[20] but during the century, especially the latter half, confidence in theoretically based numerical calculations increased until it became the way to check the adequacy of a particular structure.

Famous engineers of the 19th century, such as Robert Stephenson (1803-1859) and Isambard Brunel (1806-1859)[21] in Britain and Gustave Eiffel (1832-1923) in France calculated their structures. Without modern calculating aids these calculations had to be carried out by hand. To this end many handbooks were produced providing standard formulae for common structures, plus tables of allowable loads on elements such as beams, columns and slabs.

Fig. 0.16 Royal Albert Bridge, Saltash 1859 by IK Brunel

Today detailed hand calculations have largely been superseded by calculations made by computer programs; however, conceptual hand calculations should still form the basis of conceptual choices. How this can be done is explained in **Chapter 12**. But first the behaviour of structures **must be understood conceptually**.

0.6 The conceptual understanding of structural behaviour

The conceptual understanding of how structures behave when loaded can be achieved **without the need for any mathematics**. The conceptual understanding is gained by finding the answers to a series of questions about the structural behaviour.

● **What is the function of a structure?**

The most common answer to this question would be to **carry loads**. Whilst there is truth in this it needs to be extended to the concept of carrying loads from one place to another, which is **transferring loads**. A simple example illustrates this. If people want to cross a stream then a plank could be used as a bridge. Whilst people are on the bridge their weight (**the loads**) are transferred from a point over the water, which cannot directly support them, to points on the banks that can.

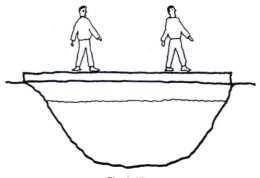

Fig. 0.17

The purpose of the plank is to **transfer** the point of load application to the point of load support. The plank does this by acting as a **structure**. This load transferring function is the main purpose of all structures, whether it is a chair or the Forth railway bridge.

- **What are the loads and the load paths?** – see **Chapter 1**

The source of loads on buildings is a combination of **natural loads,** that is those caused by nature – snow, wind, gravity, etc. – and those caused by the specific use of the building, which are **useful loads**. In the case of the simple plank bridge, the natural load is the bridge's own weight and the useful load is the weight of the people on the bridge.

Each load on a building structure is eventually supported by the foundations of the building, which is where the building joins the 'rest of the world'. In the case of the plank bridge the 'rest of the world' is the banks of the river. The sequence of structural elements that join a specific load to the foundations is called the **load path**. The load path may be different for different loads. For example the load from the weight of people standing on the first floor of a five storey building will not be exactly the same as for those standing on the fourth floor.

- **How does the structure transfer loads?** – see **Chapters 1, 2 & 7**

The structure transfers loads by **forces that exist within each element** in the load path and by **forces between the elements** where they meet.

- **What are these forces in the structural elements?** – see **Chapters 2, 3, 4, 5 & 7**

There is more than one way of regarding the forces in structural elements; however, in the majority of cases, the force in an element can be considered to be a combination of a force **along** the element, a force **across** the element, a force **bending** the element and, sometimes, a force **twisting** the element.

The idea of conceptual analysis is to identify which of these forces are acting on any particular element of any structure for any load. The modern approach finds numerical values for these forces and from known data checks if each element can support these forces and so verify that a proposed structure is satisfactory.

- **Does the structure have overall stability?** – see **Chapter 6**

When people amuse themselves by building towers of children's bricks or playing cards they build the tower higher and higher until it collapses – 'like a pack of cards'. This loss of overall stability can occur in a number of ways in building structures and clearly they must be avoided.

- **Is any element too slender?** — see **Chapter 6**

If a column is short and fat, increasing the load on it will eventually cause it to 'squash', but if the column is long and thin it will 'buckle' at a load lower than the 'squash' load. For a structure to be satisfactory, slender elements must be identified in any load path to ensure that they will not buckle in some way.

References – Introduction

1   B Rudofsky – **Architecture without architects** – Academy Editions 1964, p4 of the Preface

2   L Mumford – **The city in history** – Penguin 1966

3   RW Mainstone – **Structural theory and design before 1742** – Architectural Review April 1968, – p 303-310

4   **Vol.1 – A history of technology & invention** – Crown Publishers 1969 – ISBN 0-517-507277, p 536

5   M White – **Leonardo the first scientist** – Little Brown & Company 2000 – ISBN 0-349-11274-6, p 111

6   P Galluzzi – **The career of a technologist IN Leonardo Vinci: Engineer & Architect** – Montreal Museum of Fine Arts 1987 – ISBN 2-89192-084-8, p 41-43

7   B Gille – **The renaissance engineers** – Lund Humphries 1966 – ISBN 0-262-05024-5

8   Ref.6 – p 72-76

9   SP Timoshenko – **History of strength of materials** – Dover 1983 – ISBN 0-486-61187-6, p 31-36

10   ibid. – p 31-36

11   A de Coulomb – **Essai sur une application des règles de maximis & minimis etc** – Mémoires de Mathématique et de Physique, l'Académie Royale des Sciences par divers Savants – 7, 343-382 – 1776

12   WJM Rankine – **Applied mechanics** – Griffin 1858

13   J Heyman – **Structural analysis; a historical approach** – Cambridge University Press 1998 – ISBN 0-521-62249-2, p 48-49

14   CLM Navier – **Lectures of the application of mechanics** – Paris 1826

15   RJ Mainstone – **Development of structural form** – Penguin 1975 – ISBN 0 14 00 65032 E, p 283

16   H Straub – **History of Civil Engineering** – Leonard Hill Ltd 1952, p 111-116

17   ibid. – p 116

18   BF de Belidor – **The science of engineering** – Paris 1729

19   TM Charlton – **A history of theory of structures in the nineteenth century** – CUP1982 – ISBN 0-521-23419-0

20   D Smith – **Structural model testing and the design of British railway bridges in the 19th century** – Transactions of the Newcomen Society 48 – p 73-90

21   D Beckett – **Brunel's Britain** – David & Charles 1980 – ISBN 0-7153-7973-9, p 99

CHAPTER 1 *Loads and load paths*

A structure's main function is to **transfer loads**, but before considering the form of a structure, a clear idea of what loads it has to transfer is required: in other words an answer to the question '**what are the loads?**'

The sources of loads can be divided into **natural**, **useful** and **accidental** loads. Natural loads occur due to the existence of the structure in the world; useful loads are ones that occur from the purpose of the structure; and accidental loads occur from the misuse of the structure.

1.1   Natural loads

All structures on the surface of the Earth have to resist the force of **gravity**. This force acts through a body in a line joining the body with the centre of the Earth. However, at the local level these forces can be considered vertical.

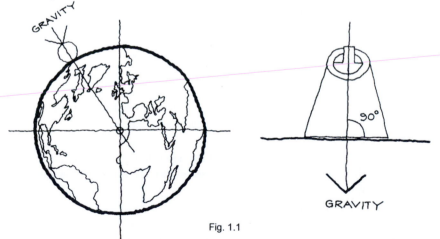

Fig. 1.1

So the first source of **natural** loads is the **gravity load**. For the example of the plank across the stream – see **Fig. 0.17** – this means that the plank has to transfer its own weight, usually called **self-weight**, to the support points.

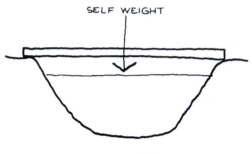

Fig. 1.2

Due to regular and continuous changes in atmospheric pressure from place to place on the Earth's surface air flows across the surface of the Earth, that is, wind. All structures built on the Earth's surface have to resist forces from wind. Near to ground level the wind can be considered to blow along the surface: this is not true for the whole of the atmosphere, as any pilot knows.

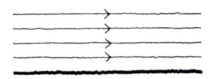

Fig. 1.3

If an obstruction is placed in the path of the wind it alters the pattern of the wind flow. This is why kites and planes fly and boats sail. If the object is fixed to the Earth's surface, like a building, the wind must flow around and over it.

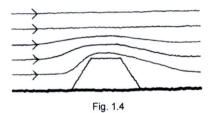

Fig. 1.4

How the wind flows around and over an object depends both on the wind speed and the shape of the object. These are the basic questions considered by the complex subject known as **aerodynamics**. But the alteration in wind flow pattern will always cause a **force** on the interrupting object.

It is an intellectual feat to see the alteration of the wind flow pattern around and over a building as a force or **wind load**. But this view allows the action of the wind on a building to be clear.

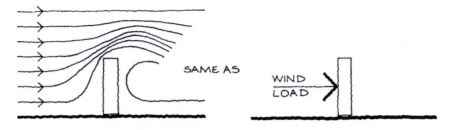

Fig. 1.5

This effect can readily be felt by holding a flat object in the flow of a stream. This is why canoes and people can propel themselves through water.

Although the pattern of wind flow around buildings is complex (very!) the resulting loads from the alteration of wind flow are predominately at right angles to the surfaces of the building.

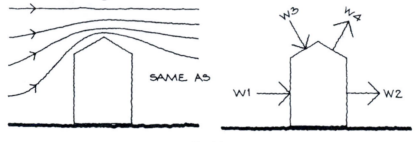

Fig. 1.6

So, for the pitched roofed building shown in **Fig. 1.6**, the alteration in wind flow will cause four loads. The loads **W1** and **W2** are on, and at right angles to the walls, and the loads **W3** and **W4** are on, and at right angles to the roof slopes. These are **wind loads**.

As far as buildings and their supporting structures are concerned, **gravity** and **wind** loads are two types of **natural** loads they always have to resist.

There are other natural loads that the structure may have to resist. These are **earth** or **water pressure, earthquakes, temperature**, and **ground movement**.

If the local shape of the Earth's surface is altered to site the building, as it often is, then parts of the building and its structure may be subject to loads from **earth pressure**. This is because the natural surface has found a shape that is at rest (not over geological time of course). So, rather like the wind flow, an alteration will cause forces. If dry sand is piled into a heap, there is a maximum slope for the sides.

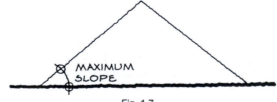

MAXIMUM
SLOPE

Fig. 1.7

What is happening inside the heap is complex, and is further complicated by the addition of water (which is why sand castles can be made). If, however, a heap with a vertical side is required, forces are needed to keep the heap in the **unnatural** shape.

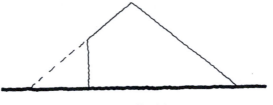

Fig. 1.8

This is usually done by building a (retaining) wall. Because the heap wants to return to a natural shape, shown by the dotted line in **Fig. 1.8**, the wall must hold back all the sand above the dotted line in **Fig. 1.9**.

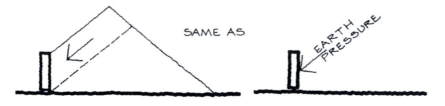

Fig. 1.9

This causes loads on the wall. In buildings, this occurs when the building has a basement, or is built into a sloping site.

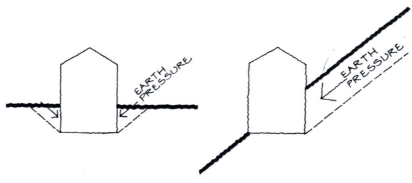

Fig. 1.10

In these cases the structure has to resist **natural** loads from **earth pressure**.

Under the surface of the Earth, depending on the local geology and climate, there will be, at some level, water. The top level of this water is called the **water table**. This level may be at the surface in swamps, bogs and beaches, or many metres down in deserts. If the siting of the building interrupts the natural water table, an **unnatural water table** is created around and under the building.

GROUND LEVEL

WATER TABLE

UNNATURAL
WATER TABLE

Fig. 1.11

Not only are the walls loaded by the water pressure but it also causes **upward** loads on the floor. The building is trying to **float**.

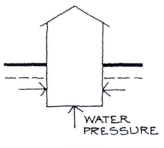

WATER
PRESSURE

Fig. 1.12

The structure has to resist natural loads due to **water pressure**.

The general shape of the surface of the Earth is the same over the life-span of most buildings, but may alter slightly due to climatic or geological changes. As the building is attached to the surface of the Earth, local changes will force a change in the shape of the structure, as the building is hardly likely to prevent the Earth changing shape! In particular, load may be caused if the local shape changes differentially. It is **not obvious** how this causes a load on the structure, if indeed it does. For example, suppose the plank bridge has a support in the stream.

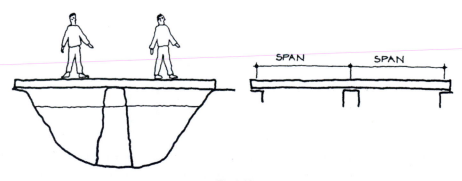

SPAN   SPAN

Fig. 1.13

If this central support were to sink into the stream bed, depending on the fixing, it may pull the plank down (load it) or cease to be a support at all.

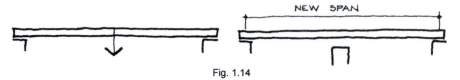

Fig. 1.14

So **ground movements** can alter the load-carrying behaviour of a structure, and so can be considered, in a rather roundabout way, to load the structure.

Another form of ground movement that can load a structure is an earthquake. Earthquakes are caused by sudden internal movements within the Earth's crust. This causes a shock to the system and results in shaking the crust of the Earth over a certain area. The Earth's surface will both bounce up and down and move backwards and forwards.

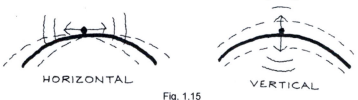

Fig. 1.15

In general the vertical movement is small compared with the horizontal movement. A building, during an earthquake, undergoes an experience similar to a person standing unaided on a cakewalk.

Fig. 1.16

Again, it is not obvious where or what the load is but the effect, as far as the building or the person is concerned, is the same as being pushed horizontally to and fro with the foundations (feet) kept still.

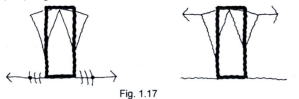

Fig. 1.17

So earthquakes cause horizontal loads similar, to some extent, to wind loads.

The last type of natural load is caused by differential dimensional changes in the structure. All structural materials expand when heated and contract when cooled. As structures are often exposed to the ambient climate, their **temperature** may vary considerably, from a hot summer day to a cold winter night, and in some cases this may cause loads. An example illustrates how this may happen. Suppose a structure consists of two parts firmly joined by a spanning structure.

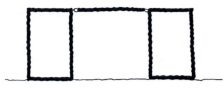

Fig. 1.18

As the temperature varies, the spanning structure will expand and contract. As it is firmly joined to the supporting structures, it will push them and pull them causing loads.

Fig. 1.19

So, as with ground movements, temperature, in a rather unobvious way, may be a load. To avoid these loads, bridges are often provided with systems of sliding bearings at the tops of the supporting columns. On large bridges these can often be seen.

A successful structure must be able to resist the effects of some or all of these natural loads for the whole of its useful life. On the whole, these loads cannot be avoided and are an integral part of the structure's existence.

1.2   Useful loads

Unlike natural loads, which cannot be avoided and so must be tolerated, **useful loads** are ones that are welcomed. These loads happen because the building and hence the structure have been constructed for a useful purpose.

With the plank bridge, it has been constructed for people to cross the stream. If it couldn't do this it would be of no use, so the previous figures can be re-drawn showing **natural** and **useful loads**.

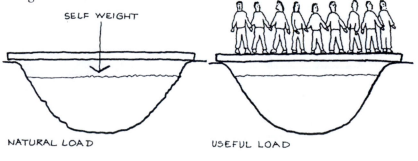

Fig. 1.20

The amount of useful load can be altered by how many people are 'allowed' on the bridge at any one time; and whether people are allowed to take their pet elephants on the bridge. It is often practical for the useful load to be the maximum load that is likely to occur. Practically the useful load would be a bridge full of people, but no elephants allowed.

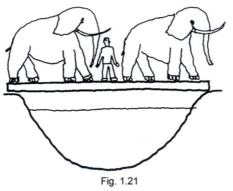

Fig. 1.21

So, unlike natural loads, there is a choice for useful loads. Of course if everyone using the bridge had an elephant (or a car!) it would be sensible for the useful load to be a bridge full of people or full of elephants. As gravity acts on the people and the elephants, the effect of this useful load will be towards the centre of the Earth, or locally vertical.

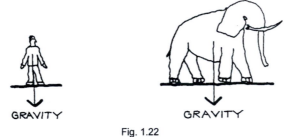

GRAVITY   GRAVITY

Fig. 1.22

Unlike natural loads, useful loads can vary enormously, depending on the use of the building which may have to carry anything from railway trains to sleeping people.

Whilst the majority of useful loads act vertically, sometimes they act horizontally. It may be useful to store sand, grain or water and these will cause useful earth or water pressure loads.

Fig. 1.23

Also, rather like earthquakes, machinery housed in a building may tend to shake a building sideways, causing another type of useful horizontal load.

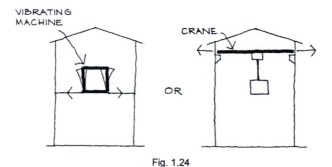

Fig. 1.24

Again, industrial processes may increase or reduce the ambient temperature, giving 'useful' temperature loads.

1.3 Accidental loads

The occurrence of **accidental loads** is inextricably bound up with concepts of **safety**. How safe anything is, driving a car or drinking water, is a matter for society to decide, or at least keep under review. If accidents are thought to be likely and unavoidable then the structure should be able to resist loads that these accidents cause. For instance, in a multi-storey car-park, it is likely and unavoidable that someone will hit the edge barrier whilst parking.

Fig. 1.25

The edge barrier should be able to cater for 'run of the mill' collisions but not suicide attempts. Similar situations occur at railway stations and ship berthing jetties.

Another unavoidable accident is a minor (!) explosion. Minor explosions in kitchens and bomb factories are of different orders of magnitude, but both should be expected and allowed for. Other unavoidable accidents are crowd panics which require the installation of panic barriers, or tanks bursting which require lower structures to carry the extra liquid load.

It is impossible for an individual to decide which accidents, and hence accidental loads, are unavoidable and which aren't and any society is never clear. Compare the numbers of people killed on the roads in 'unavoidable' accidents and the relatively few killed in train 'disasters'.

1.4 Loading summary

The major function of a structure is to transfer loads and the main sources of these loads have now been identified. Whilst each load or set of loads can be considered to act independently, buildings are usually loaded by combinations of the various loads. As the building must carry any combination it is usual to consider a range of combinations called **load cases**.

The only load case that will always be present is the **natural gravity load**. That is the effect of gravity on the building construction and to this load must be added **all other loads**. All the other loads that have been identified may or may not be acting at any particular time. Therefore an almost endless variety of load combinations may act. For example:

Loadcase 1 – Natural gravity load + Useful gravity load on all floors
Loadcase 2 – Natural gravity load + Wind load in a particular direction
Loadcase 3 – Natural gravity load + Useful gravity load on some floors + Natural temperature load

However, the purpose of considering these different load cases is not to find as many load cases as possible but to ensure that the building structure will safely carry all possible load cases. This apparently contradictory statement means that only the load cases that cause the biggest effect on the structure need to be considered. In other words only the **worst load case** is of interest. This presents two difficulties that are:

1   One load case may cause the biggest effect on one part of the structure whereas another load case may have the biggest effect on another part, so there may be more than one worst load case.

2   How can the worst load case or cases be found without considering **every** possible load case?

Unfortunately there is no automatic process to overcome these difficulties for every situation but guidance is given in technical documents. For buildings it is usual to consider:

1   Natural gravity load + Maximum useful gravity load
2   Natural gravity load + Wind load in direction 1
3   Natural gravity load + Wind load at right angles to direction 1

It is unusual to have to consider loads due to earth or water pressure, ground movement, temperature or accident. But for particular types of building or sites these may have to be considered, and incorporated into the load cases. For example, for a two-storey factory building, the following loads would be considered for the structural design.

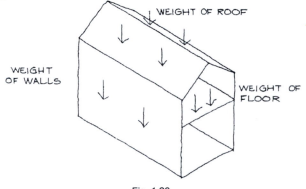

Fig. 1.26

The ground floor often bears directly on to the ground and does not load the structure.

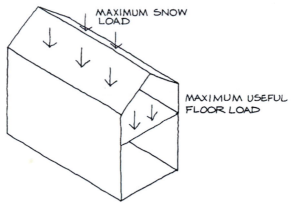

Fig. 1.27 Maximum useful gravity load

The natural gravity plus maximum useful gravity loads usually, but not always, give the **worst vertical load**.

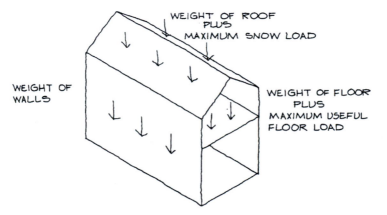

Fig. 1.28 Worst vertical load

The combination of natural gravity load and the maximum wind loads usually gives the **worst horizontal load**.

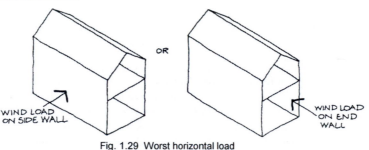

Fig. 1.29 Worst horizontal load

It may seem surprising that only two directions are chosen for the wind, because, after all wind blows in any direction. So the maximum wind load, which has been decided, can act in **any** direction.

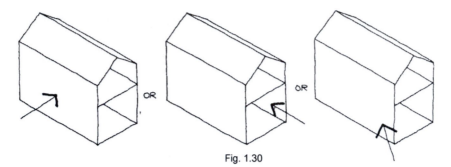

Fig. 1.30

But if the building structure is strong enough to carry the maximum wind load separately in two perpendicular directions, then **all** other wind loads can be considered to be smaller proportions of the maximum loads.

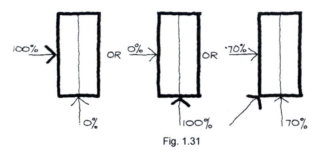

Fig. 1.31

The same principle of **load combinations** applies to all buildings.

1.5   Reaction loads

In the same way that people stand on a floor and usually don't fall through, buildings also have to stand on something strong – the foundations.

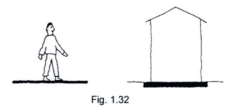

Fig. 1.32

But what is the floor doing to stop people from falling through? What it is doing is to provide a **reaction force**, or a **reaction load**. The idea of reactions is due to Isaac Newton who, in 1687, stated three fundamental laws, which together with his discovery of gravity, provided the basis of what has come to be known as **Newtonian mechanics**. These were used extensively by scientists in their pursuit of knowledge about the natural world. They formed the backbone of physics and still provide the backbone of structural engineering thought.

(It was only at the beginning of the 20th century that Albert Einstein postulated a system of mechanics that were non-Newtonian. This system came to be known as

relativity, which is used for calculations about the Universe. Fortunately structural engineers can still use Newtonian mechanics for building structures on the Earth.)

One of Newton's three laws (the third), states:

- **To every action there is always an equal and opposite reaction.**

So when a person stands on a floor, the weight of the person pushes down on the floor with a force equal to their bodyweight. For equilibrium, the floor must push back with an **equal and opposite force**.

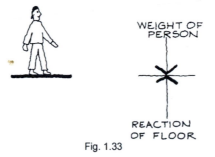

Fig. 1.33

An understanding of this statement is fundamental for an understanding of how building structures carry loads.

Whilst it is true that the load and the reaction have to act at the point of the application of the load, a structure transfers the load to another point. Returning to the example of the plank bridge:

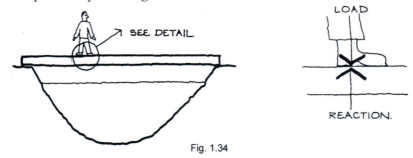

Fig. 1.34

The reaction to the person's weight is **in the structure**, and the structure transfers this reaction to the banks.

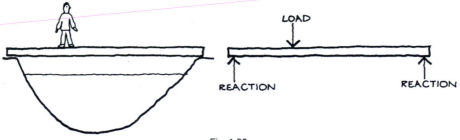

Fig. 1.35

Because of Newton's law, the numerical sum of the loads and the reactions must be equal.

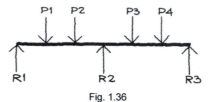

Fig. 1.36

For vertical equilibrium of the 2-span beam in **Fig. 1.36**:

- P1 + P2 + P3 + P4 = R1 + R2 + R3

When loads are acting horizontally, a reaction is required for equilibrium. It is to upset this equilibrium that tug-of-war contests are held.

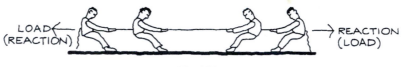

Fig. 1.37

Here it is unclear which is the load and which is the reaction. This is why the (applied) load and the reaction (load) should be thought of as a balanced system of loads.

Fig. 1.38

Here the pull of the team is the (applied) load and the tree provides the reaction (load).

Not only are there vertical and horizontal reactions there are also **moment** reactions! What is a moment? A moment is a **force times a distance**. Moments abound in structural engineering but the concept of a moment is often found hard to understand. However, it is because of moments that things can be weighed or people can enjoy see-saws.

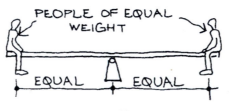

Fig. 1.39

The fun in see-sawing can only be enjoyed if the people are of equal weight and sit at an equal distance from the support. This is because they are in moment equilibrium.

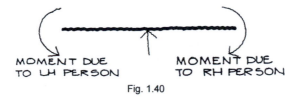

Fig. 1.40

In other words, the left-hand person causes an **anti-clockwise** moment and the right-hand person causes a **clockwise** moment about the central support. Because both people are of equal weight and are sitting at equal distances from the support, the anti-clockwise and clockwise moments are equal in magnitude but opposite in direction and so are in **moment equilibrium**. By pushing from the ground this equilibrium is upset and the people 'see-saw'.

The same principle can be used for weighing scales, this time to find the unknown weight of some goods.

Fig. 1.41

To balance the scales the moments must be equal. As the distances are equal the weights must equal the weight of the goods.

The idea of **moment reaction** occurs at the support of a **cantilever**.

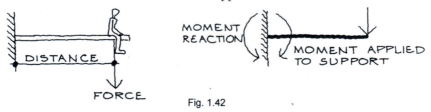

Fig. 1.42

The person standing on the end of the cantilevered plank causes a moment at the support (**force** × **distance**). The fixing of the plank must balance this moment with a moment reaction, otherwise the plank will rotate away from the wall.

Moment reactions are also required to prevent flag poles, fences and signs from being blown over by the wind.

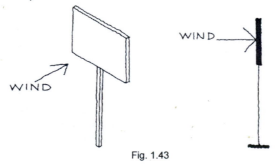

Fig. 1.43

In this case the post is acting as a **vertical cantilever** from the ground. The wind force acting on the sign at some height (distance) above the ground causes a moment at ground level, so the post must be dug into the ground to provide a moment reaction.

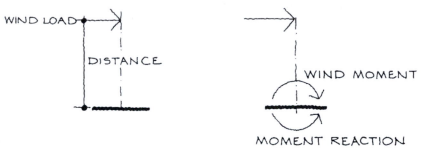

Fig. 1.44

Notice that the moment reaction is in the opposite direction to the moment caused by the wind force × height.

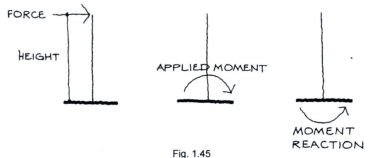

Fig. 1.45

Many structures require more than one type of reaction. Using the example of wind blowing on a sign, the support must provide **vertical**, **horizontal** and **moment reactions**. These resist the **weight** of the **sign**, the **wind load** and the **wind moment**.

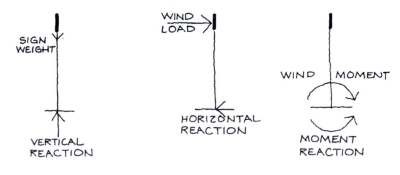

Fig. 1.46

The idea of moment equilibrium also plays a part in apportioning vertical reactions for spanning structures. Suppose a weightless (!) plank spans between two weighing scales and a person stands at different points along the plank.

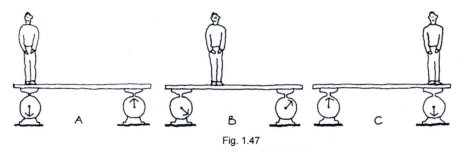

Fig. 1.47

The person is the load and the reaction forces occur at the supports on the weighing scales. As the person moves from position **A** to **B** and then to **C**, the readings on the scales will vary, giving the values of the reactions for each position. But the fact that the sum of the readings on the scales for each position will equal the weight of the person **does not indicate how they are shared**. If the person stands in position **A**, directly over the left-hand weighing scale, it is reasonable to expect this scale to give a reading of **100%** of the person's weight and the right-hand weighing scale to give a reading of **0%** of the person's weight. But vertical equilibrium would equally be satisfied by the right-hand scale reading **100%** of the person's weight and the left-hand scale reading **0%**!

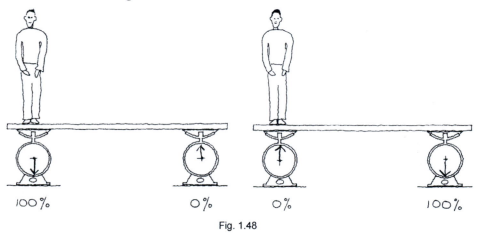

100%   0%   0%   100%

Fig. 1.48

This seems unlikely to be true, but why not? The answer is because only 100% at the left-hand scale gives moment equilibrium. But where are the moments? These are far from obvious, but suppose the left-hand weighing scale was removed.

Fig. 1.49

Now the person causes an anti-clockwise moment about the right-hand weighing scale and the plank would hinge about the right-hand end. To prevent this, the left-hand weighing scale provides a reaction that causes a clockwise moment about the right-hand weighing scale.

Fig. 1.50

As these two moments must balance, the left-hand reaction must balance the person's weight, as the distance from the right-hand end is the same for the load and the reaction so:

Person's weight × **length of plank = left-hand reaction** × **length of plank**

So the left-hand diagram of **Fig. 1.48** gives vertical **and** moment equilibrium whereas the right-hand one gives vertical equilibrium **but not** moment equilibrium. So **every time there are loads on structures there must be reactions (vertical, horizontal and moment) and these reactions must balance the loads**.

In other words:

- **Sum of vertical loads = Sum of vertical reactions**
- **Sum of horizontal loads = Sum of horizontal reactions**
- **Moments due to loads = Moments due to reactions**

These three statements must be true for all structures and the understanding of these statements unlocks the door to an understanding of structures.

1.6   Load paths

To understand how loads are transferred through complex structures the **concept of load path** is used. This is basically a sequence of loads and reactions between structural elements. The important point here is one element's reaction to the next element's load.

For the simple example of a beam on two walls, the reactions of the beam 'cause' loads on the walls.

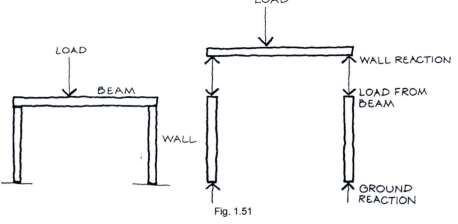

Fig. 1.51

The double-headed arrow between the beam and the walls represents the reaction and the load. The **upper arrow** represents the wall providing a **reaction** to the beam and the **lower arrow** represents the beam causing a **load** on the wall.

Fig. 1.52

Fig. 1.53 shows a more complicated situation of two beams supported by walls, all sitting on a longer beam.

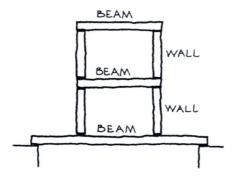

Fig. 1.53

First, what are the loads? These are natural, the self-weight of the beams and walls, and useful, the loads applied to the beams.

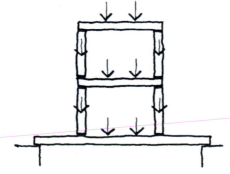

Fig. 1.54

Loads **P1**, **P2** and **P5** are the self-weight of the beams and **P3** and **P4** the self-weight of the walls. Loads **P6**, **P7** and **P8** are the loads applied to the beams. For vertical equilibrium, all the loads **P1** to **P8** must be balanced by the reactions of the lowest beam.

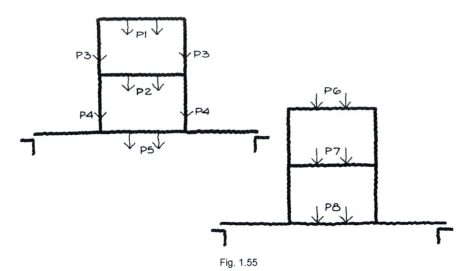

Fig. 1.55

For the lowest beam:

The sum of the reactions = P1 + P2 + P3 + P4 + P5 + P6 + P7 + P8

But how do the loads get to the reactions? First the upper beam.

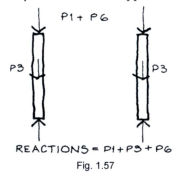

Fig. 1.56

Loads to the upper walls $=$ P1 + P6

The upper walls are loaded by the loads on the upper beam plus their self-weight.

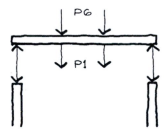

REACTIONS = P1 + P3 + P6

Fig. 1.57

The tops of the lower walls are loaded by and provide a reaction to the upper walls and the middle beam.

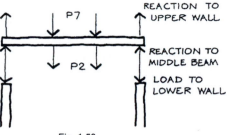

Fig. 1.58

So for the lower walls,

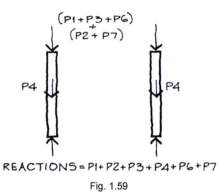

REACTIONS = P1 + P2 + P3 + P4 + P6 + P7

Fig. 1.59

And the reactions to the lower walls are:

Load from the upper wall + Load from the middle beam + Self-weight of the lower wall

Reaction = (P1 + P6 + P3) + (P2 + P7) + P4

The lower beam is not only loaded by its self-weight, **P5**, and the applied load, **P8**, but also by providing reactions to the lower walls.

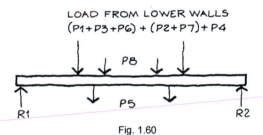

Fig. 1.60

So for vertical equilibrium of the lower beam:

The **REACTIONS** = Self-weight of the upper beam
+ Self-weight of the middle beam
+ Self-weight of the lower beam
+ Self-weight of the upper walls
+ Self-weight of the lower walls
+ Useful load on the upper beam
+ Useful load on the middle beam
+ Useful load on the lower beam

that is:

$$R1 + R2 = P1 + P2 + P3 + P4 + P5 + P6 + P7 + P8$$

The load path of load **P6** can now be identified. First the upper beam transfers the load to the upper wall, which transfers it to the lower wall, which transfers it to the lower beam, which transfers it to the supports.

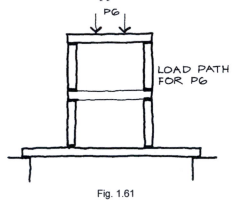

Fig. 1.61

And for **P2**, the self-weight of the middle beam:

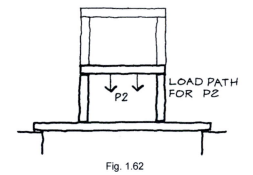

Fig. 1.62

The load path joins the load from its **point of application** to the **final support point**. There are two facts to be considered about load paths.

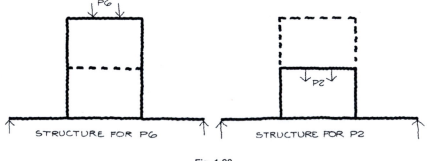

Fig. 1.63

Firstly **all loads** must and will have a load path from their point of application to the final support. The structural designer must identify these paths for **all loads** and **all load cases**.

Secondly, as the function of the structure is to transfer loads, then the **load path is the structure** for each load. So the answer to the question **'what is the structure?'** may vary with each load. For the loads **P2** and **P6** the structures are different.

The identification of vertical load paths for most buildings is relatively straightforward. Oddly it can be quite complex for 'simple buildings' like houses.

Not only do vertical loads need load paths but so do horizontal loads. These loads are usually caused by wind. How does the signboard shown in **Fig. 1.64** resist wind forces? The main wind load is caused by the wind blowing on the actual sign, and only the load path for this load is considered. This means the effect of the wind on the rails and posts is ignored.

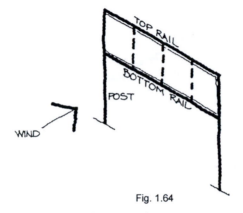

Fig. 1.64

The actual signboard spans horizontally between the vertical stiffeners and the stiffeners act as vertically spanning beams supported by the top and bottom rails.

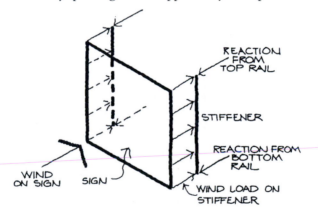

Fig. 1.65

The reactions from the stiffeners become horizontal loads on the top and bottom rails. These rails act as horizontally spanning beams supported by the vertical end posts.

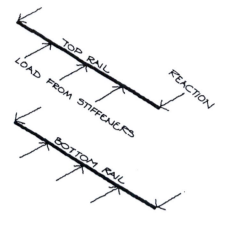

Fig. 1.66

The reactions from the top and bottom rails now cause loads on the vertical posts that act as vertical cantilevers from the ground. For the signboard, the wind load path is the whole structure.

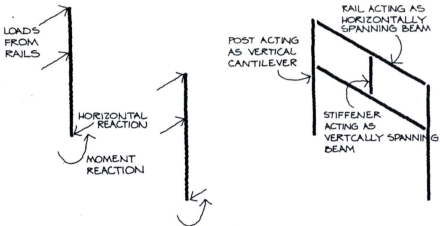

Fig. 1.67 Loads on post (left) and whole structure (right)

But even in simple buildings the load paths for vertical and horizontal loads are rarely the same. As the **load path is the structure**, this means there are usually **different structures** resisting vertical and horizontal loads.

CHAPTER 2   *Internal forces*

So far, loads, reactions and load paths have been identified for structures. But how does the structure transfer the load to the reaction? And what happens to the structure when it transfers loads? The structure transfers loads by **forces** that are **'in the structure'** and these forces cause **stresses** in the structural material. The structure also deforms under the effect of the loads, and the size of the deformation depends on the **stiffness** of the structure.

2.1   Axial forces

To illustrate the idea of **internal force** consider a simple column supporting an end load.

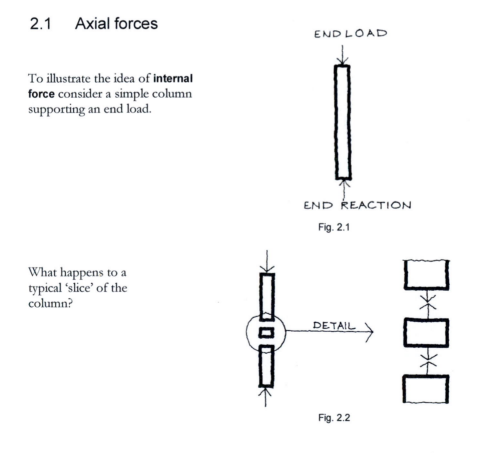

ENDLOAD

END REACTION

Fig. 2.1

What happens to a typical 'slice' of the column?

DETAIL

Fig. 2.2

The slice is being squashed, or compressed, and furthermore **all slices** are being squashed.

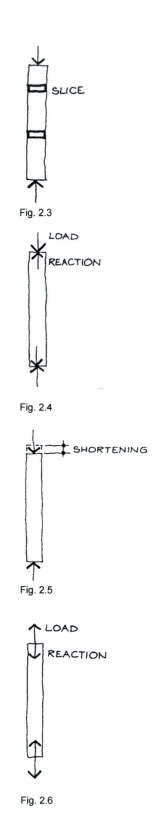

Fig. 2.3

The column transfers the end load to the reaction by a system of 'squashed slices', or to use the engineering description, the column is **in compression**.

Fig. 2.4

Not only is the column in compression but also deforms by **shortening**. This happens because each slice becomes thinner on being squashed.

Fig. 2.5

If the direction of the load is reversed then each slice is being stretched, and the end load is transferred to the reaction by a system of 'stretched slices'. Or, to use the engineering term, the column is **in tension**.

Fig. 2.6

Forces that stretch or compress elements in the direction of their longitudinal axis are called **axial forces** and these always act **along** the element.

2.2   Bending moments and shear forces

Looking again at the load path for load **P6** (see **Fig. 1.61**), the walls supporting the upper beam are in compression.

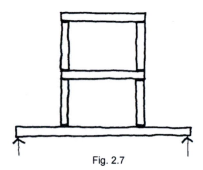

Fig. 2.7

But what is happening to the upper and lower beams? These beams are transferring the loads to the supports by a combination of **bending moments** and **shear forces**. Although bending moments and shear forces act together, conceptually they can be considered separately. To understand what is happening to the beam it helps to see what happens to a slice.

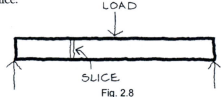

Fig. 2.8

Each side of the slice is being bent by a moment.

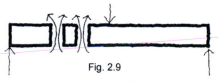

Fig. 2.9

The moments at the slice are the forces multiplied by their distances from the slice.

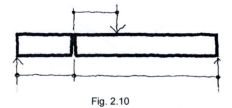

Fig. 2.10

So the moments on the slice are:

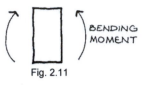

Fig. 2.11

This causes the slice to be squashed at the top and stretched at the bottom. In other words the top of the beam is in compression and the bottom in tension, and a pair of bending moments is bending the slice.

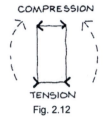

Fig. 2.12

Because the top is in compression it **shortens**, and because the bottom is in tension it **lengthens**. These effects cause the sides to **rotate**.

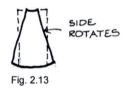

Fig. 2.13

In general, the size of the bending moment varies from slice to slice. This varying size can be represented by drawing lines at right angles to the beam, with the length of the line indicating the **size of the bending moment**.

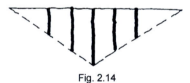

Fig. 2.14

Because there is a bending moment at every slice and the beam is 'made' of slices, there is a bending moment at every point of the beam. A clearer picture of the bending moments on the beam can be obtained by joining the ends of all the bending moment size lines shown in **Fig. 2.14**. This diagram is called a **bending moment diagram**.

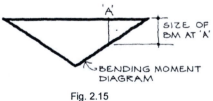

Fig. 2.15

And because each slice changes shape, as shown in **Fig. 2.13**, the beam takes up a bent shape.

40 Building structures

Fig. 2.16

Bending moments in a beam resist the effects of the moments caused by external loads, and reactions acting at different distances from each other. Bending moments **do not** resist the vertical effect of loads on beams; **shear forces** resist these. When a **rectangle** is distorted by an angular change into a **parallelogram**, it is **sheared**.

Fig. 2.17

Returning to a slice of a beam, not only does the slice have to transfer the bending moments from one face to the other, it also has to transfer the vertical load from one face to the other.

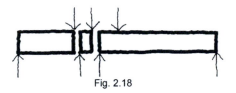

Fig. 2.18

The beam either side of the slice has to be in **vertical equilibrium**.

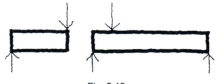

Fig. 2.19

And the balancing forces themselves have to be balanced by forces on the face of the slice.

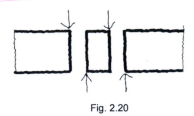

Fig. 2.20

It is these pairs of **up and down forces** that are called shear forces, because their effect is to shear the slice.

Fig. 2.21

Like bending moments, shear forces will, in general, vary along a beam. So, in a similar way to bending moment diagrams, **shear force diagrams** can be drawn.

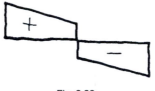

Fig. 2.22

To make more sense of bending moment and shear force diagrams, the vexed question of the **sign** of a bending moment or shear force must be answered.

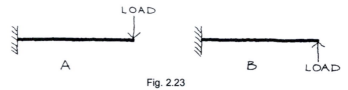

Fig. 2.23

The figure shows two cantilevers that are exactly the same except the loads are being applied in **opposite** directions. Some agreement has to be made to distinguish the fact that cantilever **A** is being bent down, and cantilever **B** is being bent up! This could be done by deciding that cantilever **A** deforms in a **negative** way, causing negative bending moments and vice versa for cantilever **B**.

Fig. 2.24

In **Fig. 2.24** the bending moments have been drawn on the **tension side** of the beam. Although these decisions are supposed to aid clarification, this is not always the case! Especially as the decisions about positive and negative are made by personal whim. However, they have to be made and adhered to or the bending moment diagrams become chaotic.

Similar decisions have to be made about shear forces, but here the situation is more incomprehensible. As shear forces are pairs of forces, the sign decisions have to be made about these pairs. A possible sign convention is shown in the following figure.

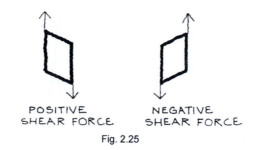

POSITIVE
SHEAR FORCE   NEGATIVE
                   SHEAR FORCE

Fig. 2.25

Again this decision is made by personal whim. Using the stated sign conventions the bending moment and shear force diagrams can be drawn for a simple beam with point load, and these diagrams show the signs of the bending moments and shear forces.

LOAD

BENDING MOMENT
DIAGRAM   SHEAR FORCE
                   DIAGRAM

Fig. 2.26

It is sets of diagrams like this that give engineers pictures of what is happening inside a structure. **The conceptual meaning of sets of bending moment and shear force diagrams is central to the understanding of structural behaviour.** Being able to sketch the correct shapes for these is a skill to be learnt, as is being able to calculate numerical values – guidance on how to obtain these skills is given in **Chapter 12**. A deep understanding of structural behaviour is only obtained when the correct diagrams can be drawn for real or proposed structures.

2.3   A simple plane frame

For the more complicated structure of a goal-post, known as a **portal frame,** diagrams can be drawn showing what is happening inside the structure when it is loaded.

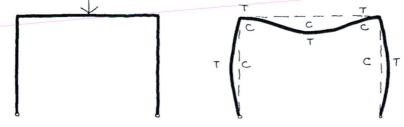

Fig. 2.27

Here, although there is only vertical load there are **horizontal reactions**. These exist because otherwise the legs would move apart at their bases.

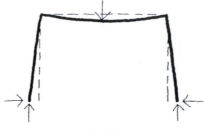

Fig. 2.28

The deformed shape (**Fig. 2.27**) shows which sides of the legs and cross-bar are in tension and compression. Using this as a guide the bending moment diagram can be drawn.

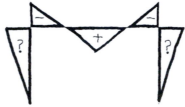

Fig. 2.29

The bending moment diagram is drawn on the tension side of the legs and cross-bar. Although the sign convention used for the beam shown in **Fig. 2.24** can be used for the cross-bar, it is unclear what sign should be given to the bending moments in the legs. Not only will there be bending moments in the frame but there will also be axial forces and shear forces. There are axial forces in the legs due to the vertical load and an axial force in the cross-bar due to the horizontal reaction.

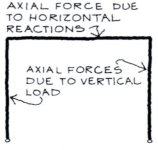

Fig. 2.30

As well as the bending moment diagrams, an axial force diagram can be drawn on the portal frame. For axial forces there is no agreed convention for the sign of axial forces or even the way the diagram should be drawn! In some ways the sign convention for axial forces is simpler than for bending moments and shear forces because compression forces are either positive or negative, and similarly for tension forces. Traditionally, axial force diagrams are drawn with a system of arrows on the structure, with numbers written alongside the member indicating the size of the force. To be consistent axial force diagrams should be drawn in the same way as bending moment and shear force diagrams. Both types of diagrams are shown in **Fig. 2.31**. The arrow convention is for **arrows pointing away** from the end of a member to indicate compression and, for the diagram, compression is assumed to be positive.

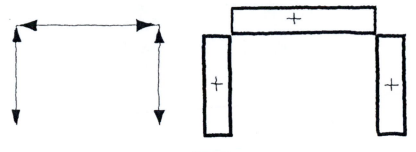

Fig. 2.31

Also a **shear force diagram** can be drawn, here the beam sign convention shown in **Fig. 2.26** can be used for the cross-bar but again, as for the case of the bending moment, the sign of the shear force in the legs is unclear.

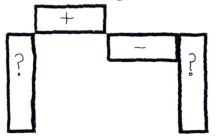

Fig. 2.32

It is impossible to have fully consistent sign conventions and diagrams without having agreed local and global axes systems for the whole structure. The importance of this point becomes clear when computer programs are used to find the forces in a structure, and this is commonplace these days.

Further understanding of how the internal forces are acting on a structure can be obtained by considering the parts of a structure as 'free bodies'. In the case of the portal frame, the **free bodies** are the beam and the two legs.

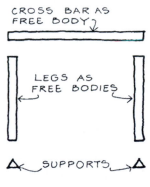

CROSS BAR AS FREE BODY

LEGS AS FREE BODIES

SUPPORTS

Fig. 2.33

The forces acting on these free bodies to keep them in equilibrium are shown in **Fig. 2 34**.

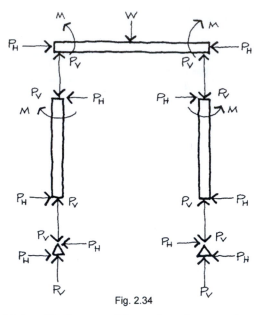

Fig. 2.34

The meaning of this bewildering set of forces is easier to understand by considering the forces due to the load and the forces due to the horizontal restraint separately. For the vertical load **W**, its effect on the beam is balanced by the end forces P_v. These in turn cause forces equal to P_v on the tops of the legs that are balanced by forces, also equal to P_v, at the bottom of the legs. The forces at the bottom of the legs are balanced by forces on the supports that, in turn, are balanced by the reactions.

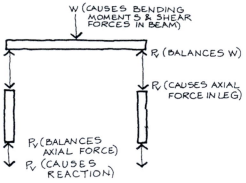

Fig. 2.35

The reasons for the existence of **M** and P_H are less clear. They exist because the joints between the legs and cross-bar are **stiff**, that is, the joints are **at right-angles before and after loading**. Due to the vertical load **W**, the cross-bar bends and the ends rotate. To maintain the right-angles at the joints, the legs want to move outwards, as is shown in **Fig. 2.28** (if this did happen **M** and P_H would not exist). But the connection at the bottom of the legs prevents horizontal movement and this causes the legs to bend.

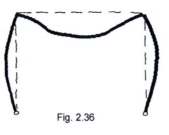

Fig. 2.36

And just looking at one leg:

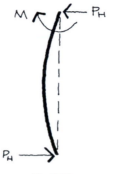

Fig. 2.37

This effect can be simulated by holding one end of a flexible stick between two fingers of one hand and rotating the other end with the other hand.

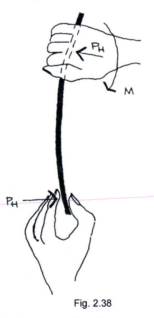

Fig. 2.38

So the effect of connection is to cause bending moments in the leg due to **M** and shear forces due to **P**$_H$. A free body diagram can be drawn showing the effect of **M** and **P**$_H$ on all the parts of the structure.

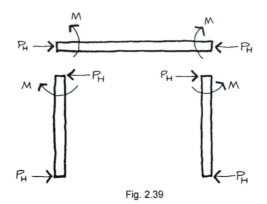

Fig. 2.39

The diagrams showing the bending moments, shear and axial forces can be separated into those caused by the vertical load **W**, and those caused by the horizontal restraint of the legs. Firstly the effect of the vertical load with no horizontal restraint at the base of the legs.

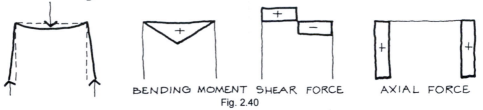

BENDING MOMENT   SHEAR FORCE   AXIAL FORCE

Fig. 2.40

And secondly the effect of pushing the bottom of the legs together.

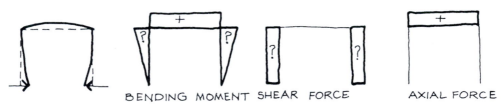

BENDING MOMENT   SHEAR FORCE   AXIAL FORCE

Fig. 2.41

As both effects happen together, the diagrams can be combined to give the complete picture.

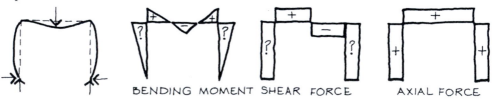

BENDING MOMENT   SHEAR FORCE   AXIAL FORCE

Fig. 2.42

It is sets of diagrams like these, together with the magnitude of all the forces, that provide the engineering information on how any structure behaves under any form of loading.

2.4 Slabs

The concepts of bending moments, shear and axial forces are not confined to one-dimensional elements, such as beams and columns; they can be applied to all structural forms. For instance a two-dimensional element such as a floor slab resists lateral loads by a system of internal bending moments and shear forces.

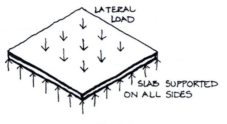

Fig. 2.43

Because the slab is two dimensional, bending moments and shear forces can be considered as acting in two separate directions. For example a rectangular slab, supported on all sides and loaded by a central point load, will span in two directions.

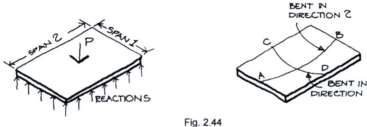

Fig. 2.44

A 'strip', **AB**, of the slab acts rather like a beam spanning from **A** to **B**. This strip will have bending moment and shear force distributions that can be represented by bending moment and shear force diagrams.

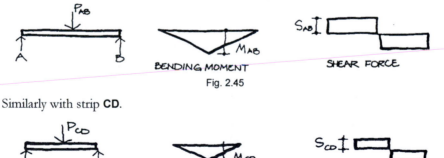

BENDING MOMENT   SHEAR FORCE

Fig. 2.45

Similarly with strip **CD**.

BENDING MOMENT   SHEAR FORCE

Fig. 2.46

Because the whole slab is carrying the load **P**, the amount of load the strips **AB** and **CD** carry is less than **P**. The diagrams drawn for the strips can be compared with those shown in **Fig. 2.26**. These diagrams can be drawn for the two strips.

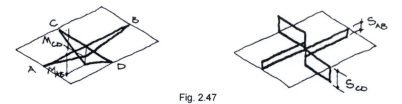

Fig. 2.47

Remember that this is for one strip in each direction and the width of the strip is arbitrary. For the real slab, these bending moments and shear forces will vary continuously throughout the slab. Unfortunately this is difficult to show as a clear diagram, but an idea can be given by drawing the diagrams for a series of strips. In the next diagram, bending moments are drawn for the two directions for a series of strips.

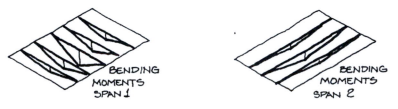

Fig. 2.48

Similarly a series of shear force diagrams could be drawn.

2.5 The structural action of load paths

Often beams support the edges of floor slabs and columns support the beams. The slab spans two ways on to the beams and the beams, together with the columns, form a series of portal frames.

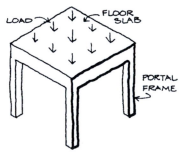

Fig. 2.49

The slab carries the load to the beams by a system of bending moments and shear forces acting in two directions. At the edges of the slab there are vertical reactions that balance the load on the slab. In turn, these reactions cause loads on the portal frames.

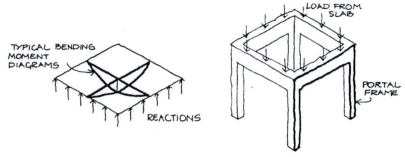

Fig. 2.50

The portal frames resist these loads by internal bending moments, and shear and axial forces. These internal forces are distributed throughout the portal frames and are summarised by diagrams like those shown in **Fig. 2.42**. The columns are now part of two portal frames!

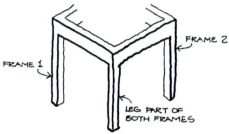

Fig. 2.51

The bending moments and shear forces from the action of portal **FRAME 1** are in the plane of **FRAME 1** and those from **FRAME 2** are in the plane of **FRAME 2**.

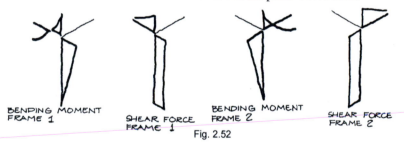

Fig. 2.52

As the column can't bend in two different directions at the same time it actually bends in a third direction that is not in the plane of **FRAME 1** or **FRAME 2**.

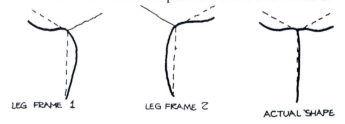

Fig. 2.53

This illustrates the fact that whilst it may be conceptually convenient to view the slab supports as a series of portal frames, the structure acts in a way that is most structurally 'convenient'.

The example of the slab supported by beams and columns, shown in **Fig. 2.49**, has a simple load path. With the new concepts of structural actions it can be seen that this load path carries the loads by a sequence of these structural actions.

Now two essential skills required for the understanding of structures have been presented and these are:

- **Identifying the load path for each load — this is what carries the load**

- **Identifying the sequence of structural actions in the load path — this is how the load is carried.**

To see how the concept of structural actions shows how the load path carries the load, the earlier example of the wind-loaded signboard, see **Fig. 1.64**, is re-examined using these concepts.

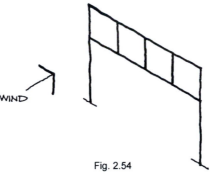

Fig. 2.54

The sign itself is a two-dimensional structural element which is supported by three stiffeners and the posts. As these lines of support are parallel, the element acts like a one-dimensional element.

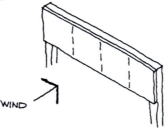

Fig. 2.55

The bending moments and shear forces caused by the wind vary along the sign but are constant across it.

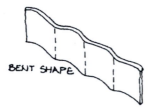

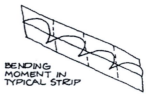

Fig. 2.56

It may be clearer to draw as a view from above.

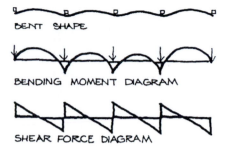

Fig. 2.57

The reactions from the sign load the stiffeners, and these act as beams spanning between the rails. Bending moment and shear force diagrams can be drawn for a typical stiffener.

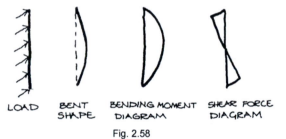

LOAD   BENT SHAPE   BENDING MOMENT DIAGRAM   SHEAR FORCE DIAGRAM

Fig. 2.58

The reactions from the ends of the stiffeners act as three point loads on the top and bottom rails. These act as beams spanning between the posts so bending moment and shear force diagrams can be drawn for the rails.

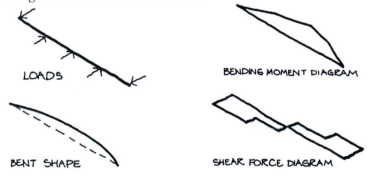

LOADS

BENT SHAPE

BENDING MOMENT DIAGRAM

SHEAR FORCE DIAGRAM

Fig. 2.59

The posts act as cantilevers carrying the loads from the ends of the rails plus the load from the sign. The bending moment and shear force diagrams are drawn for the posts.

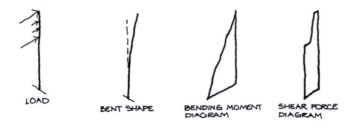

LOAD   BENT SHAPE   BENDING MOMENT DIAGRAM   SHEAR FORCE DIAGRAM

Fig. 2.60

So each part of the load path transfers the load by some form of structural action – these may be bending moments and shear forces or axial forces or some combination of these. Not only is the load path the structure, but also as a sequence of internal structural actions, the **load path acts as a structure**.

2.6   Twisting forces

The internal forces that are axial forces, bending moments and shear forces are the 'usual' forces. However, there is another internal force that **twists** a structural element about its longitudinal axis. This internal force is a moment and is called a **torque** or, more commonly, a **torsional moment**.

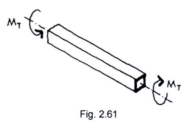

Fig. 2.61

That this internal force is a moment, that is, a force acting at a distance, can be seen by considering an element loaded by equal and opposite forces applied to the element by rigid arms.

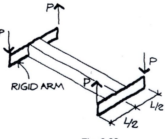

Fig. 2.62

Here the torsional moment applied to each end of the element is:

$$2(P \times (L/2)) = P \times L = M_T$$

54   Building structures

There are no other forces in the element as all the loads are equal and opposite.

Torsional moments are often applied in daily life, think of the action of a screwdriver or a spanner (torque wrench), they are rarely used as part of the primary load carrying systems in building structures however, they can occur. Consider a slab cantilevering from a beam that is spanning between two columns.

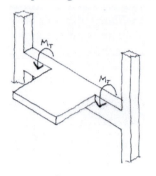

Fig. 2.63

But torsional moments frequently occur as a result of the geometry of the structure. In the case of the structure shown in **Fig. 2.49** the supporting beams will be subjected to these 'secondary' torsional moments. The beam will rotate due to the connection with the slab and with the column. At each point the rotation will vary so that the beam is being twisted which will cause these secondary torsional moments.

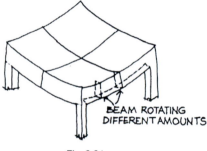

Fig. 2.64

These types of torsional moments, those that are not part of the primary load carrying system, are usually regarded as 'secondary effects' and are ignored at the 'discretion' of the structural designer provided there is confidence that they will not cause unwanted results.

In the case of beams curved in plan, torsional moments are part of the primary load carrying system in all cases and cannot be ignored – see **Section 3.7**.

2.7   Summary

It is the prediction of the structural behaviour of the load path that is the major skill required for successful structural engineering design. When structures are proposed, the structural action of each load path must be predicted as part of the proposal. The more complex the proposed structure, the more difficult it is to predict the structural behaviour of the load paths. In very complex structures it may even be difficult to identify the load paths! Severe problems can arise in the design process when complex structures with unpredictable structural behaviour are proposed. A prime example of this was the structural design of the Sydney Opera House (see **Section 11.4**) for which thirteen different structural schemes were proposed before an acceptable structural design was found; this took six years and an estimated 375,000 hours of engineering design time. Often it is wise to propose simple and therefore easily predictable structures unless there is ample time, and money, during the design process for the inevitable modifications to be made.

CHAPTER 3   *Structural element behaviour*

In this chapter the behaviour of the structure that is part of a load path is examined in detail. The understanding that is obtained from this examination makes it clear how parts of structures resist the internal forces. It also gives guidance on the best shape or **structural form** for any particular part of the load path. The choice of overall structural form for any particular structure is one of the basic tasks of the structural designer but before the behaviour of whole structural forms can be understood, the behaviour of very simple structures must be clear. To do this it is helpful to think of structures being **assemblies of elements**.

3.1   Structural elements

For structural engineering 'convenience', elements are considered to be one dimensional, two dimensional or three dimensional. The basic element can be thought of as a rectangular block, with sides of dimensions **A, B** and **C**.

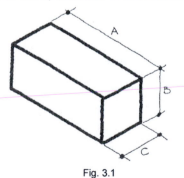

Fig. 3.1

If the three dimensions are very approximately equal then such an element is a **three-dimensional element**. Examples of three-dimensional elements are rare in modern building structures but often occur in older buildings, such as wall buttresses or thick stone domes.

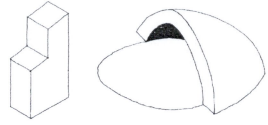

Fig. 3.2

If one of the dimensions, say dimension **C**, is small compared with dimensions **A** and **B**, then the element is a **two-dimensional element**.

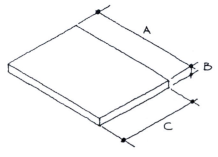

Fig. 3.3

Many parts of modern building structures are two-dimensional elements such as floor slabs, walls or shell roofs.

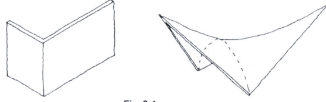

Fig. 3.4

If two of the dimensions of the basic element, say **B** and **C**, are small compared with dimension **A**, then the element is a **one-dimensional element**.

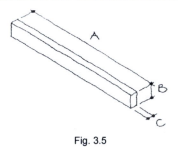

Fig. 3.5

One-dimensional elements are used abundantly in nearly all buildings; examples are beams, bars, cables and columns. Using the concept of elements, structures can be conceived as assemblies of elements. Examples can be found both in traditional and modern structures.

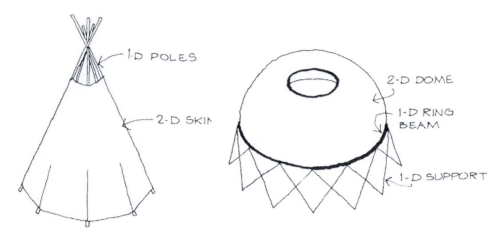

Fig. 3.6   Fig. 3.7

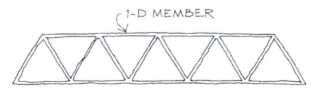

Fig. 3.8

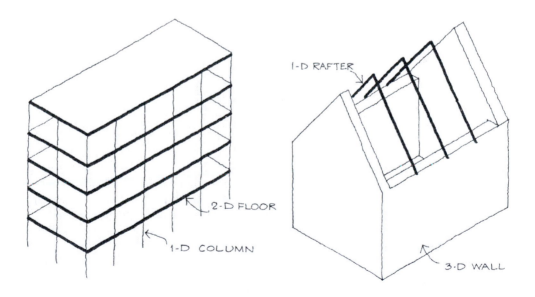

Fig. 3.9   Fig. 3.10

Nowadays structures are usually conceived and designed as assemblies of structural elements. This means the structural behaviour can be quantified by considering the behaviour of each **structural element** in each load path.

3.2   Concepts of stress and stress distribution

For any structure, all the elements that make up each load path must be strong enough to resist the internal structural actions caused by the loads. This means detailed information is required about the structural behaviour of different materials and of the structural elements.

To obtain this knowledge a new concept has to be introduced, this is the concept of **stress** and the related idea of **stress distribution**. Stress is a word in common usage but for engineering it has a particular meaning and that is **force per unit area**. Stress distribution describes how the sizes of stresses vary from unit area to unit area.

To begin to understand these ideas it is helpful to look at the slice of a column shown in **Fig. 2.2**.

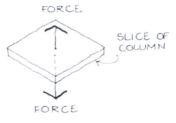

Fig. 3.11

Suppose the cross-section of the slice is gridded into squares of the same size (unit squares), then a force can be attached to each square.

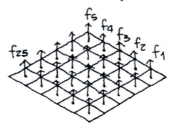

Fig. 3.12

The slice is divided into **25** unit squares, so the force shown in **Fig. 3.11** is divided into **25** forces per unit area, f_1 to f_{25}. For equilibrium, the numerical sum of the sizes of the twenty forces per unit area must equal the total force on the cross-section. So far there is no requirement that any of the forces per unit area, f_1 to f_{25}, are numerically equal. **Fig. 3.12** is redrawn as **Fig. 3.13** showing a possible **pattern of variation** for f_1 to f_{25}.

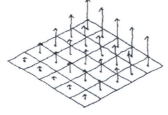

Fig. 3.13

The length of each force arrow indicates the size of the force in each unit square and it can be seen that these forces (stresses) vary in a pattern. Suppose, for clarity, just one strip of squares is drawn and the tops of the arrows are joined with a line.

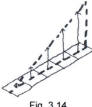

Fig. 3.14

As can be seen the resulting shape is a triangle, so along this strip there is a **triangular stress distribution**. **Fig. 3.13** shows the stresses varying in both directions across the cross-section so the tops of all the arrows can be joined with lines as shown below.

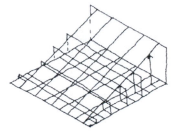

Fig. 3.15

These lines show triangular shapes in one direction and rectangular ones in the other direction.

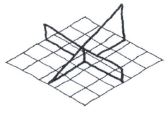

Fig. 3.16

It usual to simplify these diagrams of stress distribution by just drawing the outline along the edges.

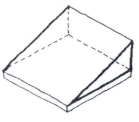

Fig. 3.17

Notice that the stress distribution is drawn right across the section. The stress distribution shown in **Fig. 3.17** is **triangular** in one direction and **uniform** in the other.

Uniform, or constant, stress distribution means that the sizes of the stresses do not vary in that direction.

In general there is no restriction on how stresses vary across any cross-section of any structure, except that the sum of the stresses must be equal to the internal force acting at the section and the internal force acts at the **centre of gravity** of the stresses. This new concept of centre of gravity has been used, in a different way, for the see-saw (see **Fig. 1.39**). Suppose a see-saw has people of different weights all along its length, their weights are indicated by their sizes.

Fig. 3.18

In this figure the see-saw is divided into ten equal spaces and, to balance, pairs of people of equal weight sit at equal distances from the balance point.

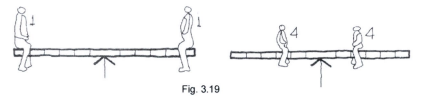

Fig. 3.19

Two such pairs are shown. Provided the equal pairs sit at equal distances from the balance point, the order of the pairs does not matter. **Fig. 3.20** shows two different seating arrangements both of which balance and that is because the centre of gravity of the ten people is at the balance point of the see-saw.

Fig. 3.20

As the seated height of the people relates directly to their weight, these diagrams are conceptually similar to the diagrams of stress distributions. For instance the left-hand seating arrangement shown in **Fig. 3.20** relates to a triangular stress distribution.

Fig. 3.21

If the seating arrangement were altered to have all the heaviest people at one end, **Fig. 3.22**, then the balance point would have to be moved.

Fig. 3.22

The new balance point will be nearer the end of the heavier people than the lighter. This is because the centre of gravity of this new seating arrangement is no longer at the centre of the see-saw. In the same way the internal force at any point of any structural element must act at the centre of gravity of the stress distribution. Where stresses vary in two directions across the section, the centre of gravity will also vary in two directions.

This new concept of stress allows checks to be made along each load path to ensure that it is strong enough to resist the internal forces caused by the loads. This is checked by making sure that the stresses in the structural elements that are in the load path are less than the **maximum stress** allowed for the structural material being used. In other words the structure must not be **over-stressed**. How a maximum stress is decided is far from straightforward and is discussed later.

Using the concepts of load path, structural action and maximum stress, the main parts of the **process of structural design** can be outlined. Once the reason for the existence for the structure has been identified – building, water tank, bridge – then the process can be used.

Step 1 Choose a structural form and material or materials.

Step 2 Identify the loads that the structure has to carry.

Step 3 Find the structural actions in the load path for each loadcase.

Step 4 Check that each load path is not over-stressed.

The details of the process of structural design are examined later but now the concept of stress has been explained, the main steps of the process can be stated. This gives the basic framework that allows the overall behaviour of structures to be understood or designed.

The main point about the size of stresses is that they can be varied without altering the force. Carrying out **step 4** of the design process may indicate that some part of a load path is over-stressed. If this is the case then it may be convenient to alter the structure locally, by altering the geometry, so that the stress is reduced below the maximum stress that is allowed.

This idea is used widely in everyday life; stresses are increased or reduced purposely. For example, the weight of a person may be constant, but the stress under the person's feet will vary with the area of the shoe in contact with the ground. This variation may have good or bad effects. **Fig. 3.23** shows three types of shoes, normal shoes, high-heeled shoes and snow shoes.

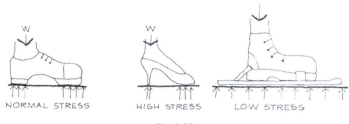

NORMAL STRESS   HIGH STRESS   LOW STRESS

Fig. 3.23

Normal shoes cause normal stresses and can be used on surfaces that can resist these stresses. High-heeled shoes, as they provide a much smaller area to carry the same weight, cause higher stresses under the shoe, particularly under the heel. With very slender (stiletto) heels the stresses can be high enough to permanently damage some types of normal floor surfaces. Where stresses must be kept low, for walking on snow for instance, the area under the foot must be increased. This is why snow shoes prevent people from sinking into snow.

The meaning of 'comfortable' shoes, beds and chairs etc. is partly based on limiting the stresses on the human body to 'comfortable' ones. Padded chairs with large seat areas are more comfortable than hard chairs with small seat areas.

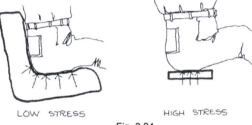

LOW STRESS   HIGH STRESS

Fig. 3.24

The idea of deliberately **altering** stress sizes by geometric methods is also widely used in many other objects used by humans. For example drawing pins are provided with large heads, to allow comfortable stresses on the thumb, and pointed shafts to cause high stresses under the point. The point stress is so high that the base surface fails and allows the drawing pin to be driven in.

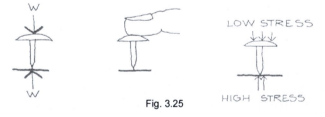

Fig. 3.25

The important idea is that for equilibrium, the force on the head must equal the force on the point, but the stresses vary. The stresses are varied by changing the geometry (of the drawing pin). The provision of handles, points, sharp edges and wide shoulder straps are all familiar devices for deliberately raising or lowering stresses.

Returning to engineering structures, the task is to provide a structure that will carry the prescribed loads down the load path with 'comfortable' stresses everywhere.

Depending on the material used, the size of the comfortable stress will vary. For instance as steel is stronger than timber, the allowable (comfortable) stress for steel is higher than for timber. So, in a general sort of way, timber structures will have larger structural elements than steel structures if they are to carry the same load.

As it is usually impractical to arrive at satisfactory structures by guesswork or by testing whole structures, the modern approach is to calculate the size of the stresses on each load path and to check that all the stresses are within set limits. For this to be a practical proposition rather than a research project, many simplifying assumptions have to be made. These assumptions allow what is usually known as **Engineer's theory** to be used for stress calculations. Some of these assumptions are concerned with the nature of the material from which the structure is made. These are:

- **The material is isotropic**. This means that the mechanical behaviour of the material is the same in all directions.

- **The material is linear elastic**. An elastic material is one which after deforming under load returns to exactly the same state when the load is removed. If an elastic material deforms as an exact proportion of the load then it is linear elastic. This is discussed further in **Chapter 6**.

There are also assumptions about the geometry of the structure. These are:

- **The structure is homogeneous**. This means there are no cracks, splits or holes or other discontinuities in the structure.

- **The deflections of the loaded structure are small**. This means that using the shape of the unloaded structure for calculations to determine structural behaviour will not lead to any significant errors. This does not apply to very flexible structures; think for example of a washing line.

- **Plane sections remain plane**. This rather cryptic statement means that certain parts of a structure that are flat before loading are still flat after loading. This is explained more fully in this chapter.

The Engineer's theory is used for most structural design because it leads to simple stress distributions in structural elements when they are subjected to internal forces of bending moments, shear and axial forces.

3.3   Axial stresses

An axially loaded structural element has axial internal forces and these cause axial stresses across the element (see **Figs. 3.11** and **12**). Using the Engineer's theory this leads to a very simple stress distribution.

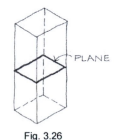

Fig. 3.26

This plane cross-section remains plane after the column is axially loaded. This is visually implied in **Fig. 2.2** where a slice of a loaded column is shown. What the 'plane sections remain plane' assumption means in this case is that the flat faces of the unloaded slice are flat after the slice is loaded.

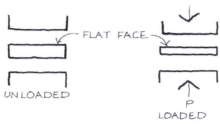

Fig. 3.27

This assumption gives a very simple stress distribution for an axially loaded column. Because the loaded faces remain flat, all parts of the column cross-section deflect by the same amount.

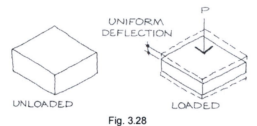

Fig. 3.28

Because the deflections are equal over the cross-section, the stress (load/unit area) is the same everywhere, in other words there is a constant (or uniform) stress distribution.

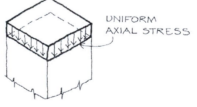

Fig. 3.29

The constant stress over the cross-section of an axially loaded column gives a very simple relationship between force and stress and this is:

- **Axial stress = Axial force divided by the cross-sectional area**

This means that for a given force, the size of the stress can be varied by increasing or decreasing the cross-sectional area of the column.

The assumption that plane sections remain plane also gives guidance as to when a structural element should be regarded as one, two or three dimensional (see **Figs. 3.1, 3.3** and **3.5**).

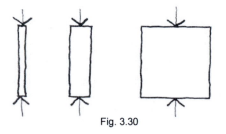

Fig. 3.30

The assumption implies that the whole cross-section is equally stressed. **Fig. 3.30** shows three columns each subjected to a local load. For the widest column it does not seem reasonable to assume that the whole cross-section is equally stressed or even that the whole cross-section is stressed.

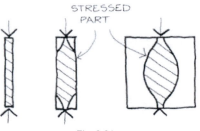

Fig. 3.31

This figure shows the stressed part of the three columns. Very approximately the stress 'spreads out' at about 60°. This means that for the widest column, plane sections do not remain plane. The faces of the loaded slice of the widest column **do not remain plane**.

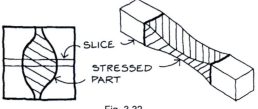

Fig. 3.32

From an engineering point of view this gives guidance as to whether structural elements are one, two or three dimensional. Where simple stress distributions are reasonable then elements can be regarded as one dimensional, but where the stress distributions are no longer simple the elements are two or three dimensional. In **Fig. 3.32** the widest column has to be regarded as a two dimensional element. This effect can be seen by pulling on progressively wider and wider sheets of paper. The stressed part of the paper will become taut; the unstressed areas will remain floppy.

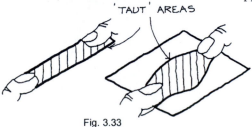

Fig. 3.33

Structural element behaviour 67

3.4　Bending stresses

Where parts of the load path are spanning elements, beams and slabs, the elements will have internal bending forces (moments). The top and bottom surfaces of these elements become curved; however, plane cross-sections still remain plane.

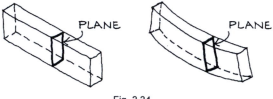

Fig. 3.34

Again looking at unloaded and loaded slices (see pages **40** to **42**), the plane sections can be identified.

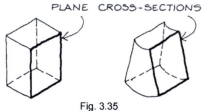

Fig. 3.35

By viewing the slice from the side it can be seen that the plane sections rotate.

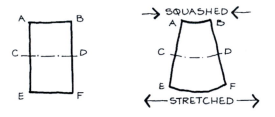

Fig. 3.36

When the slice is bent by an internal bending moment, **AB** is squashed, **EF** is stretched and **CD** remains the same. Because the cross-sections remain plane, the amount each part of the slice is squashed or stretched varies directly with the distance it is from **CD**.

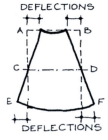

Fig. 3.37

68 Building structures

As the structural material is linear elastic, the force is directly proportional to the deflection, so the maximum compression is at **AB** and the amount of compression decreases constantly from **AB** to **CD**. Similarly the maximum tension is at **EF** and the tension decreases constantly from **EF** to **CD**. The maximum compression is at the top of the slice and the maximum tension is at the bottom of the slice and at **CD**, the change point, there is neither compression nor tension. Using this information a stress distribution diagram can be drawn for the side view of the slice.

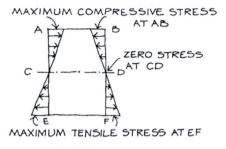

Fig. 3.38

If it is also assumed that these stresses that are caused by an internal bending moment do not vary **across** the beam, a three-dimensional diagram of the stress distribution of the compressive and tensile stresses can be drawn.

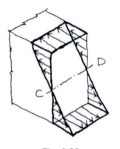

Fig. 3.39

This stress distribution, which is based on the assumptions of linear elasticity and plane sections remaining plane, is widely (but not exclusively) used in structural engineering. It can be viewed as being in two parts, a triangular distribution of compressive stress and a triangular distribution of tensile stress. **Figs. 3.22** and **3.23** explain how a stress distribution balances a force at the centre of gravity of the stress distribution. The two parts of the stress distribution give a new concept which is the **moment as a pair of forces**. In **Figs. 2.9** to **2.12** a bending moment is shown as a rotating force. Now the bending moment acting on a slice of a beam can be thought of in three alternative ways – as a rotating force, as a double triangular distribution of compressive and tensile stresses, or as a pair of forces.

Fig. 3.40

This figure illustrates a **key concept** in the understanding of structural behaviour and applies, often disguised, to almost all structures. These three alternative views are logically connected by the various concepts that have been introduced, really **three steps** have been made.

Step 1 Connects the idea of a bending moment in a beam with plane sections remaining plane and the sides of the slice of a beam rotating.

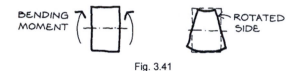

Fig. 3.41

Step 2 Connects the deflection of the slice caused by the rotation of the sides to ideas of linear elasticity and stress distribution.

Fig. 3.42

Step 3 This uses the idea that if a force causes a stress distribution, then where there is a stress distribution there must be a force. And this force must act at the centre of gravity of the stress distribution.

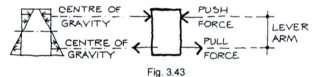

Fig. 3.43

In this figure the **distance** between the 'push forces', which are the effect of the compressive stresses, and the 'pull forces', which are the effect of the tensile stresses, is called the **lever arm**. Remembering that any moment is **a force times a distance**, the push and pull forces 'give back' the bending moment. Here, rather confusingly, the force can be the push or the pull force and the distance is the lever arm.

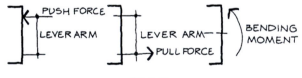

Fig. 3.44

The push and pull forces and the lever arm show how by altering the local geometry of the beam, the **size** of the stresses can be altered for any bending moment. From **Fig. 3.44** two statements can be made about the sizes of the forces from the requirements of equilibrium. Firstly the forces on each face must be in horizontal equilibrium.

Fig. 3.45

So the first statement is:

- **the size of the push force must equal the size of the pull force.**

Secondly, from moment equilibrium, the bending moment must equal a force times the lever arm. So the second statement is:

- **the size of the push force times the lever arm must equal the size of the pull force times the lever arm must equal the size of the bending moment**

The size of the bending moment is 'fixed' by the position of the element in the load path and the size of the loads the load path has to carry. So, from the second statement, if the lever arm is made bigger, the push (or pull) force is smaller and vice versa.

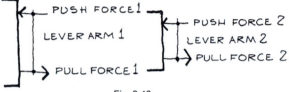

Fig. 3.46

Because of statement two, the size of **PUSH FORCE 1** times **LEVER ARM 1** must equal **PUSH FORCE 2** times **LEVER ARM 2**. As **LEVER ARM 1** is bigger than **LEVER ARM 2** then **PUSH FORCE 1** will be smaller than **PUSH FORCE 2**. The relationship between the size of stresses and forces is dependent, for any force, on the area and the shape of the distribution. For bending stresses the distribution shown in **Fig. 3.39** has been used.

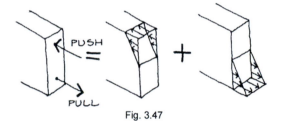

Fig. 3.47

All the compressive stresses (force per unit area) on the upper part of the beam must add up to the push force, and all the tensile stresses on the lower part of the beam must add up to the pull force. By varying the **depth** and therefore the lever arm, the size of the push and pull forces can be altered, which means the sizes of the stresses can be altered. This is only true if the width of the beam is not altered. The size of the stresses can also be altered by varying the **width** because this alters the area. Or the size of the stresses can be altered by varying both the depth and the width.

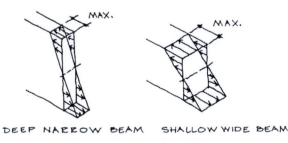

Fig. 3.48

Unlike axially loaded elements that are equally stressed over the whole cross-section (**Fig. 3.29**), beams bent by moments have varying stresses that are at a maximum at the top and bottom. As all structural materials have a maximum usable stress, rectangular solid beams like those shown in **Fig. 3.48** are 'under-stressed' except for the top and bottom faces.

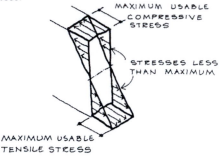

Fig. 3.49

It is one ambition of structural design to try and stress all parts of a structure to the maximum usable stress of the structural material being used. In this way no structural material is 'wasted'. This is a sensible ambition provided it does not lead to geometrically complex structures that are expensive to build.

Not only can material be wasted within the depth of a beam but it can also be wasted along its length. Suppose a beam of constant depth and rectangular cross-section is used to carry a load over a simple span. The size of the bending moment will vary along the length of the beam.

Fig. 3.50

For this simple structure, the maximum stress only occurs at one place where the bending moment is at its maximum. Almost the whole of the beam has bending stresses less than the maximum. This contrasts sharply with a column with end loads. Here the whole of the cross-section and the whole of the length of the column can be at maximum stress and so none of the structural material is wasted.

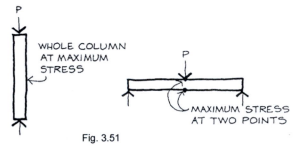

Fig. 3.51

To try and make beams more 'stress effective', non-rectangular shapes have been developed. Although there is some visual evidence that ancient builders were aware of the effect of cross-sectional shapes on the bending performance of beams, the pioneers of modern engineering in the early 19th century took some time to evolve efficient shapes. As the maximum stresses for bending are at the top and bottom of a beam, more efficient beam sections have more structural material here. These efficient sections are I, channel or box sections.

'I' BEAM   CHANNEL   BOX

Fig. 3.52

The exact details of these shapes depend on the structural material used, as the methods of construction are different. Furthermore where bending efficiency is not of paramount importance or for a variety of other reasons, such as cost and speed of construction, other shapes such as tubes, rods and angles may be used.

To understand why the shapes shown in **Fig. 3.52** are 'bending efficient' it is helpful to compare an **'I'** shaped section with a **'+'** shaped section. Both have the same depth and the same cross-sectional area.

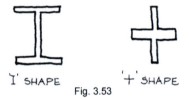

'I' SHAPE   '+' SHAPE

Fig. 3.53

As plane sections are assumed to remain plane and both sections are assumed to have the same maximum usable stress, the side view of the stress distribution is the same as **Fig. 3.38** for both the sections.

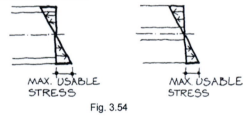

MAX. USABLE STRESS   MAX. USABLE STRESS

Fig. 3.54

However, if the three-dimensional stress diagrams are drawn, similar to **Fig. 3.39**, dramatic differences appear.

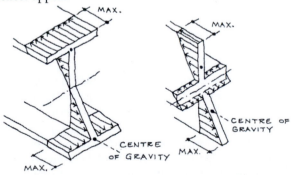

Fig. 3.55

The **I** section has large areas of the cross-section with stresses near to the maximum, but the **+** section has large areas with stresses near to zero. This means that the push and pull forces of **Fig. 3.43** are much bigger for the **I** section than for the **+** section. Also the positions of the centres of gravity of these stresses are different and this gives the **I** section a larger lever arm than the **+** section.

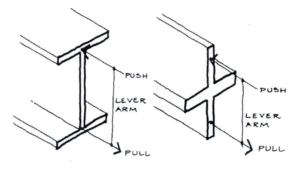

Fig. 3.56

The maximum bending moment a beam with any particular cross-section can carry is given by the second statement stated on **page 71** and this moment is:

- **the push force, with the maximum usable stress, times the lever arm**

which is the same as:

- **the pull force, with the maximum usable stress, times the lever arm**

Both the lever arm and the push force (or pull force) are greater for the **I** section than for the **+** section. Because of this, if beams have the same depth, the same cross-sectional area and the same maximum usable stress, then those with **I** sections will be able to resist larger bending moments than those with **+** sections. Although **I** beams, as they are called, can be made from timber or reinforced concrete they are readily made from steel. Due to the bending efficiency of **I** beams they are very widely used in steel construction as any visit to a steel construction site will show.

By adopting more efficient cross-sections, more structural material is used at, or near to, the maximum usable stress. But as the size of the bending moment usually varies along a beam, higher stresses can be achieved away from the position of maximum bending moment by reducing the width or the depth of the beam.

Fig. 3.57

By reducing the depth the lever arm is reduced, so that the push and pull forces are higher for the smaller bending moment. Reducing the width has the effect of reducing the stress area for the push and pull forces and so increasing the stresses.

Building a beam with an **I** section and varying the depth or width to keep the bending stresses high where the size of the bending moment reduces, is an efficient use of structural material compared with using a solid rectangular section of constant depth and width. Whether it is worthwhile using the more complex bending efficient beam depends on cost, both of the material and cost of construction. It is common to see beams of varying depth used for road bridges but unusual in building structures. It is also common to see steel **I** beams, but timber structures, particularly in houses, nearly always use timber beams of rectangular cross-section of constant width and depth.

As with columns (see **Section 3.3**), the assumption that plane sections remain plane is not always valid. There are two situations where it may not apply. The first is when the span of the beam is not more than about five times the depth of the beam. As the plane sections are no longer plane, the bending stress distribution is not the one shown in **Figs. 3.28** and **3.29**.

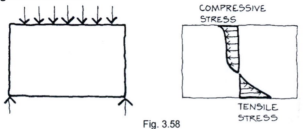

COMPRESSIVE STRESS

TENSILE STRESS

Fig. 3.58

These beams, called **deep beams**, cannot be regarded as one-dimensional elements but are two-dimensional elements (see page **58**).

If a beam is not deep but is made from an **I** or similar section, again plane sections may not remain plane. If the widths of the top and bottom parts of the section are increased eventually they will become 'too wide' and not all of the section will be stressed by the bending moment.

NORMAL I BEAM   'TOO WIDE' I BEAM

Fig. 3.59

For a normal **I** beam the bending stresses are assumed to be constant across the top and bottom parts, but for wide beams only part of the beam may be stressed and the stress is not constant across the beam.

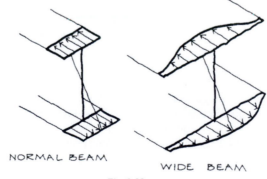

NORMAL BEAM

WIDE BEAM

Fig. 3.60

The effect that causes this varying stress across wide beams is called **shear lag** and the part of the beam that is stressed is often called the **effective width**.

3.5   Shear stresses

Axial forces cause axial stresses (see **Fig. 3.29**) and bending moments cause bending stresses (see **Fig. 3.39**), so it is not unreasonable to expect shear forces to cause **shear stresses**. Shear stresses resist vertical loads so it is to be expected that shear stresses act vertically. For the vertical shear force acting on the face of the slice of the beam, ideas similar to those shown in **Fig. 3.12** can be used. Here, unlike the column, the shear stresses (force per unit area) act in line with the face of the slice.

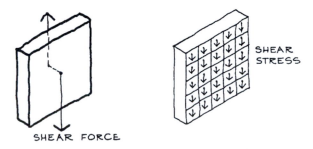

Fig. 3.61

Unfortunately the distribution of shear stress cannot be deduced from the straightforward assumptions that were used for axial and bending stress. At the top and the bottom the shear stress must be zero otherwise there would be vertical shear stresses on the surface of the beam, which is impossible! So what shape is the distribution of shear stress? Mathematical analysis shows that for a rectangular beam the shear stress distribution has a curved shape, accurately described as parabolic. The maximum is at the middle of the beam and it is zero at the top and bottom and is constant across the width of the beam.

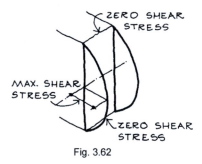

Fig. 3.62

It is common to assume for 'practical' structural engineering design that the shear stress distribution is rectangular rather than curved. This means that this shear stress is 50% less than the maximum shear stress and that there are vertical shear stresses at the top and bottom faces. In spite of these inaccuracies this assumption is thought to be worthwhile as it simplifies the numerical calculation of shear stresses.

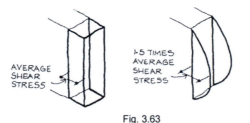

Fig. 3.63

With this assumption there is a similar relationship between shear force and shear stress as that used for the axial forces and stresses (see page **66**) and this is:

- **Shear stress = Shear force divided by the shear area**

The term **shear area** is introduced because for non-rectangular cross-sectional shapes the 'vertical' area is used rather than the total area.

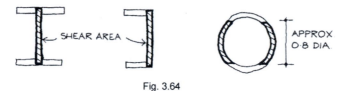

Fig. 3.64

This figure shows typical shear areas for a few common structural cross-sections and illustrates the general idea of vertical shear area.

3.6   Torsional stresses

When a one-dimensional element is twisted by torsional moments (see **Section 2.6**) the internal forces in the element cause torsional stresses. To see what is happening cut a slice from a circular bar that is being twisted by torsional moments.

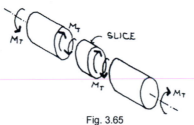

Fig. 3.65

If the circular cross-section is divided into small areas by radial and circumferential lines then each area has a force in the tangential direction to the circumference. Compare this with the diagram for shear stresses – **Fig. 3.61.**

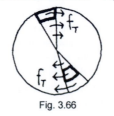

Fig. 3.66

At the centre these tangential forces are zero and it is assumed that they increase linearly towards the outside of the bar. Compare this with the variation of bending stresses shown in **Fig. 3.38.**

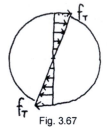

Fig. 3.67

If a circular tube, with a wall thickness that is 'small' compared with its diameter, is twisted by torsional moments then it could be considered reasonable that the tangential stresses are constant across the wall of thickness **t**.

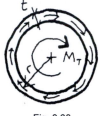

Fig. 3.68

In this case the relationship between the torsional moment, **M$_T$**, and the tangential torsional stress, **f$_T$**, is particularly simple;

Torsional moment = Circumference at wall centre x wall thickness x torsional stress

or $$M_T = 2\pi r \times t \times f_T$$

The tangential torsional stresses in circular elements can be thought of as a number of 'loops' or circles of constant stress, with the stress in each circle being proportional to the distance from the centre. The circular tube is then a special case of just one circle of constant stress.

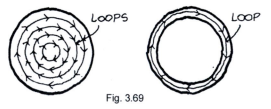

Fig. 3.69

As far as torsional stresses are concerned, circular rods and tubes are special cases because their cross-section is symmetrical about **all** radial axes. The faces of slices cut from these elements are flat (plane) before being twisted and remain flat after the element has been twisted – this is a special case and is not true for sections of other shapes. This should be compared with the idea of plane cross-sections shown in **Fig. 3.35** for the case of a bent beam. If a rod with an elliptical cross-section is twisted, the face of a slice that is flat before the rod is twisted by a torsional moment will not remain flat. In this case the face will deform into a curved surface technically called a hyperbolic paraboloid. In other words the cross-section warps and the element deforms unequally in the longitudinal direction.

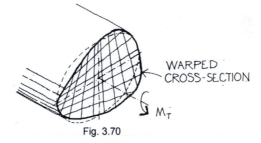

Fig. 3.70

In the case of non-circular rods, the torsional stresses can still be thought of as a series of 'loops' but in this case these loops are elliptical.

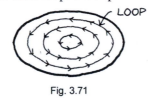

Fig. 3.71

In the case of a rectangular bar, the loops are not all of the same shape and the cross-section warps in a more complex manner.

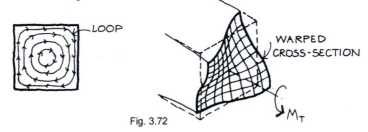

Fig. 3.72

Where cross-sections of an element are made up of a number of rectangular elements which do not form any type of tube – **I** beams and channels for example – they are called open sections (see **Fig. 3.52**). For these sections the torsional stresses are loops round the whole section and the cross-section warps.

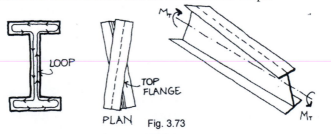

PLAN   Fig. 3.73

The torsional behaviour just described has two important features that are:

- **the torsional stresses form 'loops' within the section**

- **in general a plane cross-section warps when the element is twisted**

This type of torsional behaviour is often called **Uniform Torsion** or **St. Venant's Torsion** (after the French mathematician Saint-Venant (1797-1886) who presented the mathematical theory of torsion in 1853). Torsion is looked at again, from a different point of view, in the next chapter.

3.7 Curved elements

When structural elements are curved vertically or horizontally the internal forces, axial forces, bending moments and torsional moments cannot always be considered as separate internal forces as they can be interconnected. To see how this happens, two cantilevers, one curved vertically, one curved horizontally and each loaded at the end with a point load **P**, are considered.

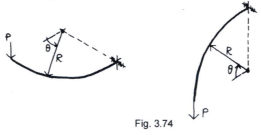

Fig. 3.74

Looking at the horizontal cantilever, first consider an 'L' shaped cantilever with straight elements **AB** and **BC**. Using the definition that a bending moment is a distance times a force – see page **27** – the bending moment will increase linearly along **AB** and be constant along **BC**. There will be no twisting effect in element **AB** but a constant one in element **BC**. The bending moment and torsional moment diagrams are drawn in the next figure. A constant shear force of **P** also exists, but the diagram is not drawn for this structure.

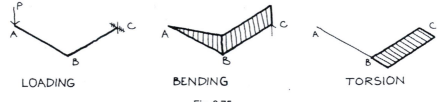

LOADING   BENDING   TORSION

Fig. 3.75

But with the curved cantilever, the bending and torsional moments are present throughout the element and vary continuously as trigonometrical functions of the angle θ.

LOADING   BENDING   TORSION

Fig. 3.76

A similar approach is used for the vertical cantilever, firstly an 'L' shaped cantilever is considered. In this case only an axial force exists in element **AB** whereas bending moments and shear forces exist in element **BC**.

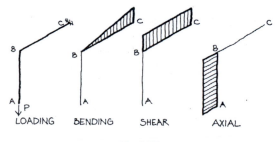

LOADING   BENDING   SHEAR   AXIAL

Fig. 3.77

Like the horizontal curved cantilever, all the forces in the vertical cantilever are present throughout the element again varying as trigonometrical functions of the angle θ.

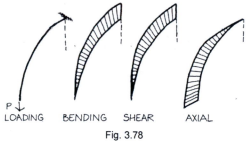

LOADING   BENDING   SHEAR   AXIAL

Fig. 3.78

If a curved member is bent to a tight radius, the distribution of stresses across the section, even using the assumption of the **Engineer's theory** (see page **65**), will not be linear, however the linear distribution is accurate enough for most situations. Curved elements are not considered further in this book – the interested reader should consult the specialised literature. This brief section has been included to show how a structure with curved elements has a more complex and interactive behaviour than those structures that only have straight elements.

3.8   Combined stresses

When a one-dimensional element is part of a load path it will have internal forces and these may be axial forces, bending moments or shear forces. These internal forces can be thought of as distributions of axial stress, bending stress and shear stress. With the simplifying assumptions that have been made these stresses have very simple **stress distributions**.

For axial forces and axial stresses:

AXIAL FORCE

UNIFORM STRESS

Fig. 3.79

for bending moments and bending stresses:

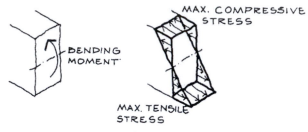

Fig. 3.80

and for shear forces and shear stresses:

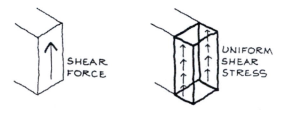

Fig. 3.81

Fig. 2.42 shows how axial forces, bending moments and shear forces vary around a portal frame when it is loaded with a point load. Each part of the portal frame has an axial force and a bending moment and a shear force. This means that at each part of the structure there are distributions of axial stresses **and** bending stresses and shear stresses. Can, and if so how, can these stresses be combined to give the total stress distribution? One way is to combine the stresses on the face of a slice; this type of combination is frequently used in engineering.

This way of combining stresses is relatively straightforward as it 'just adds' stresses that are in the same direction on the face of the slice. Both axial stresses and bending stresses act at right angles to the face of the beam, which is along the beam, so they are combined by adding the stress distributions together.

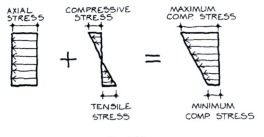

Fig. 3.82

In this figure because the size of the axial compressive stress is bigger than the maximum tensile bending stress, the whole of the cross-section is in compression. The effect of combining the stresses gives a combined **maximum stress** and a combined **minimum stress**. The sizes of these stresses are:

- **Maximum stress = Axial compressive stress** plus **Maximum compressive bending stress**

- **Minimum stress = Axial compressive stress** minus **Maximum tensile bending stress**

Because the shear stress is at right angles to the face of the slice it is not added to the axial and bending stresses but is kept separate. Depending on the relative sizes of the axial and bending stresses and whether the axial stress is tensile or compressive, the combined stress distribution is all tensile, tensile and compressive, or all compressive.

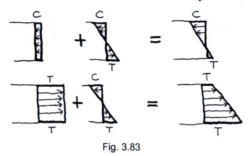

Fig. 3.83

The axial stress distribution can be thought of as an axial force acting at the centre of gravity of the axial stress distribution and the bending stress distribution can be thought of as a pair of push-pull forces acting at the centres of gravity of the tensile and compressive parts of the bending stress distribution.

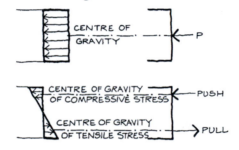

Fig. 3.84

As the stress distributions have been combined to give one stress distribution, can the forces be combined to give one force? If so, what is this force and where does it act? As **Fig. 3.45** shows the push equals the pull so the combined force can only be the axial force. But this force must act at the centre of gravity of the combined stress distribution.

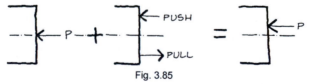

Fig. 3.85

And this centre of gravity is not at the centre of gravity of the axial stress.

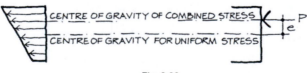

Fig. 3.86

Structural element behaviour 83

The effect of the moment is to 'move' the axial force by a distance, **e**, from the centre of gravity for uniform axial stress. This distance **e** is called the **eccentricity** and with this new concept many common engineering situations can be better understood.

Before combining the forces there was an axial force **P** and a bending moment **M**. Now there is an axial force **P** that has 'moved' by a distance, the eccentricity **e**. What has happened to **M**, the bending moment? The bending moment still exists but now as **P** times **e**. This is the by now familiar force **P**, times distance **e**.

Fig. 3.87

This idea of the axial force acting at an eccentricity can be used for both internal forces and external forces. If a structural element has an internal axial force and a bending moment then this can be viewed as being the same as the axial force being applied at a point eccentric from the centre of gravity for uniform stress. Alternatively if an external axial load is applied to a structural element at a point eccentric from the centre of gravity for uniform axial stress then this can be viewed as being the same as applying an **axial load plus a moment**. This gives a very simple relationship between axial force, bending moment and eccentricity, which is:

- **bending moment = axial force times the eccentricity**

or

- **eccentricity = bending moment divided by the axial force**

Suppose a beam is supported on a wall as in **Fig. 1.53**. Then, for the wall only to have uniform axial stress from the reaction of the beam, the beam must be supported exactly at the position of the centre of gravity for this uniform stress distribution.

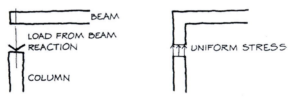

Fig. 3.88

This is usually impossible in any real structure unless very precise precautions are taken. This means the reaction from the beam that the wall is supporting will be applied to the wall at an eccentricity. So the wall is loaded by an axial load plus a bending moment.

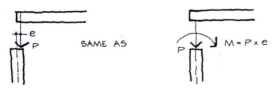

Fig. 3.89

In this figure the eccentricity is within the width of the wall but this will not always be the case. What happens at the base of a garden wall or any other free-standing wall, when the wind blows? The axial force is caused by the weight of the wall itself and the bending moment is caused by the wind blowing horizontally on the wall.

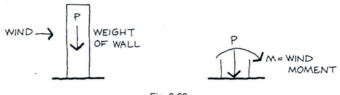

Fig. 3.90

Here the eccentricity could be of any size depending on the relative sizes of the axial force caused by the weight of the wall and the moment caused by the wind. The top diagrams in **Fig. 3.91** show a cross-section with only compression stresses whilst the lower ones with compressive and tensile stresses. This means that the eccentricity is greater in the lower diagram.

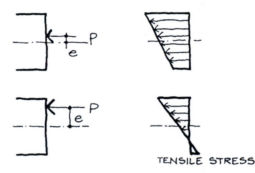

Fig. 3.91

For rectangular sections the eccentricity must be kept within the middle third of the cross-section if there is to be no tensile stress.

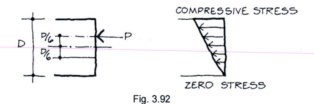

Fig. 3.92

This has very important consequences for structures made from structural materials such as masonry or mass concrete that cannot carry significant tensile stresses. For structures made from these materials, axial forces must be 'kept' within the central part of the cross-section or the structure will crack or collapse. This is why brick chimneys and walls sometimes blow over in high winds.

This way of combining stresses makes it easy to check that the stresses in a structure are within the limits of the usable stress for the material. Of course all parts of every load path have to be checked in this way for all load combinations, to ensure that the stresses in the structure are always within the limits of the material.

CHAPTER 4   *Advanced concepts of stress*

In the last chapter the concept of stress was introduced and it was shown how axial forces, bending moments and shear forces could be related to stress distributions in a structural member. By making simplifying assumptions, the **Engineer's theory** in particular, simple stress distributions were obtained. At the end of the chapter the idea of combining stresses was used to show how axial loads and moments are related. Most engineering design is carried out just using these concepts, however, the idea of stress can be used to understand more complicated structural behaviour.

This chapter could be omitted on first reading but the concepts used in this chapter give a deeper understanding of structural behaviour. These concepts can be used to understand more complicated structures than those made of simple beam and column elements, but they also give deeper insights into how simple structures behave.

4.1   Principal stresses in one-dimensional elements

Section 3.8 of the last chapter gave one way of combining stresses but there is another way of combining stresses at points in a structure by using the idea of **principal stress**. The idea of principal stress is both conceptually and mathematically more difficult than just adding the axial and bending stresses and keeping the shear stresses separate, but it does give much more information on how a structure acts.

To try and understand how a structure acts, slices of the structure have been examined and the idea of stresses has been presented as the effect of forces acting on the face of a slice. The structure does not 'know' that the human brain has decided that it is stressed by axial, bending and shear stresses, nor does it 'think' that it is made up from a series of slices. When a structural element is loaded by being part of a load path it deforms. Some parts squash and others stretch and internal forces do exist. However, the idea that three types of stress exist on the face of a slice cut at right angles to the length of the element is simplistic.

To get a better idea of what is happening inside a structure a 'small part' of the structure is examined. This is similar to the approach used for slices cut at right angles to a one-dimensional structural element only this time there is no restriction on the position of the part examined. This approach can apply to one, two or three-dimensional elements.

What is meant by a small part is usually taken as a small cube. How small is small is never stated explicitly but it is larger than molecular size but small enough for stresses not to vary across the faces of the cube. Because the stresses do not vary, a stress on a face can be represented by a single **force arrow**.

As before, if a beam is subjected to lateral loads it resists these by internal forces called bending moments and shear forces. Using simplifying assumptions these cause constant shear stress and linearly varying bending stresses on a face cut at right angles to the length of the beam.

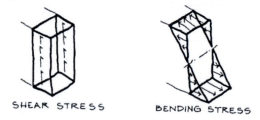

SHEAR STRESS   BENDING STRESS

Fig. 4.1

If two small cubes are cut from the beam, one near the top and one near the bottom, then these cubes would be subjected to axial stresses from the bending moment and shear stresses from the shear force.

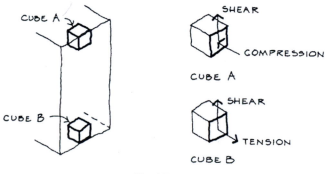

Fig. 4.2

Because the cubes have been cut from a beam rather than a more general structure and because they have been cut at right angles to the length of the beam, it seems that only two of the six faces of the cube have been stressed. Each of the two faces is stressed with a shear stress and an axial stress.

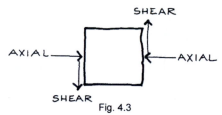

Fig. 4.3

The cube is in horizontal equilibrium and vertical equilibrium as the stresses balance but the cube is not in moment equilibrium, as the shear stresses are tending to rotate the cube.

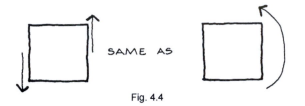

Fig. 4.4

As this cannot happen there must be other stresses to balance the rotation. These 'new' stresses are shear stresses on the top and bottom faces of the cube.

'NEW' SHEAR STRESS

Fig. 4.5

So the small cubes when cut from the beam in the positions shown are stressed by axial stresses, vertical shear stresses and the new **horizontal shear stresses**. For moment equilibrium the horizontal shear stresses must be numerically equal to the vertical shear stresses. Because there are no forces across the beam there are no further stresses.

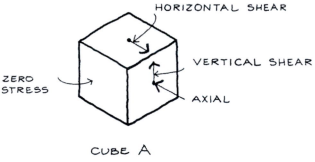

HORIZONTAL SHEAR

VERTICAL SHEAR

ZERO STRESS

AXIAL

CUBE A

Fig. 4.6

Before exploring these ideas further the effects of 'rotating cubes' must be clear. If a square flexible sheet is pulled on two opposite sides it will stretch and if pushed it will squash.

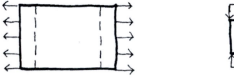

Fig. 4.7

If the sides of the sheet are subjected to shear forces, the sheet will take up a lozenge (or parallelogram) shape.

Fig. 4.8

Draw a square on the sheet at **45°** to the sides. If the sheet is pulled on one pair of opposite sides and pushed on the other pair, then the square sheet becomes a rectangle, but the square drawn on the sheet becomes lozenge shaped.

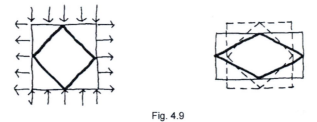

Fig. 4.9

And if the sheet is subjected to shear forces, the square sheet becomes lozenge shaped and the square drawn on the sheet becomes a rectangle.

Fig. 4.10

This shows that for push and pull forces the sheet 'thinks' it is in tension and compression but the drawn sheet 'thinks' it is in shear. When the sheet has shear forces on the sides the situation is reversed and the drawn sheet 'thinks' it is in tension and compression. So, depending on how the element is cut from the structure, the type and the sizes of the stresses depend on the angle at which it is cut. The sheet example illustrates the two-dimensional case (as in the beam). In general the element is a cube and the stresses are in three directions, the concept of rotating is the same but the diagrams would be distorted cubes.

When shear stresses are absent, that is, there are **only axial stresses**, these stresses are called **principal stresses**. At some point in a structure a small cube positioned in some particular direction will, in general, have axial and shear stresses acting on the faces of the cube. To find the principal stresses at this point the cube must be rotated so that the shear stresses are zero. For the previous examples, push and pull forces cause principal stresses so no rotation is needed, but for shear the element must be rotated by 45°.

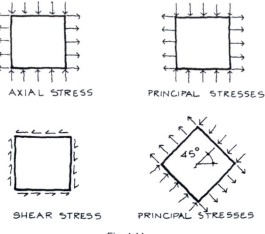

AXIAL STRESS   PRINCIPAL STRESSES

SHEAR STRESS   PRINCIPAL STRESSES

Fig. 4.11

Generally, at any point in a structure, axial and shear stresses will exist. Depending on the numerical size of these stresses, the cube will have to be rotated a specific amount for the shear stresses to be zero. The stresses on the rotated cube will be principal stresses.

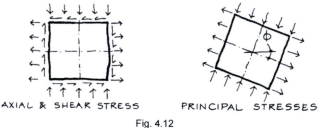

AXIAL & SHEAR STRESS   PRINCIPAL STRESSES

Fig. 4.12

As the stresses vary in type and size from point to point of a structure under load, the principal stresses will vary in size and direction from point to point. To see what information principal stresses give it is helpful to look at a simple beam loaded with a constant lateral load.

LOAD

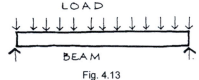

BEAM

Fig. 4.13

The beam transfers the lateral load to the supports by a system of internal forces that in this case are bending moments and shear forces. As before, the variation in the size of these forces is shown by bending moment and shear force diagrams.

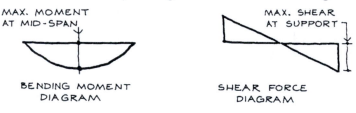

MAX. MOMENT
AT MID-SPAN

MAX. SHEAR
AT SUPPORT

BENDING MOMENT
DIAGRAM

SHEAR FORCE
DIAGRAM

Fig. 4.14

If the beam has a rectangular cross-section, the stresses on a face at right angles to the length of the beam are those shown in **Figs. 3.49** and **3.62**. That is, linearly varying for bending and curved (parabolic) for shear.

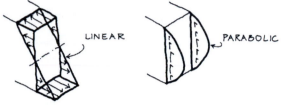

Fig. 4.15

The size of the bending moment and shear force vary along the length of the beam so the size of the stresses varies both across the depth and along the length of the beam. For bending stresses, the maximum is at the top and bottom faces in the centre of the beam and the shear stress is at a maximum at mid-depth at the ends of the beam.

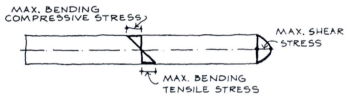

Fig. 4.16

For the top and bottom faces, the shear stress is always zero and at the centre of the beam the bending stress is always zero. For these points on the beam the principal stresses are horizontal or at 45°, see **Fig. 4.11**.

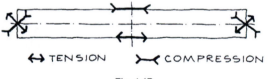

Fig. 4.17

For other points on the beam, the size and direction of the principal stresses can be calculated and these can be plotted. To indicate how the directions of these stresses change, lines can be drawn connecting the stresses at each point.

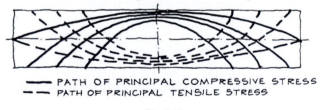

Fig. 4.18

The paths of stress (sometimes called stress trajectories) show that for this load case near the middle of the beam the principal stresses are nearly horizontal whilst near the supports the influence of the shear forces causes the stress paths to curve. The size of the stress varies along each path. **Fig. 4.18** shows that for the beam shown in **Fig. 4.13,** the two sets of principal stresses act in a series of 'arch like' curves – each curve crossing at right angles with every other curve.

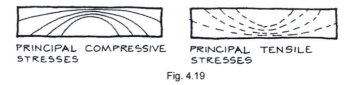

PRINCIPAL COMPRESSIVE STRESSES

PRINCIPAL TENSILE STRESSES

Fig. 4.19

These diagrams give a far clearer picture of what is happening to the beam than do a series of bending moment and shear force diagrams.

If a rod is subjected to a torsional moment, as shown in **Fig. 3.65**, then the rod will have principal stresses. The explanation follows directly from **Figs. 4.2** to **4.6**, which deal with vertical shear.

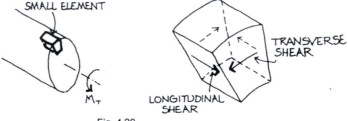

SMALL ELEMENT

M_T

TRANSVERSE SHEAR

LONGITUDINAL SHEAR

Fig. 4.20

A 'small element' of the torsionally loaded rod will become lozenge shaped which can be interpreted as 'diagonal' principal stresses – see **Fig. 4.11**.

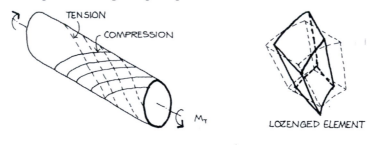

TENSION

COMPRESSION

M_T

LOZENGED ELEMENT

Fig. 4.21

The 'lozengeing' of the element can be thought of as being 'caused' by principal tensile and compressive stresses whose direction is at 45° to the longitudinal axes. Therefore a torsional moment is resisted by principal stresses that 'spiral' around the rod.

4.2 Principal stresses in two-dimensional elements

Pictures of the paths of principal stress can be drawn for any structure including those for which bending moment and shear force diagrams do not apply. Suppose a plate (a two-dimensional element) has a hole in it and the plate is stretched in one direction. The principal stress paths give a clear picture of how the plate behaves under this loading.

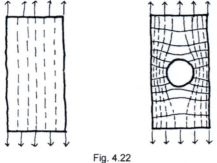

Fig. 4.22

For the plate without a hole the lines of tensile stress are parallel, but for the plate with the hole these lines have to curve around the hole. Because the lines of principal tensile stress curve there are curved lines of principal compressive stress near the hole.

Using the idea of principal tensile and compressive stresses diagrams can be drawn showing how a column 'changes' into a beam. Both a column and beam are considered to be one-dimensional elements, but the intermediate stages are two-dimensional elements.

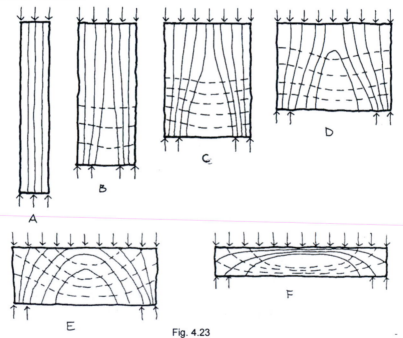

Fig. 4.23

Fig. 4.23A shows the stresses for a column, a one-dimensional element, and **Fig. 4.23F** shows the stresses for a beam, also a one-dimensional element. **Figs. 4.23B** to **E** show the stresses for various intermediate stages, and all these are two-dimensional elements. Whilst bending moment, axial and shear force diagrams make sense for the column and beam they cannot usefully be drawn for the intermediate structures.

Without the use of a computer program it is very laborious to calculate numerical values for the magnitude and direction of principal stresses. However, it is possible to make relatively simple calculations by introducing fictitious compressive and tensile members – struts and ties. **Fig. 4.23D** shows a structure that resembles a 'deep beam' – see **Fig. 3.58**. By introducing struts, shown dashed, and ties,[1] shown as full lines, it is possible to approximate the two-dimensional element with a simpler structure.

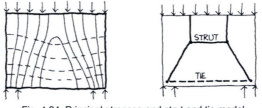

Fig. 4.24 Principal stresses and strut and tie model

What the actual cross-section is for each strut and tie obviously cannot be determined precisely so 'engineering judgement' has to be used. Specialist literature gives guidance on this. However, even without needing to make numerical calculations, drawing possible strut and tie models can lead to an increased conceptual understanding of these two-dimensional structures.

Principal stresses can also be drawn for curved elements like a shell. If a curved shell is spanning between end supports and loaded laterally the pattern of principal stresses will be similar to those for the beam shown in **Fig. 4.18** but the stresses will be curved across the shell.

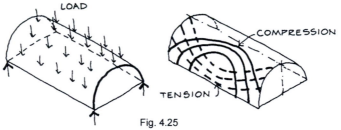

Fig. 4.25

As with the beam, the two sets of tensile and compressive stresses act as 'arch-like' curves. The compressive stresses move together at the top of the centre of the shell whereas the tensile stresses move apart to the bottom of the shell at the centre.

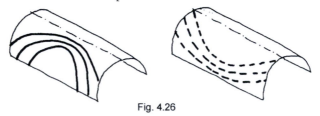

Fig. 4.26

It is often quite difficult to calculate the size and direction of the principal stresses for structures in general, however, if the pattern of the paths of the principal stresses can be visualised this gives a clear picture of how the structure is acting. With materials such as concrete or masonry, which cannot resist significant tensile forces, principal stress paths show where problems may occur or tensile reinforcement is needed.

4.3   The role of shear stresses in beams

When beams do not have simple rectangular cross-sections, as is often the case, the actual behaviour can be quite complex. **Fig. 3.52** shows a number of common non-rectangular shapes used for beams and **Fig. 3.55** shows the distribution of the bending stresses for an **I** beam. **Fig. 3.64** illustrates the idea of shear area used in the simple design of non-rectangular cross-sectional shapes.

The idea of the new shear stress shown in **Fig. 4.5** is crucial to the understanding of the complex behaviour of beams with non-rectangular cross-sections. Although this shear stress is required for the equilibrium of a small cube cut from a beam, what does it contribute to the behaviour of a beam with a rectangular cross-section? Suppose there are two beams of equal depth, one on top of the other and separated by a perfectly slippery surface.

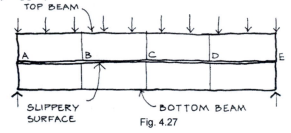

Fig. 4.27

The bent shape of the two beams will be the same, with the top of each beam shortening and the bottom lengthening (see **Fig. 2.13**). This means **ABCDE** of the top beam gets longer and **ABCDE** of the bottom beam gets shorter. Note that point **C** is at midspan.

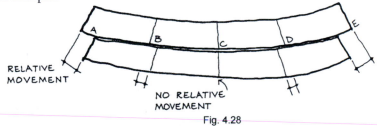

Fig. 4.28

Along the slippery surface **ABCDE** there will be a relative movement between the top and bottom beams. At midspan the movement is zero and the relative movement increases to become a maximum at the ends **A** and **E**. If the two beams are to act as one beam there would no relative movement along **ABCDE**. If this movement is to be zero there must be a force to stop the movement and the force will be proportional to the relative movement. So the force will be zero at midspan and a maximum at the ends.

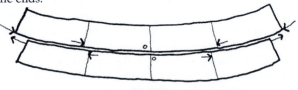

Fig. 4.29

It is the existence of these forces that causes the new shear stress. Because it is acting along the beam it is often called **horizontal shear** (or in timber design rolling shear). It is this horizontal shear stress that alters the bending stress distribution from a 'two beam' to a 'single beam' one.

ZERO HORIZONTAL   HORIZONTAL
SHEAR STRESS   SHEAR STRESS

Fig. 4.30

Not only does the size of the horizontal shear stress vary along the beam but it also varies within the depth of the beam. The size of the stress at any point within the depth of the beam is related to the size of the horizontal force being transferred. This force is due to the change in size of the bending stress across a slice. The difference in the size of the bending stresses has an out of balance horizontal force on any horizontal cut and this force is balanced by the horizontal shear stresses at the cut.

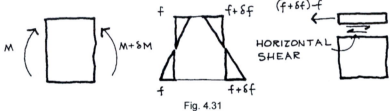

Fig. 4.31

By taking a series of horizontal cuts across the slice, the size of the horizontal shear stresses can be found. At the top and bottom faces of the beam this stress is zero whilst at mid-depth it is at a maximum. The actual shape of the distribution is parabolic, the same shape as the distribution of the vertical shear stress (see **Fig. 3.62**).

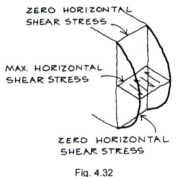

ZERO HORIZONTAL
SHEAR STRESS

MAX. HORIZONTAL
SHEAR STRESS

ZERO HORIZONTAL
SHEAR STRESS

Fig. 4.32

If an **I** section is used for a beam the horizontal shear stress still exists but the distribution is rather different. Because of the changed distribution of bending stresses, the largest part of the bending stress is in the top and bottom flanges (see **Fig. 3.55**). The maximum horizontal shear stress is still at mid-depth but because the section is 'made up' of flanges and a web the horizontal shear force has to be transmitted from one part of the beam to another. If the section is 'exploded' it can be seen how the horizontal shear forces 'join' it together.

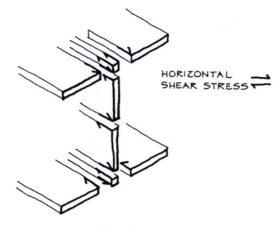

Fig. 4.33

What is happening is that the change in push force in each half of the top flange is being transmitted to the top of the web by a horizontal shear force.

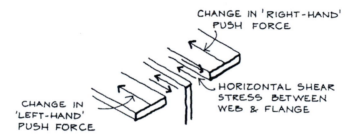

Fig. 4.34

The total change in flange force is then transmitted by a horizontal shear force to the web underneath the flange.

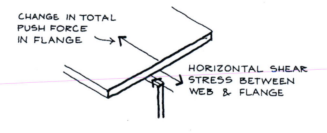

Fig. 4.35

At the mid-depth of the beam, the total change in web and flange force is being transmitted by a horizontal shear force.

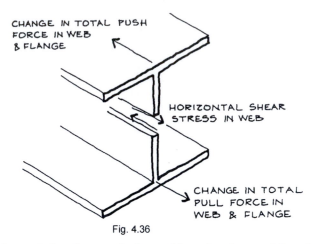

Fig. 4.36

Similarly for the change in bending tensile forces. Note that the word force has been used rather than stress because the stress will depend on the relative thickness of the flanges and the web. The horizontal shear stress in the web is balanced by the vertical shear stresses, but the horizontal shear stresses in the flange are acting in the plane of the flange and have to be balanced by shear stresses acting **across** the flange.

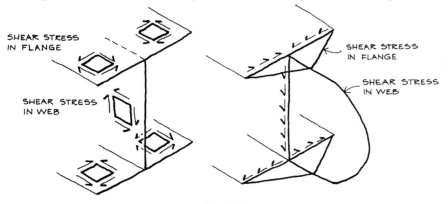

Fig. 4.37

The cross flange shear stress is zero at the outer edges and increases linearly towards the web. Because the web shear under the flange is the sum of the change of both the left and right-hand push forces, there is an increase at this point. The stress in the web then varies parabolically with a maximum at mid-depth. These shear stresses can be plotted on the cross-section. These shear stresses in built-up sections are often called the **shear flow**. Strictly the shear flow is a force, as it is the shear stress times the thickness.

Fig. 4.38

The horizontal forces in each flange are in horizontal equilibrium and the vertical shear stresses are in vertical equilibrium with the shear force. However, if a channel section is used for a beam, the shear flow can be obtained from the diagram for the **I** beam.

Fig. 4.39

Here, although the horizontal forces in each web are in overall equilibrium, these forces are some distance apart which means there is a moment.

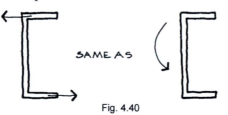

Fig. 4.40

This moment is trying to twist the channel rather than bend it. This example of the channel has been introduced to show how structural actions can become complicated even for a 'simple' beam and a 'simple' section like a channel.

4.4 Effect of beam cross-section

The reason the channel wants to twist and the **I** beam does not, is because the **I** beam is symmetrical about a vertical line and the channel is not.

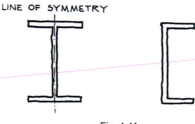

LINE OF SYMMETRY

Fig. 4.41

More generally, the effect of the cross-sectional shape of a structural element interacts with the type of loading to produce different types of structural behaviour. This structural behaviour can become extremely complicated for general shaped elements. The important point is to appreciate what causes simple or complex behaviour.

For axially loaded elements, if all parts are to be equally stressed, that is, uniform stress distribution (see **Fig. 3.29**), then the load has to be applied to the element at a particular point. This point is confusingly called the centre of gravity of the cross-section, a better term is **centre of area**. This point is the same point that balances a uniform stress distribution. To illustrate this concept imagine a tee shaped platform carrying people of equal weight equally spaced on the platform.

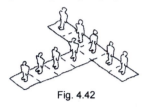

Fig. 4.42

These people are supposed to represent a uniform stress distribution. But where is the balance point? Unlike the see-saw the balance point has to be found in two dimensions. Two pictures can be drawn, one along the tee and one across it.

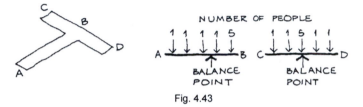

Fig. 4.43

In the **AB** direction the balance point will be nearer **B** than **A**, but for the **CD** direction the loading is symmetrical so the balance point is midway between **C** and **D**. The balance points are really lines and where these lines intersect is the centre of area.

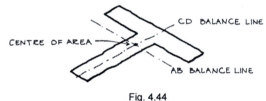

Fig. 4.44

So if the axial loads are applied through the centre of area a uniform stress distribution will be caused. If another shaped cross-section (or platform) is used then the centre of area will move. The balance lines will always be along any axes of symmetry, so for shapes with two axes of symmetry the centre of area will be at the intersection of the axes.

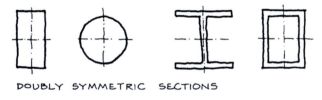

DOUBLY SYMMETRIC SECTIONS

Fig. 4.45

Notice that for the box section the centre of area is not actually within the cross-section. Where there is only one axis of symmetry, the unsymmetrical balance line will vary with the geometrical dimensions of the cross-section.

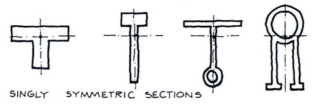

SINGLY SYMMETRIC SECTIONS

Fig. 4.46

And where there is no axis of symmetry, the centre of area can only be found by calculation.

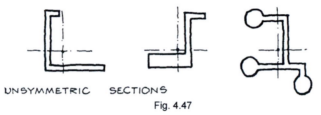

UNSYMMETRIC SECTIONS

Fig. 4.47

For each cross-sectional shape there is only one position for the centre of area and the position depends on the shape and, if the section is not doubly symmetric, the dimensions of the cross-section. In other words the centre of area is a **section property**. In actual structures it is not easy to ensure that axial loads are always applied through the centre of area.

As well as affecting the behaviour of elements when axially loaded the cross-sectional shape also affects the way they behave when they bend as beams. When a beam bends, part of the cross-section is in compression and part is in tension (see **Fig. 3.38**). Where the stress changes from compression to tension the stress is zero. The question is where is this point? And the answer is where it needs to be to satisfy horizontal equilibrium (see **Fig. 3.46**). This is not a helpful answer but if no simplifying assumptions are made the position of zero stress is not easy to find. If the **Engineer's theory** (see page **65**) is used the position can be found. With this theory, plane sections are expected to remain plane and the structural material to be linear elastic. This results in the points of zero stress due to bending being in a straight line. Because this is a line of zero stress it is often called the **neutral axis**. For a rectangular beam loaded laterally there has been a tacit assumption (see **Section 3.4**) that the neutral axis is across the beam at mid-depth.

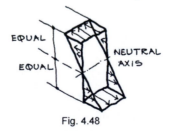

EQUAL

EQUAL

NEUTRAL AXIS

Fig. 4.48

Because the horizontal (push/pull – see **Fig. 3.45**) forces must balance, then, for cross-sections that are symmetric about a horizontal axis that are being loaded vertically, the neutral axis will be at mid-depth.

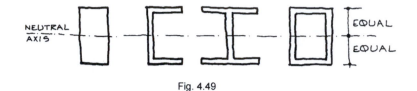

Fig. 4.49

Because of this symmetry, the stress due to bending at the top of the section will be equal to the stress at the bottom of the section.

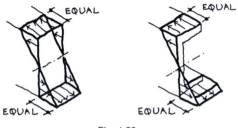

Fig. 4.50

For sections that are not symmetrical about a horizontal axis, the neutral axis will not be at mid-depth, but where will it be? Surprisingly and very fortunately it passes through the centre of area.

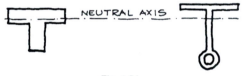

Fig. 4.51

As the **Engineer's theory** is being used, the bending stresses vary linearly with the depth of the beam. Where the neutral axis is not at mid-depth this linear variation means that the stresses at the top and the bottom will no longer be equal.

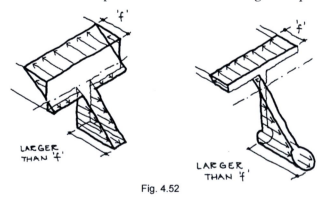

Fig. 4.52

That the neutral axis passes through the centre of area may seem fortuitous but this is not so. To see why consider a cross-section in two parts, one double the area of the other. The centre of area is the balance point for constant stress over the whole area of the cross-section. In this case it means the stress **f** is constant over the two parts of the section.

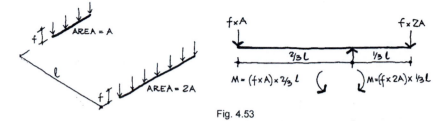

Fig. 4.53

The force in each part of the cross-section is the area multiplied by the constant stress **f**. The moments about the balance point (see **Fig. 1.41**) will be equal if the position is as shown in **Fig. 4.53**. For bending, plane sections remain plane and due to linear elasticity the stress is directly proportional to the movement. For this section, if it is rotated about the balance point (centre of area – see **Fig. 3.37**) the movement of one part will be twice that of the other. This means where the movement is double, the stress will be double.

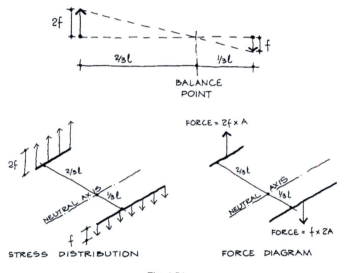

Fig. 4.54

This diagram shows that for the part of the section with area **A**, the stress is **2f** giving a force of **2fA** in one direction. For the part of the section with an area of **2A** the stress is **f** giving a force of **2Af** in the opposite direction. Therefore the push/pull forces are equal and opposite as required for horizontal equilibrium (see **Fig. 3.45**). This in principle is why the neutral axis goes through the centre of area and this principle applies to a cross-section of any shape or any number of 'parts'.

4.5   Biaxial bending

Whilst the neutral axis goes through the centre of area, its position rotates depending on the loading. For a rectangular beam loaded 'vertically' the neutral axis is 'horizontal', that is at right-angles to the load direction. The same is true for the

beam if it is loaded 'horizontally'. The associated stress diagrams due to bending are
drawn as before.

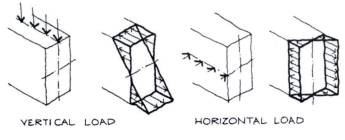

VERTICAL LOAD   HORIZONTAL LOAD

Fig. 4.55

If both the vertical and horizontal loads (not necessarily of the same size) are applied
to the beam simultaneously the beam will have a 'new' neutral axis. The position of
this neutral axis can be found by adding together the two bending stress diagrams.
This addition is similar to the addition of stresses shown in **Fig. 3.82**.

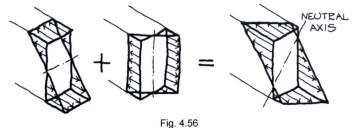

Fig. 4.56

Whilst this is relatively straightforward what is not obvious is that now, except for a
few special cases, the new neutral axis is not at right-angles to the axis of loading.
Why is this? The answer is the beam has 'provided' push/pull forces at the centres of
gravity of the now rather odd-shaped stress distributions. These forces are also on
the line of the load axis. This neutral axis is no longer at right-angles to the load axis
which means that the beam does not deflect in the direction of the load.

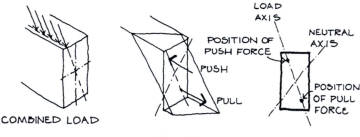

Fig. 4.57

The reason for this is that any cross-section will have axes of bending called **principal
axes**, and these are another section property. When the load is applied through a
principle axis, the neutral axis will be at right-angles to the load axis but for loads in
other directions this will not be true. To predict the bending behaviour of beams of
different cross-sections, the positions of the principal axes need to be known. They
intersect at the centre of area but in what direction do they go? They will go through
an axis of symmetry, so for sections with an axis of symmetry, the directions of the
principal axes are clear.

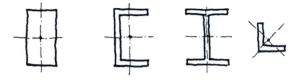

Fig. 4.58

For sections with no axis of symmetry, the direction can only be calculated.

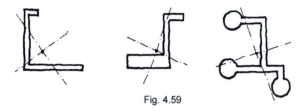

Fig. 4.59

When a beam bends there will be bending stresses and, except for very special cases, there will also be shear stresses. The effect of shear stresses on beams has been described in **Section 4.3**. **Fig. 4.40** shows that shear stresses may also cause twisting even when only vertical loads are present. This is because of another section property called the **shear centre**. The shear centre is the point through which the load axis must pass to avoid any twisting caused by the shear stress distribution. (Conversely the shear centre is the point about which the section will twist if loaded with twisting loads – see **Sections 2.6** and **3.6**.) For doubly symmetric or skew symmetric cross-sections, the shear centre will coincide with the centre of area. For cross-sections with only one axis of symmetry, the shear centre will be on this axis of symmetry but will not in general coincide with the centre of area.

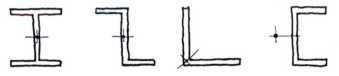

Fig. 4.60 Shear centres

Three important **section properties** of cross-sectional shapes have been identified and these are:

- **Position of the centre of area**

- **Directions of the principal axes**

- **Position of the shear centre**

For doubly symmetric cross-sections these properties are readily found but for general cross-sectional shapes these properties can only be found by calculation.

Knowing these section properties, the distributions of axial, bending and shear stress can be drawn provided the assumptions of the **Engineer's theory** are used. Even when the Engineer's theory is used, for structural elements of general cross-sectional shape, the structural behaviour is quite complex. If the element itself is curved or varies in cross-sectional shape along its length, engineering analysis, both conceptual and mathematical, rapidly becomes extremely difficult. This analysis is the subject matter of advanced texts or even research papers.

4.6   Torsion and warping of open sections

Some of the effects of twisting one-dimensional elements have already been described in **Sections 2.6**, **3.6** and **4.1**. In **Section 3.7** it was seen that torsion can also occur in curved elements. For **Uniform Torsion**, see page **79**, the two important features were noted as the formation of 'loops' of torsional stress and the warping of non-circular sections.

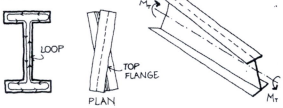

Fig. 4.61 Torsion loops and warping of a built-up section

It can be seen why tube-like sections are torsionally stiff for uniform torsion and built-up sections are not. For a tube, the resistance to the torsional moment **M$_T$** is due to the circumferential torsional stresses times the radius – see page **79**. The same thing is happening in the **I** beam, but the lever arm is now very small as it is within the thickness of the flange or web.

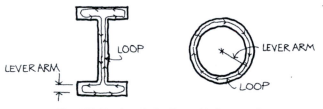

Fig. 4.62 Torsion of tube-like and built-up sections

If however a built-up section is supported in such a way that it cannot warp, the torsional rigidity increases enormously. This can be seen by considering a cantilever **I** beam, which is supported in a way that prevents the flanges displacing longitudinally, and is loaded by a torsional moment. In this case the torsional moment is resisted by the top and bottom flanges acting as horizontal cantilevers.

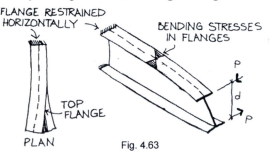

Fig. 4.63

The torsional moment **M$_T$** can be thought of as a pair of point loads **P** acting on the flanges, giving the moment **P** × **d**. Now the torsional moment is being resisted by longitudinal stresses rather than spiral principal stresses. Although this case of horizontal restraint, or **warping restraint**, may seem an unusual one in fact it is very common in building structures. This is because a torsional moment applied between the supports of a beam gets this restraint because the flanges act as horizontal beams even if there is **no longitudinal restraint** at the support.

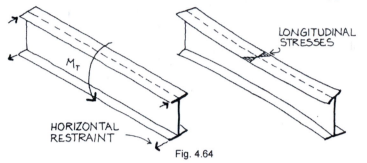

Fig. 4.64

Few computer programs in current use take this common situation into account.

4.7   Composite elements and pre-stressing

Often structural elements are made from more than one type of structural material to form composite structural elements. These combinations are made to exploit the different qualities of the materials to produce an element that performs better than one made from only one material. The usual combination is of a relatively cheap material such as concrete or masonry with a relatively expensive material such as steel. In these elements, the concrete or masonry carries the compressive stresses and the steel carries the tensile stress.

By far the most common form of composite construction for building structures is **reinforced concrete**. Reinforced concrete, together with structural steelwork, is widely used throughout the world for a great variety of structures both large and small. Because concrete has no useful engineering tensile strength, the steel, usually called reinforcement or re-bar, is placed in areas of the structural element where calculations predict tensile stresses. This is where diagrams like **Fig. 4.18** are useful. This shows that there are tensile stresses along the bottom of the beam near the centre and these slope near the ends of the beam. So, to make a reinforced concrete beam, there would be longitudinal reinforcement in the bottom of the beam and sloping reinforcement towards the ends.

Fig. 4.65

Historically the sloping bars shown in **Fig. 4.65** were used, but it is now more usual to resist the sloping tensile stresses by vertical reinforcement. This vertical reinforcement is bent into rectangles called links. The reinforcement is made into a cage by tying the bars together with wire.

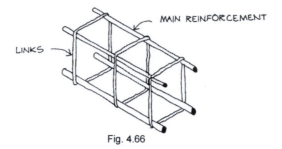

Fig. 4.66

The cage is placed into a mould or form and the wet concrete is poured around the reinforcement thus forming a composite element. As the concrete dries it shrinks and 'grips' the reinforcement. To aid this grip the reinforcing bars are often made with a rough pattern.

Fig. 4.67

When the composite beam is bent by a moment, the principle of push/pull forces (see **Fig. 3.43**) still applies but because concrete cannot resist tensile stresses, the pull force is resisted by tensile stresses in the reinforcement.

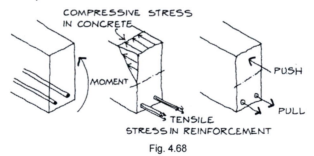

Fig. 4.68

For the steel and concrete to act compositely the steel must not slip in relation to the concrete. This is the same effect as that shown in **Fig. 4.30** for horizontal shear stresses. The relative slip is resisted by horizontal shear stresses on the face of the reinforcement, these stresses are often called **bond stresses**.

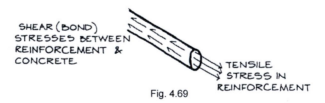

Fig. 4.69

The behaviour of reinforced concrete when subjected to shear forces is very complex but, as can be seen from the principal stress diagram (**Fig. 4.18**), in areas of high shear there are diagonal tensile stresses. In unreinforced concrete these would cause cracks at right angles to the lines of tensile stresses.

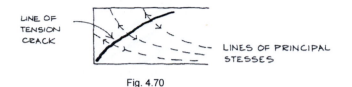

LINE OF TENSION CRACK

LINES OF PRINCIPAL STESSES

Fig. 4.70

The role of the diagonal reinforcing bars or links is to provide tensile strength across these lines of tensile force.

TENSILE FORCES IN REINFORCEMENT PROVIDING TENSILE STRENGTH ACROSS TENSION CRACK

Fig. 4.71

Although in theory concrete only needs reinforcement in areas of tensile stress, except for very minor elements, it is usual to provide a complete cage of reinforcement. The reinforcement that resists the tensile stresses is called the **main reinforcement** and the other reinforcement is called **nominal reinforcement**. For the portal frame shown in **Fig. 2.27,** loaded on the cross-beam, the bending moments cause tensile bending stresses in both the cross-beam and the columns.

LOADING

BENDING MOMENT DIAGRAM

POSITIONS OF TENSILE STRESS

Fig. 4.72

Here the main reinforcement is placed in areas of tensile stress, but for practical reasons whole cages of reinforcement would be used for the cross-beam and the columns.

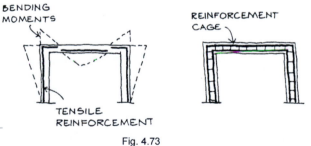

BENDING MOMENTS

REINFORCEMENT CAGE

TENSILE REINFORCEMENT

Fig. 4.73

It is not always possible to provide continuous reinforcement in areas of tensile stress, so reinforcing bars are 'joined' by lapping. The bars are laid next to each other in the mould and the concrete is poured around both bars. The force is transmitted from one bar to another by bond (shear) stresses in the surrounding concrete.

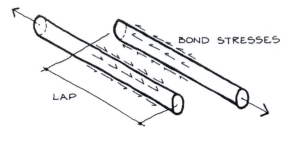

Fig. 4.74

By lapping bars, parts of the reinforced concrete structure can be cast in a preferred sequence. In the case of the portal frame, the sequence would be foundations, columns and then the cross-beam. Bars would be left projecting from each part to be lapped with the reinforcement of the next part.

Fig. 4.75

Whilst reinforced concrete is the most common form of composite construction, structural steelwork and reinforced concrete can also be combined to form structural elements. This form is frequently used in spanning structures where the floor slab, a two-dimensional reinforced concrete element, is also used as part of the main beams, acting compositely with the one-dimensional structural steel elements.

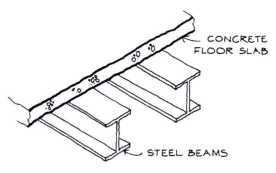

Fig. 4.76

To achieve composite action, the slab is joined to the top of the floor beams by what are known as **shear connectors**. These are pieces of steel, usually in the form of studs, welded to the top of the beam.

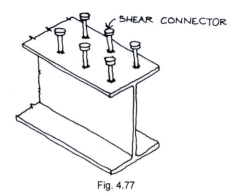

Fig. 4.77

The concrete slab is cast around the shear connectors and these prevent the slab and the top of the steel beam moving in relation to each other. This allows horizontal shear stresses to develop between the slab and the steel beam as is explained on pages **95-96.**

Fig. 4.78

Now the floor beam is the steel beam and the concrete slab. By the addition of the shear connectors, the concrete slab becomes part of the compression flange.

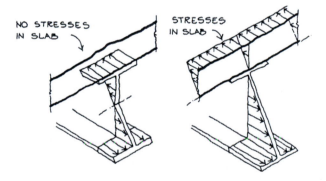

Fig. 4.79

Another form of composite construction is to **pre-stress** materials such as concrete (or less often masonry). This is a technique that causes stress in structural elements **before** they are loaded. Like the addition of reinforcement, the purpose of pre-stressing is to add tensile strength to elements made of materials that can only resist compressive stresses. The principle can be illustrated by stressing together some match boxes with an elastic band. This pre-stressed element can now act as a beam.

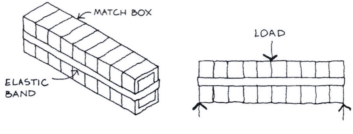

Fig. 4.80

Here the stretched elastic band causes compressive stresses between the match boxes before there are stresses due to beam action. When the lateral load is applied it is resisted by internal push/pull forces that cause tensile and compressive bending stresses (see **Fig. 3.40**). Provided the numerical size of the pre-stressed compressive stress is equal or greater than the bending tensile stress the match boxes, with the pre-stress, will act as a beam. The stresses due to pre-stress and bending can be combined as shown in **Fig. 3.83**.

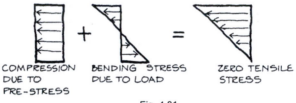

COMPRESSION   BENDING STRESS   ZERO TENSILE
DUE TO   DUE TO LOAD   STRESS
PRE-STRESS

Fig. 4.81

Exactly the same principle is used to make pre-stressed concrete elements. The pre-stress is caused by tensioning the steel reinforcement and this can be done in two ways called **pre-tensioning** and **post-tensioning**. For pre-tensioning the steel reinforcement is tensioned by jacking against strong points fixed to the ground, then the concrete is poured around the tensioned reinforcement. When the concrete has hardened the jacks are released.

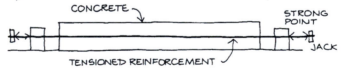

Fig. 4.82

When the jacks are released the stretched reinforcement tries to shorten. But, because the hardened concrete has shrunk around tensioned reinforcement (see **Fig. 4.68**), it prevents the reinforcement shortening and by doing this goes into compression. So in the case of pre-tensioned pre-stressed concrete there are bond (shear) stresses between the (tensioned) reinforcement and the concrete before any load is applied.

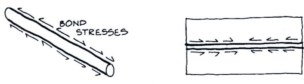

Fig. 4.83

Concrete can also be pre-stressed after it has hardened, this is called post-tensioning. The concrete element is made with a hole through it, this hole is usually called a duct. The reinforcement to be stressed is then threaded through the duct, in many cases the reinforcement is put in the duct before the concrete is cast. When the concrete is hard enough the reinforcement is tensioned by jacking it against the end of the concrete element. This causes tension in the reinforcement and compression in the concrete. When the required tension force has been obtained, the reinforcement is 'locked off' and the jacks removed. There are several methods of locking off and these depend on the proprietary method being used.

In the pre-tensioned method, the force in the tensioned reinforcement is transferred to the concrete along the whole length of the element but in the post-tensioned method, the force is transferred at the jacking points. This can sometimes require special end details to make sure the concrete is not over-stressed locally.

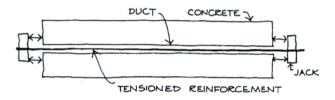

Fig. 4.84

In the same way as eccentric applied loads cause axial stresses and bending stresses (see **Fig. 3.75**), if the tensioned reinforcement does not go through the centre of area of the section then the pre-stress will not be a constant axial stress. This can be an advantage as it can increase the size of the compressive stress in the part of the element that will have tensile stresses due to the applied load.

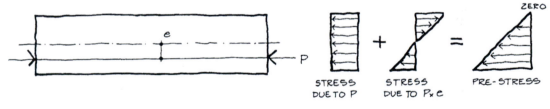

Fig. 4.85

The idea is that the stress distribution due to pre-stress is completely reversed under maximum applied lateral load. This means that, for a simple beam element, the stress at the top is zero due to pre-stress, and the stress at the bottom due to pre-stress and applied load is zero.

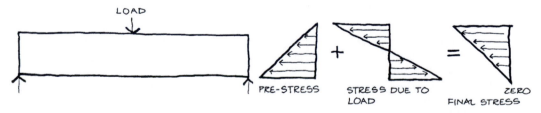

Fig. 4.86

Advanced concepts of stress 113

The effect of the eccentrically applied pre-stress is to apply a moment to the element and this moment can be used to counteract the effect of the bending moment caused by the self-weight of the element. For concrete elements, the self-weight is a significant part of the total load. By careful adjustment of the pre-stress force and its position, the stress distribution due to pre-stress and self-weight can be made triangular, with zero stress at the top face.

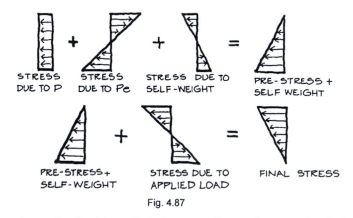

Fig. 4.87

When the maximum live load is applied, the stress diagram is reversed as before. It is usual for the maximum compressive stresses to be the maximum allowable for the concrete. By using pre-stress in this way the concrete member can be used more effectively than a reinforced element because the maximum stress in a reinforced element has to include both self-weight and live load. Because of this the pre-stressed element can carry higher loads or alternatively be shallower for the same load than a reinforced element.

The pre-tensioning method means that the pre-stressing reinforcement has to be straight, but there is no restriction on the shape duct that can be cast into a concrete element. This means that the post-tensioning method allows the position of the pre-stressing force to be varied along the element. As the lines of the principal tensile are rarely straight, the ducts can be cast into the concrete along these lines.

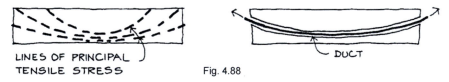

LINES OF PRINCIPAL TENSILE STRESS   Fig. 4.88   DUCT

This has the advantage of putting compressive stresses into the element which directly counteract the tensile stresses caused by the applied load.

The method of pre-tensioning is ideally suited to the production of **standard** pre-stressed elements made in pre-casting yards. These types of elements are used extensively as floor spanning members or beams, usually called lintels, over openings in masonry walls. The method of post-tensioning is slower so its use in building structures is relatively rare and is limited to unusually large elements in major buildings. It is used extensively for large bridges. Often these are made from a number of pre-cast units that are stressed together exactly like the matchboxes (see **Fig. 4.80**).

Composite action can also be used to increase the 'size' of a beam in a masonry wall. This is done by making the masonry that is built on top of the concrete beam act with the beam.

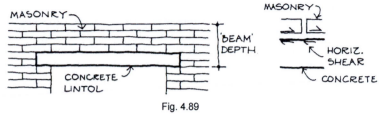

Fig. 4.89

This is similar in principle to the action between the concrete slab and the steel beam shown in **Fig. 4.78**. Here the horizontal shear stresses that are essential for the composite action are resisted by the mortar joints, the beam and the masonry units (bricks or blocks).

Many other examples of composite action could be given but the essential point is to understand the role played in the total structural action of the element by the different materials. This is done by understanding how each part of the element is stressed when it acts as part of a load path.

As buildings are constructed by joining together a variety of elements, walls, floors, windows, stairs, etc. it is important to be sure that loads do go down the chosen load paths and not into non-loadbearing elements that are not capable of carrying the loads. This is really composite action in reverse. For example, the portal frame when loaded will deflect. If the portal frame is glazed as part of the building design, the glazing would try and prevent the portal frame from deflecting. This means that the glazing is acting compositely with the portal frame to 'make' a two-dimensional wall element.

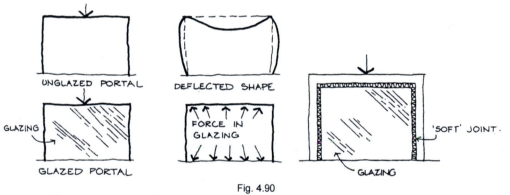

Fig. 4.90

Unless the glazing is designed to be part of the load path it may fail as it tries to carry a share of the load due to composite action. In these cases special 'soft' joints or other devices must be introduced to prevent the composite action. These are exactly opposite to the idea of the shear connectors shown in **Fig. 4.77**. In this case the joint between the glazing and the portal frame must be designed so that the portal frame can deflect without loading the glazing.

4.8　Summary

This section shows how structural elements act when they are loaded as part of a load path. This behaviour has been characterised by the stress distribution at each point of the element. These stresses are caused by the structural actions, axial bending and shear forces described in **Chapter 3**. The stress distributions in this section have been obtained by using the **Engineer's theory**. These assumptions have been used by several generations of structural designers. Whilst the Engineer's theory is still widely used, non-elastic theories are now also used. These theories are outlined in **Chapter 6**.

Part of the skill of designing structures is the prediction of the stress distribution in each element as it acts as part of a load path (or paths!). The accuracy of prediction will vary depending on the stage of the design process. For instance the exact size of elements may not need to be calculated at preliminary stages. However, it should be clear to the structural designers that the proposed types of elements, shells, slabs, **I** beams etc., will act effectively as their part of the load path. This is clarified if the stress distribution is known in principle. For instance if load-bearing walls are used at different levels and they cross at angles, then the whole wall will not be effective (see **Fig. 3.31**).

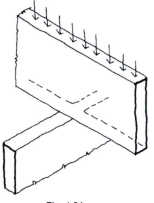

Fig. 4.91

Or again if an element is acting as a beam, then an **I** section is better than a **+** section (see page **73**) and it might be worthwhile to vary the depth (see **Fig. 3.57**).

The central point is that structural design is not the result of a logical process but the result of an imaginative concept. For this concept to be successful it must be informed by a conceptual understanding of how the imagined structure will behave.

References – Chapter 4

1　　J Schlaich, K.Schäfer, M. Jennewein – **Towards a consistent design of structural concrete** – PCI Journal 32, N° 3, May/June 1987 – p 74-150

CHAPTER 5   *Structural materials*

To build any structure, whether it is a chair or the Forth Bridge, it has to be constructed of a suitable material. That is a material that at least has the necessary structural properties. The two basic properties that are required are: **strength and stiffness.** Because the structure has to transfer forces it has to be **strong enough**, and because, on the whole the structure is expected to maintain its shape, it has to be **stiff enough**.

Strangely, strength and stiffness of a material are unrelated. The reason for this is that the molecular structure varies from material to material. However, structural designers usually consider the macroscopic rather than molecular level of behaviour. The behaviour of materials at the molecular level is the concern of material scientists and is beyond the scope of this book.

5.1   Types of material behaviour

Engineering materials are classified by comparing the relationship between strength and stiffness or 'stretchiness'. Everyone is familiar with stretching rubber bands or pulling pieces of Plasticine®. After being stretched the rubber band and the piece of Plasticine behave quite differently. The rubber band returns to its original size whereas the piece of Plasticine stays stretched.

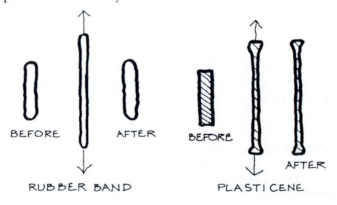

Fig. 5.1

This is because the rubber is **elastic**, hence elastic band, and Plasticine is **plastic**. Elastic and plastic are technical engineering terms. The elastic and plastic behaviour are best described by drawing graphs of the **load/deflection** behaviour.

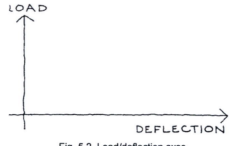

Fig. 5.2 Load/deflection axes

It is usual to plot the load on the vertical axis and to plot the deflection on the horizontal axis. If the load/deflection graph is plotted for an elastic band, the deflection will increase with load.

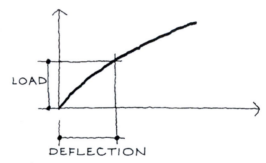

Fig. 5.3 Load/deflection graph of an elastic band

However, once a piece of Plasticine starts to stretch, it can be continuously stretched with a constant load. So the load/deflection graph is more or less a horizontal line.

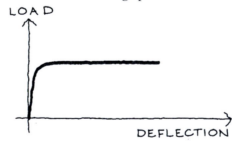

Fig. 5.4 Load/deflection graph of a piece of Plasticine

Naturally it is preferable for structures to act elastically rather than plastically when loaded, otherwise the structure would be permanently deformed.

Some materials can be both elastic and plastic, steel for example. This can readily be demonstrated with an ordinary paper clip. When being used to hold papers together the clip acts **elastically**, returning to its former shape when the papers are removed. But the clip can easily be permanently deformed by being bent out of shape – to achieve this steel acts **plastically**. The load/deflection graph has two parts, an **elastic part** and a **plastic part**.

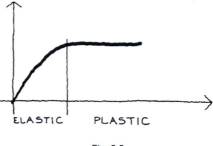

ELASTIC   PLASTIC

Fig. 5.5

Some materials will act elastically and then, on further loading, suddenly break. Glass and plaster are examples of these materials. These materials are called **brittle** materials. This type of material is unsuitable for important structural elements as accidental overloading may cause sudden, and therefore catastrophic, failure.

To aid the process of numerical structural design, structural materials are idealised, where possible, as **linear elastic/perfectly plastic** materials.

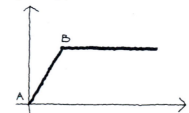

Fig. 5.6 Load/deflection graph of a linear elastic/perfectly plastic material

For this **idealised** structural material, the load/deflection graph consists of two **straight** lines. A sloping line **AB**, which is the linear elastic part, and a horizontal line, starting at **B**, which is the perfectly plastic part. The fact that **AB** is straight means the **load is directly proportional to the deflection**. So if the load doubles then the deflection doubles. In the **AB** part of the graph, how load is proportionally related to deflection is given by a number. This number varies from material to material and indicates how 'stretchy' it is. It is named after Thomas Young (1773-1829) and is known as **Young's modulus of elasticity** and is often denoted by **E**. A low number or low **E** indicates a material is 'stretchy' and a high number or high **E** indicates a material is 'stiff'. For example the number for timber is low and the number for steel is high.

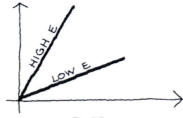

Fig. 5.7

At point **B**, on **Fig. 5.6**, the material's behaviour changes from linear elastic to perfectly plastic; this point is called the **yield point**. From point **B** the material deflects (forever) under constant load. The vast majority of building structures are expecting to spend their entire useful lives within the elastic part of their behaviour. Otherwise the structure would change shape permanently after every loading and this would be rather inconvenient.

5.2   Actual structural materials

Every stiff physical object is a structure; the choice of suitable materials is immense. A slice of toast, a pair of shoes, flowers, aeroplanes and bicycles are all structures. However, for a building structure the choice of suitable materials is very limited. This is because the materials must be strong, stiff, durable and cheap. These are relative terms but building structures must be strong and stiff enough to carry the required loads without deflecting excessively; they must be sufficiently durable to last for the structure's useful life and cheap enough to make the structure affordable. Because building structures consume considerable amounts of material they, unlike materials for musical instruments and racing cars, must be cheap which means plentiful.

Few materials comply with these requirements in any culture at any historical time. The original traditional buildings were constructed from **natural** materials. These were vegetation (trees, grass, leaves, etc.), animals (skins and less commonly bones), rocks and stones (including caves) and, in the case of the Inuit people, ice and snow. Slowly **man-made** materials were evolved so mud-dried bricks and woven cloth were used and stones were shaped rather than used as found. Later, kiln-dried bricks and lime-based mortar and concrete were used. Even though bronze, first smelted about 4500 BC and iron first smelted about 2500 BC, are strong, stiff and durable they were far too expensive for use in building structures. Even as late as 1750 AD the use of iron nails was rare. Thus, for thousands of years building structures were constructed of timber, brick and stone.

This was changed by what is wrongly called the **Industrial Revolution**; a better word would be evolution (because it took about 150 years). In 1709, Abraham Darby discovered a method of smelting iron ore using coal (actually using coke, a product of coal). Previously iron ore, which is plentiful, was smelted using charcoal which was neither cheap, and as the supply of trees ran out, nor plentiful. This crucial discovery meant that iron became a plentiful and cheap material. Therefore iron, or more correctly **cast iron**, could be used for building structures. This was dramatically demonstrated by the erection, in 1779, of the Iron Bridge at Coalbrookdale in Shropshire. What is revolutionary about this bridge, which still stands, was not its size or method of construction but the fact that it is wholly constructed of iron. See also **Section 11.2**.

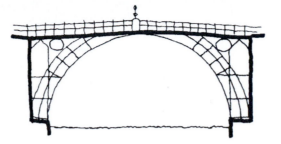

Fig. 5.8 Iron Bridge at Coalbrookdale

The evolving manufacturing and transport industries required a variety of new types of buildings and structures. These included mills, bridges, workshops, chimneys and railway buildings.

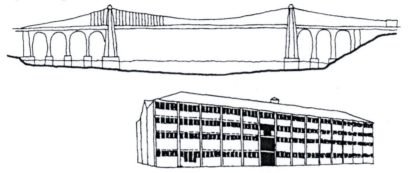

Fig. 5.9 Menai Straits Bridge and The Boat Store at Sheerness

Because the size of these structures and the magnitude of the loads were much greater than traditional buildings, there was pressure to produce both new types of structure and new structural materials. After the availability of cast iron, **wrought iron**, due to Henry Cort in 1784 and later **steel**, due to the Bessemer process (1850) became cheap enough for building structures. About 1811, Joseph Aspdin invented artificial **cement** made from Portland stone which allowed strong mortars and mass concrete to be made. In 1892, Françoise Hennebique patented the use of concrete reinforced with iron and steel, now known as **reinforced concrete**. Thus by about 1900 all the 'modern' building structural materials were available.

Nowadays, building structures are constructed using concrete, both mass and reinforced, timber, brick or block masonry and steel. So a combination of new materials, steel and concrete, and traditional materials, brick and timber are used. Cast iron, wrought iron and stone are now rarely used for building structures. Although there are constant efforts being made to find 'new' materials for building structures, none have been found mainly due to lack of cheapness. Many developments have taken place since 1900 but these have mainly been either new uses or methods of design and construction.

On the whole the behaviour of structures in the real world is too complicated to be modelled by structural theory; so theories are derived that are based on various simplifying assumptions. This provides theories that are simple enough (but not necessarily simple) to be used for structural design.

Although structural theory exists that can predict behaviour of structures built of non-linear elastic materials, computations are enormously simplified if **linear elasticity** is assumed. But is this a valid assumption for the limited range of materials used in building structures?

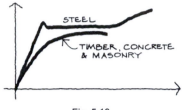

Fig. 5.10

The figure shows that only steel, and mild steel at that, closely approximates the idealised linear elastic/perfectly plastic behaviour. However, all exhibit some type of elastic behaviour at the beginning of the load/deflection graph. Therefore, for design rather than research purposes, **steel, concrete, timber and masonry are assumed to be linear elastic**. This means that 'ordinary' structural theory can be used for the structural design of all the commonly used materials. (It should be noted that **Fig. 5.10** only shows the relative shape of the load/deflection graphs rather than the relative numerical values.)

The most important concept to grasp for an engineering understanding of structural materials is the **load/deflection behaviour**. For designing structures it is also necessary to know the **strength** of the materials. Of the four common structural materials steel is the strongest with concrete, masonry and timber very roughly the same strength. All the materials can vary considerably in strength depending on the process of manufacture, or in the case of timber, the species. Again steel is the stiffest material with concrete about one tenth, masonry about one twentieth and timber about one thirtieth as stiff as steel. Again these values, apart from steel, vary considerably.

Not all the materials are equally strong in tension and compression, that is pulled or squashed. Steel and timber are equally strong in tension but masonry and concrete although strong in compression are very weak in tension; so weak in fact that their tensile strength is usually ignored in structural design. This difference in material behaviour has a great influence on the choice of structural form because if the loaded structure has to carry tensile forces then steel or timber must be used.

Another influential characteristic is the **strength to weight ratio**. The self-weight of structures constructed from steel or timber is usually not more than 15% of the total load carried, whereas the self-weight of masonry and concrete structures can be 40% of the total load carried. This is because steel and timber have high strength to weight ratios and masonry and concrete have low strength to weight ratios, so **timber and steel are lightweight materials and masonry and concrete are heavyweight materials**.

5.3   Soil as a structural material

All building structures rest on the surface of the Earth and the foundations are the final part of the structure. Loads imposed on the planet Earth by buildings are trivial but locally the behaviour of the surface of the Earth matters. The purpose of the foundations is to ensure that the stress on the local surface is within the safe bearing stress of the soil. The concept of foundations is the same as using snowshoes – **Fig. 3.23**.

If a hole is dug in the surface of the Earth rock will eventually be found. This rock may be many metres below the ground level so the foundations are usually placed on the soil that lies above the rock. This layer of soil may be very compressible under load so the foundations will move downwards causing them to settle. This means that the building may move downwards as a rigid body or it may settle differentially causing the building to tilt and distort. So not only strength but foundation movement has to be considered by the engineering designer. Unfortunately for engineering designers, the behaviour of soils under load is complex. Due to this complexity a specialist subject has come into existence called **soil mechanics**.

The first stage in understanding the engineering behaviour of soils is to identify the types of soil that are found. These are broadly classified as **rocks, granular soils and clayey soils**. These are often found in layers or **strata**, so immediately under a building site there usually several different types of soil.

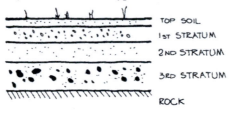

Fig. 5.11

Examples of rocks are granite, sandstone and chalk, granular soils are sands and gravels and clayey soils are various types of clay. Foundations on rock are rarely a problem for buildings as they are strong and stiff, but foundations on granular or cohesive soil need careful consideration.

There are two basic differences between the behaviour of structural elements and the structural behaviour of soil. The first is that the part of soil loaded by the foundations of a structure cannot act in isolation in same way a column can. The loaded part of the ground is affected by adjacent 'unloaded' parts of the ground.

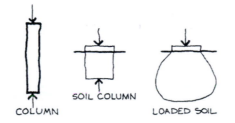

Fig. 5.12

How much of the adjacent soil is affected by the load is hard to determine but it can be significant. To see why this happens look at two simplified models of soil. One is of unlinked elastic coil springs and the other of elastic spheres. Both are in pits with completely rigid sides.

Fig. 5.13

For the first model the behaviour is quite simple. As the load is applied through the rigid foundation each coil spring deflects vertically under its share of the load. As the load increases so does the deflection. The bottom and sides of the pit do not move.

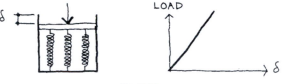

Fig. 5.14

This model assumes that the soil under the foundation **does** act as an isolated structure; the springs. This is the same as assuming there is a finite column of elastic soil under the foundation and that soil outside the 'rigid box' is unaffected.

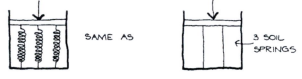

Fig. 5.15

The second model using elastic spheres is more complex as there are three phases of behaviour. The pit of elastic spheres will not be tightly packed so the load causes compaction of the spheres. This compaction can be seen by shaking a jar of rice or sugar and noting the depth before and after shaking.

Fig. 5.16

The second effect is the restriction on the shape into which the spheres can deform. Because the spheres are touching each other and the sides of the pit, each sphere cannot deform freely.

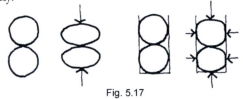

Fig. 5.17

As the confined spheres are compressed, the restriction on their lateral deformation causes horizontal loads on the rigid pit walls. As the spheres deform, the foundation moves down into the pit, this reduces the overall volume of the pit and the size of the voids between the spheres.

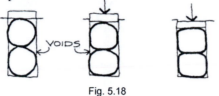

Fig. 5.18

When all the voids are filled the pit will be completely filled with the elastic material. This is quite a different structure from the pit filled with barely touching spheres. This means that the pit filled with elastic spheres will have three phases of behaviour.

Phase 1   Reduction of voids by compaction.
Phase 2   Deformation of spheres until the voids are filled.
Phase 3   Deformation of pit filled with elastic material.

This gives a three-part load/deflection diagram.

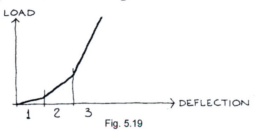

Fig. 5.19

It is possible to find single-sized spherical stones occurring naturally, these can be seen on some shingle beaches. For this 'soil', the model of elastic spheres is reasonable but the rigid pit restriction is not. A new model of this soil would be an 'infinitely wide' layer of elastic spheres with finite thickness. This layer rests on a rigid base.

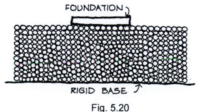

Fig. 5.20

As the foundation is loaded, the spheres compact locally. Then the touching spheres begin to deform. With no rigid pit walls the adjacent, 'unloaded' spheres have to provide lateral forces.

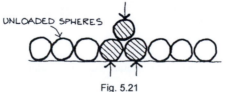

Fig. 5.21

The lower spheres will provide the lateral force if they are heavy enough. Each layer of spheres transfers its load to a lower layer and each lower layer will have more spheres.

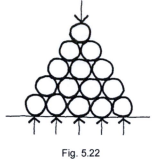

Fig. 5.22

In this way the area of loaded spheres increases with depth and the level of load in the spheres reduces.

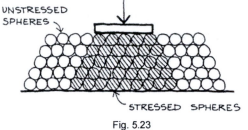

Fig. 5.23

As soil is not usually made from elastic spheres and there is not a rigid base, the stressed volume under a single foundation becomes bulb shaped.

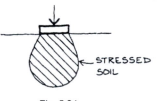

Fig. 5.24

For an elastic sphere to deform into an elastic cube, thus filling all the voids, the material has to be very elastic. A stone sphere could not deform into a cube as it would split first. If the foundation load is increased, the highly stressed spheres will fail or the lateral forces required will become too high for the 'unloaded' spheres and these will heave upwards.

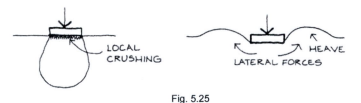

Fig. 5.25

The load/deformation curve can be drawn for this model and again this has three phases.

Phase 1	Reduction of voids by compaction.
Phase 2	Deformation of spheres.
Phase 3	Failure by crushing or heaving.

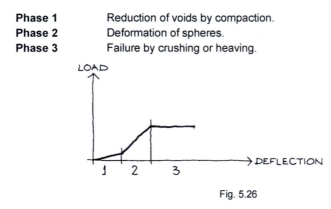

Fig. 5.26

So far the models have been used to understand the behaviour of the **soil skeleton**. If, as is often the case, there is water in the soil, the behaviour of the soil skeleton **plus water** has to be modelled. The behaviour of this composite structure can be quite different from the behaviour of the soil skeleton. Fill the pits of the first two models with water and assume that the foundations fit into the pits in a watertight manner.

Fig. 5.27

Water is almost incompressible so the load from the foundations is carried by water pressure in both of the models with almost no deformation.

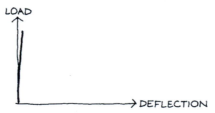

Fig. 5.28

The behaviour will be altered if holes are made in the foundation which relieve the water pressure and allow some water to escape.

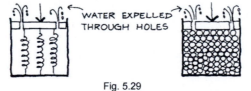

Fig. 5.29

Now the water that is filling the voids in the soil skeleton has a **drainage path**. As the water is expelled from the voids, the soil skeleton carries the load as before. If the holes are large then the water will be expelled immediately, but if the holes are very small the water will only seep through the foundation slowly.

For the coil spring model with no water, the deflection will double if the load is doubled. This is because the model is linear.

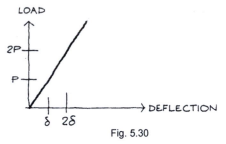

Fig. 5.30

If the pit is filled with water and only very small holes are made in the foundation, the water will take time to seep through. Initially the water will carry the entire load but as the water pressure is gradually reduced by seepage, the load is transferred to the coil springs. Now the deformation is **time dependent**, and under a constant load will deform in a non-linear way until the springs are carrying the entire load.

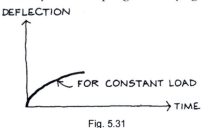

Fig. 5.31

If further load is applied the process will be repeated.

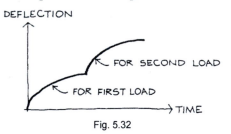

Fig. 5.32

In the water-filled soil skeleton, the pressure of the water in the voids is called the **pore water pressure**. Before loading, the pore water pressure is just the hydrostatic head, but the loads cause an increase in the pore water pressure. This increase is relieved by the drainage until the pressure returns to the hydrostatic pressure. How long this takes is called the **seepage rate**. The smaller the drainage holes, the longer it takes. In a real soil there is no rigid pit, so the water drains away laterally as well as vertically.

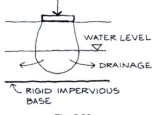

Fig. 5.33

Even with the first model, the presence of water and a low seepage rate dramatically alters the soil structure behaviour. With all the variations of underlying strata, particle size and shape and rate of loading, if water is present the soil structure behaviour of a real soil can be complex.

Just to complicate matters further, if the particle size is smaller than **0.002 mm** and the particles are made from certain chemically complex minerals, then the presence of water is always a consideration. If water is poured over a heap of large stones, apart from a small part that wets the surfaces of the stones, all the water will drain away.

Fig. 5.34

However, with a heap of very small particles this will not happen as the wetted area of the particle is enormous compared with its volume.

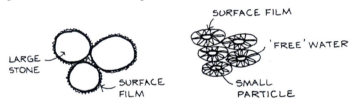

Fig. 5.35

The water does not drain away but is adsorbed on to the surfaces of the particles. Complex electro-chemical actions between the wetted particles now cause them to cohere together to form a **clayey soil**. In soil mechanics, soils are divided into freely **draining soils – non-cohesive or granular soils** and **non-draining soils – clayey soils**. Examples of granular soils are sands and gravels and examples of clayey soils are clays and marls. The difference can be physically experienced by squeezing handfuls of wet sand and clay. The water is readily squeezed from the sand but cannot be squeezed from a clayey soil. This is because the proportion of 'free' water in clayey soil is small and the diameters of the drainage paths are also small which causes very low permeability.

For non-cohesive soils, water may or may not be present but in clayey soils water is **always** present. If a clayey soil is loaded by a foundation, the load is initially carried by an **increase** in pore water pressure. As with granular soils the pore water pressure in cohesive soils reduces by draining laterally to unstressed areas. But due to the extremely low seepage rate in cohesive soils this may take years.

In summary three broad statements can be made about soil as a structural material and these are:

- **The engineering behaviour of many real soils is difficult to formulate analytically. Many aspects are not fully understood and these are subjects for research by specialists.**

oxygen can penetrate the concrete sufficiently to allow this corrosion to occur. The growing interest in the repair of concrete structures indicates that this is neither a small nor rare problem. This problem could be solved by using stainless steel reinforcement but unfortunately, except for special circumstances, this material is not cheap enough.

Rather like masonry and concrete, timber can last for hundreds of years. But timber can also deteriorate, usually due to attacks from animals or plants. Various animals, such as insect larvae or termites, eat the timber. Various plants, mainly fungi, can grow in the timber. The action of these plants and animals alters the structure of the timber. This alteration usually means that the timber can no longer serve its constructional purpose. Some species of timber are more readily attacked than others and susceptible timbers can be preserved with various forms of chemical treatment. But the best way of ensuring timber is durable in building is to avoid using it in positions where attack is possible.

Not only do the material properties affect the choice for a particular structure, the choice is also affected by the process of building with the material. The four main structural materials are available in quite different forms.

The shape and size of steel structures is almost unlimited (think of super-tankers). Steel is generally available in various standard forms, these are plates of standard thicknesses and rolled members of particular cross-sectional shapes and sizes. Whilst these can be assembled into structures of any size they are usually fabricated in workshops rather than the final site. The size of the largest part is usually limited by the maximum size that can be transported.

Like steel, concrete structures are unlimited by size or shape. Concrete can either be formed on site, in-situ concrete, or made off site in special pre-casting yards – pre-cast concrete. Again like steel, the maximum size of pre-cast parts is limited by transport restrictions.

Timber sizes are determined by the natural size of trees. Larger timber structures can be made by laminating timber. This technique involves gluing natural sized timber together to form large structures. Laminated timber can also be made into curved or bent structures.

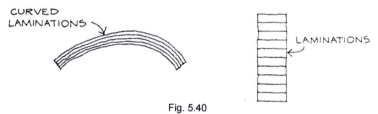

Fig. 5.40

Theoretically, the size of masonry bricks and blocks is not limited, but masonry is constructed manually. This means the size of individual units is limited by human dimensions of the bricklayers, both their size and strength. Strangely this has resulted in bricks sized to be held in one hand whilst blocks come in a range of sizes, including some dense concrete blocks that are so heavy that it takes two people to lift them.

This section shows that the choice of a particular structure, made from a particular structural material, cannot be made without consideration of the non-structural behaviour. For example, the non-structural behaviour may restrict choice in highly corrosive or highly flammable environments. Again restrictions of size may require joints or complete separation of structural elements, thus altering the structural behaviour. When proposing a structural system for a particular application, the structural designer must be sure that the chosen system satisfies the requirements of the non-structural behaviour.

CHAPTER 6 *Safe structures and failure*

A major aim of structural design is to provide structures that are strong enough, that is, they can carry the loads imposed on them by their use without failure. This may seem obvious but there are many difficulties associated with this simple requirement, and unless they are resolved, the possibility of failure remains.

6.1 Basic concepts of safety

In industrial societies, building structures are expected to be very safe and the occurrence of failures, especially causing loss of life, must be almost unknown. To achieve this, the possibility, or more correctly the probability, of failure must be quantified. This is attempted by using a **statistical approach**.

The first question to be answered is how big is the load on a particular structure. If this question cannot be answered then all attempts at structural design will be meaningless. But accurate answers can only be obtained if the use of the building is somehow controlled. For example, the density of water does not vary so, for a water tank, the load from the liquid can be known accurately, unless someone decides to store mercury in the tank. This illustrates the difficulty of knowing how a structure will be loaded during its life which may be 100 years or more.

Other important loads such as those from snow or wind are beyond the control of humans so can never be 'known'. To overcome this serious problem, attempts are made to estimate possible loads from natural phenomena by making a statistical analysis of past records. In many areas of the world no useful records exist so the prediction of these loads becomes hazardous.

To understand how real structural design is done the basic principles of the statistical approach must be understood. These principles attempt to use past data to predict **probable future data**. Because the prediction is one of **probability** it is, by definition, uncertain. To illustrate the principles a non-structural engineering example is used. Anyone who has visited ancient buildings may have noticed that the heights of doorways are often lower than those of modern buildings. This is often explained by the 'fact' that people were smaller when these buildings were constructed. So how high should a doorway be? Should every doorway be high enough for the tallest person who ever lived – Robert Wadlow who was 272cm (8ft 11in) tall – to walk through upright?

Fig. 6.1

As this person was so tall, 'most' people would agree that all doorways do not need to be this high. But what percentage of doorway users should be able to walk through the doorway upright? For convenience, most users should be able to walk through the doorway upright. To arrive at an actual height some data are needed. Suppose 100 randomly chosen adults have their heights measured. There will be an average height, but how much shorter or taller than the average height will any person be? The first step is to draw a **histogram** of the data. This is a diagram that shows how many of the 100 people there are of each height. If the heights are taken for 4cm intervals and the number of people in each height interval is recorded, the histogram can be drawn.

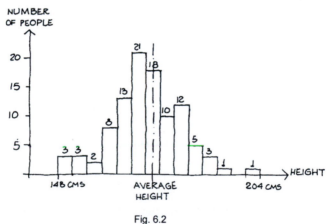

Fig. 6.2

All the histogram does is to record the **distribution** of the heights of the **population**, as the sample is called. In this population there is one person over 2m tall, so if all doorways used by the group were made 204cm high everyone could walk through all doors upright, but if they were made 192cm high, 98 people could walk through upright and 2 could not.

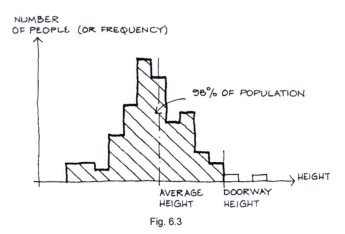

Fig. 6.3

It may seem reasonable that 98% of the population can walk through all the doorways upright and the chosen door height is 14cm higher than the average height. This choice has not used probability because the heights of **all** the users are known. But can the data be used to predict anything? Is a random sample of 100 people enough? In **Fig. 6.3** the histogram is 'heaped' around the average height but would this always be true and would the average height be 174cm? Suppose the top of the histogram is made into a smooth curve by joining the middle of each step to the next.

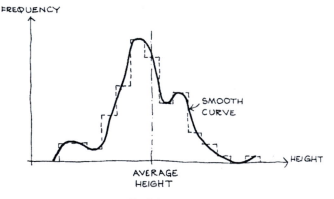

Fig. 6.4

If a mathematical expression could be found for this rather odd-shaped curve it would be called a **probability density function**. From the mathematical expression for the curve, the **mean** can be calculated and so can something called the **standard deviation**. In this case the standard deviation would be a length in centimetres. By adding or subtracting a number of standard deviations to the mean, a relationship can be established between the mean, a number of standard deviations and a percentage of the population.

136 Building structures

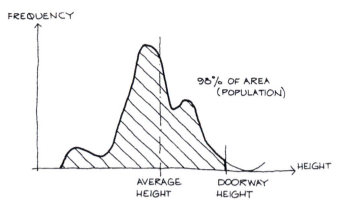

Fig. 6.5

As the population increases in size the size of the interval can be reduced and the smooth curve may become simpler. Anticipating this simplification a bell-shaped probability density function is often used. This is called the **normal** curve and it is the probability density function of the **normal** (or **Gaussian**) **distribution**. This is used as it is straightforward to calculate the standard deviation, and two standard deviations from the mean give 98% of the population.

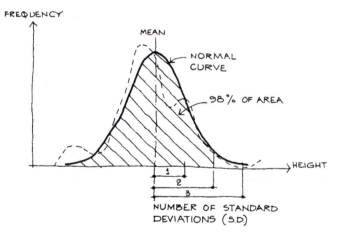

Fig. 6.6 Normal distribution

Using the standard calculations for the normal distribution (often available on pocket calculators) any data can be processed to produce the **mean** and the **standard deviation**. So the data used to draw the histogram could be processed as a normal distribution to give the mean and the standard deviation.

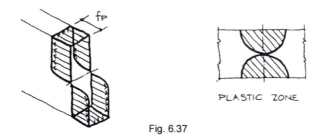

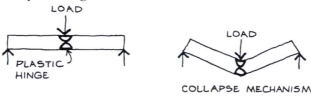

PLASTIC ZONE

Fig. 6.37

When full plasticisation is reached the beam cannot be stressed further and a **plastic hinge** has formed. The beam now collapses 'gradually' as it becomes a mechanism rotating about the plastic hinge.

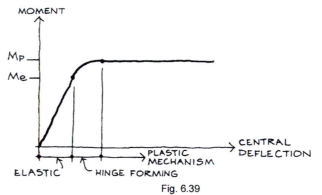

Fig. 6.38

The bending moment at the formation of the plastic hinge is called the **plastic moment**. The ratio between the elastic moment, M_e, the moment at the elastic limit, and the plastic moment, M_p, varies with the cross-sectional shape. For a rectangular cross-section the ratio is 1.5. The behaviour of the beam through the loading range can be illustrated by drawing a graph of the bending moment plotted against the central deflection.

Fig. 6.39

What happens to the structure is that a local failure of an element in the load path causes the structure to become a plastic mechanism. The prediction of the plastic mechanism forms the basis of the **collapse design method**. For the simple beam the elastic behaviour directly predicts the plastic mechanism.

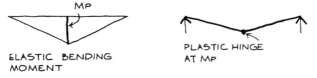

Fig. 6.40

150 Building structures

But for slightly more complicated structures, such as a two-span beam, the formation of one plastic hinge will not cause the structure to become a plastic mechanism.

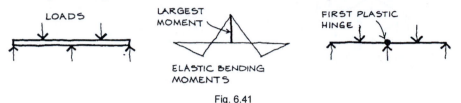

Fig. 6.41

Here the first plastic hinge forms at the central support but the structure is not yet a mechanism.

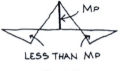

Fig. 6.42

The load on the structure can be increased until one of the span moments reaches the plastic moment. A second plastic hinge now forms and the structure becomes a mechanism and collapses.

Fig. 6.43

For a pitched portal frame loaded both horizontally and vertically there are three different possible collapse mechanisms. Which one will form depends on the rates of loading for each load.

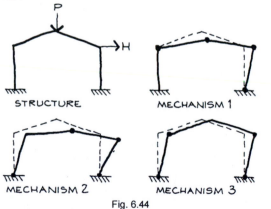

Fig. 6.44

This idea of plastic hinges can be used for laterally loaded two-dimensional structures to predict collapse mechanisms. The plastic moment, instead of being at a point forming a plastic hinge, is along a line. This 'line of plastic moment' is usually called a **yield line**. For a rectangular slab spanning between opposite supports the yield line position is similar to that of the hinge in the beam shown in **Fig. 6.38**.

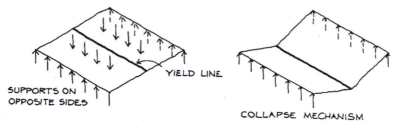

Fig. 6.45

For this simple case, the position of maximum bending moment is in a straight line across the slab which gives the position of the yield line. A plan of the slab showing the yield line (or lines) is called the **yield line pattern**. For the slab shown in **Fig. 6.45** the yield line pattern has just one line.

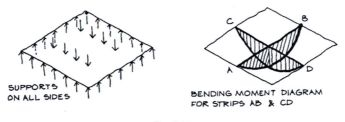

Fig. 6.46

A 'free edge' of a laterally loaded slab is one that is unsupported. If the rectangular slab is supported on all sides then it will span two ways (**Fig. 2.44**). This will cause bending moments in two directions (**Fig. 2.47**).

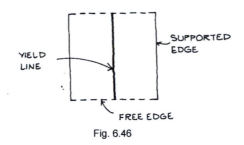

Fig. 6.47

But what is the yield line pattern? Whilst the slab is acting elastically the maximum bending moment will be at the centre, but as the load is increased the slab will become plastic at this point, the moment cannot be increased (see **Fig. 6.39**) and a yield line begins to form.

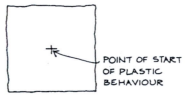

Fig. 6.48

But how will the yield lines 'grow' into a yield line pattern that allows the slab to collapse? For the one-dimensional structure shown in **Figs. 6.43** and **6.44**, the hinges allowed the structure to 'fold' into a collapse mechanism. Similarly the slab must be able to fold to be able to collapse. As the supported sides must remain level, the fold lines (yield lines) must go to the corners.

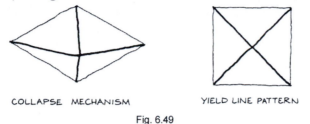

COLLAPSE MECHANISM   YIELD LINE PATTERN

Fig. 6.49

The fact that the yield lines go diagonally across the slab is because it is necessary for the fold pattern, but these are also lines of **principal moments**. The idea of principal moments is not described here, but it is similar to the idea of principal stresses (**Section 4.1**). Moments are applied to the 'sides of a small element' and this is rotated in plan to find the maximum and minimum moments on each side.

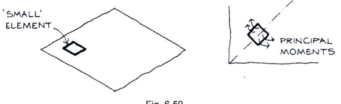

'SMALL' ELEMENT   PRINCIPAL MOMENTS

Fig. 6.50

For a square slab with a uniform load, the yield line pattern may be 'obvious' but a rectangular slab can be folded in several different ways.

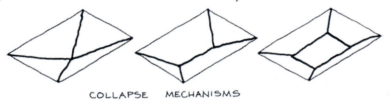

COLLAPSE   MECHANISMS

Fig. 6.51

These three different foldings of the slab give three different yield line patterns and three different collapse loads.

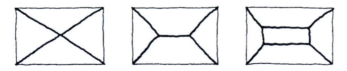

Fig. 6.52 Yield line patterns

Because the mathematical prediction of the elastic behaviour of slabs (usually called 'plates' in the technical literature) is difficult or often impossible, the mathematical elastic analysis of slab structures is not usually carried out as part of structural design. In contrast, **yield line analysis**, developed for reinforced concrete by the Danish engineer FW Johanssen, is relatively simple to carry out. Of course the correct yield line pattern must be chosen to make sure that the lowest collapse load is calculated.

The collapse mechanisms for these one- and two-dimensional structures rely on the formation of plastic hinges (yield lines) at positions of maximum bending moments. The formation of these hinges allows geometrically simple foldings of the structure into a collapse configuration. This means that these simple types of structural collapse are only possible if internal axial forces are absent or negligible and the geometry of the structure allows a simple folding.

For instance the ideas of plastic hinges and folding do not give any guidance on how a simple column collapses. Again the ideas of yield lines give no guidance on how the curved shell shown in **Fig. 4.25** collapses. To see how these structures collapse, the effect of **axial forces** must be examined.

6.4   Axial instability

When a straight one-dimensional structural element is loaded by axial end loads, it either stretches or squashes (see pages **37-38**). If the structural material is linear elastic/perfectly plastic (**Fig. 5.6**) the element deforms elastically as the load is increased until the elastic limit is reached. The element then becomes plastic and deforms without limit under the collapse load. Because the axial stress distribution is assumed to be uniform (**Fig. 3.29**) the whole of the cross-section becomes plastic at the collapse load.

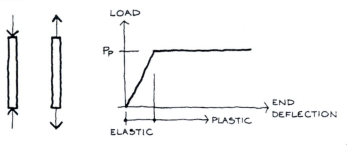

Fig. 6.53

At collapse load **P$_p$** the element fails by 'endless' stretching or squashing. This is always true for elements in tension but for elements in compression it is only true for certain types of element. This is because compressed elements can be affected by the 'Pe effect' which caused the stack of bricks, shown in **Fig. 6.29**, to topple. If there are two columns of the same cross-section, made of the same material, and one is 'short' (stocky) and the other is 'long' (slender), the difference in length will not alter the collapse load, **P$_p$** of **Fig. 6.53**. Both will resist axial forces by uniformly distributed axial stresses. As the cross-sections and the material are the same, both columns will become 'plastic' at the same load.

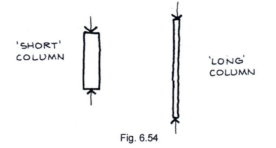

Fig. 6.54

But a simple experiment with a slender rod will show that as the end load is increased, that a slender rod begins to bow, that is, it starts to bend.

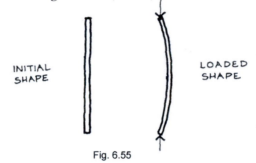

Fig. 6.55

The rod (column) is still carrying load but because the rod is bent, the internal forces are axial and bending moments. The size of the bending moment depends how much the axial load bends the column. So far the behaviour of structures has been described using the **unloaded shape** of the structure and the deflection has not altered the behaviour. This assumption is part of the **Engineer's theory** mentioned on page **65**, and this theory makes no distinction between stocky and slender columns. For this distinction to be made, a more sophisticated theory is required. The general name for this bending behaviour under axial load is **buckling** (from 'to buckle'; 'to bend out of shape'). Because of the technical difficulties of buckling it has fascinated and frustrated mathematicians and engineers for over 200 years. The first mathematical analysis was carried out by the great Swiss mathematician Leonhard Euler (1707-1783) who used it as an illustration of the calculus of variations which he was developing. His work remained unknown to engineers for over 100 years but such was its importance, Euler's name (pronounced 'oiler') is still associated with the buckling behaviour of structures.

But why has the initially straight rod (column) buckled? According to Euler's analysis, the **perfectly straight** rod will remain straight under increasing load until the **Euler buckling load** is reached.

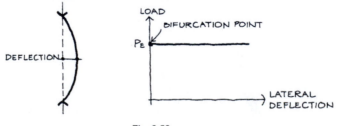

Fig. 6.56

The rod can then either buckle or stay straight. The Euler buckling load is often called the **elastic critical load** and the point on the load/deflection graph where the rod can buckle is called the **bifurcation point**. The deflection is now the lateral deflection and not the axial deflection of **Fig. 6.53**.

Euler's analysis was based entirely on mathematical theory and the fact that the rod has a choice at the bifurcation point is a 'quirk' of the mathematics, no real rod behaves like this. Euler's analysis also required that the rod is perfectly straight, but real rods are not, they are **imperfect**. The reason that a stack of bricks topples (**Figs. 6.30, 6.31** and **6.32**) is that it cannot be perfectly made, stacked or loaded. These imperfections cause the 'e' of **Fig. 6.30** and the toppling of the stack. Similarly columns cannot be made perfectly or loaded perfectly. This means columns are never perfectly straight, as Euler's theory requires, but are always bent (imperfect).

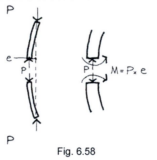

Fig. 6.57

This imperfection 'e' has the same effect on the column as that shown in **Fig. 3.89**.

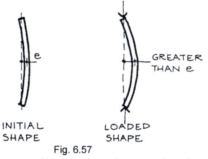

Fig. 6.58

In the case of the eccentric loading shown in **Fig. 3.89** the eccentricity 'e' remains constant no matter how big the axial load **P** becomes, and the **Engineer's theory** applies. For the imperfect column, as the axial load increases the dimension 'e' increases and so the bending moment, **M = P × e**, also increases. If the Engineer's theory is used for an imperfect column, the bending moment in the column is **Pe** where 'e' is the initial imperfection. As the axial load increases, the increase in 'e' is ignored and the moment increases in direct proportion with the load.

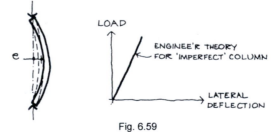

Fig. 6.59

If the effect of the increase in 'e' due to increasing load is taken into account the load/deflection behaviour is not represented by the straight line of **Fig. 6.59** but by a curve. As the axial load reaches the Euler buckling load (**P_E**, the **elastic critical load**) the curve meets the horizontal line of **Fig. 6.56**.

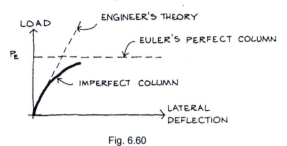

Fig. 6.60

The **slenderness** of a column depends on the length, the structural material and the cross-sectional shape. As the buckling effect causes a bending moment in the column, the better the column is at resisting bending, the less slender it will be. Unlike a beam that is loaded in a particular direction, a column can buckle in any direction, so columns that are good at resisting bending in any direction will be the least slender. For the same reasons for preferring **I** sections to **+** sections for beams (see pages **74-75**), columns with circular tubular sections are the least slender and those with **+** sections the most slender. This was not realised by 19th century engineers who frequently used **+** section columns. And as the column becomes more slender, the elastic critical load **P_E** reduces.

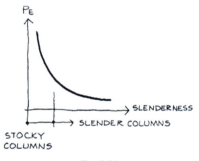

Fig. 6.61

This figure indicates a point on the slenderness axis where a column alters from a stocky column to a slender column. For a stocky column the buckling effect can be ignored and the Engineer's theory can be used to predict the column behaviour. As is explained later, the reason that this distinction can be made is because stocky columns fail at loads well below their elastic critical loads.

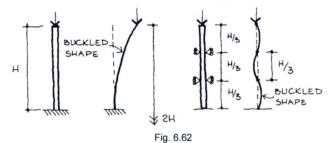

Fig. 6.62

Columns that are cantilevers or horizontally restrained within their height will have buckled shapes that are different to each other and to the column shown in **Fig. 6.57**. For the cantilever, the slenderness would be based on a length of **2H** whereas for the column restrained at third points, the length would be **H/3**, a sixfold difference. So, depending on how a column is joined to the rest of the world, a column could be stocky or slender. To make sure that the appropriate theory is used, the following questions must be answered for **all parts of structures in compression**.

- **What is the buckled shape?**
- **Is the structure slender?**

And as with many structural engineering questions they are easier to ask than to answer.

For columns, the whole structure buckles into a shape that depends on how the column is joined to other parts of the total structure. But how does a beam buckle? As already explained, when a beam is loaded, part of the beam is in compression and part is in tension (**Fig. 3.36**).

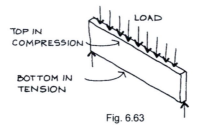

Fig. 6.63

For this simple beam, the whole of the top of the beam is in compression, so it will be the top part of this beam that will buckle. As the bottom is in tension it can only be displaced by an external force so the top can only buckle sideways.

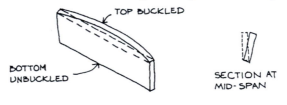

Fig. 6.64

If, like the column in **Fig. 6.62**, the top of the beam is restrained at third points, the top of the beam will buckle into a different shape.

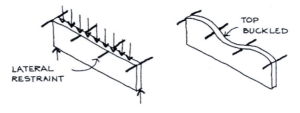

Fig. 6.65

Having found the buckled shape, it has to be decided whether the compressed part of the structure is slender or stocky. As with the column, this depends on the (buckled) length, the structural material and the cross-sectional shape. The compressed part of the beam buckles by a combination of sideways bending and twisting (**Fig. 6.64**) so this type of buckling is often called **lateral-torsional buckling**. The resistance to this buckling depends on the torsional stiffness of the beam. Beams that have cross-sections that are good at resisting this combined action are the least slender. For solid rectangular beams, deep narrow sections are more slender than square ones, for non-rectangular sections, tubes or sections with wide flanges are less slender and **+** sections are more slender – see **Sections 3.6** and **4.5**.

Where stress effective sections (see page **73**) are used, flanges or webs that are in compression may have buckled shapes in part of the element, this is often called **local buckling**. If an **I** beam is used for a simple beam, compressive stresses will be high in the top flange at the centre of the beam and in the web at the supports.

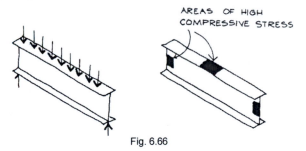

Fig. 6.66

So the top flange or the web could buckle locally in these areas of high compressive stress.

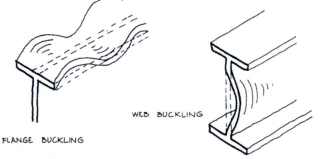

Fig. 6.67

This local behaviour can happen anywhere in a structure if there are high compressive stresses and the structure is **locally slender**. This could happen in the wall of a box column or the crown of a cylindrical shell.

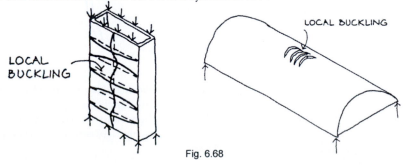

Fig. 6.68

Safe structures and failure 159

These various forms of buckling can be combined by considering slenderness in the compressed part of the structure. Whether it is local is then a matter of definition rather than concept. For the box column, the whole of the wall has buckled locally.

As with other structural engineering concepts, slenderness has to be quantified before it can be a factor for making structural decisions. The importance of identifying slenderness is shown by redrawing **Fig. 6.60**.

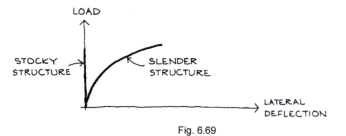

Fig. 6.69

Although a stocky structure will not be perfect, the imperfections can be ignored for structural design and axial forces only cause axial shortening and uniform axial stress. For a slender structure, imperfections cannot be ignored for structural design and axial forces cause axial shortening and lateral displacement, hence non-uniform axial stresses. Most importantly, the bending of slender structures under axial forces means the type of collapse will be different from a similar stocky structure and **at a lower load**.

Whether elastic, collapse or limit state design methods are used (see pages **142** to **144**), to be successful they all depend, in one way or another, on the collapse strength of the structure. Structures collapse by becoming mechanisms (see **Section 6.2**) and if they are slender, the bending due to axial forces must be considered in the formation of these mechanisms. This bending may cause a slender structure to collapse in quite a different way to a similar but stocky structure. For example the two columns shown in **Fig. 6.54** will collapse differently. The stocky structure, the short column, will collapse by squashing as the axial stress reaches the elastic limit and becomes plastic. The slender structure, the long column, will collapse when a plastic hinge (see **Fig. 6.38**) forms in the column bent by the effect of the axial load.

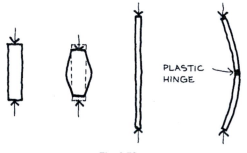

Fig. 6.70

A structure will always collapse due to plastic behaviour before the **elastic critical load** is reached. The more slender the structure, the nearer the collapse load will be to the elastic critical load. Recent research into the behaviour of steel columns has been collated to produce a graph showing the relationship between the collapse load and the elastic critical load (also see **Fig. 12.46**).

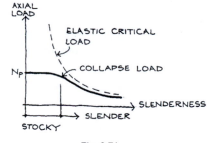

Fig. 6.71

Here N_p is the squash load of a stocky column, the maximum collapse load of the column. As the column becomes more slender, the collapse load reduces and is nearer the elastic critical load which is also reducing with increased slenderness. For beams the situation is similar, that is, a stocky beam will collapse with a plastic hinge when the bending moment reaches M_p (see **Fig. 6.40**). As the beam becomes more slender, the effect of buckling on the part of the beam in compression (see **Fig. 6.65**) reduces the collapse moment. A diagram similar to **Fig. 6.71** can be drawn for beams.

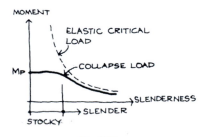

Fig. 6.72

These diagrams show that if the failure strength of a column or a beam (**P**LOAD2 of **Fig. 6.17**) is calculated without considering slenderness, then the factors of safety used in the design process may be dangerously wrong. In fact safe structures have collapsed for this reason. One of the best known collapses of this type was the failure, in 1907, of the St. Lawrence Bridge in Canada.[2] This bridge collapsed twice during construction with the loss of 88 lives. As the bridge structure was being cantilevered out, one of the compression elements failed as a mechanism caused by the buckling effect.

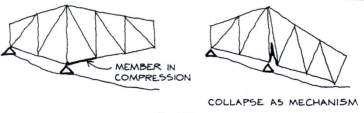

Fig. 6.73

Slender structures may have a 'light' appearance but are rarely light in terms of structural material. This is because the permissible stress of the structural material has to be reduced to avoid the possibility of buckling-induced collapses. Slenderness in structures presents the designer with a number of practical difficulties:

- **The theoretical analysis is mathematically difficult and at present incomplete.**

- **The matching of theoretical predictions to laboratory experiments is also incomplete and has only been attempted for elementary structures such as beams and columns.**

- **The design process does not automatically identify parts of the structure that are slender.**

The first two difficulties mean that the structural designer may not have reliable technical data for use in quantitative analysis. The third difficulty means that the structural designer must be able to **identify** structures, or parts of structures, that are slender.

The various aspects of the effect of buckling on structures has generated a vast amount of technical literature. Unfortunately in most introductory texts, the buckling effect on structures is either ignored or treated as an isolated topic. Although the basic behaviour of structures can be understood without considering the buckling effect, it leads to a naive understanding of structural design. This is because both overall conceptual design and detail design are concerned with the control of slenderness by either the choice of element or the specific introduction of slenderness-controlling elements or systems.

A simple example explains how this happens. At the end of a simple beam, the shear force is at its maximum – **Fig. 2.26**. If the chosen beam has an **I** section, then this shear force is mainly carried by the web, **Fig. 4.38** and the web may buckle locally, **Fig. 6.67.**

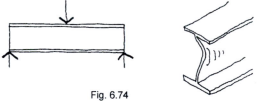

Fig. 6.74

This buckling behaviour may have to be controlled by making the web thicker, choice of element, or by adding slenderness-controlling elements. As the web wants to bend sideways, these extra elements need to stiffen the web against this bending.

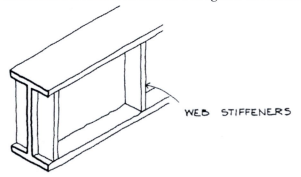

WEB STIFFENERS

Fig. 6.75

In effect, the stiffener now acts as a beam spanning between the top and bottom flanges and because it is stiff in the direction that the web wants to buckle, it prevents the web buckling. These web stiffeners can often be seen on steel railway bridges or other large steel beams.

Although the most widely used structural materials are still steel, concrete, timber and masonry (see **Section 5.2**) there is an increasing availability of these materials with higher strengths. This may result in more slender structures, but to use the higher strengths, more slenderness-controlling strategies are needed.

6.5   Relationship of structural theories

No matter what theories of structural behaviour are proposed, a real loaded structure will behave in a way that suits the structure and not the theory. To design structures by using a theory there are two conditions. The predictions of the theory must have a **reasonable correlation** with the behaviour of real structures and the theory must be **simple enough** to be usable as a part of the design process. But how close is a reasonable correlation and how simple is simple enough? There is no definitive answer to these questions but by comparing how the various theories apply to a simple structure, an opinion can be formed. The simple structure used for this comparison is the portal frame shown in **Fig. 2.27**. The loads are applied both vertically and horizontally.

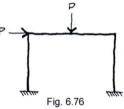

Fig. 6.76

The structural material is idealised as linear elastic/perfectly plastic (see **Fig. 5.6**). The behaviour shown in **Fig. 5.10** indicates the reasonable correlation obtained by this idealisation. Under the loading, the portal frame will deflect sideways at the beam level.

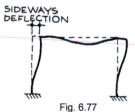

Fig. 6.77

As the size of the loads, **P**, is varied, the size of the horizontal deflection will also vary. The response of this deflection to the variation of the load will indicate how the frame is behaving. The most widely used theory for the prediction of structural behaviour is the **linear elastic theory**; this uses the assumptions of the **Engineer's theory**. This analysis predicts that the size of the deflection will vary in **direct proportion** to a variation in the size of the load. There is no limitation to the size of load, which means that there is no prediction of collapse. This theory predicts a **linear** response.

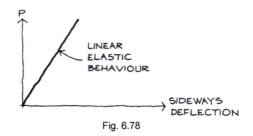

Fig. 6.78

For simple framed structures, the **rigid/perfectly plastic theory** can be used. This assumes a collapse mechanism from which a collapse load is predicted. For the portal frame with the loading shown in **Fig. 6.76**, the collapse mechanism would have four hinges.

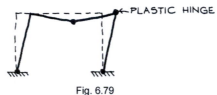

Fig. 6.79

This theory predicts a collapse load and at this load the frame would deflect without limit. This theory would not predict the frame's behaviour before collapse.

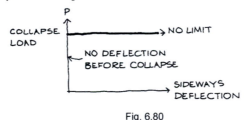

Fig. 6.80

The predictions of these two theories can be combined to give a **linear elastic/ perfectly plastic** response.

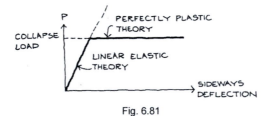

Fig. 6.81

These theories can also be combined to predict **linear elasto-plastic** behaviour. Really this is just alternating applications of the two theories. The linear elastic theory is used until the largest elastic moment equals the plastic moment (see **Figs. 6.41** and **6.42**). The structure used for analysis is now modified by the formation of the first plastic hinge but acts elastically until the second plastic hinge forms. Again the structure for elastic analysis is modified and another hinge forms, this process is repeated until the frame becomes a mechanism. Each phase of elastic analysis will only predict the position of the next plastic hinge and will not automatically identify the collapse mechanism. The response alters with the formation of each hinge.

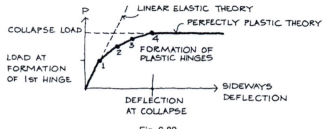

Fig. 6.82

This elasto-plastic analysis gives additional information such as the loads at which each hinge forms. The formation of the first hinge, which is a form of local failure, may occur at a load that is much lower than the collapse load. Because now there is a deflection history, the rotations at each hinge are predicted.

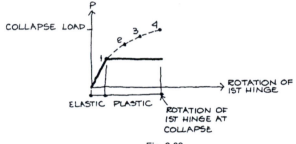

Fig. 6.83

In a real structure, there may be a limitation on the rotation of a plastic hinge due to a lack of ductility. This may cause the first hinge to fail due to excessive rotation before the final hinge forms to cause the collapse mechanism. In this case the failure would not be the frame collapse but a local collapse and the collapse load would be lower.

The analysis will take into account the bending moments and deflections caused by the **Pe** effect (see **Figs**. **6.57** and **6.58**). The response will be non-linear and will follow a similar curve to that shown for the imperfect column in **Fig. 6.60**. An elastic critical load can also be predicted for the frame under the specific loading and this limits the size of the load the frame can carry.

Alternatively an elastic analysis can be carried out for simple frames that take the buckling effect into account; this is a **non-linear elastic** analysis.

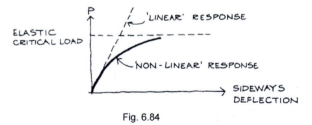

Fig. 6.84

The elastic critical load will always be greater than the collapse load as **Figs. 6.71** and **6.72** show for columns and beams. However, the elasto-plastic analytical process can use the non-linear elastic analysis between the formation of plastic hinges. The response will be similar to that shown in **Fig. 6.82** except the behaviour between hinge formation will now be non-linear.

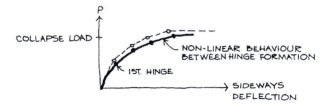

Fig. 6.85

This theory may predict a collapse load that is lower than the one predicted by the linear theory as the buckling effect may increase the bending moments at critical sections. This will cause the hinges to form at lower loads. The responses predicted by the five types of analysis can be compared by combining **Figs. 6.81, 6.82** and **6.85** into one diagram.

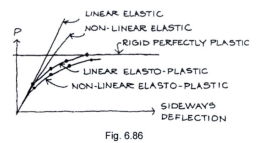

Fig. 6.86

The analytical dilemma facing the structural designer is now clear. A reasonable correlation between theory and real behaviour is best obtained by the use of the non-linear elasto-plastic analytical process which predicts the response shown in **Fig. 6.85**. The only general theory that is simple enough for general use is the linear elastic theory which predicts the response shown in **Fig. 6.78**.

The reasonable correlation of the non-linear elasto-plastic theory is approximate as it idealises the true material behaviour, ignores local buckling effects, ignores the effect of residual stresses and ignores the effect of axial and shear stresses on the formation of plastic hinges. Theories that take account of these effects are in the realm of research rather than structural design. The linear elastic theory is only simple enough for quite simple structures unless computing facilities are available. In spite of these shortcomings, the linear elastic theory can be used because the difference in the predicted behaviour and the actual behaviour is small in the phase before the formation of the first plastic hinge.

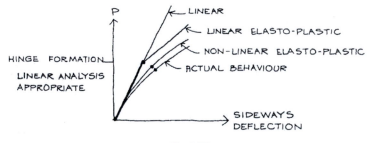

Fig. 6.87

As the majority of building structures are expected to behave elastically during ordinary use, their behaviour is adequately predicted by the linear elastic theory. However, safe structures can only be designed by using factors of safety against collapse (see pages **142-144**). The factors of safety are applied to linear elastic analysis by the use of a range of numerical coefficients. These coefficients are based on current analytical and experimental research and take account of the non-linear effects of material and structural behaviour. These coefficients are published in technical documents specifically prepared for structural design and are called **Codes of Practice**. In countries that have sufficient technical resources, these are prepared as national codes and their recommendations are often legal requirements as they are part of national building laws. In Europe, the national codes are being superseded by trans-national European codes.

References – Chapter 6

1   JE Gordon – **Structures or why things don't fall down** – Penguin 1978 p 328
2   RM Francis – **Quebec Bridge** – Conf. Canada. Soc. Civil Eng. Vol III, 1981 – p 655-677

CHAPTER 7   *Geometry and structural behaviour*

A structure may be considered to be an assembly of elements and these elements can be one, two or three dimensional. Depending on whether the loading is lateral or axial, each element has a particular type of structural behaviour (see **Chapter 3**). This behaviour may also be affected by the slenderness of parts of the structures that are axially loaded, as this can lead to instability (see **Section 6.4**).

The structural behaviour of any structure is dependent on a number of factors and these are:

- **The shape of the structure**
- **The type of loading on the structure**
- **The slenderness of the structure**

To conceive structures, the structural designer must be able to understand the consequences of structural geometry and structural assembly. This can be achieved by knowing how structures can be varied geometrically and understanding the overall behaviour of different assemblies of elements.

7.1   Geometry of structures

For structures to exist in the real world they must have a shape or **form**. Not only must the overall structure have a **geometry**, but also each part of the structure must have a shape or form.

Fig. 7.1

For a simple goal post structure, there is a choice for the cross-sectional shape for the posts and the cross-bar. They could be rectangular, circular or any other shape. Furthermore, the posts and cross-bar could have the same (constant) cross-section throughout their length, or a variable (that is, tapered, etc.) cross-section.

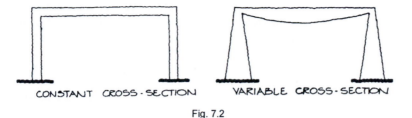

CONSTANT CROSS-SECTION   VARIABLE CROSS-SECTION

Fig. 7.2

Or again the basic goal post geometry could be altered by sloping the posts or curving the cross-bar.

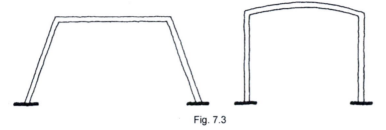

Fig. 7.3

It is worth making a distinction between **defined** and **organic geometry**. What is meant by a defined geometry is one whose shape can be expressed mathematically. Examples are rectangles, circles, ellipses and so on. Thus with a defined geometry the exact shape can be determined by mathematical calculation. This contrasts with organic geometry which has no mathematical basis. All natural objects such as trees, fish, humans, rocks and beetles have this geometry. This geometry can be created by drawing or modelling the structure without mathematical constraints. The exact numerical geometry can, if necessary, be obtained by measuring the drawing or model. This is often done for such natural objects as car body shapes.

Traditional building tends to use organic geometry, for example tepees, igloos and thatched cottages, and this is part of their charm and 'naturalness'. This is not to say traditional building has random geometry, often traditional geometry complies with a strict geometry but it is not mathematically based. This contrasts with civilised building which has a strict defined geometry. Often the geometry is something of a fetish. Research has highlighted the amazing accuracy of the geometry of the ancient Egyptian Pyramids and Classical Greek temples. Indeed the main secrets of the masons who built the great Gothic cathedrals were geometric.

Many attempts have been made to build modern civilised organic buildings, such as the original scheme for the Sydney Opera House – see **Section 11.7**. However, these attempts appear contrived rather than natural.

Fig. 7.4   Sydney Opera House

There are obvious advantages for a civilised society to use defined geometry. This is because civilisation uses extended lines of communications and a defined geometry is easier to communicate than an organic one. The majority of civilised building structures are based on rectilinear forms and there are practical and economic reasons for this. Due to the lack of skill of the designers, the vast array of non-rectilinear but still mathematically based geometries are rarely used. Again because the engineering analysis of non-rectilinear structures is difficult, therefore time-consuming and costly, engineering designers prefer rectilinear geometries.

7.2   The behaviour of structural systems

To understand the overall behaviour of any structural system it must be clear how the basic concepts apply. These concepts are:

1   **The function of a structure is to transfer loads** (see page **11**)
2   **The load path is the structure for each load** (**Section 1.6**)
3   **The structure transfers loads by forces in the structure** (see **Chapter 2**)
4   **Forces in the structure can be considered as a combination of direct forces, shear forces and bending moments** (see **Chapter 2**)
5   **The structure must have overall stability** (see **Section 6.2**)
6   **Collapse initiated by slender structures must be avoided** (see **Section 6.4**)

The choice of structural materials, concepts of structural safety and the stress distribution all affect the actual design but not the overall behaviour of the structural concept.

The first step towards understanding the overall behaviour is to extend the concepts of direct forces, shear forces and bending moments to more complex structures than the beam element. The behaviour of a simple spanning beam can be characterised by drawing the bending moment and shear forces diagrams (see **Fig. 2.26**). The shape of these diagrams will depend on the pattern of loading and the magnitude on the size of the span and the loads. Looking yet again at the simple beam with a central point load, the bending moment and shear force diagrams are those shown in **Fig. 7.5**.

BENDING MOMENT
DIAGRAM

SHEAR FORCE
DIAGRAM

Fig. 7.5

These diagrams plot the size of the internal forces which balance slices of the beam (**Figs. 2.9** and **2.18**).

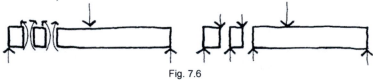

Fig. 7.6

It is important to understand the equivalence of bending moments with push/pull forces acting a lever arm apart (**Figs. 3.40** and **3.43**).

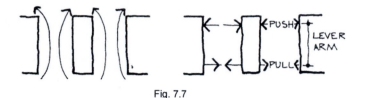

Fig. 7.7

These concepts have been explained by their effect on a simple beam, but a more general statement is:

- **When any structure carries loads over a span, bending moments and shear forces or THEIR EQUIVALENT will be present.**

The key is to find '**THEIR EQUIVALENT**'. Suppose that instead of using a beam to transfer the load **P** to the support points, a 'loose' cable is used. As anyone who has hung out washing knows, the line changes shape as each item is hung up. For a central point load, the shape is particularly simple.

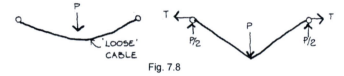

Fig. 7.8

The cable will be in tension (a direct force) and the supports must be capable of resisting vertical and horizontal loads. This seems to be a completely different structure from a beam, so where is the equivalent of the bending moment and shear force? Where is the push force and where is the pull force? Using the slicing technique of a section, what happens to a slice of cable?

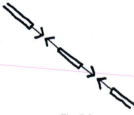

Fig. 7.9

Everything is nicely balanced but suppose that the sloping forces are thought of as a combination of horizontal and vertical forces.

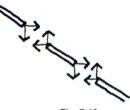

Fig. 7.10

Now the vertical forces on the slice look rather like shear forces.

Fig. 7.11

But where is the bending moment? All there is are some pull forces and these are not in the same line.

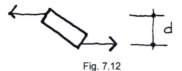

Fig. 7.12

The push force is in mid-air in line with the supports.

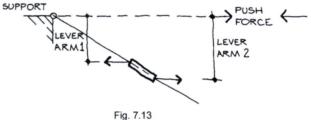

Fig. 7.13

This seems completely unreasonable, after all how can there be a push force in mid-air? Clearly it isn't there as such, only conceptually, and this allows the comparison with a bending moment and bending moment diagram.

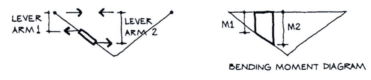

Fig. 7.14

Because the force in the cable cannot vary, the variation in the size of the bending moment is achieved by the variation in lever arm. This rather fantastic concept makes more sense if a strut is introduced 'to hold the supports apart'.

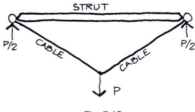

Fig. 7.15

Now the supports only resist vertical forces and the tension force **T** of **Fig. 7.8** becomes a compression force in the strut.

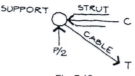

Fig. 7.16

Now the strut/cable assembly can be sliced.

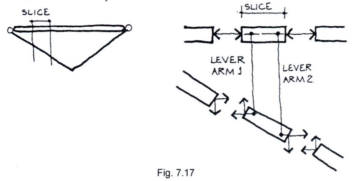

Fig. 7.17

The whole structure could be turned upside down, with sloping struts and a horizontal tie.

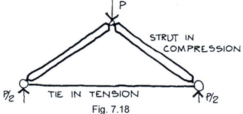

Fig. 7.18

Here a slice would show that the shear is now carried by the vertical force in the sloping strut and the tensile force in the tie. This is the pull force of the bending moment. If the supports can resist horizontal forces, then the tie could be removed.

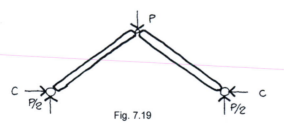

Fig. 7.19

A slice of this structure would now require a pull force in mid-air to allow comparison with a bending moment. These five different structures, all carrying the same load over the same span provide a basic palette of structural types. These five structures are:

1   A beam
2   A hanging cable
3   A hanging cable with a compression strut
4   Sloping struts with a straight cable
5   Sloping struts

Geometry and structural behaviour 173

Structures **3** and **4** are **trusses** and are simple forms of the structure shown in **Fig. 3.8.** Structure **5** is an **arch**, these are usually curved shapes. These five structures can now be compared for the structural actions of bending moments and shear forces.

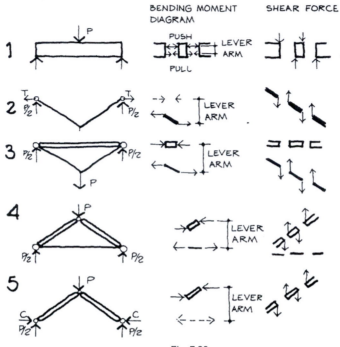

Fig. 7.20

It is worth noting that in structures **3** and **4** the shear forces are carried by the sloping members, the horizontal member making no contribution.

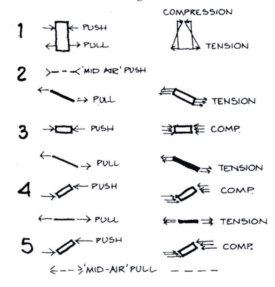

Fig. 7.21

Similarly the stress distribution for shear for structures **2**, **3**, **4** and **5** is the 'vertical' stress in the sloping member.

Fig. 7.22

For a beam, the paths of principal stress give arch-like curves for tension and compression (see **Fig. 4.19**).

PRINCIPAL COMPRESSION   PRINCIPAL TENSION

Fig. 7.23

Because of the simplicity of the stress paths of the structures **2** to **5**, they only crudely approximate the beam patterns. For comparison they are drawn on beam shapes.

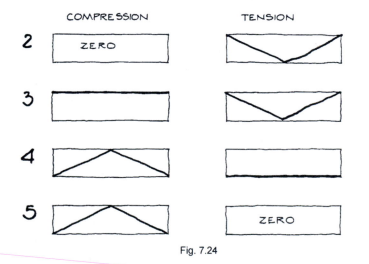

Fig. 7.24

All these structures are in two dimensions but they can be extended to form similar three-dimensional structures.

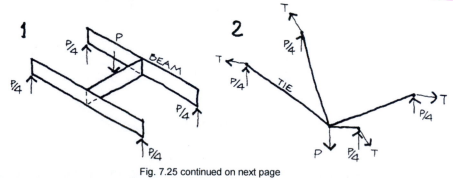

Fig. 7.25 continued on next page

Geometry and structural behaviour 175

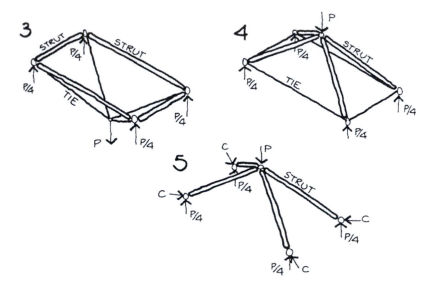

Fig. 7.25 continued

Structure **1** now has bending moments and shear forces in two directions.

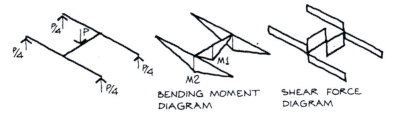

BENDING MOMENT
DIAGRAM

SHEAR FORCE
DIAGRAM

Fig. 7.26

For the tetrahedron-shaped structures, it is difficult to draw the slices and the push and pull forces but **M1** and **M2** must exist. These structures can be thought of as having four simple triangles.

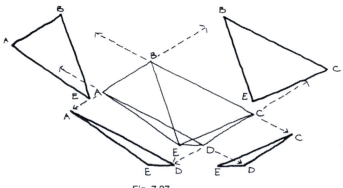

Fig. 7.27

The inclined triangles share the inclined members **AE**, **BE**, **CE** and **DE**. The inclined trusses **ABE** and **DCE** resist the bending moment **M1**, and **ADE** and **BCE** resist the bending moment **M2**. This is achieved by the horizontal part of the tension force in the inclined ties **AE**, **BE**, **CE** and **DE**. The push forces are supplied by the compression forces in the struts **AB**, **BC**, **CD** and **DA**.

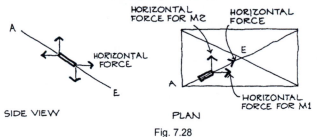

Fig. 7.28

Because the structure is now **three-dimensional**, the five basic **two-dimensional** structures can be combined to form many different structural systems. Here are three (the bold numbers indicate the type of structure used – see **Fig. 7.20**):

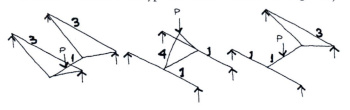

Fig. 7.29

These simple structures can also be used to illustrate concepts **5** and **6** (see page **170**). Structures **2** and **5** depend for their action on the existence of the support reactions **T** and **C** shown in **Fig. 7.20**. These reactions could be resisted by massive blocks.

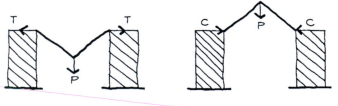

Fig. 7.30

The massive blocks must be stable under the disturbing forces that tend to turn the blocks over.

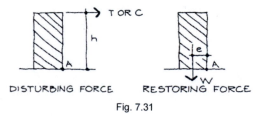

Fig. 7.31

From page **148** the factor of safety would be:

- **F.o.S = Restoring force ÷ disturbing force**

The structure could fail by the blocks overturning or sliding.

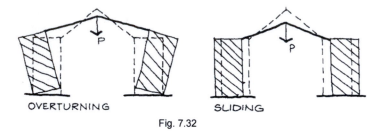

OVERTURNING   SLIDING

Fig. 7.32

Again structures **4** and **5** could fail by falling over sideways if there was eccentricity in the construction.

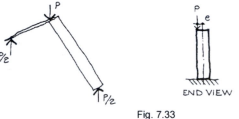

END VIEW

Fig. 7.33

If the dimension **e** was significant then the truss would lose overall stability.

In structure **1**, if the beam was slender then a collapse could be initiated by lateral buckling of the top of the beam (see **Fig. 6.64**). In structures **3**, **4** and **5** if the compression struts are slender then a collapse could be initiated by overall buckling of the strut (see **Fig. 6.55**). This is what happened in the collapse of the Quebec Bridge (see **Fig. 6.73**).

7.3   Trusses and frames

It is now possible to see how the concepts of bending moments and shear forces enable the structural action of a variety of physically dissimilar structures to be understood. In **Fig. 7.20** the structures **3** and **4** are trusses and trusses can be made in a range of **triangulated** arrangements of straight members.

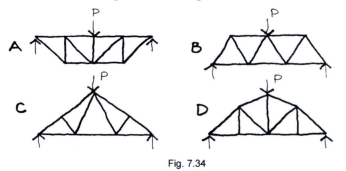

Fig. 7.34

These trussed structures are used widely and can be seen in all types of buildings, particularly as roof structures. As with the simple trusses, the sloping members carry the shear forces and also part of the push/pull forces of the bending moment whilst the horizontal members only carry the push/pull forces. This can be shown by examining the forces in **truss type A**.

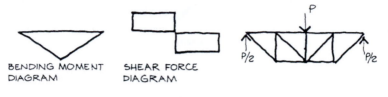

BENDING MOMENT DIAGRAM

SHEAR FORCE DIAGRAM

Fig. 7.35

If the truss is sliced then the slice of the truss must be in equilibrium with the bending moment and the shear force.

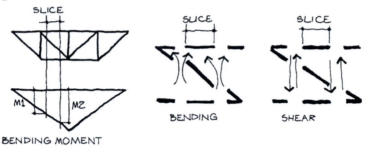

BENDING MOMENT

BENDING   SHEAR

Fig. 7.36

Of the three truss members cut by the slice, only the sloping member has a vertical force and can carry shear.

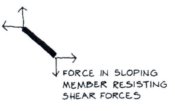

FORCE IN SLOPING MEMBER RESISTING SHEAR FORCES

Fig. 7.37

The forces in the top and bottom members only contribute to the push/pull forces, but there is also a contribution from the sloping member. So there are three push/pull forces.

 PUSH FORCE IN TOP MEMBER

PULL FORCE IN SLOPING MEMBER

 PULL FORCE IN BOTTOM MEMBER

Fig. 7.38

As the forces do not vary along each member, the variation from **M1** to **M2** comes from the variation in the lever arm caused by the different positions of the pull force in the sloping member.

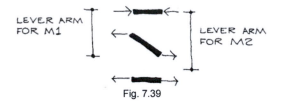

Fig. 7.39

This shows the top member in compression and the bottom and sloping members in tension. The complete distribution of compression and tension forces for such a simple truss is relatively easy to discover.

Fig. 7.40

Again the forces in the members can be considered to be paths of principal stress (see **Figs. 7.22** and **7.23**). Because the truss is now more beam-like, the paths are more beam-like.

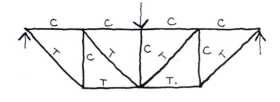

PRINCIPAL COMPRESSION   PRINCIPAL TENSION

Fig. 7.41

For this truss there is overall stability but there are several possibilities that slender parts could initiate collapse. The whole of the top part of the truss could buckle laterally, similarly to the top of a beam.

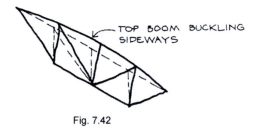

Fig. 7.42

Or any of the seven members that are in compression could buckle individually.

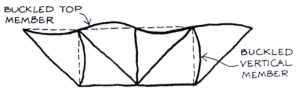

Fig. 7.43

Sometimes it is more convenient, for practical reasons, to support this type of truss at the level of the bottom member.

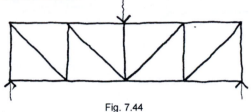

Fig. 7.44

The pattern is not altered, but the extra vertical members are in compression, basically just transferring the reaction force. The extra horizontal members are unloaded.

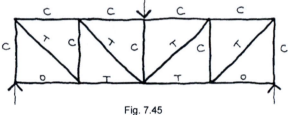

Fig. 7.45

This would be altered if the diagonals were reversed.

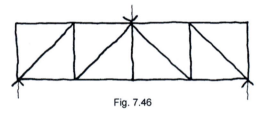

Fig. 7.46

The force pattern is similar for the top and bottom members but the forces in the diagonals now change from tension to compression and vice versa for the verticals.

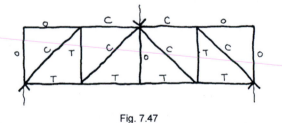

Fig. 7.47

This shows how a structural designer can alter, to some extent, the force pattern by choice of structural arrangement. But the truss still has to provide vertical forces for shear and push/pull forces for bending moments. This means the top and bottom members will always have tension and compression forces.

The trusses have axial forces in the individual members of the truss but a beam has bending moments and shear forces. As has been explained, there are similarities between the structural action of spanning trusses and beams, but physically they are quite different. It is possible however to physically change them into one another. Suppose a beam has small holes drilled through it and a truss has thicker members with large joints.

Fig. 7.48

These two structures do not appear to be similar and it would quite reasonable to expect the beam to act like a beam and the truss like a truss. In the region of the small holes, the beam stresses would be slightly altered and in the region of the joints the direction of the direct forces may be altered. But the overall behaviour would be beam-like and truss-like. However, if the holes in the beam were made larger and the members of the truss made thicker, the behaviour would change.

Fig. 7.49

Both these structures have to carry bending moments and shear forces but the stress distributions are no longer like beams or trusses. The large holes in the beam will invalidate the assumptions made for a beam (**Section 3.4**). The thick members and the large joints mean that the truss members will no longer only carry axial forces because the joints are no longer pinned. By making the holes in the beam square or removing the truss diagonals, the structures become the same – a **frame**.

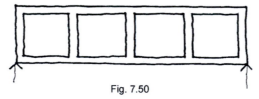

Fig. 7.50

But how does this unbeam-like/untruss-like structure carry the overall bending moments and shear forces? Again, slice the structure.

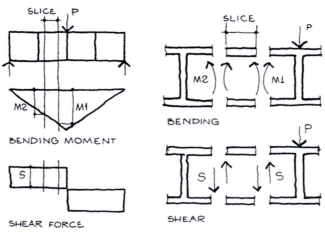

Fig. 7.51

Now the top and bottom parts of this structure have to carry the effects of **M1** and **M2** by axial push/pull forces and also the shear forces.

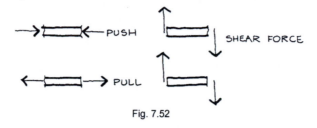

Fig. 7.52

It may appear that these are the only forces that act on the structure, but by carrying the shear forces, the top and bottom members are also subjected to bending moments – this is far from obvious. In the truss with diagonals, the individual members may be joined to each other in such a way that they are hinged to one another. This is called **pin-jointed**. However, if the frame was pin-jointed, it would be a mechanism and collapse.

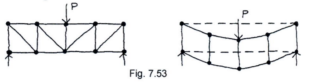

Fig. 7.53

But if the frame members have stiff joints, the structure will not collapse. What is preventing the collapse is the stiffness of the joint stopping each panel lozenging, but to do this the stiff-jointed members must bend.

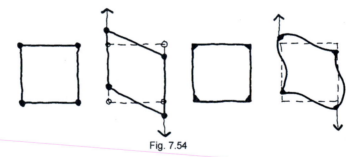

Fig. 7.54

Each member bends into an **S shape**, with the maximum bending moments at each end and a zero bending moment in the middle. Drawing the bending moment on the tension side of each member gives a rather confused bending moment diagram for the whole panel.

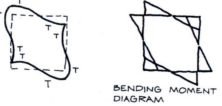

BENDING MOMENT DIAGRAM

Fig. 7.55

Not only are there bending moments in all members of the structure but there are also (horizontal) shear forces in the vertical members.

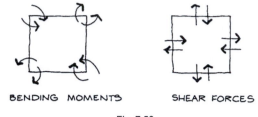

BENDING MOMENTS   SHEAR FORCES

Fig. 7.56

This should not be too surprising as this is similar to the horizontal shear forces that were required for the beam (see **Fig. 4.29**).

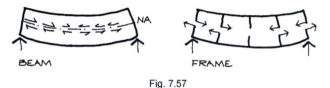

BEAM   FRAME

Fig. 7.57

For the whole frame, the bending moments are a sequence of those shown in **Fig. 7.55** for one panel. For clarity, the bending moment diagram is split into two, one for the top and bottom members and one for the vertical members.

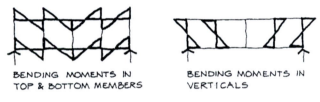

BENDING MOMENTS IN   BENDING MOMENTS IN
TOP & BOTTOM MEMBERS   VERTICALS

Fig. 7.58

In the truss, the variation in the overall bending moment either side of the slice was catered for by the variation in the lever arm (see **Fig. 7.39**). The lever arm varied because of the varying position of the force in the sloping member. In the frame this is achieved by the bending moments in the top and bottom members. The axial forces are constant in each panel and cater for the overall moment at the point of zero moment in the top and bottom members.

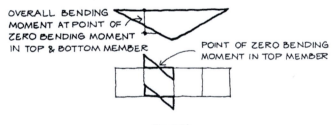

OVERALL BENDING
MOMENT AT POINT OF
ZERO BENDING MOMENT
IN TOP & BOTTOM MEMBER   POINT OF ZERO BENDING
MOMENT IN TOP MEMBER

Fig. 7.59

For each panel, the overall bending moment is the sum of the moment due to the axial forces **plus** or **minus** the bending moments in the top and bottom members.

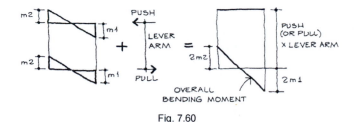

PUSH
LEVER ARM
PULL

PUSH (OR PULL) X LEVER ARM

OVERALL BENDING MOMENT

Fig. 7.60

This frame action with bending moments at the stiff joints which connect the individual members of the frame is used widely in structural engineering. The portal frame (see **Fig. 2.27**) is a common example of a framed structure. It is the loss of joint stiffness by the formation of plastic hinges (see **Fig. 6.44**) that causes frame structures to collapse.

Three types of structure have been identified – beams, trusses and frames.* Each type carries the overall bending moment and shear forces of **Fig. 7.5**: beams by internal forces of bending moments and shear forces; trusses by internal forces of axial tension and compression; and frames by internal forces of bending moments, shear forces and axial forces. This means that if any part of a load path has to carry an overall bending moment and shear forces then any of these types of structure can be used. For example, the vertical legs of the sign board shown in **Fig. 1.64** could be beam-like, truss-like or frame-like.

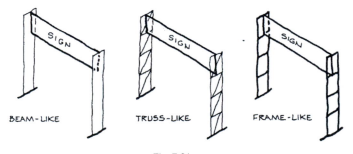

BEAM-LIKE   TRUSS-LIKE   FRAME-LIKE

Fig. 7.61

Or again the portal frame (see **Fig. 2.27**), whilst itself a frame could also be beam-like, truss-like or frame-like.

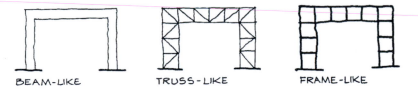

BEAM-LIKE   TRUSS-LIKE   FRAME-LIKE

Fig. 7.62

The types can be mixed to make a portal frame with beam-like legs and a truss-like beam, or any other mixture.

---

*   This type of spanning frame is often called a Viereendel girder

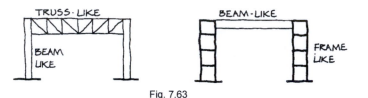

Fig. 7.63

All these portal frames are the same! That is they all have to carry the applied load and do so by overall bending moments and shear forces. Where part of the structure is beam-like they are carried by internal bending moments and shear forces, where it is truss-like they are carried by internal axial forces and where it is frame-like they are carried by frame action. Even one structural element could be a mixture of structure types.

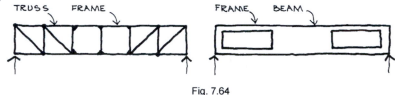

Fig. 7.64

By using these mixtures a great variety of structural systems are available to the structural designer.

7.4   Cables and arches

There is another type of structural behaviour which is not beam-like, truss-like or frame-like but **funicular**. Funicular comes from the Latin for rope – funis. The behaviour has already been described for the washing line/cable structure (see **Fig. 7.8**). For a cable (or rope) the shape of the structure changes with a change in the load pattern.

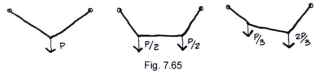

Fig. 7.65

This is because the cable is flexible and can only have internal forces of axial tension. It would be rather surprising if the cable took up different shapes from those shown in **Fig. 7.65**.

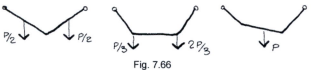

Fig. 7.66

The shapes shown in **Fig. 7.66** would require that the structure was stiff rather than flexible, then the structure would be a frame – but a cable is not a frame it is a funicular structure. Like any spanning structure it has to carry the overall bending moment and shear forces. For a cable this has already been described on pages

173-174. If a cable is loaded by a uniformly distributed load, the cable will take up a parabolic shape. This is the **funicular shape** for this load pattern.

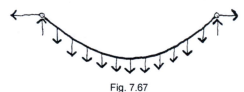

Fig. 7.67

If the load is non-uniform then other curved shapes would be the funicular shapes.

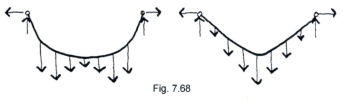

Fig. 7.68

Because all these cables are in direct tension, if they were turned upside down they would be in direct compression.

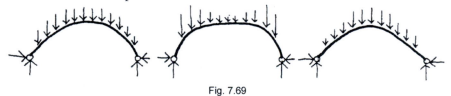

Fig. 7.69

Of course this would not be possible for a cable but if the structure could carry compression then the funicular shape obtained from the hanging cable gives the correct shape for an arch that is in direct compression everywhere. Although the arch was the main spanning structure for construction from the Roman period to the 19th century, the idea of inverting cables to find arch shapes was only stated in 1675 by the English genius and eccentric Robert Hooke (1635-1703). There is a sketch in the British Museum by Christopher Wren (1632-1723) – see **Fig. 11.10**, of a funicular line drawn on the dome of St. Paul's but there is no direct evidence that he used this for the design. The first application of this principle seems to have been by G. Poleni in 1748 as part of his investigation into the structural behaviour of the dome of St. Peter's in Rome. He used a correctly loaded chain to determine the funicular shape of the dome.

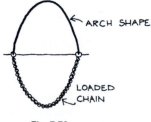

Fig. 7.70

If an arch is built to the shape of the funicular line for a particular loading, the whole of the arch will be in direct compression. If, however, the loading changes, or the arch is built to the wrong shape and the funicular line moves outside the arch, then the arch will have to maintain its shape by frame action or collapse.

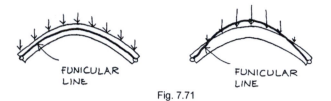

Fig. 7.71

Because funicular arches are in direct compression they are suited to materials that are good in compression but have little tensile strength, that is, brick, stone or mass concrete. To ensure that tensile stresses or cracks do not occur with arches made of these materials, it is important to keep the funicular line within the middle third of the cross-section (see **Fig. 3.92**).

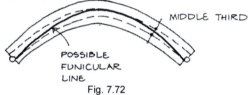

Fig. 7.72

As the funicular line changes shape with a change in loading, for compression – only arches the load variation can only be small. For heavyweight structures the permanent load is usually large compared with the applied load. If this is not the case, the arch structure must be capable of resisting the bending moments and shear forces that result from the frame action required to maintain the arch shape. It must be remembered that funicular structures need supports that can provide a horizontal reaction. In fact funicular structures must be seen as a combination of the funicular part and the horizontal restraint. Casual viewing of a curved structure does not always reveal whether the structure is funicular or just a curved beam.

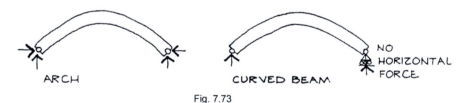

Fig. 7.73

7.5   Three-dimensional structures

Beam-like, truss-like, frame and funicular structures can be two-dimensional or three-dimensional. For three-dimensional structures the basic principles of the different types of behaviour still apply. The structure now has overall bending moments and shear forces in two directions. Schematically this can be illustrated for a structure, rectangular in plan and supported at the corners.

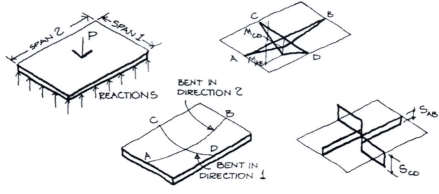

Fig. 7.74

This has already been described for slabs (see **Section 2.4**). The basic pattern of behaviour will be the same. The different types of structure can be used to span a rectangle and be supported at the corners.

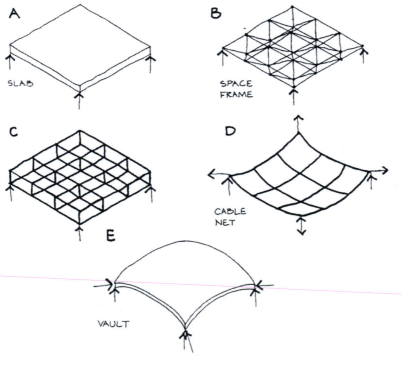

Fig. 7.75

The three-dimensional truss is often called a **space frame**, the cable system a **cable net** and the curved surface a **shell** or **vault**. Structures **D** and **E** are funicular surfaces which will be a different shape for each different loading pattern if bending moments and shear forces are to be avoided.

The action of each type of structure follows from the two-dimensional types. The slab resists the loads by internal forces of bending moments and shear forces like a beam. The space frame resists load by axial forces in the individual members, the top and bottom members resisting the bending push and pull forces and the diagonal members resisting the shear and the bending. The three-dimensional frame has axial forces with bending moments and shear forces at the stiff joints. The cable net only has axial tension forces and the shape varies with loading pattern. The shell is the cable net 'turned upside down'. Provided the shell is a funicular shape, the loads will be resisted by compression forces only. Like the two-dimensional funicular structures the supports of the cable net and the shell must be able to resist horizontal as well as vertical forces.

The variety of structures that can be derived from these basic types is almost limitless. Not only is there a choice for the overall structural system, but every part of the structure can be one of the different types. This is just an extension of the ideas shown in **Figs. 7.61** to **7.64**. However, these structures must not be conceived visually; the conception must be based on an understanding of the structural behaviour. This is illustrated by **Fig. 7.73**, as it is no good expecting a curved structure to be a funicular structure unless the supports can resist horizontal forces; again a truss without diagonals has to behave as a frame therefore must have stiff joints (**Fig. 7.54**).

7.6   Prevention of axial instability

Even if the conception of a structural system is based on an understanding of structural behaviour, the structure may be slender and prone to buckling-initiated collapse. Part of conceptual design is to provide stiffness against these slenderness-induced failures. The designer must ensure that parts of the structural system that are in compression have **stiffening structures** to keep the slenderness within sensible limits. The example of a beam with a **U-shaped** cross-section illustrates this point.

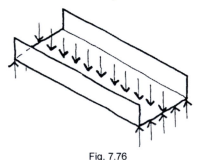

Fig. 7.76

The structure has to resist the overall bending moment due to the load. As it is a beam-like structure, this bending moment will cause longitudinal tension and compression stresses and the compression stress will be in the top part of the structure.

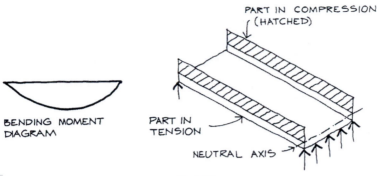

BENDING MOMENT
DIAGRAM

PART IN COMPRESSION
(HATCHED)

PART IN
TENSION

NEUTRAL AXIS

Fig. 7.77

If the top part is slender it could buckle sideways, initiating collapse. To prevent this the top of the structure must have some lateral stiffness. This stiffness could be continuous or discrete. Continuous stiffness can be provided by giving the top lateral stiffness or by making the joints between the vertical and horizontal parts of the 'U' stiff.

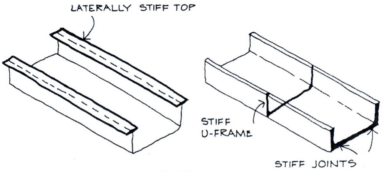

LATERALLY STIFF TOP

STIFF
U-FRAME

STIFF JOINTS

Fig. 7.78

For the stiff top structure to buckle sideways, the top must deflect sideways and this is resisted by the top acting as a horizontal beam. For the stiff jointed 'U' to buckle, the 'U' must open or close and this is resisted by bending moments at the stiff joints.

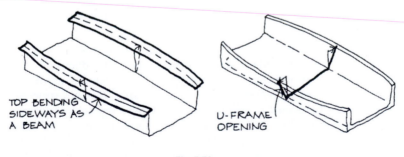

TOP BENDING
SIDEWAYS AS
A BEAM

U-FRAME
OPENING

Fig. 7.79

Alternatively the structure can have discrete stiffening structures which have the effect of providing lateral restraint at each point.

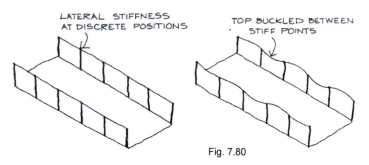

Fig. 7.80

Again these stiffening structures can be beam-like or truss-like.

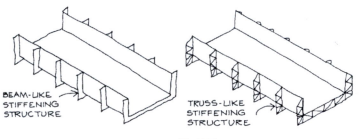

Fig. 7.81

The stiffening **U-frames** provide stiffness in the same way that the continuously stiff-jointed structure does, but at discrete points. This shows that if the structural concept was the **U-shaped** structure, it would be incomplete **as a concept** without the provision of stiffness against buckling. How any structure is stiffened against buckling-initiated collapse is a matter of choice for the designer but it must be part of the concept rather than something that is added at a later stage to 'make the structure work'. If the structural designer is unable to conceive where this stiffening is required then the original concept is likely to be flawed. Radical re-design may be required at the detail design stage often with unfortunate results for the initial concept; for instance at the WD & HO Wills factory in Bristol.*

Using all the concepts that have been described it is possible to understand how building structures behave when they are loaded. This understanding does not give any quantitative information about the structures. It does not answer questions about the sizes of the individual structural elements; this information can only be obtained by numerical calculations.

Because structures are built into buildings, it is not usually possible to see how the structure acts without additional information such as drawings or written descriptions. If this information is available, usually from technical journals, then the concepts can be used to understand how any particular building structure works. Investigating the behaviour of existing structures gives the inexperienced designer important insights into how building structures are designed and built. Because there is such an enormous variety of possible structures, this knowledge does not mean that all designs need to be slavish copies – but perhaps a 'good' copy is better than an ill-conceived 'innovation'.

---

*   Architectural Review, October 1975, p 196-213.

CHAPTER 8   *Behaviour of a simple building*

Buildings are constructed to alter the environment locally by enclosing space and building structures give strength and stiffness to the enclosing elements. The simplest building is a single enclosed space or a single space building. If the function and behaviour of the structure of a single space building is understood then understanding building structures of more complex buildings is relatively straightforward. Although many buildings have many spaces, factories, sports halls, theatres and churches are all examples of buildings which are often essentially a single space.

The shapes of single spaces could be cubic, spherical or any defined or organic geometry (see page **169**). However, the majority of new buildings are rectilinear for a number of practical reasons so the **basic structure** is the structure for a cubic single space. The explanation for the behaviour of the structure for this single space uses the six basic concepts which are:

1   **The function of a structure is to transfer loads**
2   **The load path is the structure for each load**
3   **The structure transfers loads by forces in the structure**
4   **Forces in the structure can be considered to be a combination of direct and shear forces and bending moments**
5   **The structure must have overall stability**
6   **Collapse initiated by slender structures must be avoided**

An understanding of how these six essential concepts apply to the structure of a single space can be used to understand the structures of more complex buildings such as houses, hotels, offices or arts centres. Not only does the application of these basic concepts give an understanding of structural behaviour but it also provides a basis for the more difficult process of structural design. The design process is more difficult than understanding the behaviour of existing structures as the concepts have to be used simultaneously to produce the design.

8.1   Basic structure and loading

As these concepts apply to the whole of the structure they must be applied to every part of the structure; from each weld or bolt to the whole structure. So that the concepts can be applied to a specific example, the basic shape of the building is assumed to be rectangular with a simple pitched roof.

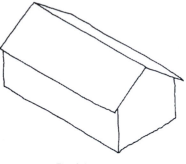

Fig. 8.1

The building has a roof covered with corrugated metal sheeting with walls of brickwork. The main structure is steelwork, the floor is of pre-cast concrete, and the foundations are of in situ concrete. This type of building is used widely throughout the world for factories and warehouses.

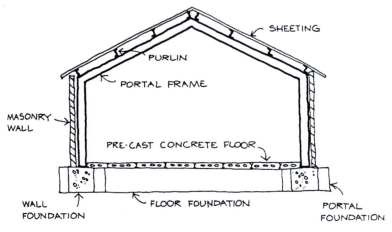

Fig. 8.2

To avoid the endless use of the word **concept** in the rest of this section concepts are put into square brackets. **So [2] in the text will mean that concept 2** – the load path is the structure – applies.

To start at the beginning **[1]**, what are the loads? The sources of loads will be gravity, the wind and the use of the space. Gravity and use will apply vertical loads (see **Figs. 1.27** to **1.32**).

W1 - WT. ROOF
W2 - SNOW
W3 - WT. WALL
W4 - WT. FLOOR
W5 - FLOOR LOAD

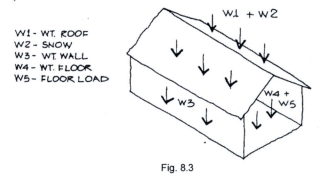

Fig. 8.3

194 Building structures

Wind will apply loads at right-angles to the roof and walls.

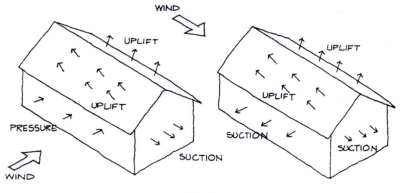

Fig. 8.4

Whether the wind causes an uplift force on the roof depends on the slope angle of the roof.

Although all these loads are applied to the building at various times, not all the loads will be applied simultaneously, so the structure must be safe under all **load combinations** (see pages **21-25**). Even for such a simple building there can be numerous different combinations. Here three combinations will be considered.

Loadcase 1   Maximum vertical load on the roof and floor.

Loadcase 2   Minimum vertical load on the roof and floor plus wind load on the side elevation.

Loadcase 3   Minimum vertical load on the roof and floor plus wind load on the end elevation.

Because of **[2]** the structure for each loadcase may be different so **[2]** has to be applied to each loadcase. As the space is three dimensional, the structure has to be three dimensional, however each element is either one or two dimensional (see pages **57-59**) and will act as one-dimensional or two-dimensional structures. For this structure, the elements can be identified as one or two dimensional and so can their actions.

ELEMENT	TYPE	ACTION
Roof sheet	2D	1D
Wall	2D	2D
Steel frame	1D	1D
Pre-cast floor	2D	1D
Foundations	1D	1D (?)

It may seem odd that two-dimensional elements like the roof sheeting or the floor units act as one-dimensional structures, but this is because of the way they are connected to the rest of the structure.

Before each load path **[2]** is identified, the structural behaviour, **[3]** and **[4]**, of each element can be clarified. Firstly the roof sheeting, this is two dimensional but spans unidirectionally.

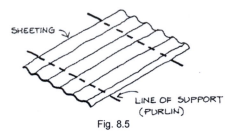

Fig. 8.5

The wall is connected vertically for vertical loads and is connected laterally for horizontal loads.

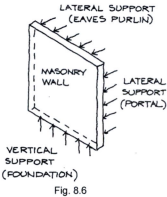

Fig. 8.6

The steel frame consists of several different parts. The purlins, the portal frames, the roof wind bracing, the wall wind bracing and the gable posts.

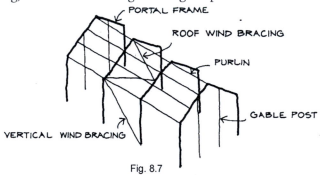

Fig. 8.7

The pre-cast concrete floor units are two-dimensional elements but span unidirectionally.

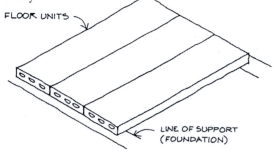

Fig. 8.8

The foundations are one-dimensional elements but their structural action, rather surprisingly, is one or two dimensional!

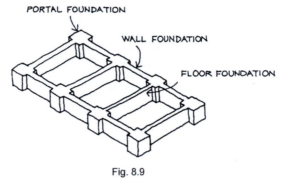

Fig. 8.9

The identification of the structural elements often provides important clues to the behaviour of the structure, but for built structures this identification usually requires more information than can be provided by visual inspection. Having identified all the structural elements it is possible to see how they become parts of load paths [2], how the structure transfers loads [3] and what type of internal forces there are in each element [4].

For **Loadcase 1**, maximum vertical load, every element will be involved because all the elements have self-weight due to gravity. Is usual to 'chase' loads down a building so the roof load path has to be identified.

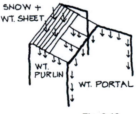

Fig. 8.10

The vertical load on the roof, snow load and the self-weight of the sheeting, is supported by the roof sheeting which spans from purlin to purlin.

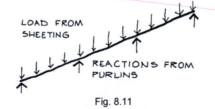

Fig. 8.11

The reactions to the sheeting become loads on the purlins, the self-weight of the purlins must be added to the sheeting reactions. The purlins span between the portal frames.

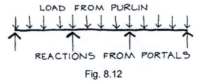

Fig. 8.12

Behaviour of a simple building 197

Now the reactions to the purlins become loads on the portal frames, again the self-weight of the frames must be added to these loads. These loads are carried by the frame action of the portal frames to the foundations.

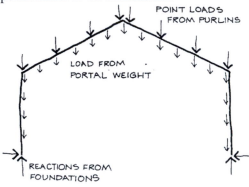

Fig. 8.13

The foundations are loaded by the reactions to the portal frames plus the reactions to the self-weight of the walls and the reactions to the floor units.

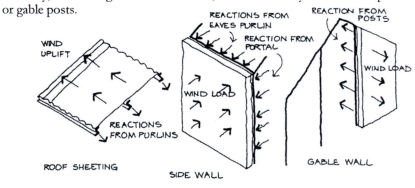

Fig. 8.14

The loadcases for the wind load include the minimum vertical load, which is the self-weight of the building construction. As the load paths for these loads are the load paths for **Loadcase 1**, only the load paths due to the wind loads are described. When the wind blows on the side elevation the walls are loaded horizontally and the roof sheeting is loaded at right-angles to the roof slope — these loads are shown in **Fig. 8.4**. Again the roof sheeting spans between the purlins but the walls span both vertically, from the ground to the eaves, and horizontally between the portal frames or gable posts.

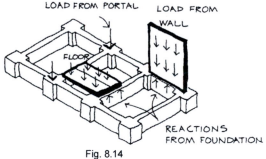

Fig. 8.15

The loads on the intermediate portals are due to the reactions to the purlins and the side walls. The self-weight of the sheeting, purlins and the portal frames must be added to the wind loads.

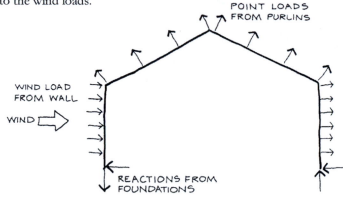

Fig. 8.16

For the end portals, the reactions from the wind load on the gable walls must be added to the loads from the wind on the side walls shown in **Fig. 8.16**.

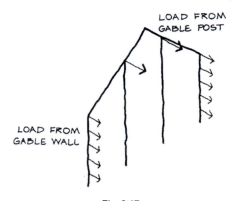

Fig. 8.17

Because the outward loads on the end walls are approximately equal, there is no overall effect along the building. The loads across the building do have the overall effect of a horizontal load.

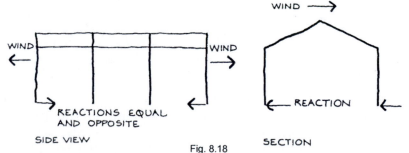

Fig. 8.18

When the wind blows on the end wall there is uplift on the roof and equal and opposite outward wind loads on the side walls. The loads on the intermediate portals are similar, but not the same as those shown in **Fig. 8.16**.

Behaviour of a simple building 199

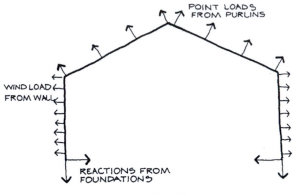

POINT LOADS FROM PURLINS

WIND LOAD FROM WALL

REACTIONS FROM FOUNDATIONS

Fig. 8.19

The loads on the end portals are similar to those on the intermediate portals plus loads from the gable wall. The gable wall loads are similar to those shown in **Fig. 8.17**. However, the overall load situation is the opposite of that shown in **Fig. 8.18**, there is now an overall force along the building, but no overall force across the building.

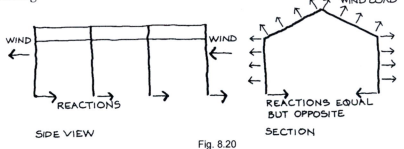

WIND

WIND

WIND LOAD

REACTIONS

REACTIONS EQUAL BUT OPPOSITE

SIDE VIEW

SECTION

Fig. 8.20

For the wind loads the foundation loads are the reactions required by the portal frames, the gable posts and the wall panels. Again it must be remembered that the self-weight loads must be added to these wind loads.

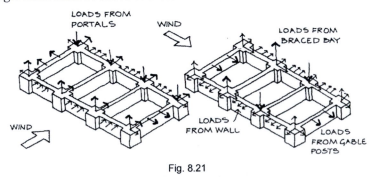

LOADS FROM PORTALS

WIND

LOADS FROM BRACED BAY

WIND

LOADS FROM WALL

LOADS FROM GABLE POSTS

Fig. 8.21

It is now possible to see how each part of the structure carries the loads **[4]** and how and stability **[5]** and **[6]** effects are dealt with. There are two approaches to this, either the whole of the load path for each loadcase can be investigated or each part of the structure can be investigated for all the loadcases. Because it is usual to design structures element by element, the second approach will be used here. As structures are usually designed **roof down**, the order of elements would be:

1	Roof sheeting
2	Walls
3	Purlins
4	Portal frames
5	Windbracing
6	Pre-cast concrete floor
7	Foundations

8.2   The roof and walls

For the roof sheeting only two of the three loadcases will apply because there will be a maximum downward loadcase and a maximum upward loadcase.

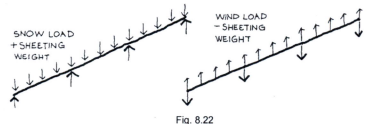

Fig. 8.22

The sheeting spans as a three-span beam between the four rows of purlins, and this spanning action will cause shear forces and bending moments in the sheeting. Shear force and bending moment diagrams can be drawn for these internal forces [3]. For brevity only the downward loadcase is shown.

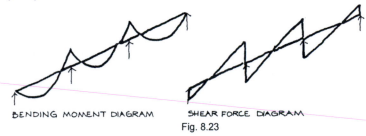

BENDING MOMENT DIAGRAM   SHEAR FORCE DIAGRAM

Fig. 8.23

As the sheeting is beam-like there will be bending stresses and shear stresses in the sheeting. The sheeting is corrugated so that it can carry these stresses in an efficient way, the bending stresses will be at a maximum at the top and bottom of the corrugations and the shear stresses will be a maximum at the mid-depth of the section [4].

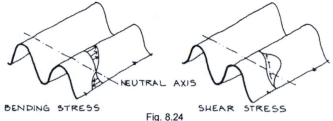

BENDING STRESS   NEUTRAL AXIS   SHEAR STRESS

Fig. 8.24

The overall stability [5] of the sheeting is provided by the fixings to the purlins. These must be strong enough to prevent whole sheets being sucked off by the upward wind loads. Due to the shape of the sheets, lateral buckling (see page **191**) will not occur but local buckling [6] could initiate collapse. This could occur at the point of maximum compressive stress or at the point of maximum shear stress.

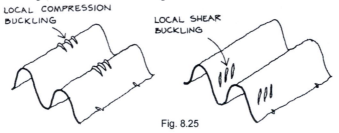

Fig. 8.25

Possible problems due to local buckling are prevented by providing a suitable thickness for the roof sheeting.

The walls are not loadbearing in the sense that they are part of the main structure however, they do have to transfer [1] wind loads to the portal frames. They also have to carry their own weight.

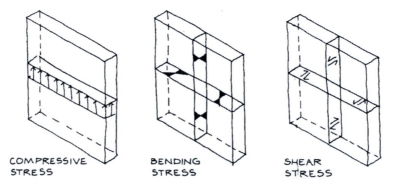

Fig. 8.26

The self-weight load is applied vertically and causes direct forces [3] and compressive stresses [4] in the wall. The wind load is applied horizontally and causes shear forces and bending moments [3] in the wall. As the wall is connected horizontally on all sides (**Fig. 8.6**), the wall spans in two directions, this means that these internal forces [3] will also be in two directions (see **Section 2.4**).

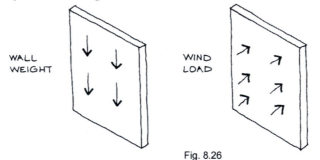

Fig. 8.27

Because brickwork has very limited tensile strength, the size of the bending moments in the wall is limited by the tensile bending stress. The bending stress depends on the span of the wall and the thickness of the wall. As walls can only be built in specific thicknesses, it is usual to choose a thickness and then limit the span. If the spacing between the main portal frames means the span of the wall is too big, then additional supports can be used to reduce the wall span.

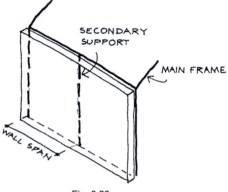

Fig. 8.28

The windload can cause bending in the wall panels in either direction so the walls must be fixed positively to the support framework, otherwise a panel could be blown (actually sucked) over [5]. The wall could also collapse by buckling [6] under its own weight if it is too thin. This form of buckling would be similar to the buckling of the wall of a box-column (**Fig. 6.68**).

The function of the purlins is to transfer the sheeting loads to the portal frames [1]. How much load depends on the spacing of the purlins along the sheet.

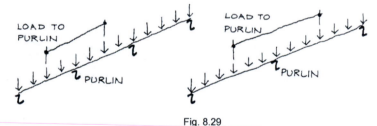

Fig. 8.29

The purlins are beams spanning between the portal frames so they have shear forces and bending moments like any other beam [3] and [4].

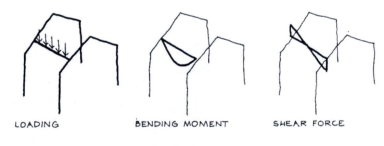

Fig. 8.30

There is a range of cross-sectional shapes that can be used for purlins.

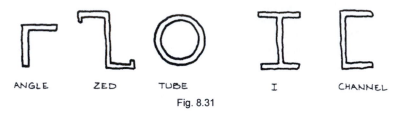

| ANGLE | ZED | TUBE | I | CHANNEL |

Fig. 8.31

If the chosen purlin is slender then the possibility of the compression flange buckling sideways [6] must be examined. Under downwards load, the roof sheeting acts as a stiffening structure to prevent lateral buckling of the compression flange. Under upward wind loading, the bottom flange is in compression and could buckle between the supports.

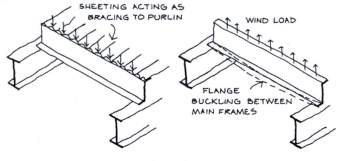

Fig. 8.32

If the span is long then a discrete stiffening structure can be used to provide lateral restraint to the bottom flange. This is often done by bracing the bottom flange of each purlin to the top flanges of the adjacent purlins with a rod.

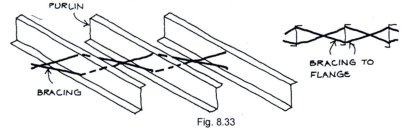

Fig. 8.33

This bracing reduces the slenderness of the bottom flange of the purlin which now has to buckle between support points.

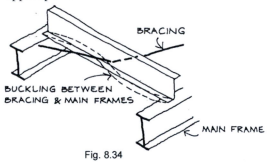

Fig. 8.34

8.3 The portal frames

The portal frames carry the loads from the purlins (**Fig. 8.30**) and the lateral loads from the walls **[1]**. This is done by frame action of the portal; this frame action only acts across the building. This means that the portal can only carry loads that are applied across the building, not loads that are applied along it.

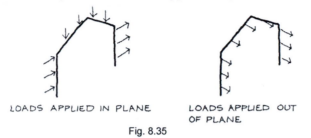

LOADS APPLIED IN PLANE   LOADS APPLIED OUT OF PLANE

Fig. 8.35

The three loadcases cause different load patterns on the portal frame **[1]**.

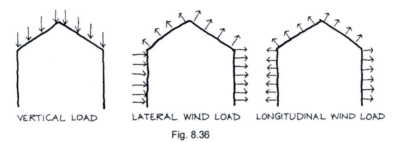

VERTICAL LOAD   LATERAL WIND LOAD   LONGITUDINAL WIND LOAD

Fig. 8.36

These load patterns will cause axial forces, shear forces and bending moments in the beam-like members that make up the portal **[4]**. The size of these internal forces will vary along the members of the frame and can be represented by axial force, shear force and bending moment diagrams similar to those shown in **Fig. 2.42**. There will also be vertical and horizontal reactions at the base of the portal frame.

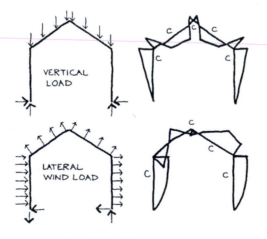

Fig. 8.37 continued on next page

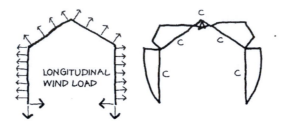

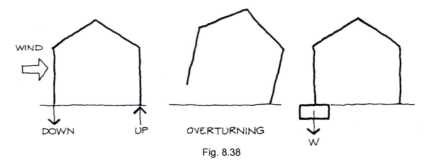

Fig. 8.37 continued

This figure only shows the bending moment diagrams, but there will be a direct force and shear force diagram associated with each of these bending moment diagrams. The positions of the tensile and compressive stresses are also shown on the diagrams. It should be noted that these vary quite dramatically from loading to loading as do the directions of the reactions at the support of the frame. Under wind loading, one vertical reaction is up and the other is down. This indicates that the whole frame could overturn under wind loading [5].

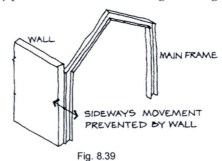

Fig. 8.38

If the frame and the cladding is 'light', the frame may need to be held down by the weight of the foundations. Where there are compressive stresses in the frame, the possibility of buckling-initiated collapse [6] must be investigated. Because different loadcases cause compressive stresses in different parts of the structure, each case must be considered separately. For compressive stresses in the top of the roof part of the frame, the purlins act as discrete stiffening structures and, depending on the connection, the walls may prevent the outside of the legs buckling.

Fig. 8.39

Under vertical load, the inside of the legs, the eaves and the ridge have compressive stresses and are not restrained in an obvious way. Under sideways wind load, different parts of the frame have compressive stresses and again some of these are unrestrained.

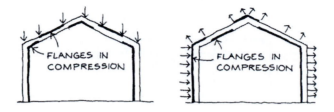

Fig. 8.40

Any of these areas of compression could buckle laterally if they were too slender.

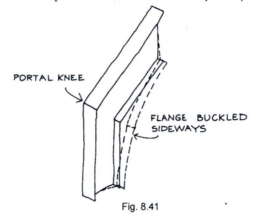

PORTAL KNEE

FLANGE BUCKLED SIDEWAYS

Fig. 8.41

8.4 The wind bracing system

The steel portals resist the force due to the wind acting on the side of the building but they cannot resist horizontal loads caused by wind loads on the gable walls (**Fig. 8.35**). The forces along the building are resisted by truss-like structures called **wind bracing**. These truss-like structures are a combination of the members of the portal frame and bracing members specifically introduced to resist the longitudinal wind forces – hence wind bracing.

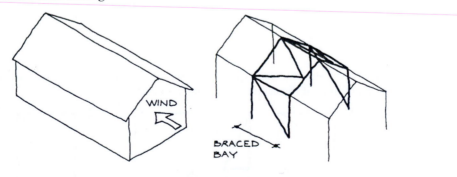

WIND

BRACED BAY

Fig. 8.42

The wind force on the end walls has to be strutted or tied to the braced bay.

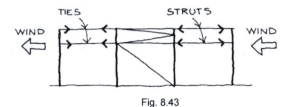

Fig. 8.43

These struts and ties may be the purlins **[2]**, in which case they have to be designed to act as part of this load path, or they may be extra members added to the roof structure solely for this purpose. The bracing in the roof is a truss-like structure often called a wind girder. The vertical bracing is also a truss-like structure which acts as a cantilever from the ground. For calculations of the wind bracing see **Example 12.21** in **Chapter 12**.

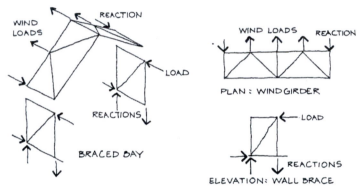

Fig. 8.44

The portal frames become part of the truss-like structures **[2]**, the roof parts of the frames become the top and bottom members of the wind girder and the legs of the portal frames become the vertical members of the cantilever trusses.

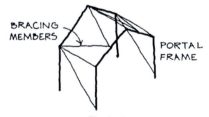

Fig. 8.45

The cantilever side bracing requires upward and downward reactions. These are the push/pull forces of the cantilever bending moment.

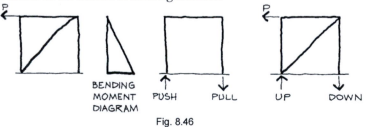

Fig. 8.46

As with the portal frame, the whole frame could overturn **[5]**. If the self-weight is low, then the downwards reaction is provided by the weight of the foundations.

Fig. 8.47

These truss-like bracing structures resist the shear forces and bending moments **[4]** caused by their spanning action by tensile and compressive forces in the individual elements of the trusses. As the wind direction is usually reversible, all the members of the bracing system will be in compression or tension for one of the wind directions. This means all parts of the bracing system have to be checked for the possibility of buckling-initiated collapse **[6]** (**Section 6.4**).

8.5   The floor structure

Like the purlins, the floor units span as simple beams between the lines of foundations **[1]** and **[2]**. The units are beam-like so the shear forces and bending moments are carried by shear stresses and bending stresses in the units **[3]** and **[4]**.

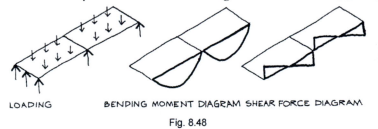

Fig. 8.48

As concrete is a heavyweight material and floors usually only have downwards loads there is no problem of overall stability **[5]**, and as no part of the structure is slender, there will be no slenderness-initiated collapse **[6]**.

8.6   The foundations

The main role of the foundations is to alter the stress level (page **64**). As the ground below the structure is usually weaker than the structural materials, the stress level has to be reduced, rather like the use of snow shoes (**Fig. 3.23**).

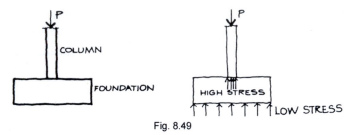

Fig. 8.49

In the case of this building the foundations also have to provide weight against uplift and resistance to horizontal forces.

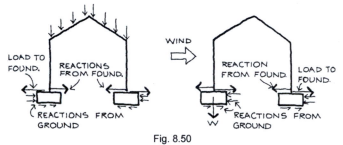

Fig. 8.50

The horizontal forces due to side wind are resisted by friction on the underside of the foundations and earth pressure on the sides of the foundations.

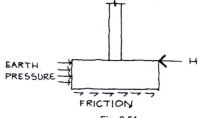

Fig. 8.51

Where the horizontal forces are acting in opposite directions, the friction and earth pressure can resist them, but if the force is high then a specific tie member may be required to resist spreading of the portal supports.

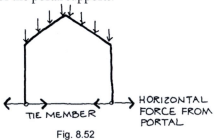

Fig. 8.52

If the supports of a portal frame move, the distribution of bending moments will alter radically. This is similar to the difference between an arch and a curved beam (**Fig. 7.73**).

Depending on the proportions of the foundations they may act as one- or two-dimensional structures.

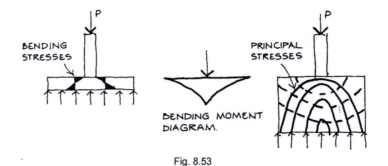

Fig. 8.53

Usually the behaviour of the ground away from the structure is not considered. This is because the stress level in the ground diminishes rapidly with distance from the foundations.

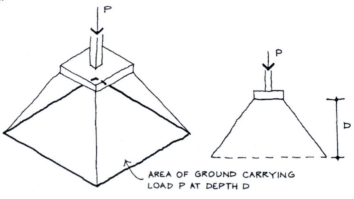

AREA OF GROUND CARRYING
LOAD P AT DEPTH D

Fig. 8.54

Whilst the ground is part of the structure, it is usual to consider that the structure ends at the underside of the foundations.

8.7   Summary

This example of a structure for a single space building illustrates how different load paths are needed for different loadings and how concepts of axial forces, shear forces and bending moments are used to understand the behaviour of each load path. The type of stress in each part of the structure depends on whether it is part of a beam-like or truss-like structure.

How any building structure behaves can be found by using the conceptual analysis used for this simple example. **It also shows how a structural designer has to choose the structure for every part of the structural system**. For instance, the chosen purlins were steel and beam-like, but truss-like steel or beam-like timber purlins could have been chosen. It is these choices and their consequential effect on the structural behaviour of the whole structural system that is the essence of structural design.

CHAPTER 9   *Real structures*

The way any structure behaves under loading can be understood by using the six basic concepts (see page **193**). The behaviour of the **basic structure** for a single space building was analysed in detail by repeatedly applying these concepts to each part of the building. This process can be used to analyse any structure provided sufficient technical information is available.

Because the process of structural design currently used for building structures is relatively recent, the structures of older buildings are often different in concept from more recent ones. Any building structure will act in the way that suits the structure rather than the designer's concept, if the concept is wrong. Recent designs answer questions raised by considering the six basic concepts, but for structures built before about 1850 the process was different. In older structures, the design was based on traditional practice (rule of thumb experience) and by the use of geometric concepts rather than structural ones. The geometry was used to size structural elements by using relationships based on proportions rather than structural behaviour. This means that the behaviour of structures conceived in this way is often difficult to clarify, their exact behaviour can even be a matter of debate amongst interested academics.

The six structures chosen for conceptual analysis are mainly from the period of engineering design because structural behaviour tends to be easier to clarify. The chosen structures are:

- **Durham Cathedral**,[1,2] England, completed 1133
- **The Palm House**,[3,4,5] Kew Gardens, England, completed 1848
- **Zarzuela Hippodrome**,[6] Madrid, Spain, completed 1935
- **CNIT Exposition Palace**,[7] Paris, France, completed 1960
- **Federal Reserve Bank**,[8] Minneapolis, USA, completed 1973
- **Bank of China**,[9] Hong Kong, completed 1990

These projects have been chosen because they all have very clear but different structural forms. Each structure is conceptually analysed in outline using the six basic concept process. These analyses demonstrate how these universal concepts apply to structures that are quite different geometrically and materially.

9.1 Durham Cathedral

Fig. 9.1 Durham Cathedral

The period of the early Middle Ages, which is from the 11th to 15th centuries, saw an enormous programme of church building in Western Europe. The buildings ranged from small parish churches to the famous, and not so famous, cathedrals. Their style is now known as Gothic and Gothic architecture has been, and still is, a subject of considerable academic and popular interest. This interest covers the historical, symbolic and aesthetic aspects of these churches and cathedrals.

There is also an interest in how the cathedrals were built and what technical knowledge the builders had. But the study of these aspects is hampered by the lack of documentary evidence of the building process. Although written material survives from this period, none of it relates to technology so either it was considered unimportant or never existed. As there was no concept of scale technical drawings the masons and carpenters must have worked from models and full-size templates.

The modern concepts of structural engineering had not been formulated so the builders could not have known about stress or bending moments but they must have known about gravity and force. The technical knowledge that did exist came from the Greeks but this had been lost in Western Europe during the so-called Dark Ages so the builders of the cathedrals were really pioneers.

The plan of Durham Cathedral follows the usual Latin cross plan of the Gothic style.

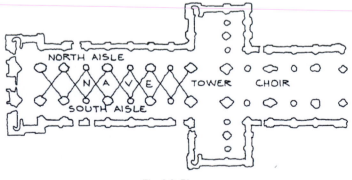

Fig. 9.2 Plan

The cross-section also follows the usual pattern for Gothic cathedrals.

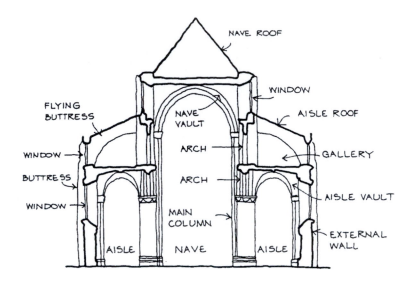

Fig. 9.3 Cross-section

The main parts of the cross-section are the roof, the main vault (ceiling), the internal and external 'walls', the side aisle roofs and vault.

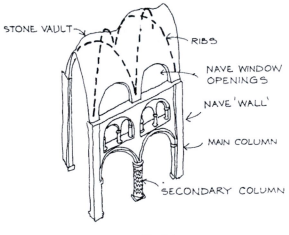

Fig. 9.4

One of the main ambitions of the builders was to flood the cathedrals with natural light, so the internal and external walls have numerous perforations which means that the walls are more like colonnades.

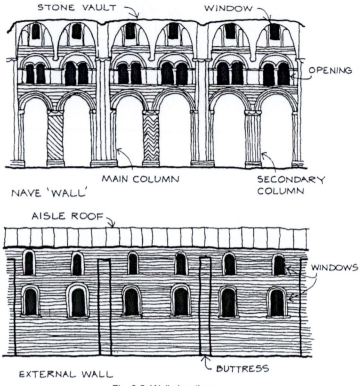

NAVE 'WALL'

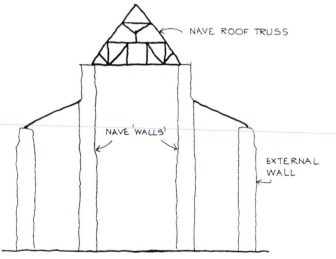

EXTERNAL WALL

BUTTRESS

Fig. 9.5 Wall elevations

The structures of the roofs of the nave and the side aisles are of timber. These structures span between the internal and external walls.

NAVE ROOF TRUSS

NAVE 'WALLS'

EXTERNAL WALL

Fig. 9.6 Roof structures

Below these roofs are stone vaulted ceilings and it is this vaulting that is one of the main interests in cathedral architecture. To allow light into the cathedral and to permit circulation at ground level, each bay of the nave vaulting is only supported at the corners.

Real structures 215

Fig. 9.7 Vaulting system

Most of the cathedral structure is built of masonry and because masonry can only carry compressive forces most of the structure must be in compression. The exception is the timber roof structures. The cathedral is essentially a single space with the main loading being from self-weight, snow and wind. As masonry is a heavyweight material and the structure is massive, self-weight is the major load. Compared with this load, snow and wind loads are negligible.

The main roof structure and the stone ceiling vaulting are independent structures spanning across the nave. The timber roof structure is a rather complicated structure which spans unidirectionally across the nave whereas the stone ceiling vault spans in two directions (**Fig. 7.75 E**). As both are spanning there will be associated bending moment and shear force diagrams.

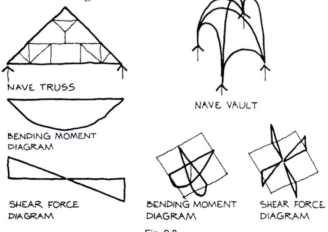

NAVE TRUSS

NAVE VAULT

BENDING MOMENT DIAGRAM

SHEAR FORCE DIAGRAM

BENDING MOMENT DIAGRAM

SHEAR FORCE DIAGRAM

Fig. 9.8

The roof structure is truss-like, so the push/pull forces are taken by the sloping and bottom members and the shear resisted by the sloping member (**Fig. 7.18**).

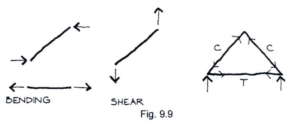

BENDING

SHEAR

Fig. 9.9

The vault, however, is funicular (see **Section 7.4**) and the push/pull forces are carried by compression in the vault and by tension in mid-air (**Fig. 7.21 - 5**). The shear is carried by the vertical component of the sloping compression force.

BENDING   SHEAR

Fig. 9.10

Because the vault acts in two dimensions, these forces will also be in two dimensions. The spans of these vaults are not great, only **9.75m** across the nave at Durham, smaller than many ancient Islamic mosques. However, the height of the nave is quite considerable, **21.4m** at Durham. It is this height that causes the major structural difficulty as the 'tension in mid-air' is supplied by a sloping thrust at the level of the vault supports.

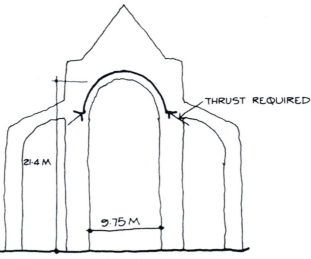

THRUST REQUIRED

21.4 M

9.75 M

Fig. 9.11

And this thrust becomes a load on the nave/external wall structure.

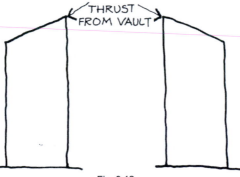

THRUST FROM VAULT

Fig. 9.12

These walls are cantilevers from the ground and the sloping thrust can be regarded as a combination of a vertical and a horizontal force applied to the top of the wall. This causes axial forces plus a bending moment and a shear force.

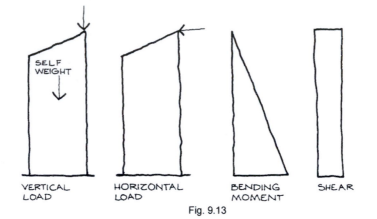

VERTICAL LOAD   HORIZONTAL LOAD   BENDING MOMENT   SHEAR

Fig. 9.13

This action is just another example of an axial load acting at an eccentricity to cause a moment (**Figs. 3.89** to **3.91**). Because the wall is of masonry the thrusts must be kept within the wall section.

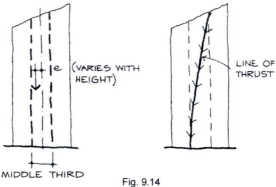

e (VARIES WITH HEIGHT)

LINE OF THRUST

MIDDLE THIRD

Fig. 9.14

The line of thrust cannot be as shown in **Fig. 9.14** as the nave/external wall is not solid across the building, so the thrust is carried by a **flying buttress** which joins the tops of the nave and external walls.

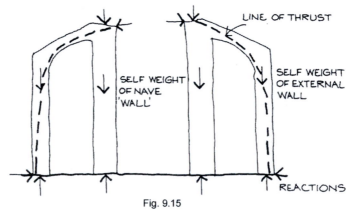

LINE OF THRUST

SELF WEIGHT OF NAVE 'WALL'

SELF WEIGHT OF EXTERNAL WALL

REACTIONS

Fig. 9.15

In this way the wall can be perforated. This system of flying buttresses became more and more complex as the Gothic period progressed and culminated with the cathedral at Beauvais. Here the height of the nave was **48m** and the vault thrust was taken by three tiers of buttresses.

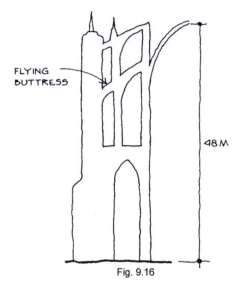

FLYING BUTTRESS

48 M

Fig. 9.16

Beauvais, see **Fig. 0.7**, is often considered the final achievement of the Gothic builders though this view must be tempered by the fact that various parts of the cathedral collapsed and it was never completed.

Whilst the forces across the structure are taken by the nave and external walls and the flying buttresses, because the vault is two dimensional there are also forces along the nave.

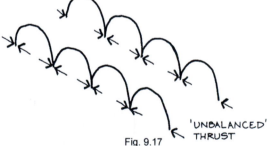

'UNBALANCED' THRUST

Fig. 9.17

As the main force is due to self-weight, the forces along the nave balance one another, that is until the end! At the ends are more solid constructions, the main tower and the West tower, and the weight of these resist the end thrusts.

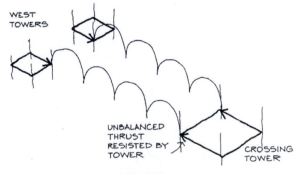

WEST TOWERS

UNBALANCED THRUST RESISTED BY TOWER

CROSSING TOWER

Fig. 9.18

The marvel of these cathedrals' structures is how the builders, without concepts of stress and moments were able to balance the various thrusts and keep them within the funicular lines. They occasionally failed to manage this with consequent collapses!

9.2   The Palm House

Glasshouses were a building type that came into existence in the 19th century being an extension of the 18th century orangeries and conservatories. As with all new building types, their emergence depended on a number of factors, technical, economic and social. The first substantial structure built of iron was the Ironbridge at Coalbrookdale in 1779 (see page **120**): by the 1840s, iron, both cast and wrought, were routinely used for structures. During this period there were also advances in the production of glass. It was the availability of iron and glass at reasonable prices that were the technical and economic factors that made glasshouses possible. During the 19th century there was also a rise in interest in science and this gave the impetus to the expansion of numerous scientific establishments. It was under these circumstances that plans for a Palm House at the Botanic Gardens at Kew were drawn up. These initial plans were abandoned and Decimus Burton, the designer of the Winter Gardens in Regent's Park, was asked to draw up plans for a new design.

Decimus Burton had already worked with the Irish iron founder Richard Turner, an astute and ambitious businessman, who ensured that the Commissioner of Works for the new Palm House asked him for a proposal for the new building. His proposal was quite different to Burton's design and was similar to the final design. For many years the design was attributed to Decimus Burton, but it is now recognised that the main influence on the design was Richard Turner.

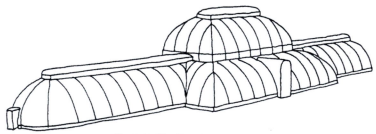

Fig. 9.19 The Palm House at Kew

The design was influenced by the work of GS MacKenzie and John Louden who had both promoted for horticultural reasons the advantages of curved glasshouses and the Palm House is curved in all directions. Turner's design also used the recently patented wrought iron **deck beam**.

Fig. 9.20

The production of these beams was, in turn, made possible by the invention of the steam hammer by Naismith in 1839. The deck beam was the forerunner of the ubiquitous **I** beam (see pages **73-74**). The deck beam was so-called as it was used to support decks in the new iron ships. The Palm House was the first building to use this new structural element.

Like the builders of Durham Cathedral, the builders of the Palm House were principally concerned with natural light. But Turner and Burton had a new structural material, wrought iron, which was much stronger than stone and could also resist substantial tensile stresses. In the 1840s, structural design was in its infancy and no evidence of the existence of technical calculations for the Palm House has ever been found, but Turner wrote *"...complete principle of mechanics for Stability"*, and beams were subjected to tests, but for what load is not known.

Whether a designer understands the structural behaviour of his structure or not does not affect the behaviour of the actual structure. Because of this the **conceptual approach** can always be used to understand the actual behaviour of the structure rather than the structural behaviour considered by the designer. The first step is to simplify the complex three-dimensional shapes into three parts; the end 'caps', the barrel vaults and the central transept.

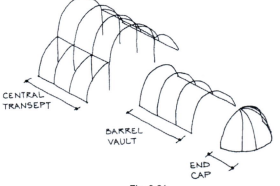

Fig. 9.21

Although these parts are connected together they do act fairly independently. The major loads on the Palm House are self-weight, snow and wind loads. Due to the curved shapes, the intensity of these loads vary continuously. The loading is conceptually similar to that on the **basic structure** (**Figs. 8.3** and **8.4**), but with no differentiation between wall and roof.

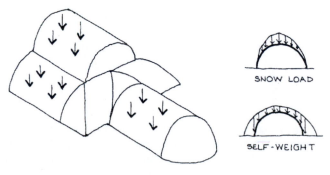

Fig. 9.22

The overall distribution of wind pressure is complex and can only be obtained from wind tunnel tests, a technique not available to the original designer! Across the barrel vault sections the pressure distribution is similar to **Fig. 8.4.**

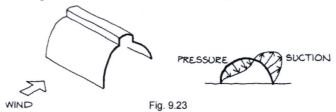

WIND   Fig. 9.23

Around the end caps and the central transept the wind pressure distribution is more complicated but there will be areas of positive pressure and areas of suction. Again, the structural behaviour of the end caps and the transept is more complicated than the barrel vaults. By regarding the barrel vaults as separate structures, a conceptual analysis can be carried out on this area. This closely follows the analysis of the roof and portal frame of the **basic structure** (see **Sections 8.2** and **8.3**).

Initially the loads are carried by the glazing (glass cladding). These loads are self-weight, snow and wind loads and the glass carries these loads by spanning between the curved glazing bars.

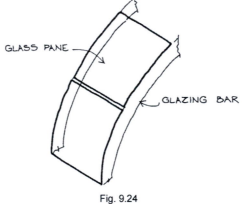

Fig. 9.24

The load and the structural behaviour of the glass vary from area to area. The self-weight and the snow load are always vertical whereas the wind load is normal (at right angles) to the surface.

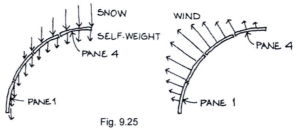

Fig. 9.25

For example **pane 2** may have the highest wind load whereas **pane 4** may have the highest snow load. All the panes have the same self-weight but near the crown this loads the pane across its width (a beam) but at the ground it loads the pane along its length (a wall).

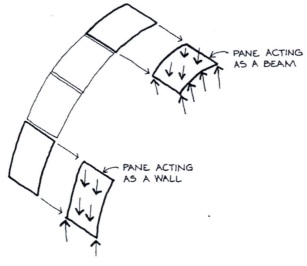

Fig. 9.26

To cater for the changing loading patterns and structural behaviour the glass panes, as structures, could be altered throughout the glass house. For a building this is too complicated so the **worst** case will determine the glass design. Depending on the numerical values this could be at the crown under self-weight and snow load or at an intermediate point under self-weight and wind load. In each of these cases the pane will act as a beam-like structure spanning between the glazing bars. This means the glass pane will have a bending moment and a shear force with the associated stresses.

LOADING   BENDING MOMENT   BENDING
                 DIAGRAM   STRESSES
                                          IN GLASS

Fig. 9.27

Like the spacing of the purlins of the **basic structure** (**Fig. 8.5**), the spacing of the glazing bars is chosen by the designer. Greater spacing means less glazing bars but thicker glass to keep the stresses in the glass within set limits; closer spacing means thinner glass but more glazing bars. There is no correct spacing.

The glazing bars are curved and run from the ground to clerestory windows. The glazing bars are supported by the intermediate tubular purlins for 'inward' loads but not for 'outward' loads. An outward load is a wind suction force. The reason for this one-way support is because the glazing bars just rest on rods which in turn just rest on the tubular purlins.

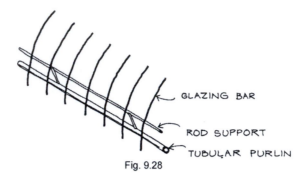

Fig. 9.28

This odd arrangement of glazing bar support shows that the designers were unaware of the suction effects of wind load. It also means that under inward load the glazing bar spans, as a beam, from purlin to purlin but for net outward load they have to span from ground to clerestory level. This is done by the glazing bar acting as a funicular structure in tension – a hanging cable (**Fig. 7.8**).

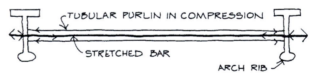

Fig. 9.29

When the purlins are loaded they span between the arch frames, but they also have a rather strange feature as they are pre-stressed (see **Section 4.7**). Pre-stressing is common for concrete but rare for steelwork. At the Palm House, the purlins are stressed by the stretching of an internal iron rod.

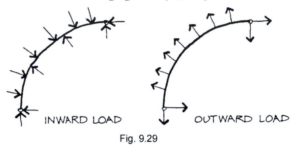

Fig. 9.30

Under inward load, the purlin system is the rod and the pre-stressed tubular purlin.

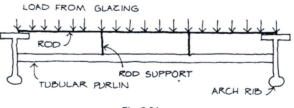

Fig. 9.31

The rod spans as a three-span beam loaded by the reactions from the glazing bars. The rod support reactions become point loads on the pre-stressed tubular purlins.

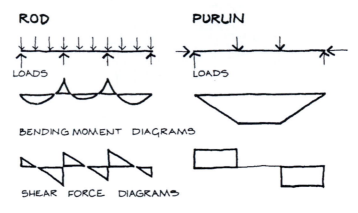

ROD   PURLIN

LOADS   LOADS

BENDING MOMENT DIAGRAMS

SHEAR FORCE DIAGRAMS

Fig. 9.32

The stresses in the rod are as for a beam but those in the purlin are altered by the pre-stress compression (**Figs. 3.49** and **3.86**).

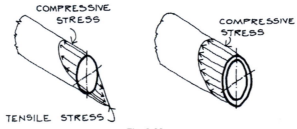

COMPRESSIVE STRESS

COMPRESSIVE STRESS

TENSILE STRESS

Fig. 9.33

The different inward/outward load behaviour of the purlin system means the loads on the arch frame are very different for the snow load and wind load cases.

SELF-WEIGHT + SNOW   SELF-WEIGHT + WIND

Fig. 9.34

These frames act like curved portal frames and not like funicular arches so their behaviour is similar to the portals of the **basic structure** (**Fig. 8.37**). This behaviour can be represented by axial force, shear force and bending moment diagrams. Only the bending moment diagrams are shown.

SELF-WEIGHT + SNOW   SELF-WEIGHT + WIND
BENDING MOMENT DIAGRAMS

Fig. 9.35

The behaviour of the central transept is quite different and has to be viewed three dimensionally.

Real structures 225

Fig. 9.36

The cross-section has an arch frame, two half-arch frames and two columns.

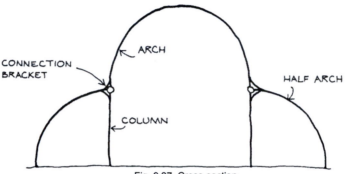

CONNECTION BRACKET

ARCH

HALF ARCH

COLUMN

Fig. 9.37 Cross-section

There are six of these frames and each is loaded by loads that are similar to those applied to the barrel vaults.

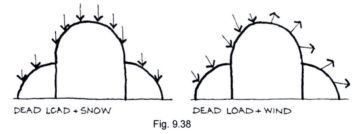

DEAD LOAD + SNOW

DEAD LOAD + WIND

Fig. 9.38

These frames could act independently, rather like more complicated versions of the barrel vault arch frames.

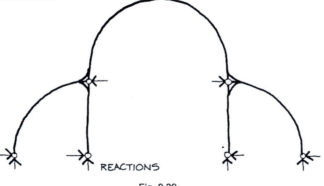

REACTIONS

Fig. 9.39

However, the structure of the central transept acts as a three-dimensional structure and this means that not only are the cross frames supported at the ground in the vertical and horizontal directions but they are also supported horizontally at the gallery level. This additional horizontal support allows the top arch frame to act in the same way as the barrel vault arch (**Fig. 9.35**) and the side arch frames to act in a similar way. Again this behaviour can be represented by axial force, shear force and bending moment diagrams and again only the bending moment diagrams are drawn.

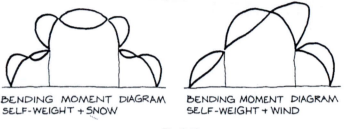

BENDING MOMENT DIAGRAM
SELF-WEIGHT + SNOW

BENDING MOMENT DIAGRAM
SELF-WEIGHT + WIND

Fig. 9.40

The horizontal reactions from the frames at gallery level become loads on the gallery which acts as a horizontal beam spanning between the main arch frames at each end of the transept.

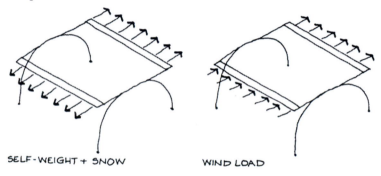

SELF-WEIGHT + SNOW

WIND LOAD

Fig. 9.41

The gallery acts as a simple beam spanning the length of the central transept. Like any other beam it has bending moments and shear forces.

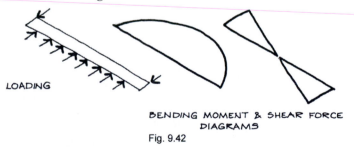

LOADING

BENDING MOMENT & SHEAR FORCE
DIAGRAMS

Fig. 9.42

The reactions from the beam become loads on the main arch frames. In the case of the vertical load, the reactions from the gallery beams do not produce any load on the arch frame, but the reactions from the wind load do cause a horizontal load applied to the arch crown.

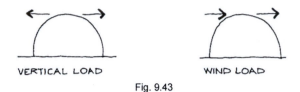

VERTICAL LOAD   WIND LOAD

Fig. 9.43

The main arch frames resist these loads by acting as curved frames. The structure for the wind load on the central transept acts like the bracing system used for the wind load on the end wall of the **basic structure (Fig. 8.45)**.

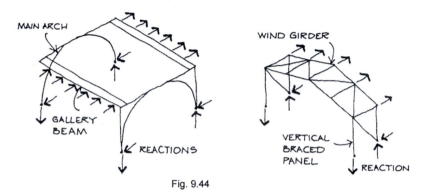

Fig. 9.44

The gallery beam spans horizontally, as does the wind girder of the **basic structure**, and each cause horizontal loads on the vertical structural elements – the main arch frames and the vertical braced panels. This is another example of similar structural behaviour but quite different structural geometries. It is the ability to recognise these systems of structural action rather than geometry, that is key to understanding how whole structures act.

The wind load acting on the Palm House, when the wind blows along it, is resisted by the end caps and the transition structures at the central transept. These wind forces cause internal forces in the various half-arch frames, which again could be represented by axial force, shear force and bending moment diagrams.

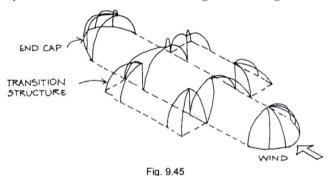

Fig. 9.45

As the structure is of iron it is quite slender, so all parts that are in compression under any loading must be examined for the possibility of buckling-initiated local or overall collapse (see **Section 6.4**). The structure must be examined element by element as was the **basic structure**.

The Palm House looks like a modern structure, and is renowned for its beauty and elegance, however its designer did not use the current rational approach. As none of the arches are near to the correct funicular shape for the loadings, a portal frame would have been more structurally appropriate. This approach can be seen at Kew with the more recent Australian and Princess Diana glass houses.

At the time of the design, the 1840s, there was considerable technical knowledge about the theoretical behaviour of structures. This knowledge was not widespread and consequently not routinely used for structural design. It is probably for this reason that no calculations were done by the original designers but in the 1980s the Palm House was completely dissembled, refurbished and re-assembled. As part of this process the structure was checked using modern analytical and wind tunnel techniques. This work showed that the original design is adequate and that no structural strengthening was required. The term re-assembled is used rather than rebuilt because the Palm House is a kit of over 7000 iron parts and the refurbishment allowed the technical and organisational genius of Richard Turner to be seen in its totality for the first time.

9.3   Zarzuela Hippodrome

The engineered structures of the 19th century were predominately of cast and wrought iron, and towards the end of the century, of steel. The first use of reinforcing concrete with metal is usually attributed to Lambot with his boat in 1849 and Monier with his garden boxes in 1865 but the idea was proposed by Coignet in 1828. But it was only at the end of the 19th century that concrete, reinforced with steel, began to be used widely. This was due to the pioneering work of the French engineer Françoise Hennebique (1842-1921) and architect Auguste Perret (1874-1954). By the 1930s, the use of reinforced concrete structures was commonplace in Europe.

Because concrete structures can be formed **in situ** by pouring wet concrete into moulds, virtually any shape can be made. Again, the reinforcing bars can be placed anywhere in the concrete and the density of the bars can be continuously varied. This means that these in situ reinforced concrete structures are quite different in concept from iron or steel ones. They are no longer an assembly of elements as the one-, two- or three-dimensional parts can be joined by smooth geometric transitions. If the structure is formed from complex shapes the conceptual analysis can be very difficult, so where possible the structure may be approximated by an assembly of elements.

The structure of the Zarzuela Hippodrome was designed by the celebrated Spanish engineer Eduardo Torroja (1899-1961) and was built in 1935, just in time to be damaged but not destroyed in the Spanish civil war.

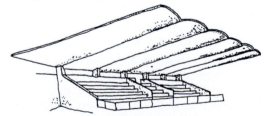

Fig. 9.46 Zarzuela Hippodrome

The building is essentially a grandstand with a betting hall underneath the seating. A cross-section through the building shows the functions of the various parts clearly.

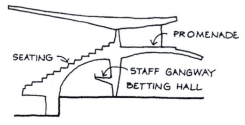

Fig. 9.47 Cross-section

This section can also be used to show where the loads are applied to the structure. As the structure is of reinforced concrete, a heavyweight material, the self-weight of the structure is a major load. Even though the roof structure is thin, its self-weight is still greater than any upward wind load.

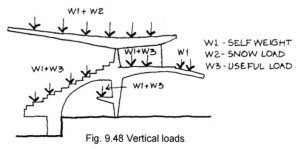

Fig. 9.48 Vertical loads

The main supporting structures are frames which are spaced regularly along the building.

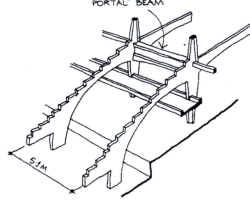

Fig. 9.49

Although much more complex in shape, these frames can be compared with the portal frames of the **basic structure** (**Fig. 8.7**).

The roof of the grandstand is a shell (**Fig. 3.4**). Concrete shells were pioneered by the German engineers Dischinger and Finsterwalder in the 1920s and are examples of funicular structures (**E** of **Fig. 7.75**). Because the shell is thin it cannot resist significant bending moments, so shells are only successful if they are good funicular shapes. If the shape of a shell deviates from a funicular shape, it may have to be

230 Building structures

thickened to resist the internal stresses caused by the bending moments. This makes a shell an inappropriate structural form. Sydney Opera House (see **Section 11.7**) and the TWA terminal at Idlewild airport in New York are well-known examples of inappropriate shapes for shell roofs. As the roof is spanning, overall bending moments and shear forces exist.

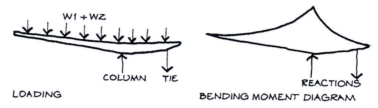

LOADING

BENDING MOMENT DIAGRAM

Fig. 9.50

A shell is a two-dimensional structure so this shell roof spans along the building as well as across it.

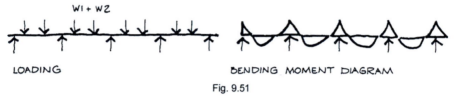

LOADING

BENDING MOMENT DIAGRAM

Fig. 9.51

For the roof to act as a funicular structure, rather than a beam-like structure, these bending moments and shear forces must be carried by internal axial forces **[4]**. The pattern of these axial forces is complex and was too difficult to be found by the mathematical techniques available at the time of the design. This meant that the designers had to resort to carrying out a load test on a large scale model. Testing was extensively used by engineers in the 19th century but it is slow and expensive compared with mathematical analysis. These tests enabled the direction and magnitude of the principal stresses (see **Section 4.2**) to be identified. The reinforcement was placed in a simplified pattern of the principal **tensile** stresses.

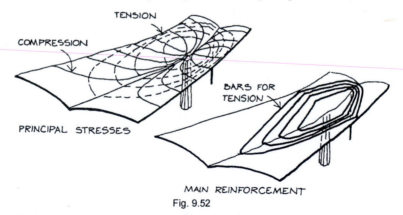

Fig. 9.52

The internal forces that result in the principal tensile and compressive stresses provide the push/pull forces that resist the overall bending moments and shear forces. They are at a maximum at the column support where the overall moments and shear are at a maximum.

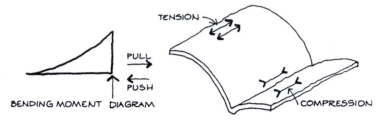

Fig. 9.53

Unlike a beam (**Fig. 3.43**) these forces are not vertically above one another, the tensile force is at the crown and the compressive force in the valley. The curved geometry of the shell roof provides the depth between these forces, which is the lever arm.

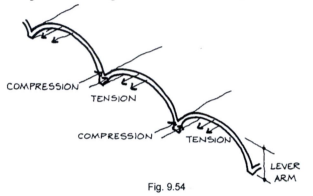

Fig. 9.54

Although the shells act as cantilevers from the support columns, the patterns of the principal stresses show that the structural action is two dimensional in the curved surface. The action of the roof causes up and down forces on the columns (**Fig. 9.50**) and these become loads on the transverse frames (**Fig. 9.49**). The other loads on the frames are from the reactions to the grandstand seating, the promenade floor and the staff gangway.

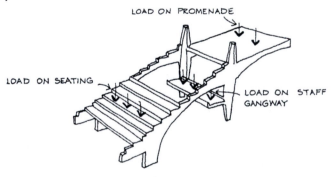

Fig. 9.55

The structural action of the transverse frames is similar to the portal frames of the **basic structure** and the arch frames of the Palm House. The frames resist the loads by internal forces which are bending moments, axial forces and shear forces. These can be represented by the appropriate diagrams. Only the bending moment diagram is shown.

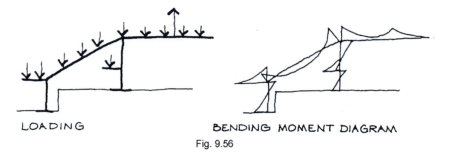

LOADING   BENDING MOMENT DIAGRAM

Fig. 9.56

Frame action is dependent on 'stiff' joints and these joints are able to resist bending moments. This stiffness is readily achieved with in situ reinforced concrete by placing reinforcing bars **through** the joint for the push/pull forces.

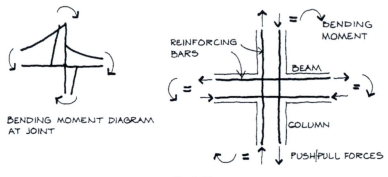

Fig. 9.57

Notice that the bending moment can change direction either side of a joint. This happens, for example, where the cantilever beam supporting the staff gangway connects to the column. If this was not a stiff joint, the beam could not be a cantilever!

Fig. 9.58

The arrangement between the roof and the promenade beam shows how the designer's understanding of structural behaviour means an effective structure is provided. The secret is the roof tie which provides the pull for the roof structure and thus reduces the cantilever moment in the promenade beam. If the tie was removed, large bending moments would be required to resist the roof load and the load on the promenade. For calculations for the tie see **Example 12.22** in **Chapter 12**.

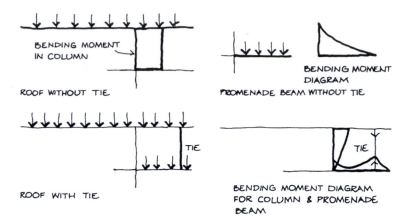

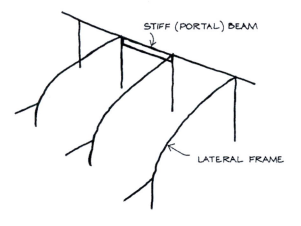

Fig. 9.59

As the building is basically open, the loads from the wind along the building are small, but all structures need some lateral strength or they could just fall over sideways. Here this lateral strength is again provided by frame action. This is achieved by using special longitudinal members, portal beams, which have stiff joints with the columns.

Fig. 9.60

Rather like the **basic structure (Fig. 8.44)** one bay is made stiff. This is done with the stiff joints forming a portal frame instead of using a diagonal bracing member.

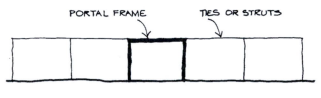

Fig. 9.61

Because concrete is a heavyweight material, concrete structures rarely have problems of overall stability. Also stresses in concrete structures are usually quite low which means the elements have to be stocky to carry the loads, so they are rarely slender enough to initiate collapse by buckling.

234 Building structures

This structure, unlike the Palm House, was designed by an engineer who was very conscious of the structural behaviour and took considerable trouble to investigate and quantify it. Where this was not possible by using analytical techniques, scientific tests were carried out. An alternative would have been to redesign the roof so that analytical techniques available at the time could have been used.

9.4   CNIT Exposition Palace

In 1950 the Federation of Industries decided that a permanent exhibition centre should be built. This centre would provide space for temporary and permanent exhibitions for all types of French industrial equipment. It would be the 'Centres National des Industries et des Techniques'; hence CNIT. A site was chosen 7km from the centre of Paris at La Defense. The design for the centre was carried out by the architects Camelot, de Mailly and Zehrfuss. Their design was triangular in plan and had a roof that spanned between the apexes of the triangular plan without intermediate supports.

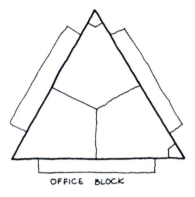

OFFICE   BLOCK

Fig. 9.62 Plan

The span of the roof is **218m** on each face of the triangular plan. This was the longest roof span ever built using the final choice of construction; this was a concrete double shell.

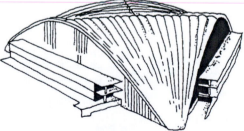

Fig. 9.63 CNIT Exposition Palace

A four-storey office block is built within each facade with the space between office block and the roof closed with a glazed facade. The structure of the office blocks is separate from the roof structure. In the late 1980s the office blocks were removed and an hotel and a shopping complex were built under the original roof.

A number of leading engineering designers were asked to submit proposals for the roof structure. Seven proposals were submitted, three using steel as the structural material, three using reinforced concrete and one proposed a composite design using steel and concrete (page **110**). The scheme chosen was of concrete and was submitted by Entreprises Boussion whose technical director was Nicholas Esquillan.

Their proposal was for a vaulted structure of reinforced concrete. To save weight, the structure of the roof was of honeycomb construction, with thin top and bottom surfaces spaced apart by a two-way arrangement of vertical webs. The whole roof is divided into three kite-shaped sections by a three-way joint.

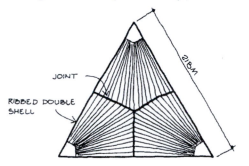

Fig. 9.64 Roof plan

Because the roof is of concrete, as with the roof of the Hippodrome, self-weight is the dominant loading. Although the wind causes loads, the building is so large that high wind pressures do not occur over the whole roof at any one time. For the effect of gravity load, the bending moments are similar to those in a triangular slab supported at the corners.

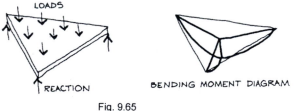

Fig. 9.65

One kite-shaped section of the slab roof could be regarded as acting as one half of a simple beam.

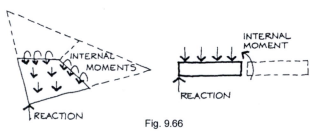

Fig. 9.66

If the roof was a flat slab then these bending moments would be resisted by push/pull forces within the depth of the slab (**Fig. 3.40**), but the roof is not flat, it is curved. The curve of the roof is the funicular shape for the self-weight; this shape is called a **catenary**. Because of this, the bending moment and the shear forces are resisted by axial forces in the structure which follow the funicular line.

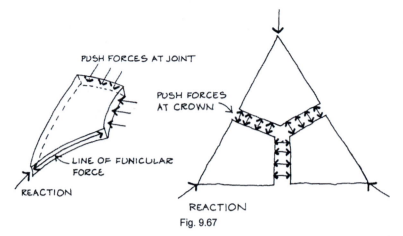

Fig. 9.67

The top and bottom surfaces are also curved in section so that the surface is corrugated.

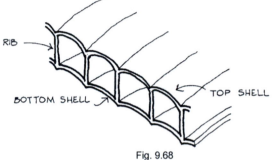

Fig. 9.68

The plan dimensions of the structure reduce towards the supports but the axial force does not, this would mean that the stresses could increase as there is less structure to carry the forces. This is avoided by concentrating the longitudinal webs and by increasing the thickness of the top and bottom skins.

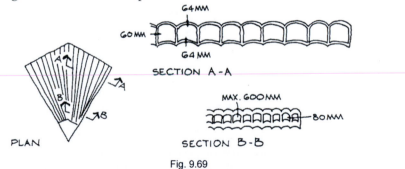

Fig. 9.69

To prevent the centre of the roof being excessively high, the curve of the roof is kept quite flat which reduces the overall lever arm.

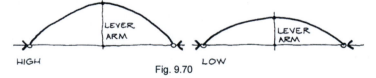

Fig. 9.70

As the shape of the vault is a catenary, the radius of the roof varies from point to point. At the crown the radius is **91m** but at the supports it is **424m**.

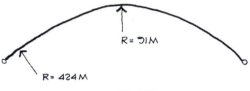

Fig. 9.71

The radius at the supports is twice as large as the one used for the bridge at Sando in Sweden. When this bridge was built in 1943 it was the largest concrete arch in the world and also had the largest radius of curvature. As the curve is flat, constructional inaccuracies could lead to the roof seriously deviating from the funicular line, so great care was taken with the geometry during construction.

Concrete structures are rarely slender but this structure is slender locally and globally, so the possibility of buckling-initiated collapse was carefully checked. The whole roof can buckle in symmetric and asymmetric modes.

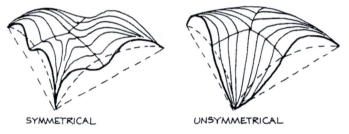

SYMMETRICAL   UNSYMMETRICAL

Fig. 9.72

As the whole of the cross-section is in compression, a collapse could be initiated by either the top or bottom surfaces buckling locally between the diaphragms.

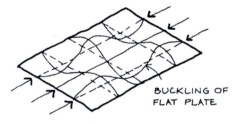

BUCKLING OF
FLAT PLATE

Fig. 9.73

This buckling pattern requires alternate panels to buckle in opposite directions. This could happen if the panels were flat but this local buckling pattern is prevented by the local curvature of the panels. This curvature means that local buckling takes place at the local crowns (**Fig. 6.68**) and this requires a much higher load than the alternate panel buckling. This was the reason that this local curvature between the diaphragms was introduced.

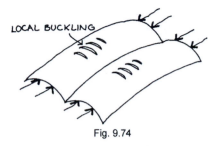

Fig. 9.74

Not only are the main parts of the roof in compression due to the arch action but the triangular geometry and the rib arrangement cause compression across the shell at the crown joint. This is far from obvious.

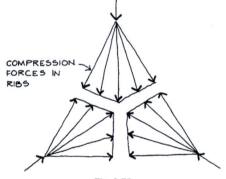

COMPRESSION FORCES IN RIBS

Fig. 9.75

Because of the fan-shaped pattern of the shells, the axial forces at the joint meet at varying angles. At the facade they are in line but the angle varies towards the centre.

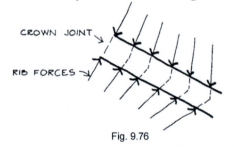

CROWN JOINT

RIB FORCES

Fig. 9.76

At the centre, the third section balances the forces, but elsewhere there is no balancing force as there are special rollers between the shells.

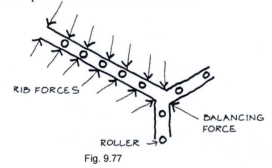

RIB FORCES

BALANCING FORCE

ROLLER

Fig. 9.77

These angled forces cause a varying compression force in the top edge members of each shell section. These edge members, the crown walls, are strengthened to carry these forces.

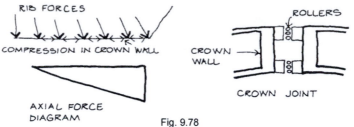

Fig. 9.78

To maintain the overall compression in the shell, the support points must provide horizontal as well as vertical reactions (**Fig. 7.19**). These horizontal reactions form the pull forces that resist the overall bending moment.

Fig. 9.79

If the shell was built between rigid abutments, natural rock for example, then the horizontal reactions could be provided by the foundations. Although the site of the building has natural rock near the surface, site limitations and the construction of underground railways in the future prevented direct use of the foundation rock for horizontal reactions.

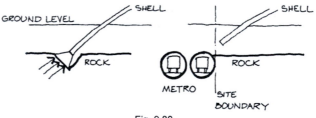

Fig. 9.80

The horizontal reactions are provided by special tie members (compare with **Fig. 8.52**). These run along the lines of the facades.

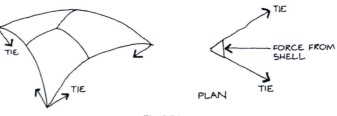

Fig. 9.81

The level of the tie at the foundation was too high along the facades, so it had to be diverted to a lower level.

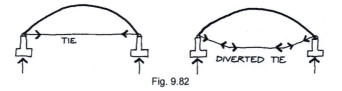

Fig. 9.82

This diversion of the tie members requires an additional tie member at the point of change in direction. This is another example of a cable shape for a particular loading.

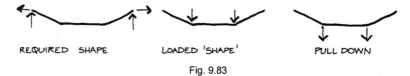

REQUIRED SHAPE   LOADED 'SHAPE'   PULL DOWN

Fig. 9.83

The pull-down members are anchored in the underlying rock by excavating undercut holes so the concrete of the tie is wedged in the rock.

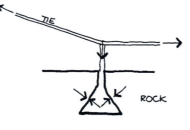

Fig. 9.84

The sides of the shell are enclosed by the four-storey office blocks and glazing.

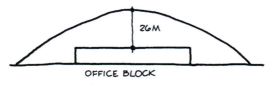

Fig. 9.85

The facade supports are substantial steel structures as they have to span up to 26m from the roof of the office block to the shell roof.

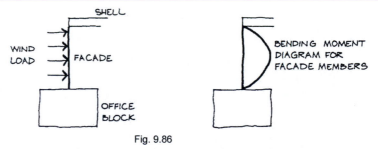

Fig. 9.86

Because the top of the shell moves vertically under different loads, there is a special joint between the shell and the facade structure to prevent the facade steelwork becoming part of the roof load path (compare with **Fig. 4.90**).

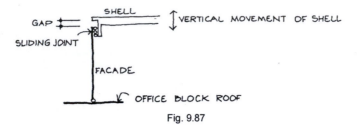

Fig. 9.87

The CNIT Exposition Palace is an enormous building and the design and construction was a considerable undertaking. Using the six basic concepts listed on page **193**, together with the necessary technical information, the structural behaviour can be understood conceptually.

9.5 Federal Reserve Bank

Most office buildings are enclosures of cellular spaces (offices) and the building is usually planned on a rectangular grid with vertical columns at the grid intersections. The structure of the floors is an arrangement of beams and slabs carrying the loads to the columns by bending moments and shear forces.

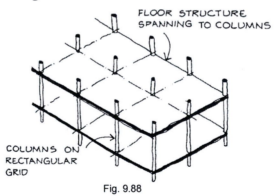

Fig. 9.88

The vertical loads are carried directly to the ground by the columns. Horizontal wind loads, which are substantial for the taller office buildings, can be resisted by a variety of structural systems. For wind loads, any building is essentially a cantilever from the ground with lateral loads (wind) and axial loads (self-weight, etc).

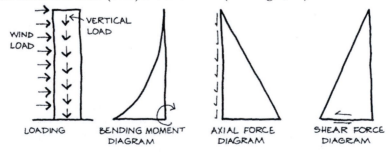

Fig. 9.89

The structural system for resisting the bending moment and shear force from the lateral wind load can be beam-like, truss-like, frame-like or, in the case of guyed structures, almost funicular.

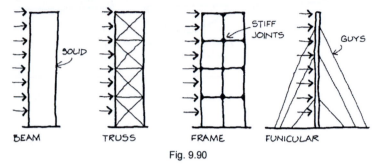

Fig. 9.90

Where beam or truss structures are used they restrict circulation so they are placed near lift shafts or at the ends of the building.

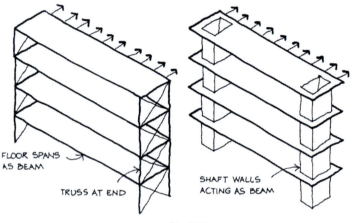

Fig. 9.91

The Federal Reserve Bank in Minneapolis, designed by architects Gunnar Birkets and Associates with engineers Skilling Helle Christiansen and Robertson, was completed in 1973. It is a ten-storey office building with underground car parking and bank vaults, quite a standard arrangement. But this building is far from standard as the whole of the office block spans across a three-storey height space under the building. Creating this space under a ten-storey building means that the column loads which would normally be supported by the ground have to be transferred laterally. The building now has to span across the space.

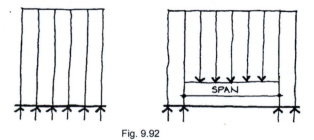

Fig. 9.92

And the loads are transferred by internal forces of bending moments and shear forces.

LOADING   BENDING MOMENT   SHEAR FORCE
DIAGRAM   DIAGRAM

Fig. 9.93

As the design requires the building to span across the space the structural designers had to choose a suitable structural system. There is no 'correct' system, just the chosen one. The choices for spanning structures are the four types: beam-like, truss-like, frame-like or funicular. As the building that spans is ten storeys high even with one type, say truss-like, there are further choices. A roof-level truss with hung floors or trusses at two levels supporting columns are examples of possible choices.

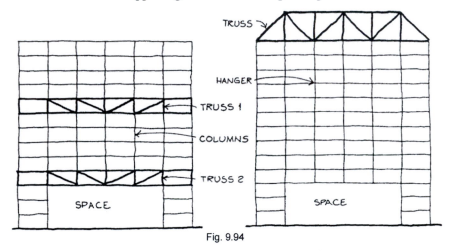

Fig. 9.94

The actual choice for the structure was quite unusual, they chose a funicular structure – a hanging cable. The cable is the whole depth of the ten-storey office building.

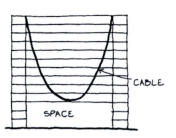
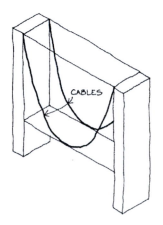

Fig. 9.95

244 Building structures

This choice means that a horizontal force must be provided at roof level so that the cable can resist the bending moment.

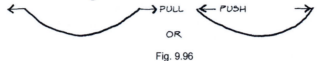

Fig. 9.96

In a suspension bridge, the mid-air push force (**Fig. 7.13**) is resisted by tensile forces in the back stays, but this would be inconvenient for this building so a strut is used to provide the push force (**Fig. 7.15**).

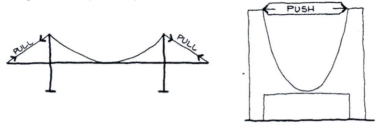

Fig. 9.97

A truss-like structure has been chosen for the strut. The floor trusses span across the building on to vertical members. These vertical members transfer the floor truss reactions to the cable. The vertical members above the cable are in compression whilst the members below are in tension.

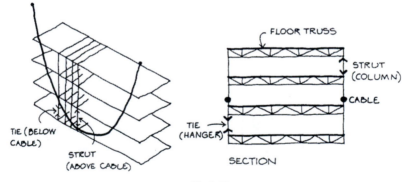

Fig. 9.98

At each end of the cable/strut structure there are vertical reactions (**Fig. 7.15**) which are resisted by thirteen-storey high concrete towers. The complete spanning structure is the cable, the strut and these end towers. The construction of the facade visually emphasises the presence of the cable part of the spanning structure.

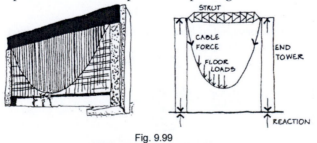

Fig. 9.99

Not only does the structure have to resist vertical loads but it also has to act as a cantilever to resist wind loads. The cantilevering action is done by the concrete end towers. Because of the vertical load from the cable structure, the forces at the base of the towers are always compressive. This is another example of combining axial and bending stresses (**Fig. 3.82**). For the calculation of the stresses in the towers see **Example 12.23** of **Chapter 12**.

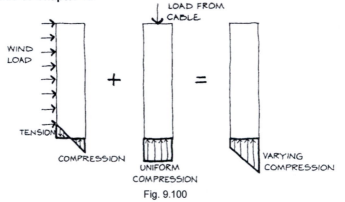

Fig. 9.100

The wind load path starts at the cladding system and ends at the base of the cantilevering end towers. The cladding system spans vertically from floor to floor. The floors are loaded by the reactions of the cladding system and span as horizontal beams between the end towers. The end towers are loaded at each floor level by the reactions from the floors acting as horizontal beams. The end towers carry these loads by acting as cantilevers from the ground.

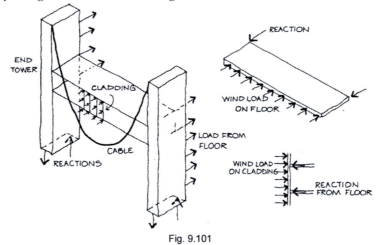

Fig. 9.101

The end towers are considered to be concrete I-beams and this affects the planning of the accommodation in the towers.

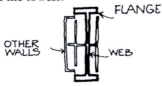

Fig. 9.102 Plan on end tower

246 Building structures

One of the main problems for the structural designer in using these core areas as vertical cantilevers is to ensure that the accommodation requirements allow horizontal shear forces to develop between the flanges and the web (**Fig. 4.32**).

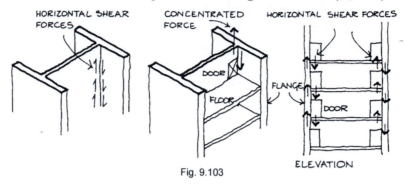

Fig. 9.103

For a cable to act as a funicular structure it must change shape with a change of load pattern (**Figs. 7.67** and **7.68**). In this building the main load is the uniform vertical load from the building construction, but the pattern can vary when different layouts of furniture and equipment are adopted on each floor and of course the occupants tend to move about. For an ideally flexible cable, each change would require a change in funicular shape and this would be difficult to achieve for a cable that is part of a building. The cables in this building can act as bending elements for the relatively small bending moments that are required to keep the cable in its basic shape. This is achieved by constructing a composite cable of a cable acting with a curved steel I-beam.

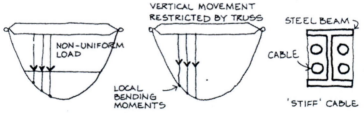

Fig. 9.104

Whilst there are only small variations in the load of the completed building, this is not the case during construction. Great care was taken by the builders to control the cable shape during construction as the cables were gradually loaded by the building elements. This was done by stressing the cable part of the 'cable' in stages as the load was applied.

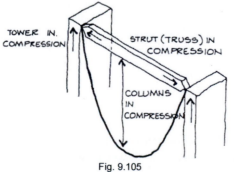

Fig. 9.105

There are a number of parts of the structure that must be checked to ensure that buckling-initiated collapse does not occur (see **Section 6.4**). The parts that are in compression are the roof level strut, the end towers and the columns. The roof level truss-like strut could buckle in a number of ways.

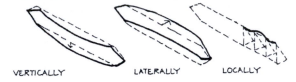

VERTICALLY   LATERALLY   LOCALLY

Fig. 9.106

The towers could also buckle locally or as a complete structure.

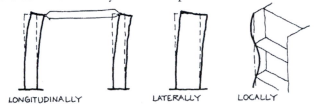

LONGITUDINALLY   LATERALLY   LOCALLY

Fig. 9.107

It is unusual to be able to see all the parts of the structural system clearly when a building is complete, however, as can be seen, this photograph taken during construction clearly shows the structural system.

Fig. 9.108 photo: Balthazar Korab

The Federal Reserve Bank is unusual as the major structural action is visually expressed by the completed building. The structure is extraordinary for an office block and it is not easy to understand why the designers went to such trouble and expense to span over a rather bleak plaza.

9.6   Bank of China

The headquarters building for the Bank of China in Hong Kong was designed by the architect IM Pei and the structural designers were the engineers LE Robertson

Associates of New York. When it was completed in 1990, it was the fifth tallest building in the world and the tallest building outside New York and Chicago.

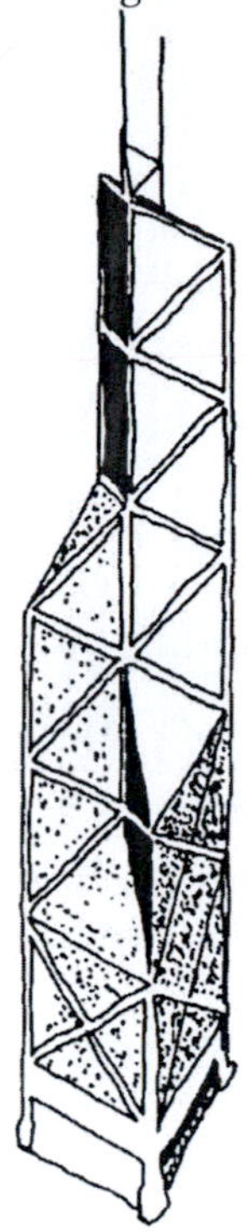

It is a massive building, 52m square on plan rising to a height, including the antennae, of 368m above road level. The gross area of the building is 133,000sq.m and there are 70 storeys.

As buildings become taller, the plan dimensions do not increase at the same rate. The reason for this is that although office workers rarely work by natural light, there is a psychological need for windows, for 'outside awareness'. This means that everyone needs to be no further than about 18m from a window. This limitation on plan dimension causes taller buildings to be more slender than shorter ones.

The combination of increased height and slenderness has two effects on the structural design of tall buildings. The first is the fact that wind speeds increase with height with a consequent increase in the wind loads on the faces of the building. The second is that all buildings act as cantilevers from the ground to carry the wind loads (**Fig. 9.89**) and, as the structure becomes more slender, this cantilevering behaviour under wind load tends to dominate the choice of structural system.

Fig. 9.109 Bank of China

Four structural systems are shown in **Fig. 9.90** for resisting lateral loading from wind and two of these systems are shown in **Fig. 9.91** for the 'slender' direction of a rectangular building. For a square building, like the Bank of China, there is no slender direction.

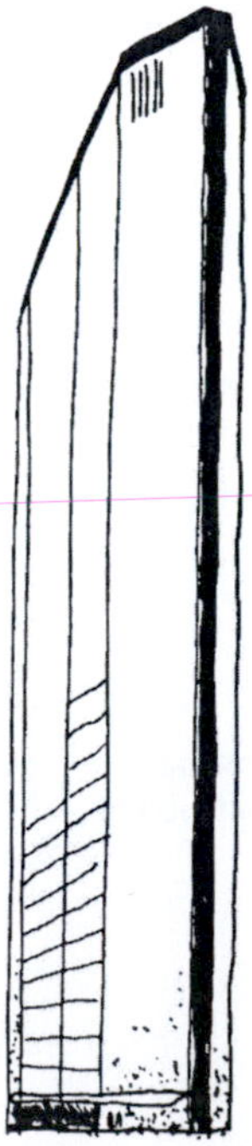

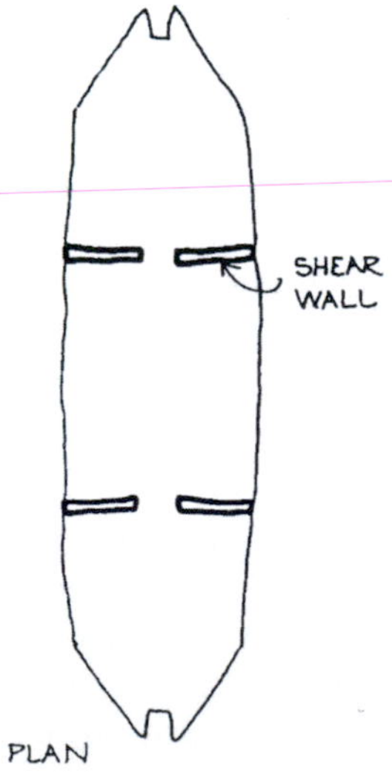

Early, very tall buildings, like the Chrysler and Empire State buildings in New York were designed as framed structures (**Fig. 9.90**). The lateral flexibility of these buildings was reduced by 'non-loadbearing' external and internal wall elements. The idea of using a vertical, beam-like structure – a **shear wall** – to carry the wind loads was first used by Pier Luigi Nervi in the structural design of the Pirelli tower in Turin in Italy.

SHEAR WALL

PLAN

Fig. 9.110 Pirelli Tower

As the external cladding became lighter and commercial pressures demanded column-free internal spaces the wind-resisting structure was sometimes moved to the facade of the building. The pioneer of this structural system was Fazlur Khan who first used it for the De Witt Chestnut building in 1965. He also used this concept for the better-known John Hancock Center built in Chicago in 1970.

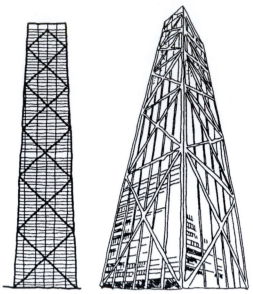

Fig. 9.111 John Hancock Center

Moving the wind-resisting structure to the external facade meant that the floors could be structure-free apart from the necessary stair/lift cores. The perimeter columns take the vertical loads directly to the ground.

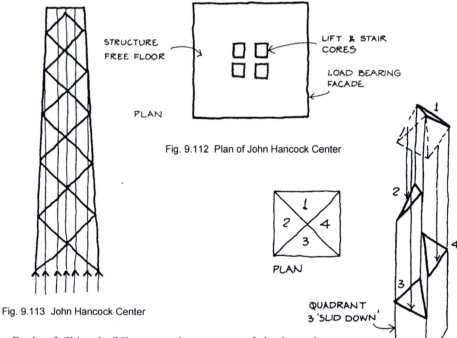

STRUCTURE FREE FLOOR

LIFT & STAIR CORES

LOAD BEARING FACADE

PLAN

Fig. 9.112 Plan of John Hancock Center

PLAN

Fig. 9.113 John Hancock Center

QUADRANT 3 'SLID DOWN'

Fig. 9.114 Bank of China

The Bank of China building uses the concept of the braced facade but with several important innovations. Before explaining the structural action it is helpful if the external shape of the building is understood. Essentially it is a cubical building with a pyramid roof but with each quadrant 'slid down' by different amounts.

This sliding means that the floor plan varies with the height.

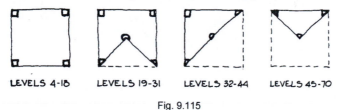

LEVELS 4-18   LEVELS 19-31   LEVELS 32-44   LEVELS 45-70

Fig. 9.115

The John Hancock Center uses the whole facade for the windbracing structure but the Bank of China building uses a **megastructure** as the primary load path for both the wind loads **and** the vertical loads.

This is really the same idea as the use of purlins and portal frames for the **basic structure** described in **Chapter 8**. The purlins are part of the secondary structure with the portals acting as a megastructure by carrying both the wind loads **and** the vertical loads.

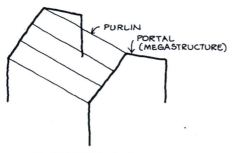

Fig. 9.116 Basic structure

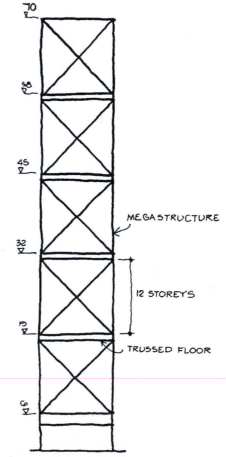

Fig. 9.117 Bank of China megastructure

The Bank of China is a 'stack' of five twelve-storey 'buildings', each of which is supported by the megastructure.

There are four megacolumns, one at each corner, but due to the changing floor shape, a fifth central megacolumn is required above **level 25**.

Real structures 251

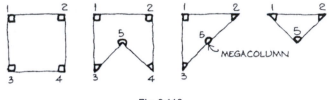

Fig. 9.118

Amazingly, the central megacolumn does not continue below **level 25**, its load being transferred to the corner megacolumns by a pyramid structure.

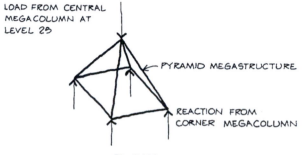

Fig. 9.119

At the bottom of each twelve-storey building is a storey-height trussed floor. This acts as the 'foundation' for the twelve-storey building, transferring the load to the megacolumns.

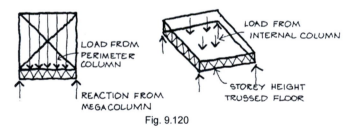

Fig. 9.120

The vertical loads in the perimeter columns are transferred directly into the facade megastructure at the points of structural intersection.

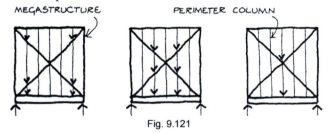

Fig. 9.121

Hong Kong is in an area of very high winds – typhoons – and these cause wind loads that are approximately double the wind loads carried by the Chicago and New York skyscrapers. These loads are resisted by the truss action of the facade megastructures. These external facades are cross-braced trusses.

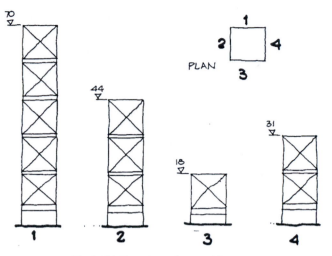

Fig. 9.122 Elevations of 'square' facades

At the higher levels there are also external facades on the plan diagonals. These facades have diagonally braced trusses.

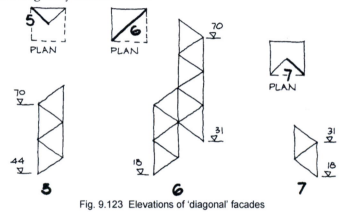

Fig. 9.123 Elevations of 'diagonal' facades

The vertical loads from the floors are transferred to the four corner megacolumns. These loads counteract the tension forces caused by the wind loads on the facade megatrusses. This maintains upward reactions at the base of the building under wind loading.

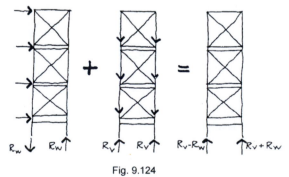

Fig. 9.124

This is another example of the role of combined stresses (**Section 3.8**). Although the external columns can carry tension forces it is difficult to provide substantial downward reactions at foundation level.

At the bottom of the tower, the horizontal wind load as well as the vertical load has to be transferred to the ground. In the Bank of China this is done by providing horizontal and vertical structures to transfer these forces to concrete walls that are below ground. These are the perimeter walls of the basement. There are five elements in the load path for the horizontal wind forces. These are:

1 **The facade megatrusses**
2 **A horizontal steel diaphragm structure at level 4**
3 **A vertical steel/concrete core between level 4 and the foundation**
4 **A horizontal concrete diaphragm structure at level 0**
5 **Vertical concrete perimeter basement walls**

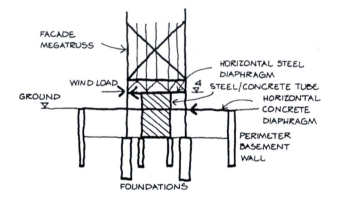

Fig. 9.125

At **level 4** the horizontal wind loads from the facade megatrusses are transferred to the vertical steel/concrete core by forces in the plane of the steel diaphragm structure.

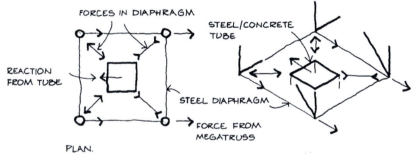

Fig. 9.126

The core transfers these horizontal loads by shear forces in the core walls to the concrete diaphragm at **level 0**.

254 Building structures

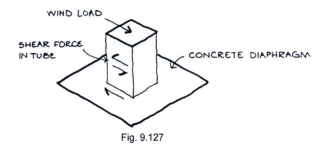

Fig. 9.127

There are also vertical forces in the core caused by the push/pull forces from the bending moment. These are carried down to separate core foundations.

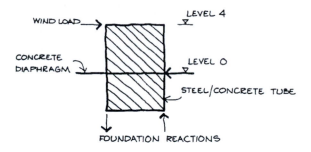

Fig. 9.128

The horizontal forces in the **level 0** concrete diaphragm are transferred to the top of the vertical basement by forces in the plane of the diaphragm structure. The forces in the walls are transferred to the ground by friction forces on the faces and the base of the walls.

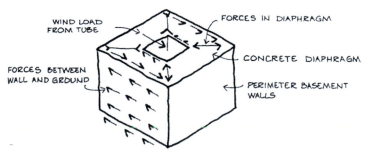

Fig. 9.129

The weight of the structural steel required for the structure of the Bank of China building was far lower than that used for other tall buildings built in the Far East. This was partly achieved by the efficiency of the overall structural form but a significant contribution was made by the way the megastructure joints were constructed. At any joint in a structure the forces in the elements have to be transferred through the joint and the cost of these joints is often a substantial proportion of the total structural cost. This is particularly true for three-dimensional structures due to the geometrical and structural complexities at the joints. This was overcome in the Bank of China building by using composite steel and concrete construction for the joints and members of the megastructure.

The facade megatrusses shown in **Figs. 9.122** and **9.123** were built as individual **plane** trusses with simple joints. Where they met at the corners to form the three-dimensional megastructure, they were connected by casting concrete around them to form the megacolumns and the joints of the megastructure.

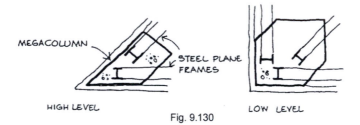

Fig. 9.130

Both the structural concepts and the finished appearance of the Bank of China are clear and simple. However, it should be appreciated that this was achieved by bold design decisions and a vast amount of complex detailed structural design.

References – Chapter 9

1   G Cook – **Portrait of Durham cathedral** – Phoenix House 1948 (out of print)
2   J Fitchen – **The construction of Gothic cathedrals** – University of Chicago Press 1961 – ISBN 0 226 252203 06102-3
3   S Minter – **The greatest glass house** – HMSO 1990 – ISBN 0 11 250035 8
4   JL Guthrie et al – **Restoration of the Palm House** – Proceedings of ICE December 1988 – p1145-1191
5   E Diestelkamp – **Richard Turner and the Palm House at Kew Gardens** – Transactions of the Newcomen Society 54, 1982 – p 1-26
6   E Torroja – **The structures of Eduardo Torroja** – Dodge Corp 1958 (out of print)
7   N Esquillan – **Shell vault of the exposition palace Paris** – Journal of Structural Division of ASCE January 1960
8   **Structure of the Federal Reserve Bank** – Architectural Record October 1971 – p106-109
9   LE Robertson et al – **Structural Systems for the Bank of China** – Proceedings of the Fourth Conference on Tall Buildings – Vol 1 – 1988

CHAPTER 10 *Structural conception*

Having an understanding of how structural systems work, what structural materials are available and what loads structures must carry does not lead to an automatic method of how to design, or more accurately how to **conceive** a structure. But as the structure is an essential part of any building and its **conceptual choice** may be part of the architectural design, the conception of the structure or the structural system is often not only made on the basis of structural economics. The interplay between structures and architecture is often complex and indeed the relationship between the engineer and the architect can lead to misunderstandings. How and why this is so is discussed in **Chapter 11**. The present chapter discusses how a **conceptual understanding** of structures can inform the process of **conception of structures** in buildings.

The term **structural designer** is used to describe the person who is responsible for the **structural concept**. This person may or may not be responsible for all the detail design and calculations for the final structure.

10.1   Structures in buildings

The only role of the structure of a crane or bridge is to carry the load, whereas the structure of a building fulfils other roles. Under the current method of building design, the 'designer' is usually more than one person, so the structural designer is part of a team. Often each member of the design team is primarily concerned with a different aspect of the overall design. A building is essentially a space that is protected from the natural environment and is constructed for a specific use. The structure of the building is part of the building construction and plays the role of giving the construction sufficient strength to withstand the loads to which the whole building is subjected. These loads are caused by natural phenomena such as wind and gravity and by the use of the building.

The structure is **part** of a building and should not be conceived in isolation, but as part of the whole design. However, it plays a specific role, that of providing strength. Whilst the structure of a building is part of the construction, the **concept** of the structure is not. Frequently design decisions are made before the structural concept is clear, often the physical size of structural members is considered without reference to an overall structure. The physical presence of the structure in a building is the concern of many members of the design team as it affects their design decisions. Often the role of structural design is seen as arriving at the physical size of structural elements rather than considering an overall design strategy.

So the structural designer of building structures is frequently faced with a difficult task. Not only is the structural design part of a whole, over which he or she may have no direct control, but the actual size and appearance of individual parts is often proscribed by others who have no concern for their structural action.

The structural designer must keep two principles firmly in mind, and these are:

- **There is no correct structure**
- **All loads must have a load path**

The first principle is often the cause of much difficulty to inexperienced designers because everyone likes to get the right answer, choose the correct structure, and it is conceptually important to realise that this is not possible. The obverse is that the chosen structure, provided that it satisfies all the requirements of the building design, is the **correct structure**. Before the structure is chosen, alternatives may be considered but these rarely eliminate themselves so the designer must choose the correct structure.

The second principle is obvious as a principle but frequently non-structural requirements alter the chosen structural concept. This means that load paths may need to be altered locally or globally. It is essential that the consequences of any alterations are accepted. A simple example illustrates this point. Suppose part of a building has floors that span on to edge beams, and these beams span between columns that are spaced at regular centres.

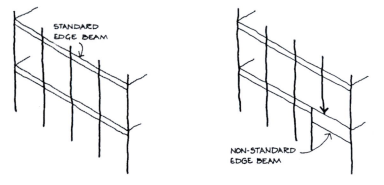

Fig. 10.1

If for some non-structural reason a column at ground level has to be moved then the upper columns will have to be carried by a beam at first floor. The beam at first floor carrying the load from the columns above will have to be far stronger and therefore bigger than the other edge beams.

The two basic principles do not give any guidance on how to conceive a structure for a building, however, the building design does. The use of a building may determine the span of the floors or roof as the internal space requirements often determine the positions of vertical supports. An office space can have internal vertical supports but planning flexibility suggests these should be columns rather than walls. An auditorium, however large, can have no internal supports but does require, for sound isolation, heavy perimeter walls. A tall building needs vertical access so these can be grouped into stair and lift towers and can be used by the structural designer to resist horizontal wind loads. These are simple examples that show how non-structural requirements for a building can guide a structural designer towards decisions about possible structural concepts.

10.2 Conceptual load paths

Before decisions are made about a particular structure, the load paths for the different load cases must be identified. Because the load path for any loading **is** the structure it must be clear how each load path structure acts. Building structures provide the strength and stiffness for the building enclosure and this means that there must be load paths to transfer **vertical** and **horizontal loads** (see **Section 1.6**). The structure transfers the loads by parts of the load path spanning to support points. As buildings are three-dimensional objects the structure also has to be three dimensional even though parts of the structure may be considered as two-dimensional.

For gravity loads the load paths are conceived 'top down'. This is because each part of the building has to be supported by the structure below and also support the building above – just like a stack of bricks. To act as a load path the structure must be **complete** – that is, no structural gaps.

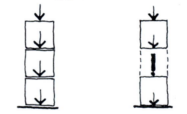

Fig. 10.2 Complete (left) and incomplete (right) load paths

A solid brick column could support a statue but is not much use as a building structure, however, the idea of a complete load path can be applied to a stack of tables.

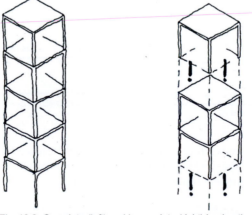

Fig. 10.3 Complete (left) and incomplete (right) load paths

The idea of a complete gravity load path may seem obvious for stacks of bricks or tables but for complex buildings it may be far from clear. For example, a hotel requires different types of space at different levels.

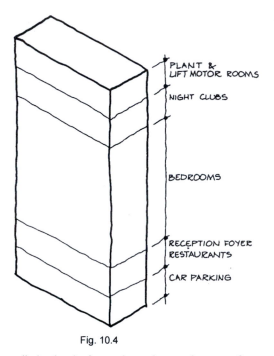

Fig. 10.4

Each part has to support all the loads from above but each type of space suggests different types and spacing of vertical structure. Bedrooms have walls at close spacings whereas a car park needs widely spaced columns that allow an efficient car parking layout. It is rare that the position of vertical structure for differing uses coincides, this means that vertical loads will have to be diverted laterally by transfer structures or the position of the vertical structure will have to be a compromise.

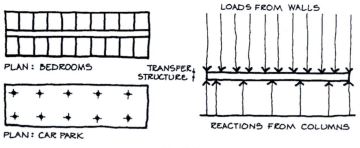

Fig. 10.5

A similar principle applies for horizontal loads, usually caused by wind loading. For horizontal loading, the building cantilevers from the ground and the cantilever structure must be complete from roof to foundation.

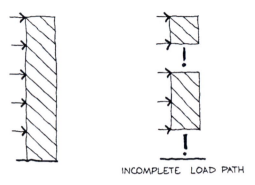

INCOMPLETE LOAD PATH

Fig. 10.6

As the wind can blow from any direction, the wind load paths must be complete in three dimensions.

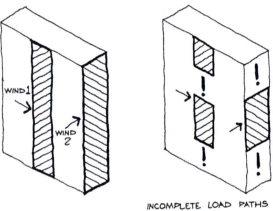

INCOMPLETE LOAD PATHS

Fig. 10.7

For wind loads there are also horizontal structural elements which transfer wind loads to the vertical cantilever structure. These may be glazing, walls, floors or roofs acting as structural elements, and again these must act as complete load paths.

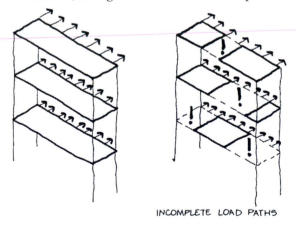

INCOMPLETE LOAD PATHS

Fig. 10.8

Structural conception 261

The conceptual load path (**Fig. 10.12**) is unaltered but the chosen load path geometry is no longer suitable. A new load path geometry has to be chosen which can act as a beam-like structure.

BENDING MOMENT DIAGRAM

Fig. 10.15

Beam-like behaviour needs elements that can resist internal forces that are bending moments and shear forces rather than axial forces. These beam-like elements will have a different geometrical shape to those chosen for the truss. Provided it is realised that this is a change in load path geometry as well as a change in building geometry, then it is just part of the design process.

This simple example illustrates how important it is to understand that an alteration in load path geometry, whilst not affecting the efficacy of the conceptual load path, may have a profound effect on the type of structural behaviour.

10.4   Overall structural behaviour

Building structures are always subjected to a number of different loads and these can act in different combinations and in different directions. These loads act vertically and horizontally. The structure must provide load paths for all these loads from the point of application to the reaction from the ground. How these loads are 'chased' has been a recurrent theme of this book first introduced in **Section 1.6**. For a simple building the various load paths are examined in detail in **Chapter 8**. The load paths for a number of real structures are given in **Chapter 9**. The load path for each load case **is** the structure and, depending on the load path geometry, it will have a particular type of structural action.

Essentially there are four types of structural action for spanning members. These are beam-like, truss-like, frame-like and funicular; **Chapter 7** explains how these different types act.

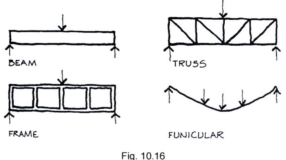

Fig. 10.16

The structures shown in **Fig. 10.16** can only be a part of an overall structure as this has to enclose space. To do this a vertical element, a column, must be added.

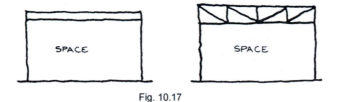

Fig. 10.17

The columns carry the vertical loads for the gravity load case but they must also provide the overall lateral stability and in doing so act as spanning structures themselves. This can be done by making the structure a portal frame or by cantilevering the columns from the ground, or both.

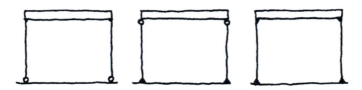

Fig. 10.18 Pinned portal (left) cantilever columns (centre) fixed portal (right)

These structures enclose space, are stable and can carry vertical and horizontal loads.

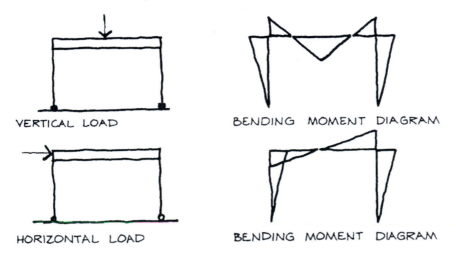

VERTICAL LOAD

BENDING MOMENT DIAGRAM

HORIZONTAL LOAD

BENDING MOMENT DIAGRAM

Fig. 10.19 Bending moment diagrams for the pinned portal

The beam-like spanning structure has become a portal frame. For both vertical and horizontal loads there is a bending moment in the 'column' which means it acts as a spanning structure.

The structural designer, when conceiving a structure has to be aware how the whole structure acts under each load case and how the choice of structural geometry causes the structure to act in different ways. This can be illustrated by examining the structure for a single-storey space.

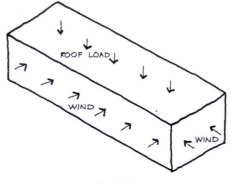

Fig. 10.20

The structure will have to carry vertical loads applied to the roof and wind loads which can act in any horizontal direction. As this building is just a flat-roofed version of the building considered in detail in **Chapter 8**, the structure already chosen (**Fig. 8.7**) would be one choice.

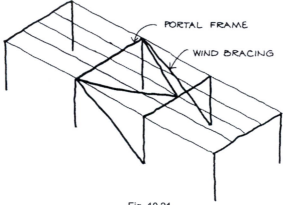

PORTAL FRAME

WIND BRACING

Fig. 10.21

But other choices can be made. The roof structure could be a three-dimensional space frame (**Fig. 7.75B**), supported on perimeter columns.

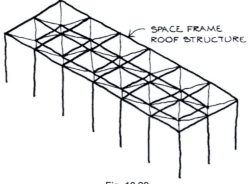

SPACE FRAME
ROOF STRUCTURE

Fig. 10.22

The columns, as with the portal frame, have to provide stability against overall collapse and also be part of the load path for horizontal loads.

266 Building structures

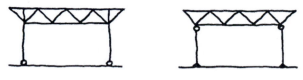

Fig. 10.23

Because the space frame is triangulated in the horizontal plane, it can act as a 'wind girder' in any direction.

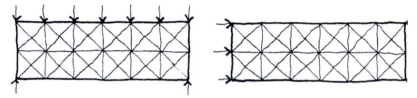

Fig. 10.24 Plans

Some columns could be chosen just to carry vertical loads whilst others, say the corner columns, could also provide stability and carry the horizontal loads.

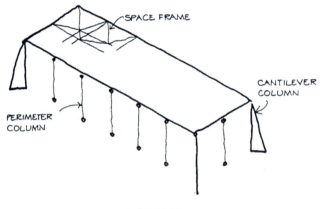

Fig. 10.25

The corner columns act as cantilevers from the ground so they are spanning structures.

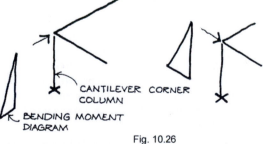

Fig. 10.26

To carry the bending moments in these corner columns, which act in more than one direction, a three-dimensional, truss-like structure could be chosen. The columns that only carry vertical loads could be simple tubular struts.

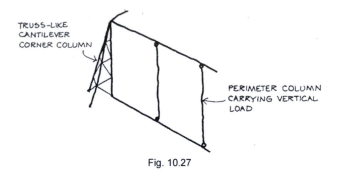

TRUSS-LIKE
CANTILEVER
CORNER COLUMN

PERIMETER COLUMN
CARRYING VERTICAL
LOAD

Fig. 10.27

Two quite different structures have been chosen for this simple building and **both are correct** as they have been conceived by using an understanding of the overall structural behaviour. Many other structures could be chosen to support the enclosure of this simple space. All these structures would be correct provided the choice of geometry was based on an understanding of the overall structural behaviour.

10.5   Choice of materials and elements

In **Chapter 5** four basic materials were identified as being suitable for building structures, these were steel, timber, concrete and masonry. The reason that the choice is limited is that the materials have to be cheap. They also have to be durable, easily altered or repaired and to be constantly available. This is because buildings are expected to last a long time, be relatively maintenance free and to be altered without recourse to specialist suppliers or technology. The situation is quite different for non-building structures. For instance, aircraft structures are very expensive, have a specific life and are regularly maintained by specialists who have ready access to the latest technology.

Fortunately this lack of choice of suitable materials has not resulted in a lack of variety either in building structures or in the buildings they hold up; after all building structures have rarely been built of anything else. The structural designer has to be aware which material is suitable for any chosen structure. Ideally the structural form and the structural material are conceived simultaneously. As each of the four materials are more suitable for different structural types, the material choice is often implicit. Timber and steel are strong compared with their weight so are suitable where tensile forces are large. Where loads are compressive, masonry or mass concrete are suitable. These materials can be used for spanning structures if they are used compositely with tensile material, steel, or are pre-stressed (see **Section 4.7**). Non-structural characteristics such as combustibility or susceptibility to chemical attack may influence choice (see **Section 5.4**). It is also necessary to know how the material can be joined (see **Section 10.6**).

With so many caveats, the inexperienced designer can feel there are more problems than solutions, so some broad guidance is needed. The main guidance is from structures that exist but each time and place favours different solutions. These will depend on material availability and the presence of suitable expertise in the chosen material. Concrete is made by mixing cement, aggregate and clean water so difficulty in obtaining any of these at an affordable price will preclude the use of concrete. The use of reinforced concrete also needs suitable steel reinforcement, expertise and technology to cut and bend the bars and material to make the formwork. These are usually readily available in industrialised areas but will not be available in remote rural areas. The choice will then be between local materials or the cost of transporting non-local materials, technology and expertise.

In the description of the action of structural systems (see **Sections 7.2** to **7.5**) no mention was made of materials. The chapter on real structures (**Chapter 9**) describes both structural systems and the use of various structural materials such as stone, wrought iron, reinforced concrete and steel.

As most parts of a structural system are required to span under some load case (see **Section 10.4**), the structural designer must be aware of how the chosen structural material caters for the resulting internal forces. The beam-like, truss-like and frame-like spanning structures all require tensile strength in some part of the structure so, for example, masonry or mass concrete cannot be used. Beams and trusses of steel or timber are commonplace.

Fig. 10.28

Frames also require tensile strength, and simple frames such as portal frames (see **Section 2.3**) are made from both steel and timber. Multistorey frames (see **Fig. 9.89**) and spanning frames (see **Fig. 7.50**) are often made of steel.

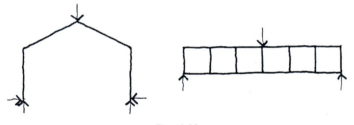

Fig. 10.29

There are two types of funicular structures (see **Section 7.4**), hanging and arching. The hanging funicular structures are in tension so timber or steel are suitable but due to jointing problems timber is rarely used. For arches, mass concrete or masonry are very suitable and this form of tension-free, spanning structure was the major form until the end of the 18th century.

Fig. 10.30

Although structural materials are commonly used on their own, they are also frequently combined to form composite materials or structures (see **Section 4.7**).

Since the 1920s, concrete reinforced with steel rods, usually called **rebar**, has become, together with steel, a widely used structural 'material' for building structures. Although heavy compared with its strength, reinforced concrete is used for beams, slabs, frames, shells and even trusses. Great care has to be taken to ensure there is rebar in all areas of tension. This means that the structural designer has to decide the size and position of every bar.

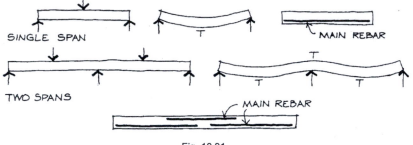

Fig. 10.31

An alternative to rebar is **pre-stress** (see pages **112-114**). Here the tensile stress caused by the structural actions is reduced to zero by using internal steel tendons to apply compressive stresses.

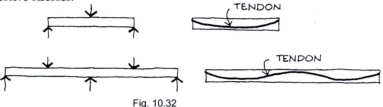

Fig. 10.32

Reinforced and pre-stressed concrete are often regarded as structural materials but there are other ways of making composite structures. Two examples have already been given, that of steel beams with concrete slabs (see pages **110-111**) and the use of reinforced concrete with masonry (see page **115**). A further example is the composite behaviour of structural steelwork and concrete used in the Bank of China (see **Section 9.6**) to form mega reinforced concrete.

Two different materials or two forms of the same material can be combined to make composite elements. A steel plate can be used with timber to form a flitch beam. Timber **I** or box beams can be made using ordinary timber sections with plywood sheeting.

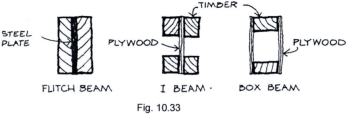

Fig. 10.33

There is also a choice for the shape of the structural element. An element's section shape should be stress effective (see pages **72-73**), the effect of cross-section shape is explained in **Section 4.4**. Section shape also has an effect on axial stability (see **Section 6.4**). Elements can also be shaped over their length (see page **74**).

Each of the four, or five if reinforced concrete is classed as a structural material, can be shaped in different ways. Mass and reinforced concrete can be made into almost any shape, limited by the skill of the makers of the formwork and the patience of the designers and the fixers of the rebar.

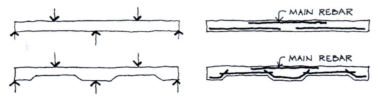

Fig. 10.34

In shaping reinforced concrete for structural efficiency, the benefit must be available to the client in the form of lower cost – this is often difficult to judge as building costs vary continuously.

Structural steelwork is available in simple bars, rods and plates of different sizes. In industrial areas **standard sections** are available. They are made by rolling hot steel into a variety of cross-sectional shapes – hence **hot rolled sections**. The size and shape may vary by producer or may comply with a national standard. In areas where a national standard applies the choice is easy for the structural designer, but where the sections are obtained from various sources the exact size and shape may only be known as construction begins. The usual range of hot rolled sections are angles, channels, I sections, tees, round and square tubes. Sizes vary from 50 to 1000mm.

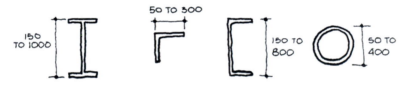

Fig. 10.35

With the use of cutting and welding equipment these sections can be altered to form structurally efficient structures. This is commonly done at the knee joint of portal frames.

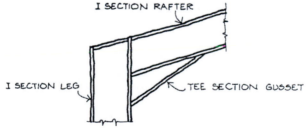

Fig. 10.36

Steelwork fabricators cut and weld steel as part of normal operations but, as with complex reinforced concrete structures, the cost of complexity must be outweighed by an overall saving.

Timber is normally cut or converted to use the correct term into lengths with a rectangular cross section. In some areas the sizes are standard which is an advantage to the structural designer. The structural performance of timber varies greatly between different species. There are two basic types – hardwood and softwood. In the Northern hemisphere, structural timber is predominately softwood but in the tropics and the Southern hemisphere structural timber is usually hardwood. Timber sheet materials are also available in many parts of the world as plywood, chipboard and hardboard, and these can be used structurally. Structural timber is most often used as simple beams with a rectangular cross-section or made into simple trusses. These can be on a large scale, for instance timber structures have been used for the construction of airship hangars.

Masonry, in the form of mud dried bricks, is one of the oldest building materials. The strength and size of blocks and bricks varies widely. The strength of masonry, rather than the units themselves, is usually limited by the strength of the mortar in which the bricks or blocks are laid. Sizes of the basic units vary but tend to be standard in an area and this will determine the overall sizes of masonry structures as it is far better to use whole units rather than cut them.

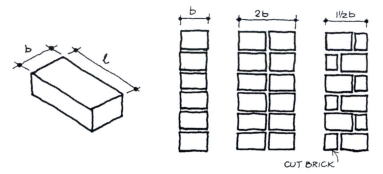

Fig. 10.37

The key to a sensible choice for a structural material is local availability and expertise. This often dictates the range of structural forms which can be used economically in any area at a particular time, requiring the structural designer to be aware of the cost and availability of materials before structural decisions are made.

Structural designers sometimes tire of the usual materials and yearn for 'new materials'. The new materials are usually sought from more high-tech industries such as aerospace. Although this pursuit of new materials is clothed in acceptable notions such as progress or innovation, often the purpose is to gain attention for the user of the 'new' material. Sometimes these new materials make their appearance in new forms of construction such as tent structures or structural glass facades.

Tent buildings date from pre-history, see **Fig. 0.2**, but from the 1970s stressed tents have been promoted by a number of designers. These require durable, strong fabrics which are now available as Teflon-coated glass fibre. This material is not cheap and has no application in ordinary building.

Another new material is toughened laminated glass which can be used as a structural element in a glass facade. This type of glass, originally developed for the windows of cars and aeroplanes, is now used as 'fins' for strengthening glass-only facades.

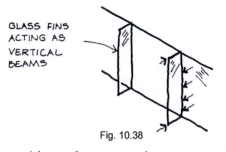

GLASS FINS
ACTING AS
VERTICAL
BEAMS

Fig. 10.38

The use of new materials produces expensive structures for clients who want attention-seeking designs. Of course there are proper innovations, new materials and processes. In the past, the introduction of iron, steel, welding and pre-stressing were all innovations that made significant differences to the way building structures were conceived and constructed. At present, the choice of structural material for most building structures is still between steel, timber, masonry or concrete, mass, reinforced or pre-stressed.

10.6   Element connection

The load path for each load case has to be complete – there can be no gaps (see **Section 10.2**). It is rare that this can be achieved without having to join parts of the structure together. They may be joints between similar or different structural materials, or they may be joints between major structural elements.

A structure transfers load by internal forces and at points of support the internal forces are balanced by reaction forces.

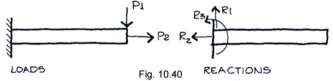

Fig. 10.39

The reactions may balance axial or shear forces or bending moments. For a cantilever beam with vertical and horizontal loads, the reactions provide vertical and horizontal forces and a moment reaction.

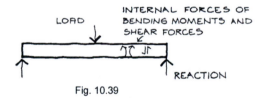

LOADS   Fig. 10.40   REACTIONS

Like points of support, joints have to transfer the internal forces to the adjacent part of the structure. Suppose, for the cantilever shown in **Fig. 10.40**, there is a joint in the beam.

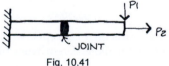

Fig. 10.41

At the joint, the forces are the same as the forces at the 'cuts' in a beam (see **Figs. 2.9** and **2.18**), except now the joint is a cut.

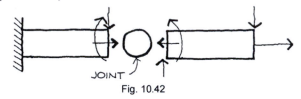

Fig. 10.42

The joint in the cantilever beam has to transfer axial and shear forces and a bending moment. For a simple spanning beam, a joint at the end only has to transfer shear forces.

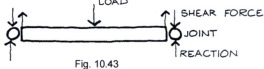

Fig. 10.43

Whilst a joint is the connection between two, or more, parts of a structure it is still part of the load path, so calling it a joint is arbitrary from the conceptual point of view. But how the elements are joined together may affect the structural behaviour. For example, a two-span beam may be continuous over the central support. At this support there is a bending moment as well as shear forces.

Fig. 10.44

If a joint is made between the two spans that can only carry shear forces then the structural behaviour will be altered. The structure now acts as two, adjacent, simply supported beams.

Fig. 10.45

The difference between an arch and a curved beam (**Fig. 7.73**) is dependent on the structural designer's choice of joint at the support points. If the designer chooses joints that can transfer vertical and horizontal forces, then the curved structure will act as an arch. If the joints can only transfer vertical forces, then it will act as a curved beam.

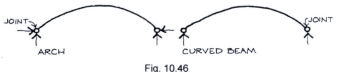

Fig. 10.46

To aid the process of using structural concepts, structural designers have evolved standard names and symbols for the different types of structural joints. Joints that can transfer all forces are called **fixed** or **encastre** joints, joints that transfer forces but no bending moments are called **pin** joints, and joints that only transfer a force in a specific direction are called **sliding** joints. These joints are drawn on structural diagrams in a standard way.

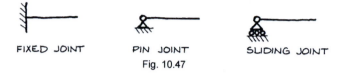

FIXED JOINT   PIN JOINT   SLIDING JOINT

Fig. 10.47

This allows structural designers to draw diagrams of structures that make their structural behaviour clear. The familiar simple structures of a cantilever beam and a simply supported beam can now be drawn as **structural diagrams**.

CANTILEVER   SIMPLY SUPPORTED BEAM

Fig. 10.48 Structural diagrams

Using these symbols, the structural diagrams of the curved structure make it obvious which is the arch and which is the curved beam.

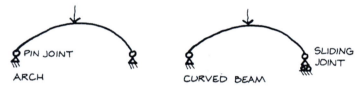

PIN JOINT   SLIDING JOINT

ARCH   CURVED BEAM

Fig. 10.49

Choosing the position and types of joints is part of the process of conceiving structures. The structural designer has to introduce joints to allow the transport and erection of the different structural elements. What structural behaviour these joints need is determined by how the structure is expected to behave at the joint positions and the practical considerations of the joint details.

How are the symbolic joints in the structural diagrams to become real joints in real structures? This largely depends on the structural material being used at the joint. Structural masonry is constructed by jointing the individual bricks or blocks to each other by introducing a bed of mortar between them.

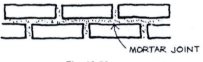

MORTAR JOINT

Fig. 10.50

Steel can be joined by welding, by heating the metal at the joint and introducing molten steel. The steel is joined so that the material becomes continuous at the joint.

WELDED JOINT   STEEL PLATE

Fig. 10.51

Welding is best carried out under workshop conditions so welded joints in steel structures are used to make steelwork elements that are transported to the site.

When reinforced concrete is constructed in its final position, that is, built in situ, joints are made simply by casting new concrete around reinforcing bars that have been left projecting from the part to be joined.

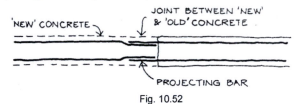

Fig. 10.52

The ease with which joints, can be made in this way is one of the main reasons for the widespread use of reinforced concrete.

As trees grow they form joints, branch to trunk, as part of the growing process. There is currently no way of growing cut pieces of timber into timber structures so it has to be joined by other means.

When different materials are to be joined, mechanical fixings have to be used. These are of two basic types – 'specific strong object' or glue. Examples of 'specific strong objects' are bolts, screws and nails whilst the range of glue types is enormous. Nowadays there is strong glue that will bond together almost any combination of materials.

To be able to design joints the structural action must be clear to the designer. Like structures in general, there is no correct joint but a number of choices. There is a load path through a joint and these can often be complex. The choices and load paths are illustrated by considering a joint between two steel I sections that are part of a beam.

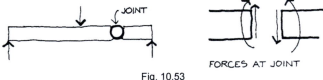

Fig. 10.53

The forces that are to be transferred through the joint are a shear force and a bending moment. The bending moment, push/pull forces, is mainly transferred by horizontal tensile and compressive stresses in the flanges (see **Fig. 3.55**) and the shear forces by vertical shear stresses in the web (see **Fig. 4.37**).

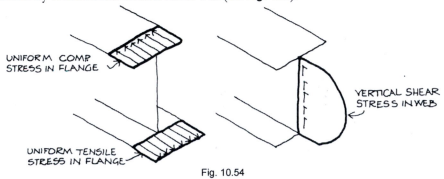

Fig. 10.54

Conceptually the joint is made by joining the flanges to take the tension and compression and the webs to take the vertical shear.

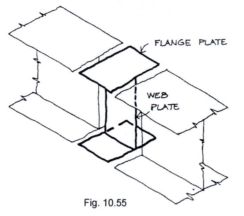

Fig. 10.55

One choice would be to weld the whole section together.

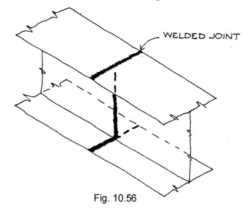

Fig. 10.56

For making joints on site, bolted connections are usually preferred. For this a number of options are available. Loose flange and web plates can be used to 'splice' the beams together.

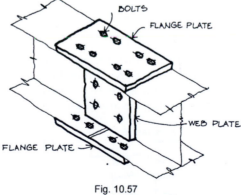

Fig. 10.57

As an example of a joint load path consider the bottom flange plate. The tensile loads in the flanges are transferred to the flange plates by shear forces in the shafts of the bolts.

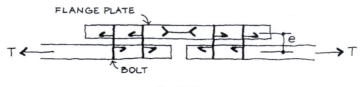

FLANGE PLATE

BOLT

Fig. 10.58

There is an eccentricity in the load path that may cause some local bending in the plate.

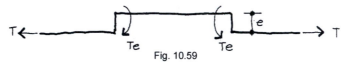

Te   Te

Fig. 10.59

The uniform tensile stress in the flange is transferred into the flange plate at the specific positions of the bolts.

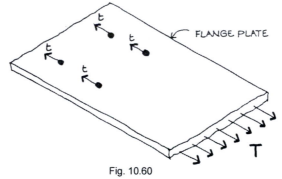

FLANGE PLATE

T

Fig. 10.60

For horizontal equilibrium $4 \times t = T$, but at the bolt positions, the tensile stress is altered from a uniform distribution to a non-uniform stress distribution.

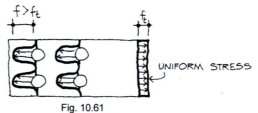

$f > f_t$ f_t

UNIFORM STRESS

Fig. 10.61

As the area near the bolts is smaller than the whole flange, the stresses are higher than the uniform stress. There is a maximum allowable stress for the steel (see page **72**) and the high stresses concentrated at the bolts must not exceed this. This indicates that it is better to make the joint in a part of the beam where the stresses are less than the maximum.

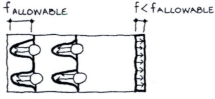

$f_{ALLOWABLE}$ $f < f_{ALLOWABLE}$

Fig. 10.62

A similar joint could be made by welding the plates to one of the beams in the fabrication shop and bolting them to the other beam on site. Another type of bolted joint can be made by welding plates across the ends of both beams then bolting the plates face to face on site.

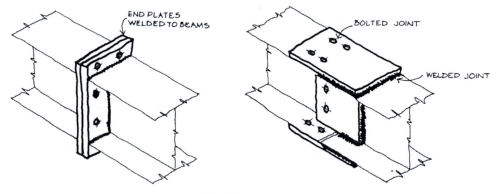

Fig. 10.63

For this joint, the load path is quite different to the load path in the plated joint. In this joint, the load transfer causes bending moments in the end plates and the bolts carry shear and tension.

There are many 'standard' ways of joining elements and these are given in technical guides. The positioning and behaviour of joints in structures can affect the overall behaviour of the structure, so the structural designer should consider them as part of the structural concept rather than an additional requirement.

10.7   Structures and building construction

The structure of a building, whilst fulfilling the specific role of giving strength and stiffness to the building enclosure, is not physically a separate part of the building construction.   The structural elements form part of building elements and the structural designer needs to know how 'the structure' will relate physically to the other elements, often designed by other members of the design team. During the design process, the structural designer often has to modify the structural design to accommodate design developments carried out by other members of the design team.

Any object that is hard is subjected to gravity forces that cause internal forces in the object. In this sense all parts of the building are structures but the structural designer is usually concerned with the **primary** structure. This is a rather nebulous concept, as all the load paths have to be complete from the point of load application. For instance, when the wind blows on a building causing wind loads these are often applied to the window panes. Except for unusually large panes, the structural designer is not concerned with the pane as a structure. What constitutes the primary structure usually becomes clear during the design process.

Sometimes parts of the structure fulfil a dual purpose, as part of the enclosure and part of the primary structure. This is particularly true for masonry walls which are part of the enclosure as well as acting as part of the primary vertical load path. This can cause difficulties as more than one member of the design team may be concerned with their design and each member may not be aware of the dual role. For example, the inner leaf of a cavity wall may carry floor loads and thus require a specific strength. Other members of the design team are concerned with the thermal insulation that the inner leaf provides. To obtain the required thermal insulation, the strength may be reduced. Or in domestic buildings some internal walls may be loadbearing whilst others are only space-enclosing elements. As the construction may be similar for both walls, this can lead to confusion.

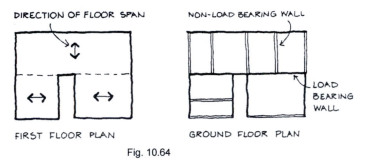

Fig. 10.64

Even with specific structural elements such as reinforced concrete columns in an office building, the building construction can influence their shape and position. This is especially true for the columns that support the floor perimeter.

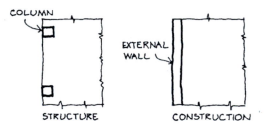

Fig. 10.65

There are various options, not always chosen by the structural designer. The columns can relate to the external enclosure in a number of ways.

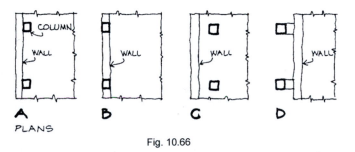

Fig. 10.66

In **A** the columns are positioned just inside the external wall which means the inner face is not flush. This will affect the layout of furniture, loose or built-in. In **B** the columns are within the wall and the wall may need extra width to accommodate the column.

280 Building structures

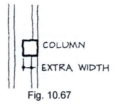

Fig. 10.67

To reduce this width, the column size needs to be the minimum possible, which may make the column slender (see page **157**).

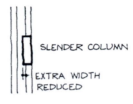

Fig. 10.68

In **C** the columns are placed within the building which means that the floor has to cantilever past the columns thus locally altering the structural behaviour.

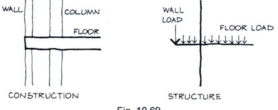

Fig. 10.69

In **D** the column is placed outside the building so it has to be connected to the floor it is supporting by a beam that penetrates the external wall.

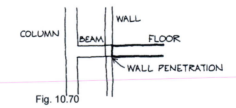

Fig. 10.70

This beam needs a 'hole' in the wall which is a potential source of rain penetration. To combat this, complicated waterproofing details have to be devised and built correctly. The beam can also create a 'cold bridge' conducting heat from the building or cold into the building. This can cause local condensation with consequent deterioration of materials. As with structural design in general there is no correct position for the column and many buildings have been constructed with columns in all the positions shown in **Fig. 10.66**.

Another aspect of building construction that frequently affects the structure is the installation of environmental services. These range from small wires, for telecommunications, to large ducts, for air handling, and all these will need openings somewhere in the primary structure. Many services are run at ceiling level.

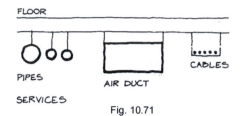

Fig. 10.71

These services are often concealed from the general building user by installing a suspended ceiling below the services.

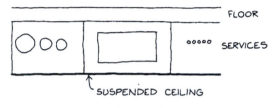

Fig. 10.72

These diagrams appear simple but services run in all directions. If there are downstand beams or trusses for large spans, the services may have to run through them to keep the construction depth to a minimum.

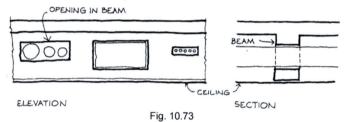

Fig. 10.73

Depending on the size and position of these openings the beam may turn into a frame (see **Fig. 7.64**). Where trusses are used, the diagonals may need to be removed locally which affects the structural behaviour (see **Fig. 7.64** again).

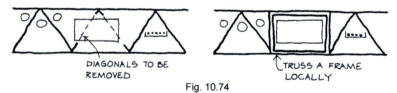

Fig. 10.74

Often ducts for small pipes have to run in reinforced concrete floors to supply perimeter radiators.

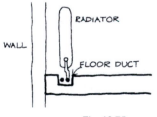

Fig. 10.75

282 Building structures

These ducts cause considerable complexity for the reinforcement as well as weakening the structure locally.

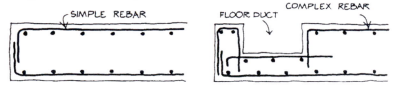

Fig. 10.76

With these local alterations to the primary structure, the structural designer must ensure that the conceptual load paths are complete and the structure at the positions of the local alterations is still strong enough to transfer the internal forces.

These examples show how the designer of building structures needs knowledge of building construction to anticipate the relationship of the primary structure to the whole construction and to be able to discuss this relationship with other members of the design team. This knowledge is not easy to acquire, especially as the structural designer rarely designs the building construction. The successful designer sees the primary structure as part of the whole design and expects that the design process will require alteration to the initial structural design. These alterations will often be made by members of the design team who do not understand the structural concepts so will be unaware of their effect. Local alterations can usually be made with some added local complexity but if an alteration in structural concept is required then it has to be made and its consequences accepted. Because of the inevitable alterations needed during the design process, it is unwise to size the structural elements so tightly that small alterations cause major structural problems. This is not being uneconomic, just sensible.

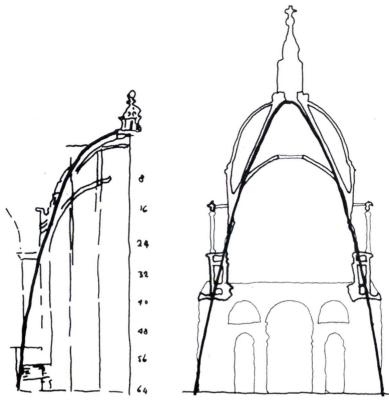

Fig. 11.10 Wren's thrust line (left) and that of a weighted chain (right)

Robert Hooke (1635-1703), who was a lifelong friend of Wren, had proposed that a hanging chain gave the shape for an arch – see **Section 7.4**. An arch is not a dome as has been shown and some think there is no definite connection between Hooke's catenary and the dome,[9] but Wren and Hooke were close friends and collaborators and there is an entry in Hooke's diary noting that Wren was altering his dome design according Hooke's arch principle.[10]

Wren's achievements were remarkable and he is regarded by many as Britain's greatest architect but his reputation as a great structural engineer seems less secure. Some have given him a place of honour in the history of structural engineering,[11] prompting Dr Thurston[12] to state that Wren "...*was simply a great natural mathematician, and it was possible that Wren was, in the same way, such a great genius that he was able to determine what was required without the need for elaborate mathematics*". This is clearly overstating the case.

There have been many structural problems with St. Paul's Cathedral, mainly with the dome support structures. Wren himself was made aware of one of these when cracks appeared in the eight large piers that support the main dome. They were 'bursting' due to the load. The piers, following usual practice, were built from a stone outer 'box' filled with rubble but, as Wren realised, the smaller upper piers were loading the rubble and not the stone of the lower piers. This produced the effect shown in **Fig. 5.13**, but here the 'rigid pit' was the stonework of the lower piers which was unable to resist the lateral forces from the rubble and so cracked or 'burst'.

There were problems due to differential settlement of the piers, as not all the foundations had been taken down to an adequate bearing stratum. But the main structural problems were with the load transfer structure between the domes and the supporting piers. There is no evidence that Wren had a clear conceptual understanding of the structural behaviour of this structure, however he decided to place extensive iron work in it. Much of this failed causing severe cracking and, after years of running repairs, the whole structure was renovated and strengthened between 1925 and 1930.[13]

Wren intended to publish a treatise on architecture which was to have included his thoughts on the behaviour of structures, however he never got round to this, though he stated in a report on Westminster Abbey that *"It is by due Consideration of the Statick Principles, and the right Poising of the Weights of the Butments to Arches, that good Architecture depends".*[14] His only known attempt at structural analysis was for the abutments of an arch and this was totally flawed.[15] He was brilliantly clever, a very able mathematician, an imaginative and dedicated experimenter and his friend Hooke was also all of these, so it is difficult to understand why Wren did not make more progress with useful aspects of structural design.

11.2   The arrival of the skeletal structure

In 1709 Abraham Darby (1678?-1717) first produced iron by using coke, a coal derivative, rather than charcoal. Charcoal was becoming prohibitively expensive with the almost complete deforestation of Great Britain. This new process was the foundation of the Industrial Revolution. Iron, now being an affordable material, allowed the development of machinery which in turn gave rise to the steam engine that provided the energy for industrialisation. In 1779 Darby's grandson Abraham Darby III built the Ironbridge at Coalbrookdale, see **Fig. 5.8**, and in 1802 the first railway locomotive. For structures and the built form, the arrival of affordable iron and the new demands of industry changed everything. Firstly with cast iron and then, with the more tension-resistant wrought iron, high strength to weight ratio structural elements, in the form of bars, rods, angles and other standard sections, became available. Secondly industrial demands brought new built forms into being, factories, railway stations, cranes and railway bridges, with structures that often had to support previously unimagined large loads, the weight of railway trains or stationary steam engines and so on. So instead of the structural self-weight being dominant, as with large masonry structures, it was now low compared with the load carried; a totally new situation. These structures, made as assemblies of relatively slender high-strength iron elements joined by metal fastenings, were **skeletal structures**.

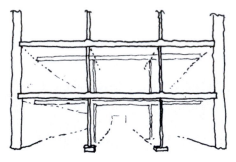

Fig. 11.11 Mill with simple internal iron framing 1801

The ability of iron skeletal structures to permit the construction of huge buildings in an incredibly short time was amply demonstrated by the erection of the Crystal Palace[16] in London in 1851 – "... *the mid-nineteenth century touchstone*".[17] In 1849 Henry Cole proposed to Prince Albert that a great international exhibition should be held in London. A site was chosen, Hyde Park, and the date set, 1851, giving less than eighteen months to stage the biggest show the world had ever seen.

In January 1850 a Building Committee was formed that included the architects, Donaldson, Robert Cockerell and Charles Barry, and the engineers Isambard Brunel and Robert Stephenson. An open international competition was held for the design of the building and 245 entries were received. After the Committee had examined the entries they announced that none was acceptable and they would design the building themselves. The design produced by this high-powered committee was a monstrous hybrid surmounted by a 62m (200 feet) diameter, 46m (150 feet) high dome designed by Brunel. When the scheme was presented to the public there was an outcry that put the whole idea of the Great Exhibition in jeopardy.

Fig. 11.12 The exhibition building designed by the Committee

The project was rescued by the remarkable Joseph Paxton (1801-1855). Lacking even elementary education he had started as a gardener's boy on the estates of the Duke of Devonshire but by the time of the exhibition he was a wealthy man, the manager of all the Duke's estates and a railway company director. Visiting his friend John Ellis, in June 1850, he mentioned his doubts about the proposed exhibition building and noted he had some ideas of his own and was wondering if it was too late to submit a design. Ellis took Paxton to meet Cole. Paxton learned from Cole that the Committee would consider a proposal provided it could be submitted, with detailed drawings, within two weeks. Paxton replied that the drawings would be ready in nine days. Three days later, at a Midland Railway board meeting, he sketched his scheme for the building that was to be 569m (1848 feet) long by 138m (450 feet) wide. When his scheme was presented to the Committee they accepted it.

Fig. 11.13 Joseph Paxton's sketch scheme

The chosen contractors, Fox and Henderson, took possession of the site on 30th July 1850 and this enormous building was ready nine months later. Everything was designed on a grid with high repetition of parts.

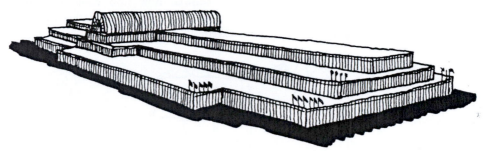

Fig. 11.14 The Crystal Palace in Hyde Park

The exhibition was thought to be a great success and the building a great achievement but it could have turned out rather differently. The frame, in spite of its enormous number of iron structural elements, was not sufficiently stiff against horizontal wind loads. Stiffness was not supplied by braced bays, see **Fig. 8.42**, but by the portal action of the joint between the columns and the trusses. This was criticised in 1850 by the Astronomer Royal George Airy (1801-1892).

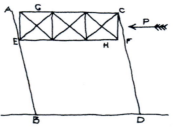

11.15 Airy's diagram for the Crystal Palace

Airy was right and when the building was dismantled and re-erected at Sydenham in South London it was stiffened but not sufficiently because part of it blew down, but rather surprisingly this did not come to the attention of the public.[18] The building stood until 30th November 1936 when it was totally destroyed by fire.

Fig. 11.16 The Sheerness Boat Store

A building constructed only nine years later, in the obscurity of Sheerness naval dockyard, in North Kent, took the idea of the skeletal iron frame forward. The Sheerness Boat Store,[19, 20] built in 1859 and still in use, has all the features of what would now be considered a modern building.. The external envelope was non-loadbearing, with strip glazing and cladding panels. This revolutionary building was designed by Colonel GT Green (1807-1896) who was neither a civil engineer nor an architect but a military engineer.

It is clear that the horizontal stability was provided by the bolted beam/column connections, these beams are called 'transverse bracing girders' on the original drawings. This modern skeletal structure showed how iron could provide a minimal primary structure that gave floors uninterrupted by loadbearing walls and external glazing patterns that were unrestricted.

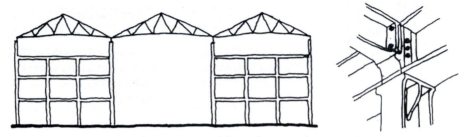

Fig. 11.17 Section and connection detail

Meanwhile in the rapidly industrialising United States of America a new building form was evolving – the skyscraper. The first skyscraper is usually considered to be the Home Insurance Company Building built in 1884-85, 11 storeys high; it was designed by William Le Baron Jenney (1832-1907). Jenney had studied in Paris, at the École Centrale des Arts et Manufactures, which trained *'ingénieurs civils'* or *'constructeurs'*. During the American Civil War he served as a military engineer. He practised as an **engineer-architect** in Chicago (1868-1905) and is regarded as the father of the Chicago School. These Chicago buildings had iron or steel frames with external elevations clad with a variety of materials, really much larger versions of the pioneering Sheerness Boat Store.

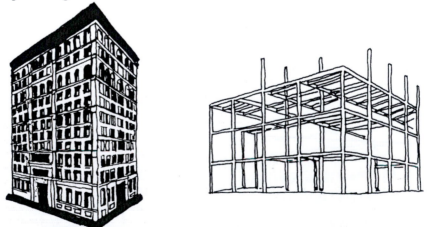

Fig. 11.18 Home Insurance Company Building and skyscraper construction

Towards the end of the 19th century, a 'new' structural material – reinforced concrete – appeared.[21] The idea of reinforcing concrete with metal was not new, but it was only in 1892 that the French engineer François Hennebique (1842-1921) patented a complete building system. This system had virtually all the features of reinforced concrete structures that are used today.

The early reinforced concrete structures were similar to the iron ones in that they were mainly skeletal; beams and columns supporting concrete slabs. The slabs were regarded as separate elements spanning from beam to beam. Reinforced concrete structures had an advantage over steel ones as they were fire-proof whereas structural steel needed some form of fire protection; also it was *"cheaper than anything available before"*. [22]

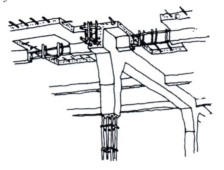

Fig. 11.19 The Hennebique reinforced concrete system

So in something like a hundred years, the idea of a separate steel or reinforced concrete primary structure became a reality. It had also brought into existence specialists in the design of these structures – the engineers – and this caused at least one architect to lament in 1907[23] that *"...where elaborate steelwork enters the architect's design he has to employ an engineer...there remains only one conclusion, that a joint production of this sort cannot be a complete success..."*.

11.3 Engineers, architects, decoration and theory

The traditional professions were medicine, law and theology but the process of industrialisation saw new groups emerging who also wanted their activities to be regarded as professions, amongst them were architects and engineers. Up to the end of the 18th century, architects, or surveyors as they were often called, were solely responsible for all aspects of building design.[24] They were strongly supported by master craftsmen who would often include the 'engineering design' of masonry and timberwork as part of their contract. The term 'engineer' was reserved for members of army engineering corps. Even then the line was not firmly drawn with many prominent architects undertaking engineering work and military engineers often being responsible for the design of buildings.

John Smeaton (1724-1792) was the first person in Britain to call himself a civil engineer, a term he used to distinguish himself from the military engineers. In 1771 he founded the Society of Civil Engineers and amongst the eleven founder members one, Robert Mylne, was an architect. The Society of Civil Engineers remained a learned society and over the years recruited military engineers and more architects. Gradually it became an elite dining club for senior canal builders so, on 2nd January 1818, eight younger men met and founded the Institution of Civil Engineers. After the election, in 1820, of the eminent engineer Thomas Telford as president, the new institution expanded rapidly due to his energy and organisational ability. In 1828, the institution was granted a charter which gave it a legal existence.

As other countries industrialised, institutions for engineers were founded. In the early stage of institutionalisation, architects and engineers often formed joint bodies: for instance in Switzerland the Société Suisse des Ingénieurs et des Architectes in 1837; in Austria the Osterreichischer Ingenieur und Architektenverein in 1848; and the American Society of Civil Engineers and Architects in 1852. But in general the institutionalisation process formed separate institutions for engineers and architects. In Britain, the Institute of British Architects was formed in 1834 from the Society of British Architects and received a royal charter in 1837.[25] In 1868 in the USA, the 'and Architects' was dropped to give the American Society of Civil Engineers, as the American Institute of Architects had been formed in 1857.

As time passed, the roles and duties of the two professions became mutually exclusive. For instance, in Britain in 1938 a government act reserved the use of the term 'architect' for those with the requisite qualifications. In some countries both architects and engineers have managed to get both these terms protected by law and frequently use Architect or Engineer as titles. Often technical submissions will not be accepted by the authorities unless they are signed by qualified architects and engineers – thus the division between architects and engineers is a legal requirement.

A basic reason for the division was the appearance of a mathematically based theory for the behaviour of loaded structures. At the beginning of the 19th century, the correct mathematical description of the behaviour of structures had been presented, principally by a number of brilliant French mathematicians and engineers. However this presentation, in the form of what are known as differential equations, did not actually provide engineers with 'answers' because the solution of the equations was another matter, nor could they be understood without special training. By the end of the 19th century, calculation procedures had been established for many common forms of skeletal structure. These were applied routinely by engineers to obtain numerical predictions that provided the required dimensional structural information. Learning these theoretically based calculation procedures became an increasing part of an engineer's training.

Not everyone was happy with this steadily increasing theoretical content. One of the founders of the École Centrale des Arts et Manufactures, Théodore Olivier (1793-1853), himself a *Polytechnicien*, heavily criticised the École Polytechnique[26] considering *"...that the sacred tradition of engineering education had been undermined by excessive devotion to pure theory...".* Over the years other engineers made similar criticisms, for example from 1952 *"...a new resource – structural theory has been added to the equipment of the structural engineer...But in acquiring that theory the engineer had temporarily or partially lost his sense of architecture and proportion",*[27] or in 1979 *"The danger in this arises when the designer's energy goes into the equations rather than the actual construction. The designer risks becoming a mere analyst...",*[28] and in 2003 *"At college students get a diet of theory, theory, theory".*[29]

This increasing interest in theory resulted in engineers gradually losing their aesthetic role. In 1844 Richard Turner, the engineer for the Palm House – see **Section 9.2** - added so much decoration to the structure that the architect Decimus Burton objected to *"…his use of a Gothic style and numerous ornamental details in fretwork, crockets etc"*.[30] Twenty years later a military engineer, Captain Fowke (1823-65)[31] was able to win an open architectural competition for a museum complex at South Kensington, which included a natural history museum and a museum to house the collection of the Commissioner of Patents.

Fig. 11.20 Captain Fowke's entry for the Museum Competition

But by 1884, when the French engineer Gustave Eiffel (1832-1923)[32] made his proposal for a 300m tower, an architect had to decorate it. The tower was initially the idea of engineers E Nouguier and M Koechlin (1856-1946), both of whom worked for the Eiffel Company, but *"Not long afterwards the two engineers asked the architect Sauvestre to give architectural form to their quick sketch, in short, to make the pylon a tower"*.[33] Amongst other things he added the arches to the base. These were decorative and did not form part of the basic structure.

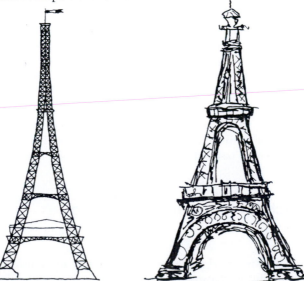

Fig. 11.21 The initial concepts of the engineer (left) and the architect (right)

During the design process the architect's decorated tower, which initially had been accepted, was altered *"…in particular the shape of the four huge arches of the base was changed…more clearly asserting the dominance of the engineer's art over that of the architect"*.[34]

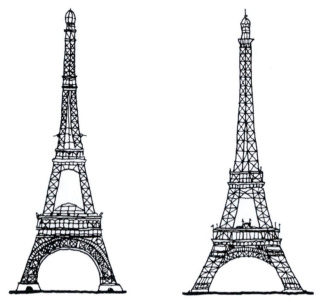

Fig. 11.22 The final design (left) and the built design (right)

By the end of the 20th century the loss of interest in the aesthetic aspects of design by engineers meant that architects were even designing bridges, *"When completed, the Millau viaduct, designed by British architect Norman Foster, will be the highest in the world…"*.[35]

With the technical aspects of structures, architects went in the opposite direction to engineers. As RMJ Sutherland wrote about beam design in the 19th century *"…it is hard to visualise the architects having either the time or the inclination to master it, let alone the necessary grasp to do the sums"*.[36] By 1986 architects often sought engineer's advice for a house *"Even here, most architects, myself included, will take the advice of a structural consultant for domestic problems"*.[37] And in 2003 a professor of architecture, Sarah Wigglesworth, stated that *"I am absolutely hopeless with structures. I know nothing about them at all"*.[38]

Thus it is often unclear who should have responsibility for the essential task of structural conception as neither architects nor engineers have made understanding the process of structural conception a priority. This cannot be an ideal arrangements and it has had and continues to have unfortunate consequences.

11.4 Architects embrace engineering

When the new structural materials appeared, steel and reinforced concrete, which provided specific load carrying systems rather than the ambiguous loadbearing systems of the Renaissance period, even renowned architect Norman Shaw

"…could not find a way of harnessing the revolutionary achievements of Victorian structural engineering to create a new architecture for his time".[39] But after the First World War, young architects appeared who thought they could – they came to be known as the Modern Movement. The principal groups were the Bauhaus[40] in Germany, De Stijl[41] in Holland, the Constructivists in Russia[42] and the Purists[43] in France. From these groups, trying to build a new society based on modern or revolutionary art and architecture, the Germans Ludwig Mies van der Rohe (1886-1969) and Walter Gropius (1883-1969), and the Swiss-French Charles-Édouard Jeanneret (1887-1965) who became better known as Le Corbusier, emerged as the founders. In 1928 a unifying organisation called the Congrès Internationaux de l'Architecture Moderne, usually denoted C.I.A.M, was formed.

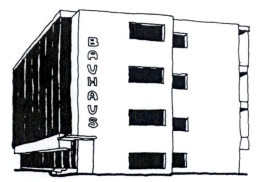

Fig. 11.23 Typical Modern Movement architecture

Perhaps the most influential was Le Corbusier. With the destruction of the First World War already in evidence, he felt a rationalised approach to housing, based on mass production principles, would be needed. To this end, in 1915, he produced a system he called Domino or Dom-ino. The drawing of this system, based on a simple reinforced structure, became a Modern Movement icon and Le Corbusier kept *"…a picture of it on his wall next to a photograph of the Parthenon: both central to his lifelong production"*.[44]

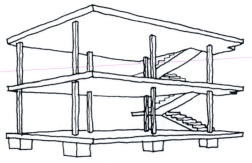

Fig. 11.24 The Dom-ino system

In 1917 he left Switzerland for Paris where he met Amédée Ozenfant. Son of a building contractor and reinforced concrete pioneer, Ozenfant was a painter and intellectual who ran a fashion shop – and he became the other Purist. They started an avant-garde magazine, L'Esprit Nouveau, and to increase the number of 'contributors' they frequently penned articles under pseudonyms, thus Jeanneret became Le Corbusier. In 1923 the book *"Vers une architecture"*[45] was published, which was based on a number of articles written by Ozenfant and Jeanneret under the joint pseudonym Le Corbusier-Saugnier.

The book, with the incorrect English title *"Towards a new architecture"*, is considered one of if not the most important document of the Modern Movement and is essential reading. It attacks recent architecture and holds up the work of engineers as things of beauty from which architects should take inspiration. The opening paragraph reads: *"The Engineer's Æsthetic, and Architecture, are two things that march together and follow one from the other: the one being now at its full height, the other in an unhappy state of regression"*. But for Kenneth Frampton *"While 'Vers une architecture' fails to sustain a tight, consequential argument, its importance as an overall primer in Purist aesthetic theory resides in the fact that here for the first time the fundamental split between engineering and architecture is set forth in dialectical terms".*[46]

Fig. 11.25 Typical illustration from Vers une architecture

In 1926 Le Corbusier published his *"Five Points of a New Architecture"*,[47] which were:

1   **pilotis** – columns that lift the building clear of the ground
2   **plan libre** – interior planning free from loadbearing walls
3   **facade libre** – exterior cladding freed from loadbearing functions
4   **fenêtre en longeur** – the horizontal strip window
5   **toît jardin** – the roof garden gaining land lost under the building

These could only be made possible by the use of a structural frame rather than any form of traditional loadbearing walls with the usual timber floor and roof structures. In this way the 'New Architecture' demanded an engineer's structure rather than that of the craftsman. Le Corbusier also wanted every part of his architecture to be based on an engineering aesthetic so, where possible, mass-produced windows, radiators and other items would be used, but frequently these had to be handmade to look mass-produced.

In spite of Le Corbusier's dedication to technology, many his projects failed technically, including the Cité de Refuge and the Pavillon Suisse, both in Paris. For these Le Corbusier and his cousin and partner Pierre Jeanneret roughly followed the five points. The **facade libre** became fully glazed on some elevations. When the proposals for the Pavillon Suisse were presented to the client M. Jungo he considered that the structure was inadequate and sought a second opinion from Dr. Ritter of Zurich Polytechnic. He was shocked by the **pilotis** and considered the scheme to be *"quite useless in its present form".*[48] After construction, environmental problems appeared in both buildings, the glazed facades turning some of the interiors into unusable ovens – the greenhouse effect which had been known for years. Remedial work had to be carried out on both buildings, but Le Corbusier considered them successful with any problems due to the buildings not being run properly.

Fig. 11.26 Pavillon Suisse 1931

The buildings of Mies van der Rohe and Walter Gropius also used the structure aesthetically in perhaps a more obvious way than Le Corbusier, especially with steel structures. But *"Architects like Mies van der Rohe believed they were akin to engineers, designing rational structures…but it was no more the product of objective scientific method than any other architecture"*.[49]

Fig. 11.27 Crown Hall at IIT by Mies van der Rohe

Often, as at the Crown Hall, the primary structure was placed outside the building to **express the structure**. Apart from being the worst position for the structure from the point of view of the waterproofing, it could introduce stability problems. The main horizontal beams of the Crown Hall have unrestrained upper flanges, see **Figs. 6.64** and **65** and **Section 7.6**, which means extra material is used to provide stiffness for this secondary effect. When it was impractical to 'express' the primary structure, a decorative 'expressed structure' would be placed on the outside of the building.

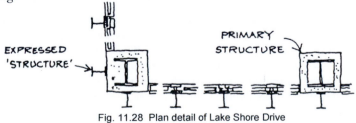

Fig. 11.28 Plan detail of Lake Shore Drive

The work of the Modern Movement, from the point of view of technology and the use of structure, reveals a puzzling situation. For instance Le Corbusier, who had taken private lessons in maths and engineering, states clearly that engineering solutions hold the key to modern architecture but he did not always apply them successfully. Frequently he tried to introduce technical innovations which were not always effective.

He wanted to be a reinforced concrete expert but seemed to have an inadequate conceptual grasp of structural behaviour, or, in fact, environmental control or building technology. Hence he left a number of buildings with technical problems that others had to try to resolve. In spite of his desire to incorporate modern technology into architecture, he still saw architecture and engineering as quite separate thought processes and in 1942 he produced a diagram showing this.

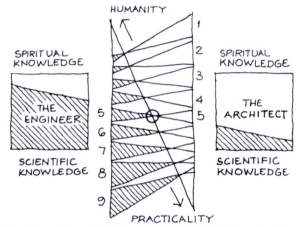

Fig. 11.29 An interpretation of Le Corbusier's view of the Engineer-Architect relationship

A basic idea of the Modern Movement was to introduce modern technology and materials into buildings to provide better environments and more durable buildings built faster and at a lower cost. Admirable aims but rarely achieved in the hands of Modern Movement architects because *"They were for allowing technology to run its course, and believed they knew where it was going, even without having bothered to acquaint themselves with it very closely".*[50] In other words the Modern Movement's real concern with technology was the visual aspects of a machine aesthetic rather than its technical functionality.

11.5 Engineering as fantasy

As has been stated several times, a built form cannot exist without a structure. The structure will influence the built form explicitly either in a demonstrative or a non-demonstrative way. Le Corbusier's houses were explicitly dependent for their built form on a structure of reinforced concrete but, perhaps with the exception of the 'pilotis' the structures were non-demonstrative whereas for the built form of the Eiffel Tower the structure is defining. In each case the structure has to fulfil its load-carrying function. But if a design is drawn with no intention of building it, then any structure the design implies does not have to fulfil this function and so can be a structural fantasy.

In 1784 the influential French architect Étienne-Louis Boullée (1728-1799)[51] made a design for a Cenotaph for Isaac Newton that was to be an empty sphere of 150m diameter, more than three times bigger than the largest existing dome, St. Peter's with a diameter of 43m. The section, see **Fig. 11.30**, is similar to St. Peter's double dome, see **Fig. 11.2**, and shows a thickness of 7.5m as opposed to St. Peter's 3m. Boullée has been criticised as a megalomaniac because of his grandiose proposals but apparently *"…these should be seen as visionary schemes rather than practical projects"*.[52] Some 150 years later, Albert Speer (1905-1981) Hitler's chief architect, projected a 300m diameter dome as part of his plan to re-build Berlin.[53] In fact it was to be built as the eighth wonder of the world and an engineering scheme existed.

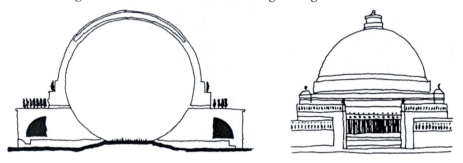

Fig. 11.30 Fantastic domes by Boullée and Speer

The designs of Futurist Antonio Sant'Elia (1888-1916)[54] and Constructivist Vladimir Tatlin (1885-1953)[55] are also scarce in structural detail. Both produced powerful images of built forms that are endlessly reproduced in architectural books, Sant'Elia in 1914 with his New City and Tatlin in 1920 with his tower for the Third International.

Fig. 11.31 Futurist and Constructivist fantasies

The New City is based on engineering imagery but not even plans exist and *"…even for him it was a dream and not a practical reality"*.[56] Tatlin whose tower was to be 400m high, that is 100m higher than the then tallest structure in the world, the Eiffel Tower, is an optimistic jumble of structural elements. Apparently Tatlin thought it was a practical project but *"…the tower was the conception of a sculptor rather than an engineer"*.[57] Sant'Elia was killed in the First World War but Tatlin went on to try to build a human-powered flying machine based on his studies of geese; needless to say it never flew.

The American Buckminster Fuller (1895-1983) had little time for architects in general *"Architecture is voodoo. The architects don't initiate anything"* [58] and Modern Movement architects in particular.

Fig. 11.32 Fuller's design for a 100 storey office block suspended from spokes of a wheel

He variously described himself as machinist, sailor, engineer, astronaut or 'trim tab' but was in effect an inventor who had several patents to his name. During 1927 due to business and family traumas he remained silent, his 'year of silence', during which he used 'four-dimensional thinking'. He summarised these thoughts in a privately published and distributed essay called 4D,[59] which few of the recipients understood. The impenetrable prose was interspersed with drawings of fantastic buildings.

Later in his life Fuller returned to mega-structures which included 3km diameter domes over cities and 1.7km diameter 'cloud structures' that would float around the world like hot air balloons each housing thousands of people. In between time he came up with numerous smaller scale technical ideas some of which worked and some that did not. Lacking technical training he seemed unable to subject his ideas to cold rational analysis.

In the 1960s, partly influenced by Fuller, a group of young mainly British architects, who became known as Archigram, produced a number of images of futuristic cities. Their work was based on Pop Art imagery and comic book science fiction and included the 'Walking City' and the 'Plug-in-City'. The *"Plug-in-City did not solve any immediate problems, nor was it intended to be built. Rather it explored and expressed ideas, beliefs…"*.[60] But for architect and detractor Denise Scott-Brown, their work was just another iconographic use of real engineering *"…or the oil-derricks, pumps and cranes of San Pedro harbour…".*[61] Nevertheless most members of Archigram subsequently pursued careers as teachers of architecture rather than the designers of built projects.

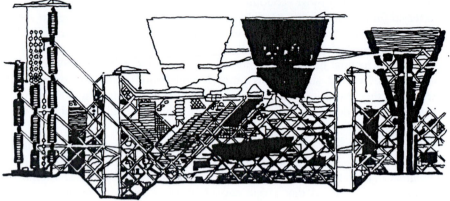

Fig. 11.33 The Plug-in-City from 1964

Not all fantasies have to be on a mega scale, a British firm called Future Systems spent years producing images based stylistically on aerospace technology. In an article written in 1983 called 'Skin', architects David Nixon and Jan Kaplicky, in the midst of photos of aeroplanes and their own drawings complained that *"One of the problems of designing innovative structures is the reluctance of many structural engineers to get involved: …it just means we have to get a different type of engineer".*[62]

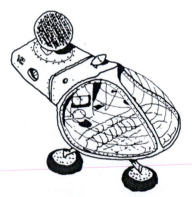

Fig. 11.34 Future Systems' 45° House

It was only in 1999 that Future Systems managed to use an 'aero-type' stressed skin structure for a building; this was for Lords Media Centre.[63] The whole structure is made of aluminium and had to be fabricated by boat builders. The main reason for the stressed skin being used was intellectual rather than structural.

It is interesting to note that all these projects were drawn to explore or express ideas, but what ideas one might ask. If these ideas were about actually building anything then why the avoidance of any credible engineering content? But in spite of their inapplicability to real buildings these projects had an enduring impact on architects whilst being totally ignored by engineers.

11.6 Engineered curved structures

The engineering skeletal frame of steel or reinforced concrete functions best if the individual elements are straight. Straight elements are also easier to construct and consequently are the most economical. Overall rectangular arrangements are also preferred for similar reasons, roof slopes being obtained by using triangular shaped trusses. Whilst curved shapes, both for single elements and overall geometry, could be used there are few strictly functional advantages. But as was seen with the dome, the structural behaviour of curved structures is not straightforward. If the behaviour of curved structures is properly understood then, for some specific structures, they can have some engineering advantages. During the 20th century, a few engineering designers did understand this behaviour and were able to use it advantageously.

Concrete, in its initial wet state, can take almost any geometric form, all that is needed is the necessary shaped formwork. In the 1920s German engineer Franz Dischinger (1887-1953), who worked for the German contractors Dyckerhoff & Widmann A.G, realised that a thin curved concrete structure, in other words a shell, could be both strong and cheap. Working with Zeiss engineer Walter Bauersfeld (1879-1959) they designed and built a thin hemispherical shell in Munich. They took out a patent for their system called Zeiss-Dywidag and also formulated a mathematical theory for domical shells. Joined by the mathematically gifted Ulrich Finsterwälder (1897-1987)[64] in 1922, he extended the theory to shells of other shapes. This enabled their company to build, between 1925 and 1962, an amazing 3,101,537sq.m of shell roofs.[65] It is important to note that these roofs were built to enable contracts to be won on a cost basis.

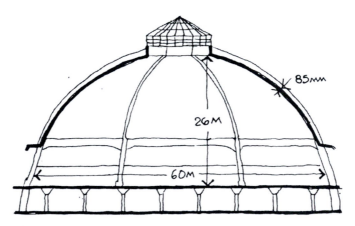

Fig. 11.35 The roof of the market at Basel built in 1932 by Dischinger & Finsterwalder

Although their shells were thin, the 'thinness' could not be seen. But with the Cement Hall, designed by Robert Maillart and built in 1939 for an exhibition in Zurich, the 'thinness' of shells could be seen. The work of the engineers Dischinger and Finsterwälder did not have any significant impact on architecture but Maillart's shell did, probably because the visual thinness of shells gave another opportunity to express the structure. Maillart built no more shells and the Cement Hall was demolished after the exhibition.

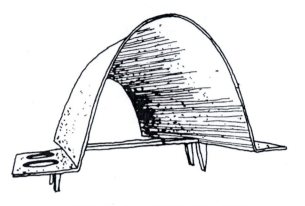

Fig. 11.36 The Cement Hall by Robert Maillart

Architectural interest in shell structures was rekindled in the 1950s when the work of Félix Candela (1910-1997)[66] began to be published widely in the architectural press. Candela caused excitement in both architectural and engineering circles not only for the range of shell roofs he had built, but also for the imaginative forms he created. In 1936 he had been awarded a travelling scholarship and hoped to go to Germany to work with the shell specialists Finsterwälder and Dischinger. Almost on the day of his planned departure, the Spanish Civil War started. An enthusiastic republican he fought on the losing side and, choosing exile rather than oppression, landed in Mexico in 1939 with little more than the clothes he stood up in. After ten years of various work, mostly related with construction, in 1950 he formed a company with his friend Fernando Fernandez called Cubiertas Ala, SA. The company was to specialise in industrial buildings, but first they built an experimental shell roof in the patio of the factory owned by Fernandez's father.

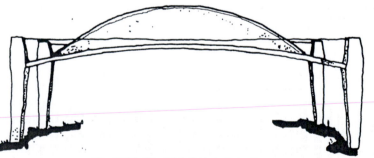

Fig. 11.37 Candela's first shell structure

Thus began the career of one of the greatest shell builders of the 20th century. Over the next twenty years Candela built a huge number of shell roofs. Working with other architects and engineers Candela would be responsible for the form and calculations of the shell roofs. The vast majority of his shells were based on the shape of the hyperbolic paraboloid or hypar for short. This is the name given to a geometric surface that can be generated by straight lines. If a square grid is drawn on a plane, with each grid intersection point being given coordinates, then the surface is defined by its distance from the plane at each point. In the case of the hypar, the vertical distance from the plane equals the product of the coordinates.

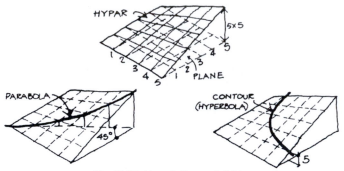

Fig. 11.38 Hyperbolic paraboloid geometry

Lines drawn on the surface of the hyperbolic paraboloid that are not directly above the basic gridlines will not be straight but curved. Two special curves may be drawn, parabolas and hyperbolas, which give the surface its name. If lines are drawn at 45° to the grid on the plane, the lines on the surface that are vertically above are parabolas. Lines on the surface that join points of equal height – contours – are horizontal hyperbolas.

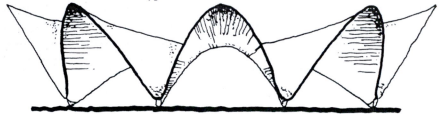

Fig. 11.39 The shell roof of Xochimilco restaurant

As this form can be generated from straight lines, concrete formwork can be erected economically or at least could be in Mexico at that time. Candela, often working on quite moderate projects, was able to produce an almost endless variety of beautiful and elegant shell roofs. These were often based on hypars; tilted, cut on the parabolas or hyperbolas or many joined together. The roof over the Xochimilco restaurant, built in 1957, is perhaps one of the most beautiful shell roofs ever built – now severely compromised by banal 'extensions'.

Candela was an architect, but in designing and building his shells he acted as an engineer-contractor. His company would build these shell roofs often on the basis of lowest cost solution. Whilst his shells were admired by architects, engineers were sometimes less happy. In 1954, Candela wrote an article entitled *"stereo-structures"*,[67] in which he outlined his conceptual understanding of structures, and in the same year presented two papers at the Massachusetts Institute of Technology. Both the article and his papers were strongly attacked by eminent engineers[68] who accused him of making conceptual and mathematical errors, to which Candela replied.[69] He could of course point to his dozens of shells and say *"there they are and they seem to work".*[70] It was not that Candela had no knowledge of the mathematical analysis of shell structures, but he thought that this analysis could be simplified by using his conceptual understanding. His shells stood, but this does not show that he or his critics were right, because many factors can make the behaviour of a real structure significantly different to that of an idealised one. By the end of the 1960s, Candela stopped building shells and, in 1971, emigrated to the United States where he taught in various universities.

Curved structures in the form of framed domes also appeared due to the invention, by Buckminster Fuller, of the geodesic dome. After various failures both technical and financial, and success with the Dymaxion Deployment Unit during the Second World War, in 1948 he was invited to tutor at a Summer School at Black Mountain College. Here he got students to build a 15m diameter geodesic dome from Venetian blinds slats – it collapsed. In spite of this failure the following year he was invited to direct the Summer School.

But what is a geodesic dome? A geodesic is the shortest line joining two points on a surface. If the curved surface is spherical then all these curves are the same – that is, circles of the same diameter as the sphere.

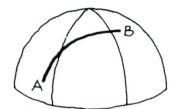

Fig. 11.40 Geodesic line joining points A and B

The idea of the geodesic dome was to create a geometry on the surface of the sphere whose nodes would be joined by geodesic lines. Fuller did this by using an icosahedron. It was known before Plato that there were only five regular solids; the tetrahedron, the cube, the octahedron, the dodecahedron and the icosahedron which has twenty faces of equilateral triangles. These solids can be put 'inside' a sphere so that their vertices touch the surface. If the faces are then 'pushed' out to the surface, the sphere is divided into regular curved regions.

Each face of an icosahedron can be subdivided with more equilateral triangles which generate more geodesic lines; the number of subdivisions is called the frequency. With this subdivision there are pentagons around the primary nodes and hexagons between them, this derived form is called a truncated icosahedron and is often used for footballs.[*] Fuller's patent application showed a dome based on an icosahedron divided with a frequency of 16.

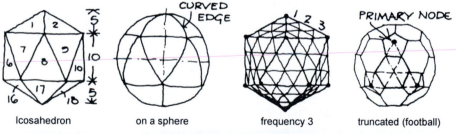

| Icosahedron | on a sphere | frequency 3 | truncated (football) |

Fig. 11.41 Geodesic dome geometry

Thousands of geodesic domes have been built, mainly by the US military, who use them for easily transported temporary accommodation and radar domes. They have also been used for many other purposes, from houses and garden greenhouses to the US pavilion for the 1967 EXPO at Montreal.

---

[*] This geometry becomes clearer if a simple model is made of a 3-frequency icosahedron

Fig. 11.42 Gardener with a geodesic greenhouse

However, it must be stressed that the geodesic dome is, in all its various configurations, just a structure transferring loads. It has no special structural qualities, its advantages being purely geometrical. The groups of members and connectors have the same geometry, but the forces in the members vary with their position in the structure so the cross-sections cannot, for economy's sake, all be equal. As the members cannot be continuous, every joint has to be designed to transmit the full force.

The geodesic dome was the beginning of Buckminster Fuller attaining *"...almost legendary status amongst architects and architectural students all over the world".*[71] Whilst Fuller's approach was in some ways similar to that of an engineer, he never attained any special status amongst engineers probably due to his penchant for incomprehensible statements like *"There are many ways of rendering geodesic structures, but all represent closed systems in which compression is comprehensively encompassed by tension. In principle, this emulates the structuring of the universe."*[72]

Occasionally, engineers would use curved forms based on the successful example of the suspension bridge, that is a hanging roof.

Fig. 11.43 Hanging roof by Schnirch, 1824

The pioneer for these roofs was B. Schnirch (1791-1868)[73] working in Moravia in the early part of the 19th century. In 1824 he proposed a hanging roof for a theatre in Strážnice. In 1896 the Russian engineer V.G. Shuckov (1853-1939)[74] designed and built three pavilions with hanging roofs at Nižnii Novgorod.

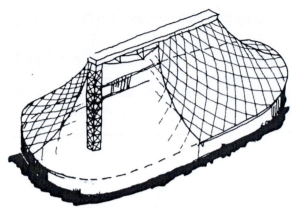

Fig. 11.44 Shuckov's pavilion at Nižnii Novgorod 1896

In 1961 the contractors Shimizu won a design and build contract for a swimming stadium to be built in Tokyo for the Olympic Games. The structure, designed by the engineers Y. Tsuboi (1907-1990) and M. Kawaguchi (b.1932), was, with a span of 126m, the longest spanning hanging roof built at the time.[75]

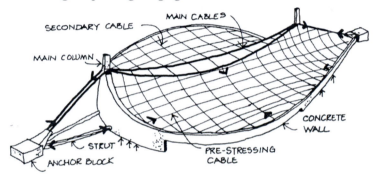

Fig. 11.45 Tokyo Olympic swimming stadium structural system

Considered by many to be one of the outstanding buildings of the 20th century, the stadium combines a brilliantly clear structural form with an architectural statement of great beauty. This combination on this scale is almost unknown and so it seems a pity that the architect involved, K Tange (b.1913) had to claim the credit for the engineering *"What made me personally decide on this structural method was the possibility I saw in it of creating an open form"*.[76]

But hanging roofs were rarely used mainly due to their cost. Whilst a hanging cable is a very economic structural element in terms of material, it needs a horizontal reaction to function structurally, see **Fig. 7.67**, and the structure that provides this, often high above ground level, is not usually cheap.

In looking at these structures that created curved built forms, it should be noted that:

- **They were used to give value for money**
- **They provide sensible and direct load paths**
- **Methods of calculation were available before conception**

These are the fundamentals of the engineering approach to built form.

11.7 Engineering fantasy becomes reality

After the Second World War Le Corbusier started to depart from his five principles and his projects took many different forms. From a structural point of view one of the oddest was the Phillips Pavilion for the 1958 Brussels World Fair.[77] Phillips, the Dutch electrical and electronics firm, contacted Le Corbusier in 1956 and he replied *"I will not make a pavilion for you but an Electronic Poem…".*[78] It is arguable that the project was not really designed by Le Corbusier but by Iannis Xenakis,[79] a Greek engineer who had been working for Le Corbusier for ten years, now better known as an composer of avant-garde electronic music.

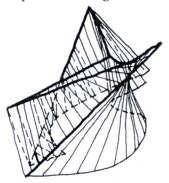

Fig. 11.46 Perspective of an early model of the Phillips Pavilion

After various ideas for the form of the pavilion had been examined, the shape evolved into a number of interlinked hyperbolic paraboloids, see **Fig. 11.38**. With the geometry defined, a method of construction was needed. The initial idea was that the intersection lines between the curved surfaces would be made as a structural steel frame with some extra vertical supports. The curved surfaces would be made from a flexible sheet material supported on a network of cables. There were only two problems with this approach, first the engineers decided that they could not calculate the forces in the frame and second it was 'discovered' that the level of sound insulation required a thickness of at least 5cm of concrete. So the curved surfaces had to become some type of shell.

Formwork for a hypar can be made by using narrow flexible pieces of wood laid along the straight lines, each piece being slightly twisted. But casting concrete at an angle steeper than about 40° needs formwork for **both** surfaces, which for a hypar is difficult.

The design and the designers were saved by Hoyte Duyster, a Dutch engineer with the contractor Strabed, who had a rare combination of imagination, practicality and theoretical ability. Working with engineers at Delft University, led by Professor Vreedenburgh, he undertook the final design. His solution was to form the shells from pre-cast concrete elements fitted between pre-stressing cables which followed the straight generators of the hypars. When everything was in place the elements and cables would be made into a shell by concreting the joints. As such a structure could not be calculated, structural load tests were carried out at Delft University. To make the elements, each diamond having a slightly different curvature, the hypar shapes were made in sand and the elements cast on top.

Fig. 11.47 Load test and element production

The structural tests showed that the structure did not need the vertical columns, so these were omitted. The structure needed a forest of scaffolding to support all the individual elements until they could be concreted together.

Fig. 11.48 The scaffolding and the completed Phillips Pavilion

Opinions about the structure are divided. A Professor of Architectural Theory writes *"The solution was not only very efficient; from the point of view of structure, it was also conducive to simplifying the process of physical construction"*[80] whereas a Professor of Engineering writes *"The Le Corbusier building, small as it is, could not be understood as a structure. The reason is simple; the building is more a work of sculpture. Le Corbusier's form did not spring from structural imagination, and even some of the finest thin shell engineers in the world could not clearly explain its behaviour"*.[81]

An international architectural competition was held in 1956 for the design of a centre for the performing arts to be built in Sydney in Australia. This new centre, which became known as Sydney Opera House, was to give the popular Sydney Symphony Orchestra a new home. Sydney Opera House is now so famous that it is difficult to think of Sydney without it, rather like Paris without the Eiffel Tower. The winning project, chosen by a panel made up of four architects, was the one submitted by Jørn Utzon (b.1918).

Fig. 11.49 Sydney Opera House – Utzon's competition entry

The design and building of the Sydney Opera House was far from a simple matter and has been told many times from various points of view. [82-86] The immediate problem was to give the client some assurance on the technical aspects of the design and in particular the dramatic roof structure. Utzon had conceived these roofs, *"apparently unaided by structural engineering advice"*.[87] But on arriving in Sydney shortly after winning the competition he was able to announce that *"The roof of the opera house will be made of concrete a few inches* thick.….This is a very economical method of construction"*.[88] He had a clear idea of how they should look saying *"I wanted to see a smooth concave surface, like the inside of an egg shell"*.[89]

Fig. 11.50   Model of Utzon's competition scheme showing thin shells

To provide the client with his scheme worked up in more detail Utzon, who had already been contacted by Ove Arup (1895-1988), recommended that Ove Arup & Partners be appointed to act as structural engineering consultants. Ove Arup was already known in architectural circles for having a 'design' rather than a 'calculation' approach to structures in buildings and his senior partner, the brilliant engineer Ronald Jenkins (1907-1975), had been responsible for a number of concrete shell roofs. But when the more detailed scheme, that came to be known as the Red Book, was presented to the client in March 1958, all the structural engineers could do was to comment that *"The superstructure of the Opera House consists partly of a series of large shells. The structural design of the latter is obviously quite a problem and has only just been touched on...".*[90]

The major problem was not the roof, though with almost any other project it would have been, but Utzon's attempts to reconcile the irreconcilable – to design a concert hall that was also an opera house. This ultimately led to his resignation in 1966 under circumstances that will always have different interpretations. The scale of the difficulties that the project designers and constructors had to overcome is measured by the facts. The project took 16 years to design and build (1957 to 1973), the final cost was $A102,000,000 whilst the original budget, set artificially low for political reasons, was just under $A10,000,000, and the structural engineers worked for an estimated 375,000 man hours on the engineering design – equivalent to one man working for nearly 200 years. But the interest here is not the whole project,. but the roof.

The shells proposed by Utzon did not comply with any of the basic requirements of a shell roof. Think of a child's balloon or a bird's egg, they are smooth and burst or break when loaded with point loads. These shells were not smooth nor did they have mathematically defined shapes, making calculations impossible. They were supported at points and were subjected to concentrated loads from the acoustic

---

* I inch = 2.54 cm.

ceiling units and ultimately, the heavy tiling units. All this was quickly recognised by the engineers who noted that *"...Utzon's intuitive technical assessment turned out to be erroneous. He had visualized the roof as thin shells..."*.[91] The first scheme prepared by the engineers used geometry based on the parabola and with the shells replaced by ribbed structures stabilised longitudinally by 'louvre' walls. These were required as some of the 'shells' in Utzon's scheme were unstable as rigid bodies in the longitudinal direction.

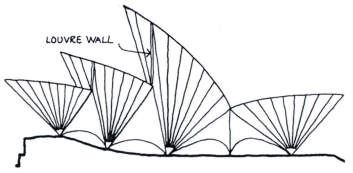

LOUVRE WALL

Fig. 11.51 The first engineering solution – scheme B

To provide Utzon with his *smooth concave surface, like the inside of an egg shell*, Jenkins, certainly one of the best shell engineers in the world at the time, tried to find a 'shell-like' solution. This was not a shell as such but a double shell with an internal steel structure. See **Fig. 9.68** for a comparison.

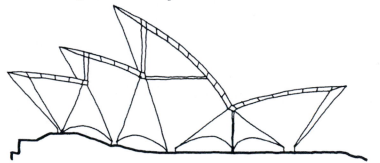

Fig. 11.52 'Shell like' engineering solution – scheme C

The analysis of this structure required Jenkins and his talented team to work at the limit of what was possible; the 'usual' problem of getting answers from complex theory. When Utzon had time to examine the result of this work he decided he did not like it as he *"...considered the steel skeleton to be structurally dishonest"*.[92] The idea of 'structural honesty', a Modern Movement edict, makes no sense to anyone who has a conceptual understanding of structural behaviour. With the rejection of the 'architect required shell-like' scheme Jenkins understandably lost interest and his chief and very able assistant H Møllmann, ironically also Danish, was so incensed that he resigned and went back to Denmark.

Amazingly Ove Arup supported the architect's decision so a new team was formed under J Zunz. This team, which saw the project to completion, initially continued to refine Jenkins' scheme whilst also developing a ribbed scheme.

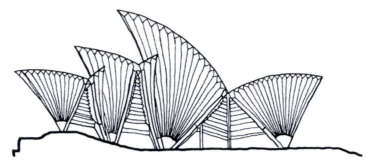

Fig. 11.53 The final engineering solution – scheme M

The final scheme was based on the geometry of a sphere and used a ribbed structure that was made of pre-cast elements stressed together after erection, and was suitably honest. This structure was so heavy that the supporting structure, which had already been built, had to be strengthened.

In terms of dimensions, there was nothing spectacular about the span or the height of the roof of Sydney Opera House. In **Fig. 11.54**, the maximum cross-section dimensions are compared with the roofs of St. Pancras railway terminus in London, built in 1868, and the CNIT exhibition hall, built in 1958 and described in **Section 9.4**.

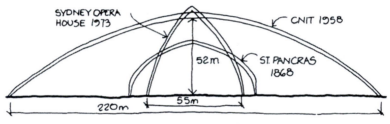

Fig. 11.54 Span comparisons

Clearly such competent engineers as Ove Arup & Partners would not require six years of work or twelve different schemes for a roof of these dimensions. But the leaders of the engineering design were convinced that this effort was justified on architectural grounds, which seems questionable, and it could never be justified on any others. Ove Arup put the whole process succinctly and rather poetically "*You may say…you should have brought Utzon down to earth. I could answer: not while there was a chance of his pulling us up to heaven*".[93]

Needless to say subsequent opinions about the roof of Sydney Opera House are divided. For architects it is technological poetry "*…Utzon demonstrated how technology can transcend itself and blossom into works of art. What is "clearer" and at the same time more poetical than the Sydney shells*"[94] but for engineers it is a technical disaster "*…many of the most prominent thin shell concrete structures designed during the 1950's by architects generally were not thin, far overran their cost estimates and often performed badly…*",[95] and even Candela remarked that "*…the Sydney Opera House is a tragic example of the catastrophic consequence of this attitude of disdain for the most obvious laws of physics*".[96]

In 1971 an open competition was held for a new centre for the visual arts to be built on the Plateau Beaubourg in Paris. The winners were the unknown architects

Renzo Piano, Richard Rogers and Gian Franco Franchini.[*] The winning submission showed a strong Archigram influence, see **Fig. 11.33**, and incorporated structural features such as a steel structure partly fireproofed by the internal circulation of cooling water, floors that would move up and down and a floor structure of only 1.6m depth spanning nearly 50m.

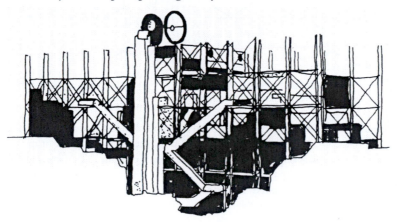

Fig. 11.55 The competition entry

The structure of the winning scheme also had another rather surprising feature in that it was a mechanism under horizontal loads, see **Fig. 6.23**, in other words the building would have fallen down.

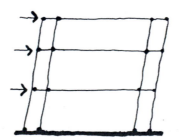

Fig. 11.56 Sway mechanism of the competition entry

All this might just have been understandable if it were not for the fact that the entry was prepared under the guidance of two engineers, Ted Happold (1930-1996) and Peter Rice (1935-1992). As the winning design was to be built, all these questions had to be addressed. In a paper written about the structure the engineers, whose concept it was, noted that it would not work *"Either solution had serious disadvantages, either by increasing an already excessive span or by seriously complicating problems of connections...".*[97] The solutions referred to were either joining the trusses with moment connections, which would have reduced the mid-span moment but generated high forces in the connecting pieces, or the trusses could be simply supported mid-way between the two columns thus increasing the span. Neither solution was practical. In the same paper it was also noted that *"the design of the*

---

[*] The inclusion of Franchini was apparently an administrative error.

structure was of the greatest importance from the architectural standpoint"[98] which makes it all the more incredible that the scheme design engineers, calling the initial design *"merely a rough draft"*, [99] could have got it so wrong.

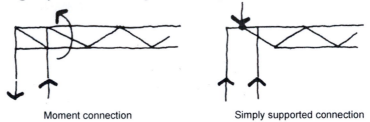

Moment connection   Simply supported connection

Fig. 11.57 Unsatisfactory truss connections

Both the ideas of the floors moving and the trusses being unprotected against fire had to be abandoned. This caused difficulties with the truss design as it now had to be wrapped in fireproofing and still appear slim and elegant. The external skin had to incorporate fire-proof panels which reduced the planned transparency. The steel work outside the skin needed a sprinkler system for fire protection; this was activated by sensors on the steelwork set to operate when the steelwork reached a preset temperature. The structure also had to be made stable under horizontal loads applied in either the longitudinal or the lateral direction.

The floor system and column arrangement were modified, the spacing between the 'columns' became 6m and the outer 'column' became a tie. The trusses were aligned with the columns, deepened to 2.3m, and supported on cantilever brackets that were called 'gerberettes'* which became emblematic of the structural brilliance of the project.

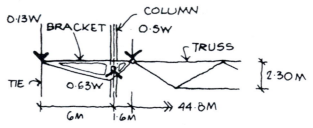

Fig. 11.58 Floor support details and forces

The matter of horizontal stability also had to be resolved. **Fig. 11.59** shows how stability was attained for horizontal forces applied in the longitudinal direction. The internal steel and concrete floor plate acted as a stiff diaphragm, but horizontal bracing had to be introduced in the external area to transmit the forces to the facades. The competition design showed facades completely braced in every bay by rod cross-bracing, this was retained. As **Section 8.4** explains, only one vertical braced bay is actually required for stability. At the time of building rod cross-bracing, the rods, only being able to resist tensile forces, had largely been superseded by a single diagonal that could resist both tensile and compressive forces as this was easier to build and cheaper.

---

* Named after the German engineer Heinrich Gerber (1832-1912).

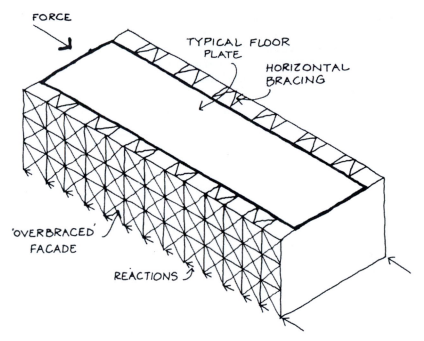

Fig. 11.59 Longitudinal stability

Even after the post-competition alterations had been made, the building was still a lateral mechanism. There was no possibility of making the lateral structures into moment-resisting frames whilst maintaining the architectural appearance, so the building had to be braced laterally as well as longitudinally.

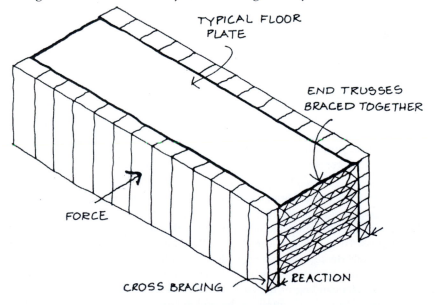

Fig. 11.60 Lateral stability

Again the steel and concrete floor plates acted as stiff diaphragms, this time spanning the whole length of the building. To make the end bays stiff, the standard truss arrangement was modified by linking them vertically with diagonal members. At the ground level, stability was achieved by introducing substantial cross-bracing in the two outer bays. As the 'standard' trusses in this bay are subjected to quite different forces, these trusses are not standard at all. The overall appearance of these end bays is not one of structural clarity.

Having made all these modifications to the competition design, the main columns were not braced sufficiently by the lateral structural system for the buckling length to be the distance between floors, which is the 'usual' situation. The buckled shapes for the main columns, the 'buckling length', was calculated to be nearly three times the floor to floor height. When the buckling length or 'effective length' increases there is always a consequent reduction in allowable stress, see **Fig. 12.46**. This means that the structural member will be less efficient in terms of material.

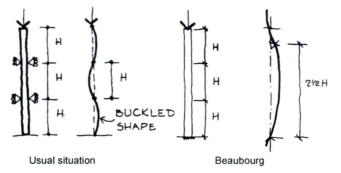

Usual situation   Beaubourg

Fig. 11.61 Buckling shapes of the main columns

The building was re-named the Pompidou Centre and is visited by more people than the Eiffel Tower. It is an example of what became known as High Tech[100] architecture: but when asked about High Tech, the eminent, and eminently sensible, engineer Frank Newby (1926-2001) put it bluntly *"I don't think high-tech has made any contribution to the development of structures at all...architects just started using structure as decoration..."*.[101] This comment could equally be applied to the other two projects described here. However, the designers, if not already famous as in the case of Le Corbusier, all went on to have illustrious careers.

It is hard to know what to make of this situation. In the 19th century, designers – whether architect or engineer, the distinction was only just being made – confronted new building forms and structural materials with commonsense and economy. Hence, previously unimaginable projects such as the Crystal Palace and the Eiffel Tower were designed and built in astonishingly short periods.

With the projects described here, all built in the second half of the 20th century; the opposite seems to have happened. None were a new type of building, an exhibition space, two concert halls or some art galleries and a library, but all involved enormous difficulty and effort both for the design and the construction – hardly progress. In the case of the Phillips Pavilion, the concept seemed to have been based purely on a geometric shape derived without any thought for the actual construction. The concept of Sydney Opera House was partially based on a complete misunderstanding of the structural behaviour of shells. The structure for the Pompidou Centre was central to the architectural concept and was prepared with constant engineering input yet the structure of the competition-winning scheme wasn't even stable.

11.8 Guggenheim, computers and beyond

In 1997 the Guggenheim Museum[102] opened in Bilbao, designed by architect Frank Gehry (b.1929). It has proved to be a great attraction for visitors from all over the world. It was conceived as a shape without mathematically defined geometry and no attempt was made to provide structural stability – the structural engineer's task was to make it stand up.

Fig. 11.62 Guggenheim Museum – Bilbao

The engineers noted that *"...the architectural themes of fractured and irregular building masses were explicitly at odds with the normal structural engineering precepts of stability, organisation and regularity...".*[103] So they had to bring structural order to chaos. Having chosen structural steel as the material, order was imposed by making horizontal and vertical lines of structure on a 3m by 3m 'grid'.

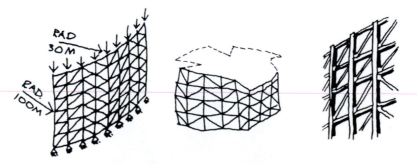

Fig. 11.63 Guggenheim Museum – Structural concept and detail

As can be seen, the structural concept is simple and sensible within the context of the randomly changing geometry. Sub-structures were shop fabricated and site bolted. The diagonals were tubes and not rod cross-bracing, as has been the economical practice for years, and the steelwork connections were 'engineering' rather than 'aesthetic', all this being possible because the structure was not visible.

The design and building of the Guggenheim could not have been easy but unlike those involved in the projects described in **Section 11.7,** the designers had a certain advantage which was computers. Computers, invented in the 1940s, were a commonplace tool by the end of the 20th century. In the case of the Guggenheim Museum it allowed the architect and engineer to function almost independently. The architect conceived the form of the building using three-dimensional models without any thought for the structural behaviour. The final shape was then digitalised using a computer program developed for aircraft geometry. Unlike the pre-computer age, when engineers needed mathematically defined shapes for structural analysis, modern structural analysis programs work on a coordinate basis. The engineers, having the geometric coordinates of the form, could, having decided on the sensible strategy shown in **Fig. 11.63**, construct their computer model.

Nowadays computer programs for structural analysis will accept enormous models that can have hundreds or even thousands of individual elements, each one being one, two or three dimensional, see **Section 3.1**. These programs can calculate the bending moments, axial and shear forces, stresses and the deflections for dozens of load cases that can be combined, again in dozens of ways. The output can be numerical or graphical and the graphical output can be coloured according to stress level. Without the benefit of computer analysis for the structure, the engineers, the Chicago office of Skidmore, Owings & Merrill, would have had a lot more problems. With the section sizes checked, the steelwork sub-contractor could prepare the fabrication drawings, which meant for this project drawing every single element.

This simplified story implies that now there is no especial need for anyone to know anything as the computer will take care of it. The architect can design a building of any old shape and the engineer loads it all, perhaps nearly automatically, into the analysis program. Naturally some data on loads, materials, and structural element sizes need to be added. The output of the computer 'lights up' hot spots, a few modifications are made, the program runs again and again until all the hot spots disappear. Working drawings are produced automatically which feed directly into machines for fabricating steelwork, bending reinforcement and cutting out formwork; all rather like a robot spot welding in a car plant. Of course it is not really like that. Computers don't always talk to each other in a friendly way and are not capable of spotting conceptual mistakes.

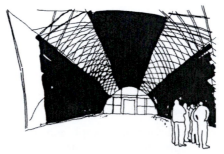

Fig. 11.64 The Downland gridshell

And even with the help of computers, unusually shaped buildings are not necessarily easy to build. The Downland Gridshell is a modest single-storey building with an incredibly complex structure made from green oak laths. A brief report [104] on the project includes *"…the slivers of timber that are the basic components of the roof…were laboriously cut into short sections…"* and *"It was repetitive and time consuming work requiring a tremendous amount of patience…"* and *"All the time the carpenters worked to printouts from the engineers…".*

Projects like this are often called innovative (which actually means something different, rather than better), but there is no useful innovation here; in the future modest single-storey work spaces will not have gridshell structures of green oak laths. However, it provides the engineers with a 'challenge' and shows that they are capable of producing 'exciting' and 'interesting' structures meanwhile giving the client a building that will be neither easy to alter nor to extend.

Nor did computers help directly with the design of a small building designed by Norman Foster, the Business Promotion Centre in Duisburg. Because the *"The complex geometry of the perimeter beam caused huge problems on site……After several ill-fated attempts and costly delays, Hoch Tief, one of Germany's leading contractors gave up…".*[105] And again with Nicholas Grimshaw's new building at Zurich airport which has a roof that is a 'croissant on stilts' which for the engineers*"…developing the croissant into a form to which numerical and engineerable properties could be applied was a huge challenge…".*[106]

It is interesting to see the use of the word **challenge** where **problem** would be more apt. This is part of a relatively new approach of engineers to architecture where they see themselves, if not exactly as servants, then as enablers, *"Helping architects achieve their dreams"*[107] as engineers Mark Whitby and Bryn Bird put it in 1988 or another engineer, Mario Salvadori (1907-1997)[108] *"I have had the good fortune to serve architects in the structural development of their dreams".* Whereas one would have thought that engineers should ensure that the client gets sensible and cost effective engineering.

When Gothic cathedrals were built they were built by master builders, later people like Brunelleschi and Wren and many others could also be regarded in the same way. They worked with no distinction between engineering and architecture, the **engineer-architects**. With the rise of professions, the engineer-architect became almost extinct, Francis Fowke and William Le Barron Jenney being rare examples in the 19th century. In the 20th century it was often considered impossible for one person to be able carry out both duties or rather see architecture and engineering as a single entity, but some did manage it – Owen Williams (1890-1969)[109] for example.

Fig. 11.65 Boots 'Wets' Factory 1930-32

In 1929, he was appointed **the engineer and the architect** for the new Dorchester Hotel to be built in the centre of London. His appointment was heralded by newspaper headlines such as *"Engineer instead of Architect"*.[110] Throughout the 1930s he worked on numerous projects as **engineer-architect**. These projects included houses, flats, office and industrial buildings. The best known are probably his factory designs for the pharmaceutical firm Boots.

In 1931 Williams wrote that *"I do not believe that an architect as an architect can collaborate with an engineer as an engineer"*[111] and Gavin Stamp wrote *"...Williams stands out and apart from Modern Movement architects in Britain for his lack of cant and for his sound, practical knowledge of building"*.[112] In fact he twice declined invitations from the MARS group, the British section of C.I.A.M, having scant respect for architects, and they repaid him by regarding him with a certain disdain. Commenting, in 1938, on the Boots factory the American critic Russell Hitchcock wrote *"his buildings remain ambivalent; brilliant seen from the point of view of the engineer, but tasteless and confusing in their architectural expression"*.[113] Williams' factory for Boots appears in many architectural histories but his later work does not; however, he continued working to the end of his life on both buildings and civil engineering projects, always as an engineer-architect. And more recently Santiago Calatrava (b.1951)[114] has become well known working as an engineer-architect.

Could the engineer-architect come back in some form to provide designs where the design concept automatically incorporates technical requirements without the intervention of specialists? Strangely computers could help this, especially with structures, but also with other engineering aspects. Before the introduction of user friendly programs for structural analysis in the early 1980s, engineers had to make hand calculations based on theory. This was onerous and difficult to apply to complex structures. When confronted with structures such as the Phillips Pavilion or Sydney Opera House even the best engineers had to carry out model tests in laboratories, an expensive and time-consuming process. Computer programs have changed this to a large extent and now someone who has a conceptual understanding can enter data into a computer and understand the output. This output can be checked against simple hand calculations that are explained in the next chapter.

It also means that architects could get involved more knowledgeably in the structural aspects of their work and would not expect that *"Our architecture comes out of our engineering and our engineering comes out of our engineers"*[115] as architect Michael Hopkins stated in 1985. Architects would no longer have to claim that they have an 'intuitive' understanding of structures – this is the *"perception of truth without reasoning or analysis"*[116] – the two things that allow the correct understanding of structural behaviour. After admitting she knew nothing about structures, see page **301**, Professor Sarah Wigglesworth stated her approach was *"totally, totally intuitive"*,[117] Dutch architect Dirk Jan Postel also thinks that *"it is much better if you have intuition about form and structure"*.[118] Jørn Utzon had an intuitive feeling for structure that cost the client dearly. This 'intuition' should be replaced by a conceptual understanding which is quite a different matter and which, even in the now traditional architect/engineer relationship, would save hundreds of hours currently wasted by talking at cross purposes. And it would also make statements by architects such as *"Architecture is only made possible through structure"*[119] or *"Structure should create the architecture"*[120] more credible.

By means of various examples this chapter shows how chosen structural systems affect any built form and how important it is that the choice is made on the basis of conceptual understanding. Without conceptual understanding it is not possible to make the numerically predictive calculations that save time and give confidence. Clear conceptual understanding has not always been available, so for example Wren could not approach his designs completely on this basis, with some consequent problems. When limited understanding became available in the 19th century, with skeletal structures, numerical calculation procedures emerged but this coincided, and was partly the cause of, the unfortunate split between engineers and architects.

This split has meant that the architectural profession has largely abandoned the idea of understanding structural behaviour in a mature way and has fallen back on an aesthetic approach based on 'intuitive' understanding. Hence conceptually flawed projects like the Phillips Pavilion, Sydney Opera House and Pompidou Centre are built, but with great difficulty due to their inherent conceptual misconceptions, in spite this they were lauded in the architectural press. Meanwhile engineers, who are constantly honing their calculating skills, now enormously empowered by computers, feel they should rise to the challenge of making these misconceptions work. This situation, which causes technical and financial problems with many projects, can only get better when everyone involved in the design process has a sufficient understanding of both technical and aesthetic aspects.

Perhaps instead of, as Berthold Lubetkin (1901-1990) put it *"...experiment for the sake of difference...endless, aimless pursuit of one stunning novelty leapfrogging over another..."*,[121] more attention should be paid to the edict of HD Thoreau (1817-1862) that *"The most interesting buildings are the most unpretending"* [122] whilst always bearing in mind FM Cornford's famous Principle of the Dangerous Precedent that states that *"Nothing should ever be done for the first time".*[123]

References – Chapter 11

The masonry dome and Christopher Wren

1   J Fitchen – **Building construction before mechanization** – MIT Press 1988 – ISBN 0-262-06102-3
2   J Heyman – **How to design a cathedral** – Proc. ICE 1992, 92, Feb – p 24-29
3   RJ Mainstone – **Engineering a cathedral** – The Structural Engineer/Vol 72/N°1/4 January 1994 p 13-14
4   CF Barnes Jr. – **Villard de Honnecourt** – Macmillan Dictionary of Art 1996 – Vol 32 – p 569-571
5   J Fergusson – **History of Indian & Eastern Architecture** – John Murray 1910 – Vol II p 273-277
6   Vitruvius – **The ten books on architecture** – Dover Books 1960 – ISBN 486-20645-9
7   E MacCurdy – **The notebooks of Leonardo da Vinci** – Jonathan Cape 1938 – p 430
8   A Tinniswood – **His invention so fertile: A life of Christopher Wren** – Pimlico 2002 – ISBN 0-7126-7364-4 – p 95
9   H Dorn & R Mark – **The architecture of Christopher Wren** – Scientific American July 1981 – p 138
10   J Heyman – **The science of structural engineering** – Imperial College Press 1999 – ISBN 1-86094-189-3 – p 41
11   SB Hamilton – **The place of Sir Christopher Wren in the history of structural engineering** –Transactions of the Newcomen Society XIV -1933-34 – p 27-42
12   ibid. p 39
13   CS Peach & WG Allen – **The preservation of St. Paul's Cathedral** – RIBA Journal XXXVII N° 18 – 9th August 1930 – p 668-9
14   see ref.9 p 137
15   RJ Mainstone – **Developments in structural form** – Architectural Press 2001 – ISBN 0-750-6545-11 – p 284

The arrival of the skeletal structure

16   P Beaver – **The Crystal Palace** – Hugh Evelyn Ltd. 1970
17   N Pevsner – **The sources of modern architecture and design** – Thames & Hudson 1968 – p 11
18   R Mallet – **The record of the international exhibition 1862** – The Practical Mechanic's Journal Special Edition 1862 – p 60

19   K Ackermann – **Building for Industry** – Watermark Publications 1991 – ISBN 1-873200-12-9 – p 24-26
20   AW Skempton – **The Boat Store, Sheerness and its place in structural history** – Transactions of the Newcomen Society Vol. XXXII – 1959-60 – p 57-78
21   JW de Courcy – **The emergence of reinforced concrete, 1750-1910** – The Structural Engineer Vol. 65A/N° 9/September 1987
22   see ref.19 – p 45
23   Martin S Briggs – **Iron, Steel & Modern Design** – Architectural Review Vol 21 1907 – p 226

Engineers, architects, decoration and theory

24   J Heyman – **Wren, Hooke & Partners** – Proc. First Int. Congress on Construction History – Madrid 2003
25   A Mace – **The RIBA Guide to its archive and history** – Mansell Publishing Ltd. 1986 – ISBN 0-7201-1773-9
26   JH Weiss – **The making of technological man** – MIT Press 1982 – ISBN 0-262-23112-3 – p 173
27   AW Skempton – Proc. ICE. Vol 1. Pt III, 1952 – p 405
28   DP Billington – **Robert Maillart's Bridges** – Princeton Univ. Press 1979 – p 47
29   C Wise in New Civil Engineer, 29 May 2003 – p 38
30   EJ Diestelkamp – **Richard Turner and the Palm House at Kew Gardens** – Transactions of the Newcomen Society 54, 1982 – p 4
31   see Chapter Five of – **Survey of London Vol XXXVIII – The Museums Area of South Kensington & Westminster** – Athlone Press 1975
32   H Loyette – **Gustave Eiffel** – Rizzoli International Publications Ltd. 1985 – ISBN 0-8478-0631-6
33   ibid. p 111
34   ibid. p 122
35   **THE WEEK** – 31 May 2003 – p 7
36   RMJ Sutherland – **The age of cast iron 1780-1850: Who sized the beams?** – Essay in **The Iron Revolution** – ed. Robert Thorne – p 28
37   HW Rosenthal – **The teaching of structure** – Building Design. 17th October 1986 – p14
38   O Popovic Larsen & A Tyas – **Conceptual structural design** – Thomas Telford 2003 – ISBN 0-7277-3235-8 – p 82

Architects embrace engineering

39   A Service – **Edwardian Architecture** –Thames & Hudson 1977 – p 14
40   M Droste – **Bauhaus** – Taschen 1993 ISBN 3-8228-0295-6
41   various – **De Stijl: 1917-1931 Visions of Utopia** – Phaidon Press Ltd. 1982 – ISBN 0-7148-2438-0
42   C Lodder – **Russian Constructivism** – Yale University Press 1983 – ISBN 0-300-02727-3
43   CS Eliel et al – **L'esprit nouveau - Purism in Paris 1918-25** – Harry N Abrams Inc. 2001
44   WJR Curtis – **Le Corbusier: Ideas and forms** – Phaidon Press Ltd. 1986 – ISBN 0-7148-2790-8 – p 43
45   Le Corbusier – **Towards a new architecture** –The Architectural Press 1927
46   K Frampton – **Le Corbusier** – Thames & Hudson 2001 – ISBN 0-500-20341-5 – p 29
47   see ref.44 – p 105
48   see ref.44 – p 69
49   L Hellman – **Architecture for beginners** – Unwin paperbacks 1986 – ISBN 0-04-7200033-2 – p 109
50   R Banham – **Theory & design in the first machine age** – Architectural Press 1962 – p 329

Engineering as fantasy

51   J-M Pérouse de Montclos – **Étienne-Louis Boullée** – Flammarion 1994 – ISBN 2-08-010075-0
52   **Enc. Brit. Micropædia Vol.** 2 – 15th Edition – p 423
53   L Krier – **Albert Speer: Architecture 1932-1942** – Aux Archives D'Architecture Moderne 1985
54   C Tisdall & A Bozzolla – **Futurism** – Thames & Hudson 1977 – Ch 6
55   see ref.42 – p 7-18
56   see ref.54 – p 132
57   B Risebero – **Modern architecture and design** – MIT Press 1983 – ISBN 0-262-68046-7 – p 167
58   New York Times – 23 April 1967
59   R Buckminster Fuller – **4D Time lock** – Biotechnic Press 1970
60   B Lawson – **How Designers Think** – Architectural Press 1980 – I SBN 0-85139-852-9 – p 65
61   D Scott-Brown – Journal of American Institute of Architects July 1968 – p 230
62   D Nixon & J Kaplicky – **Skin** – Architectural Review vol CLXIX N° 1037 July 1983 – p 54-59
63   S Lyall – **Masters of Structure** – Laurence King Publishing 2002 – p 96-103

Engineered curved structures

64   **Schalen und Behälter** in **Festschrift – Ulrich Finsterwalder** – Verlag G Braun Karlsruhe 1973 – p 75-94
65   ibid. p 81
66   C Faber – **Candela/ Shell builder** – Architectural Press 1962
67   F Candela – **Stereo-structures** – Progressive Architecture – June 1954 – p 84-93
68   **p/a views – critical discussion of stereo-structures** – Progressive Architecture – June 1954 – p 84-93
69   **critical discussion of stereo-structures parried by Candela** – Progressive Architecture – August 1954 – p 15-16
70   see ref.66 – p 14
71   M Pawley – **Buckminster Fuller** – Trefoil Publications Ltd. 1990 – ISBN 0-86294-160-1 – p12
72   J Meller ed. – **The Buckminster Fuller Reader** – Jonathan Cape 1979 – p 292
73   J Kadlcak – **Statics of suspension cable roofs** – Balkema 1995 – p 2-4
74   ibid. p 5-7

75 Y. Tsuboi & M. Kawaguchi – **Suspension structure for the Tokyo Olympics** – Proc. of Symposium on High-rise & Long-span structures – Japanese Soc. for the Promotion of Science – Sept. 1964
76 P Rianni – **Kenzo Tange** – Hamlyn 1970 – p 35

Engineering fantasy becomes reality

77 M Trieb – **Phillips Pavilion: Space calculated in seconds** – Princeton Press 1996
78 N Matossian – **Xenakis** – Kahn & Averill 1986 – ISBN 0-900707-82-8 – p 110
79 ibid.
80 A Tzonis – **Le Corbusier: The poetics of machine and metaphor** – Thames & Hudson 2001 – ISBN 0-500-283-192 – p 227
81 D Billington – **The tower and the bridge** – Princeton 1983 – ISBN 0 691 02393 – p 169
82 J Yeomans – **The other Taj Mahal** – Longmans & Green 1968
83 **The Arup Journal** – October 1973
84 F Fromont – **Jørn Utzon et l'Opéra de Sydney** – Gallimand 1998
85 Y Mikami – **Utzon's sphere** – Shokokusha Tokyo 2001 – ISBN 4-395-00712-0
86 B Murray – **The saga of the Sydney Opera House** – Spon 2003 – ISBN 0-415-32522-6
87 see ref.83 – p 5
88 see ref.82 – p 42
89 see ref.85 – p 58
90 see ref.82 – p 51
91 ON Arup & GJ Zunz – **Sydney Opera House** – The Structural Engineer March 1969 – p 101
92 A Holgate – **The art in structural design** – Clarendon Press 1986 – p 20
93 Discussion on paper by ON Arup & GJ Zunz – **Sydney Opera House** – The Structural Engineer, October 1969, N°10, vol.47 – p 421
94 C Norberg-Schulz & Y Futagawa – **Jørn Utzon - Sydney Opera House 1957-73** – Global Architecture N° 54 – ADA Edita 1980
95 see ref.81 – p 170
96 see ref.86 – p 13
97 P Rice & L Grut – **Main structural framework of the Beaubourg centre** – acier/stahl/steel 9/1975 – p 298
98 ibid. p 297
99 ibid. p 297
100 C Davies – **High Tech Architecture** – Thames & Hudson 1988
101 M Pawley – **The secret life of the engineers** – Blueprint March 1989 – p 36

Guggenheim, computers and beyond

102 H Iyengar et al – **The structural design of the Guggenheim Museum, Bilbao, Spain** – The Structural Engineer vol 78/N° 12 20 June 2000 – p 20-27
103 ibid. p 20
104 **Small project - winner** – British Construction Industry Awards – October 2002
105 G Bramante – **The Columbus Egg** – World Architecture N° 33 – p 89
106 A Mylius – **Clockwork croissant** – New Civil Engineer 27.02.2003 – p 22
107 **Helping architects achieve their dreams** – NCE CONSULTANTS FILE April 1988
108 D Gans ed. – **Bridging the gap** – Van Norstrand Reinhold 1991 – ISBN 0-442-00135-5 – p xiii
109 D Cottam – **Owen Williams** – Architectural Association 1986 – ISBN 0-904503-71-2
110 ibid. p 53
111 ibid. p 163
112 ibid. p 11
113 see ref.19 – p 71
114 L Molinari – **Santiago Calatrava** – Skira 1999 – ISBN 88-8118-525-3
115 see ref.101 – p 36
116 **The Chambers Dictionary** 1993 – p 879
117 see ref.38
118 see ref.38 – p 91
119 see ref.19 – p 177
120 R Thorne – **Structural stylists** – Building Design June 24 1988 – p 16
121 A3 Times No.10 Vol 4 1988 – p18
122 HD Thoreau – **Walden** – Princeton 1971
123 FM Cornford – **Microcosmographia Academica** – Metcalfe & Co. 1908

CHAPTER 12 *A simple approach to calculations*

In this chapter the concepts of structural behaviour are used to give a simple approach to calculations that check the fundamental points of any proposed structural system. No more than the usual arithmetic operations and simple algebra are used. The ability to make basic calculations gives 'the designer' the self-sufficiency not only to conceive structural schemes but also to arrive rapidly at sizes for the principal elements. Clearly these simple calculations will be re-done in detail for the final scheme but what is intended here is to show how, what are sometimes called 'back of an envelope' calculations, are made. Of course envelopes should not really be used, as all calculations are extremely important project information and should be numbered and filed in a proper manner. To gain full benefit from this chapter all the exercises should be done.

Calculations, even for a small project can be lengthy, so it is essential to be clear at all times just exactly what the point is of the current step. In **Section 0.6** the following questions were asked:

- **What is the function of the structure?**
- **What are the loads and the load paths?**
- **How does the structure transfer the loads?**
- **What are the forces in the structural elements?**
- **Does the structure have overall stability?**
- **Is any element too slender?**

The core of the book, **Chapters 1** to **7**, show conceptually how these questions are answered and **Chapters 8** to **10** show how the concepts apply to the structures of real projects. Now, with the conceptual understanding, the questions asked in **Chapter 0**, and returned to in **Chapter 8**, can be put more succinctly as:

- **What is the structure?**
- **What are the loads?**
- **Is the structure strong enough?**

To which has to be added:

- **Is the structure stiff enough?**

12.1 The basic questions

Before actual numbers are introduced, a strategy is required to answer the basic questions given above.

- **What is the structure?**

To enable calculations to be made the proposed structure has to be idealised by a **structural diagram** – see **Section 10.6**. Below **Fig. 12.1** shows them for a **cantilever** and a **simply supported beam**.

CANTILEVER   SIMPLY SUPPORTED BEAM

Fig. 12.1

These two structures form the basis for the simple approach to calculations.

- **What are the loads?**

Chapter 1 dealt at some length with the nature and source of structural loads. To do calculations, specific values are needed and these are available for most situations.

- **Is the structure strong enough?**

Actually this question should really be:

- **Are the stresses in the structure acceptable?**

This is really the central question. The answer involves all the concepts described in **Chapters 2** to **6**, and is what is usually called 'structural analysis'. This, together with 'section design', are the core subjects of 'official' structural engineering. They are used in this chapter in a simplified form to find the magnitude of the internal forces – axial, shear and bending moments – and to check that the stresses in each element are within those permitted.

- **Is the structure stiff enough?**

Nothing has been said so far about stiffness except from the point of view of slenderness – see **Section 6.4**. Here the phenomenon of buckling was examined in some detail. This is an important aspect of stiffness but when in use the structure must not deflect 'too much'. This is not really a conceptual question as it is obvious and 'just needs to be calculated to see if it is within acceptable limits'.

12.2 Units

When calculations are carried out, the numbers represent the **size** of a 'physical' quantity – length, axial force and area are examples. To calculate the loading on a structure not only must the physical size of the structure be known but also the size of loads – that is, the size of **forces**, and units for measuring them are needed.

In the past many systems of measurement have been used. These systems were often local or national but engineering now uses an international system of measurement called the Système International, or **SI** for short. This system is based on the metric system which uses units like metres and kilograms, but it also uses a unit of measure for force called the **Newton**. This unit is only used for calculations in physics and engineering, so is not widely known. The reason for its existence is to clarify the old problem of trying to distinguish between **mass** and **force**. They are related by the famous equation stated by Isaac Newton:

$$\text{Force} = \text{Mass} \times \text{Acceleration}$$

In the **SI** system, the standard measure of mass is the **kilogram** and the standard measure of length is the **metre**. As acceleration is the rate of change of velocity it is measured is metres per second per second or **m/s²**. The definition of a **Newton** is, from Newton's equation, the force required to accelerate **1 kilogram** by **1 m/s²**.

$$1 \text{ Newton} = 1 \text{ Kilogram} \times 1\text{m/s}^2$$

As the acceleration, **g**, due to gravity is known to be **9.81m/s²**, the force exerted by a mass of one kilogram on the surface of the earth is:

$$1\text{kg} \times \text{g} = 1\text{kg} \times 9.81\text{m/s}^2 = 9.81\text{N}$$

As 9.81 is almost 10 (!), 1 kilogram can be thought of as causing a force of 10N. Here calculations are only made for structures with static loads rather than dynamic loads – see page **18** – so there is no need to be concerned about mass and force, so loads and forces can all be measured in Newtons. In the SI system there are certain names and prefixes for useful multiples:

$$1000 \text{ times} - \text{kilo (k)} \qquad 1,000,000 \text{ times} - \text{mega (M)}$$

In structural design, it is often convenient to use units of force that are larger than the Newton:

$$1 \text{ kiloNewton} = 1\text{kN} = 1000\text{N} \qquad 1 \text{ megaNewton} = 1\text{MN} = 1,000,000\text{N}$$

These are used to keep the number of zeros that appear in the calculations under control. The **kiloNewton** is commonly used, and for large structures, **megaNewtons** are used. Forces can now be expressed as single forces in **N**, **kN** or **MN**, as forces per length in **N/m**, **kN/m** or **MN/m** and as forces per area as **N/m²**, **kN/m²** or **MN/m²**.

Description	Units	Description	Units
Loads on an area	kN/m²	Loads along a beam or truss	kN/m
Concentrated loads	kN	Reaction forces	kN
Axial or shear forces	kN	Bending and torsional moments	kN.m
Stresses in an element	N/mm²	Foundation stresses	kN/m²

Table 12.1 Typical units

12.3 Real loads

No calculation for structures makes sense if the wrong load is used. Calculating the load on a structure is not usually a fascinating process but it has to be right. In **Chapter 1**, three types of loads were identified: **Natural loads – Section 1.1**; **Useful loads – Section 1.2**; and **Accidental loads – Section 1.3**. In this chapter only **Natural** and **Useful** loads will be considered. It might seem difficult to decide what load wind, snow or the use of a room for an office will cause, but fortunately all this has been 'decided' by various authorities and form part of official **Building Codes** in many countries; therefore no hard decisions are required. This official quantifying of loads is relatively recent, mainly during the 20th century; before that, those responsible for the calculations had to decide for themselves what appropriate loads would be. Only three types of **natural loads** are used here; **gravity**, **snow** and **wind**.

Gravity loads that act vertically are due to the self-weight of the building construction, which includes the weight of the structure itself – see **Figs. 1.20**. The basis for the calculation of these loads is the **density** of the materials in kN/m^3. It is possible to find the density of any type of material in engineering handbooks – some are given in **Table 12.2**.

Material	kN/m^3	Material	kN/m^3
Water	10	Stone	27
Soil	18	Glass	28
Concrete	25	Steel	77
Brickwork	20	Aluminium	27
Plaster	18	Timber	7

Table 12.2 Typical densities of building materials

With this information, it is a simple matter to calculate the weight of any construction. Extra information can be obtained from technical literature.

Example 12.1 Calculate the gravity load of the weight of the floor construction shown in the figure. Note the dimensions are shown in millimetres but are converted to metres for the calculation.

Material	Load	kN/m^2
Timber	$0.022 \times 7 =$	0.15
Screed	$0.060 \times 22 =$	1.32
Concrete	$0.200 \times 25 =$	5.00
Plaster	$0.025 \times 18 =$	0.45
	Total =	6.92

Example 12.2 Calculate the gravity load on the beam under the wall shown in the figure. The floor construction is as Example.12.1

Element	Load	kN/m
Wall	$3 \times 0.20 \times 20 =$	12.0
Slab	$2.40 \times 6.92 =$	16.61
Beam	$0.70 \times 0.30 \times 25 =$	5.25
	Total =	33.86

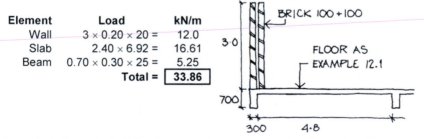

How wind acts on a building is a complex matter but has been simplified so that a static **wind load** can be calculated for any 'normal' building. There are a number of factors that influence the calculated wind load and these are:

1   **Geographical location**
2   **Local topography, height and size of building**
3   **Shape of building**

The basic data is the **basic wind speed, V**; this depends on the geographical location and is obtained from a wind map. This wind speed is then modified, by published factors, **S**, for the type of local topography – city, outskirts, open countryside, the height – wind speed increases with height – and the overall size of the building. The basic wind speed is multiplied by the factor to give the **design wind speed, Vs**. The wind pressure, **q**, is then obtained from: $q = 0.613 \times V_s^2 \times 10^{-3}$ **kN/m²**, where the wind speed is in metres per second and 0.613 is half the density of air in kg/m³. This load is then applied to the surfaces of the building after being multiplied by a pressure coefficient **Cp**, that takes into account the shape of the building.

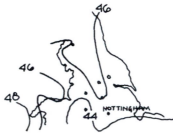

Fig. 12.2 A wind map showing contours of Basic Wind Speed **V**

Height – m	City	Outskirts	Country
10	0.62	0.74	0.88
20	0.75	0.90	0.98
30	0.85	0.97	1.03
50	0.98	1.04	1.08
100	1.10	1.12	1.16

Table. 12.3 – Typical **S** factors

Element	C_p - windward	C_p - leeward
Wall	+0.7	-0.3
Roof slope 0°	-0.8	-0.6
Roof slope 10°	-1.1	-0.6
Roof slope 20°	-0.7	-0.5
Roof slope 30°	-0.2	-0.5
Roof slope 50°	+0.2	-0.5

Table 12.4 Typical coefficients C_p

The plus signs in **Table 12.4** indicate that the wind is causing a pressure on the element and minus signs suction.

Example 12.3   Calculate the wind loads on a building 10m high with a pitched roof of 20°. The basic wind speed, from the wind map is 44m/s and the building is on the outskirts of a city.

∴ Basic wind pressure $q = 0.613 \times (0.74 \times 44)^2 \times 10^{-3} = 0.65 \text{kN/m}^2$

Element	$q \times C_p$	kN/m²
Wall - windward	0.65 × (+0.7)	+0.46
Wall - leeward	0.65 × (-0.3)	-0.20
Roof windward slope	0.65 × (-0.7)	-0.46
Roof leeward slope	0.65 × (-0.5)	-0.33

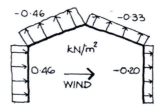

334 Building structures

Useful loads obviously depend on the use and are tabulated in the various national codes. Typical loadings for different uses are given below.

Use	kN/m^2
Residential use	2.0
Offices	2.5
Shops, showrooms, laboratories	3.0
Theatres, cinemas	4.0
Dance halls, churches, gymnasiums	5.0
Plant rooms, storage areas	6.0

Table 12.5 Typical useful floor loads

People = 2.5kN/m^2

Depending on the use of the space, the floor load for its use must be added to the gravity load from the construction. Sometimes additional loads are added to take account of loads from services or non-loadbearing partitions. Typical values are **0.3kN/m^2** for service loads and **1.4kN/m^2** for partitions. It is more common in calculations to call the gravity loads the **dead load (DL)** and the useful load the **live load (LL)** and in calculations these are often kept separate.

Example 12.4   Calculate the **live load**, the **dead load** and the **total load** for the floor shown which is to be used for a laboratory.

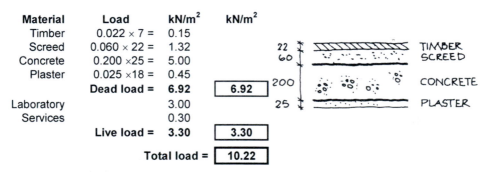

Material	Load	kN/m^2	kN/m^2
Timber	0.022 × 7 =	0.15	
Screed	0.060 × 22 =	1.32	
Concrete	0.200 ×25 =	5.00	
Plaster	0.025 ×18 =	0.45	
	Dead load =	**6.92**	6.92
Laboratory		3.00	
Services		0.30	
	Live load =	3.30	3.30
	Total load =		10.22

Roofs may also need to support **snow loads**. These will vary due to the slope and the geographical location. The density of fresh snow is **1.0kN/m^3**. Many countries produce **snow maps** similar to wind maps.

In terms of calculations, loads are somewhat problematic because at the initial stages of a project there may be many unknowns that will affect the loading. In many countries there are loading codes some of which, especially for wind and snow, can be quite complex. Therefore it is always sensible to 'err on the safe side' when computing the loads. The values shown in this section are 'typical' and are given to allow basic calculations to be made, where possible reference should be made to the applicable code.

12.4   The beam and the cantilever

In this section the bending moments and shear forces are calculated for a simply supported beam and a cantilever. These structures are shown in **Fig. 12.1**. This is the beginning of structural analysis; trying to find more and more general methods for doing this occupied engineers for a large part of the 19th century and all of the 20th.

A simple supported beam has a span of **L**, and carries a uniformly distributed load of **w** per unit length. The bending moment and the shear force are required at each point of the beam. First the reaction forces are required and then the moments and shears are found at a point **x** from the support by considering moment and vertical equilibrium.

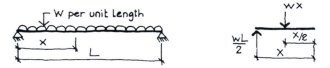

Fig. 12.3 Simply supported beam

At the position **x** along the beam, the bending moment, M_x, will be equal to the sum of all the moments from the left, or from the right. That is, from the left, the reaction **wL/2**, times the lever arm **x**, minus the load **w** × **x**, times the lever arm **x/2**, which is the equation:

$$M_x = w \times L/2 \times x - w \times x \times x/2$$

And the shear force, S_x, is the sum of the vertical forces. That is, from the left, the reaction, **wL/2**, minus the load, **w** × **x**, this is the equation:

$$S_x = w \times L/2 - w \times x$$

To find the bending moment and the shear force at the support, M_{SUP} and S_{SUP}, **x = 0** is entered into the equations and at the centre for M_{CEN} and S_{CEN}, **x = L/2**, these give:

$$M_{SUP} = 0 \text{ and } S_{SUP} = wL/2 \quad \text{and} \quad M_{CEN} = wL^2/8 \text{ and } S_{CEN} = 0$$

Example 12.5   The beam in Example 12.2 is simply supported and spans 4.8m. The slab live load is as Example 12.4. Calculate the bending moment at the centre and the shear force at the supports, also calculate the values for the bending moment and shear force 1.3m from the support. Draw the bending moment and shear forces diagrams showing the values.

Total uniformly distributed load (**UDL**) on the beam = Dead Load (**DL**) + Live Load (**LL**)
= 33.86 + 2.4 × 3.30 = **41.78kN/m**

Force	Calculation	Result
S_{SUP}	(41.78 × 4.8) ÷2	**100.27kN**
$S_{1.30}$	100.27 − (41.78 × 1.3)	**45.96kN**
M_{CEN}	(41.78 × 4.8²) ÷ 8	**120.33kN.m**
$M_{1.30}$	(100.27 × 1.3) − (41.78 × 1.3²)÷2	**95.05kN.m**

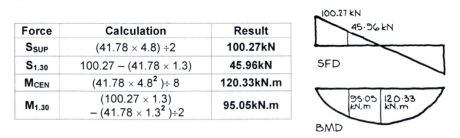

Note that the abbreviations **SFD** and **BMD** have been used for **Shear Force Diagram** and **Bending Moment Diagram**, and these will be used from now on.

The approach used for the simply supported beam can be used for the cantilever. A cantilever has a span of **L**, and carries a uniformly distributed load of **w** per unit length. The bending moment and the shear force are required at each point. First the reaction forces are required and then the moments and shears are found at a point **x** from the support by considering moment and vertical equilibrium.

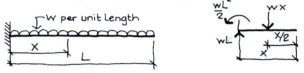

Fig. 12.4 A cantilever

So, following the process used for the simply supported beam, the bending moment and shear force at a distance **x** from the support are:

$$M_x = wL \times x - wL^2/2 - wx \times x/2 \quad \text{and} \quad S_x = wL - wx$$

To find the bending moment and the shear force at the support, M_{SUP} and S_{SUP}, **x=0** is entered in the equations and at the free end for M_{END} and S_{END}, **x = L**, these give:

$$M_{SUP} = -wL^2/2 \text{ and } S_{SUP} = wL \quad \text{and} \quad M_{END} = 0 \text{ and } S_{END} = 0$$

Example 12.6 A cantilever of 2.7m is loaded as Ex.12.5. Calculate the bending moment and the shear force at the support, and 1.8m from the support. Draw the bending moment and shear forces diagrams showing the values.

Force	Calculation	Result
S_{SUP}	41.78 × 2.7	112.81kN
M_{SUP}	$-(41.78 \times 2.7^2) \div 2$	-152.29kN.m
$S_{1.80}$	112.81 – (41.78 × 1.8)	37.60kN
$M_{1.80}$	(112.86 × 1.8) – 152.29 – $(41.78 \times 1.8^2) \div 2$	-16.91kN.m

112·81kN

37·60kN

SFD

−152·29 kN. m

−16·91 kN.m

BMD

Exercise 12.1 Check the values of the bending moments and shear forces calculated for the simply supported beam and the cantilever, in the examples above, by considering the forces to the **right**.

Exercise 12.2 Calculate values at regular intervals along the simply supported beam and the cantilever and draw shear force and bending moments to scale.

Exercise 12.3 Recalculate the values of the shear forces and bending moments assuming the concrete slab is 300mm thick and the live load is for an office with allowances for services and partitions.

In the calculations carried out so far the values of the reaction forces, **wL/2**, for the beam and **−wL²/2** and **wL**, just 'appeared'. These are true for a **UDL** of **w** along the whole of the element but suppose the loading is different. A simply supported beam with a **partial UDL** and **point load** is shown in the figure.

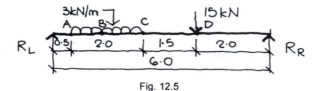

Fig. 12.5

The loads shown ignore the weight of the beam and the numbers are 'simple' to aid the explanation. Now, before the values of shear forces and bending moments can be calculated, the values of the reactions, R_L and R_R, have to be known. These are calculated using the concepts explained in **Section 1.5** for the man on the plank. They are found by considering moment equilibrium about the right-hand and left-hand supports respectively and equating clockwise and anti-clockwise moments.

Example 12.7   For the beam shown in Fig. 12.5 calculate reactions, R_L, R_R, bending moments M_B, M_D, and the shear forces, S_B, S_D at the positions shown. Draw the bending moment and shear forces diagrams showing the values.

First about the right-hand support for R_L:

$R_L \times 6.0 = (3 \times 2.0) \times (3.50 + (2.0 \div 2)) + (15 \times 2.0)$

$\therefore R_L = (27 + 30) \div 6.0 = 9.50$kN

and about the left-hand support for R_R:

$R_R \times 6.0 = (3 \times 2.0) \times (0.50 + (2.0 \div 2)) + 15 \times 4.0$

$\therefore R_R = (9 + 60) \div 6.0 = 11.50$kN

$R_L + R_R = 9.50 + 11.50 = 21$ kN

$\therefore$ **Sum of reactions = Total load** (checks)

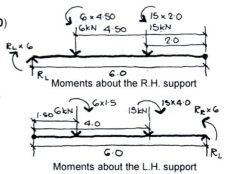

Moments about the R.H. support

Moments about the L.H. support

As the reactions are known, the shear force and the bending moment can be calculated at any point on the beam. This is done in exactly the same way as before by considering the vertical and moment equilibrium at the position on the beam where the values are required. The calculations are made using the equilibrium to the **left**.

Force	Calculation	Result
S_B	$9.5 - (3 \times 1.0)$	6.50kN
M_B	$(9.50 \times 1.5) - (3.0 \times 1.0^2)/2$	12.75kN.m
S_D	$9.50 - (3 \times 2.0)$	3.50kN
M_D	$(9.5 \times 4.0) - (3 \times 2.0 \times 2.5)$	23kN.m

Exercise 12.4   Calculate all the values for the shear forces and bending moments shown on the diagrams. Check by calculating from the **right**. Calculate intermediate values and draw the diagrams to scale.

For cantilevers, the calculation of the reactions is simpler. As there is only one vertical reaction it must equal the total load. The moment reaction is equal to the moment due to all the loads.

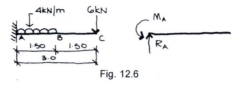

Fig. 12.6

Example 12.8 For the cantilever shown in Fig. 12.6 calculate reactions, R_A, M_A, bending moment M_B, and the shear force, S_{BL}, at the end of the UDL. Draw the bending moment and shear forces diagrams showing the values.

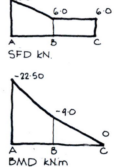

Force	Calculation	Result
R_A	$6 + (4 \times 1.5)$	12kN
M_A	$-(6 \times 3.0) - ((4 \times 1.5^2) \div 2)$	-2.5kN.m
S_B	$12 - (4 \times 1.50)$	6kN
M_B	$-22.5 - ((4 \times 1.5^2) \div 2) + 12 \times 1.50$	-9kN.m

The pinned and fixed supports of the beam and cantilever are idealisations that are rarely found in 'real' structures – see **Section 10.6**. In the case of the cantilever, instead of having a fixed support, the usual case is for a cantilever to be an extension of a supported beam. So a simply supported beam can cantilever beyond its support. To see how this affects the reactions, shear forces and bending moments, the beam shown in **Fig. 12.5** and the cantilever shown in **Fig. 12.6** can be combined to give the structure shown in **Fig. 12.7.1**.

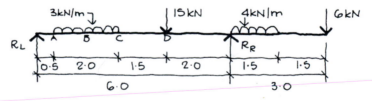

Fig. 12.7.1

Example 12.9 For the beam and cantilever shown in Fig. 12.7.1 calculate the reactions, bending moments and the shear forces at the same positions shown in Examples 12.7 and 12.8. Draw the bending moment and shear force diagrams showing the values.

The reactions, shear forces and bending moments for the beam and cantilever have already been calculated independently but the effect of the cantilever support moment now has to be taken into account. The loads on the cantilever apply a moment to the support and this is balanced at the support by the equal and opposite support moment. The beam now provides the resistance for the cantilever moment. The effect on the beam is to apply a clockwise moment to the right-hand end. This is the same as the concept explained in **Figs. 2.36 to 2.38**. This

A simple approach to calculations 339

applied moment causes equal and opposite reactions at the left- and right-hand supports of the beam and a constant shear force in the beam itself. These moments and reactions are shown in **Fig. 12.7.2.**

Fig. 12.7.2

In this case; **M_A = 22.50kN.m** and **R_L = −M_A/L = −22.50 ÷ 6.0 = −3.75kN**, the minus sign indicating that the reaction is downwards.

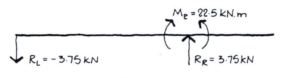

Fig. 12.7.3

For vertical equilibrium **R_R = −R_L** and, as well as a constant shear force, there is also a linearly varying bending moment in the beam due to the effect of the cantilever. The values of the bending moments, due to the cantilever, are given at the positions for which the bending moments have been calculated for the load on the beam; these are calculated directly by proportional triangles.

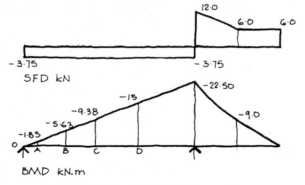

Fig. 12.7.4 SFD and BMD due to the cantilever

The final reactions and the complete shear force and bending moment diagrams can now be drawn by simply adding, with respect to sign, the values given in **Fig. 12.7.3** to those given in **Example 12.7**.

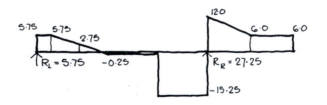

Fig. 12.7.5 Final Reactions and SFD

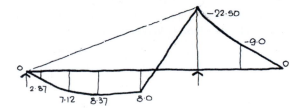

Fig. 12.7.5 (contd.) Final bending moment diagram

In **Fig. 12.7.5**, positive and negative values appear on both the shear force and bending moment diagrams. **Figs. 2.23** to **2.26** show how a sign convention for shear forces and bending moments can be introduced. **Fig. 12.7.6** shows how this sign convention applies to the beam and cantilever.

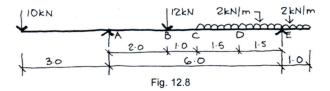

Fig. 12.7.6 Shear force and bending moment sign convention

Exercise 12.5   For the beam and cantilevers shown in **Fig. 12.8** do all the calculations and draw all the diagrams that were done for **Example 12.9**.

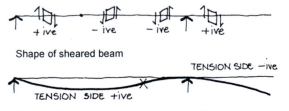

Fig. 12.8

(Partial answers: R_A = 24.33kN, R_E = 5.67kN, M_A = −30.0kN.m, M_C = 1.0kN.m)

It is essential that these examples are thoroughly understood and that all the exercises in this section are done before proceeding. This understanding may be reinforced by inventing further exercises, particularly using real loads. The understanding of this section can be used as a basis for carrying out simple calculations for an amazing array of structures, as will be shown in the following sections.

12.5   More complex beams

For the beam and the cantilevers, all the forces, shear forces and bending moments were calculated using Newton's third law which is

•   **To every action there is an equal and opposite reaction.**

Which leads to the following statements for **equilibrium** – see **Section 1.5**

- **Sum of vertical loads = Sum of vertical reactions**
- **Sum of horizontal loads = Sum of horizontal reactions**
- **Moments due to loads = Moments due to reactions**

These statements must always be true everywhere in every structure. As there were no horizontal loads on the beam or cantilever only two of these statements were used.

Suppose a beam of span **L**, loaded with a **UDL** of **w**, has a pinned joint at the right-hand support, but instead of a pin joint at the left-hand support it has a fixed support. There are now three reaction forces; vertical forces R_L and R_R at the supports plus a moment reaction M_L at the fixed support.

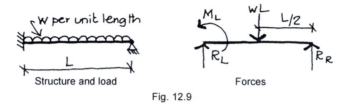

Structure and load   Forces

Fig. 12.9

Note that in **Fig. 12.9** the moment caused by the **UDL** has been shown as the total load **wL** acting at its centre **L/2**. Now the equilibrium conditions for vertical forces and moments can be used:

$$R_L + R_R = w \times L \qquad \text{and} \qquad M_L + R_R \times L = (w \times L) \times L/2$$

There are three unknowns to be calculated, R_L, R_R and M_L, but there are only two equations from the equilibrium conditions. This is a basic difficulty in structural analysis, but it is avoided here because simplification is required, not mathematical analysis. What can be done? A possibility is to make one of the unknowns zero. If $R_R = 0$ is chosen then the structure becomes a cantilever or if $M_L = 0$ is chosen the structure becomes a simply supported beam, both of which have already been calculated.

R_R = 0; Cantilever M_L = 0; Simply supported beam

Fig. 12.10

The forces calculated from either of these structures will be in equilibrium and so will be satisfactory from the statical point of view; that is they are **statically admissible solutions**. But the deflections caused at the supports seriously violate the geometric conditions because δ_R or θ_L are not zero, so they are **kinematically inadmissible solutions**.

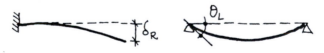

Fig. 12.11 Inadmissible deflections

However, it is possible to alter the structure in another way that allows the forces to be calculated from the equilibrium conditions. This can be done by introducing a pin joint within the length of the beam. This turns the structure into a simply supported beam with one end supported by a cantilever.

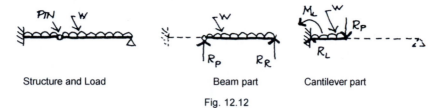

| | PIN | | | | Cantilever part |

Structure and Load   Beam part   Cantilever part

Fig. 12.12

Finding the forces in this structure follows directly from the previous examples. First the reaction forces are found; then these are used to calculate the shear forces and bending moments at any point. This is illustrated by making the calculations for the structure shown in **Fig. 12.13**.

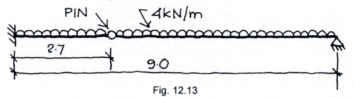

Fig. 12.13

Example 12.10 For the structure shown in **Fig. 12.13** calculate reactions, bending moments and the shear forces. Draw the bending moment and shear force diagrams showing the values

Force	Calculation	Result
R_P	$(4 \times 6.3) \div 2$	12.6kN
R_R	$(4 \times 6.3) \div 2$	12.6kN
R_L	$12.6 + (4 \times 2.7)$	23.4kN
M_L	$-(12.6 \times 2.7) - ((4 \times 2.7^2) \div 2)$	−48.6kN.m

$R_P = 12.6 \text{ kN} = R_R$

$M_L = -48.6 \text{ kN.m}$

12.6kN

$R_L = 23.4 \text{kN}$

The shear force and bending moment diagrams and the deflected shape can now be drawn.

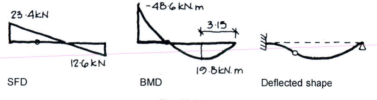

SFD   BMD   Deflected shape

Fig. 12.14

The shear forces and bending moments calculated again provide a **statically admissible solution** and the deflected shape does not violate the support geometry. But, of course, the calculations have not been done for the original structure but one modified by the insertion of a pin. Now three statically admissible solutions have been identified, the cantilever, the simply supported beam and the inserted pin structure. In **Fig. 12.15** the bending moment diagrams, together with the values of the reactions, are shown for these solutions. The last diagram is the result of a calculation based on the mathematical theory – see **Chapter 13**.

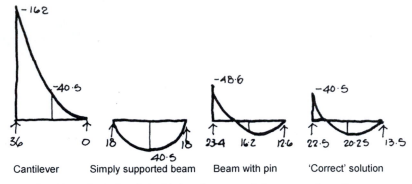

Fig. 12.15 Statically admissible bending moment diagrams and reactions

Clearly the cantilever and the beam solutions are nothing like the 'correct' solution, shown on the far right of the figure, whereas the inserted pin structure gives values within 20%. Why is this? The reason is that the pin was inserted close to the true position of the **point of contraflexure**. In **Fig. 12.7.5** the **BMD** is shown for the structure of a beam with a cantilever, and in the beam span, the sign of the bending moment changes from positive, in the left-hand part, to negative, in the right-hand part. So at one point the bending moment is zero, and at this point the deflected shape changes, as is shown in **Fig. 12.7.6**. This is the point of contraflexure and it 'functions' as a pin. As **Fig. 12.15** shows, if a pin is inserted to make it possible to use the equations of equilibrium to calculate the forces, and the pin is close to the actual point of contraflexure, the calculated forces will be approximately correct, which is good enough for the simple approach.

Another important point is the role of the bending moment calculated as if the load were applied to a simply supported beam of the same span. This is often called the **free bending moment**. For this example it can be seen how the simply supported **BMD** can be added to the support **BMD** to give the final **BMD**.

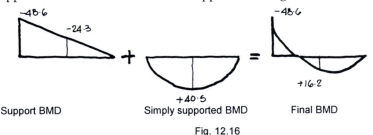

Fig. 12.16

When the forces can be calculated from statics, the structure is said to be **statically determinate**; otherwise it is **statically indeterminate**. The insertion of the pin into the statically indeterminate structure, shown in **Fig. 12.12**, made it statically determinate. To show how this can be used for a more complex beam, calculate the forces in the four-span beam shown in **Fig. 12.17**.

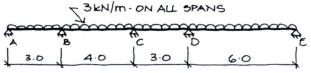

Fig. 12.17 Statically indeterminate 4-span beam

344 Building structures

If pins were inserted at supports **B, C** and **D** there would be four simply supported beams – a statically determinate system which violates the continuity of the beams. Using the previous example as a guide, insert pins to the right of **B, C** and **D** at a distance from the support of 20% of the span.

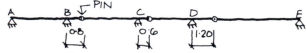

Fig. 12.18 Statically determinate 'inserted pin' 4-span beam

Example 12.11   For the structure shown in **Fig. 12.18** calculate bending moments and the shear forces. Draw the bending moment and shear force diagrams showing the values.

The support moment at **D** can now be calculated as before so:

$$M_D = (3 \times 2.4) \times 1.20 + 3 \times 1.20^2 \div 2 = \textbf{10.80kN.m}$$

But the calculation for the support moment at **C** also has to take into account the moment at **D** already calculated, as this causes a reaction at the pin between **C** and **D** so:

$$M_c = ((3 \times 1.2) \times 0.60 + 3 \times 0.6^2 \div 2) - ((10.8 \div 2.4) \times 0.6) = \textbf{0kN.m}$$

Having calculated all the support moments, the bending moment diagram can be drawn. The values at mid-span have been added.

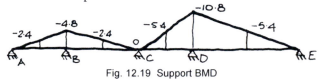

Fig. 12.19 Support BMD

The free bending moment diagrams for each span can be added to this diagram to give the final **BMD**.

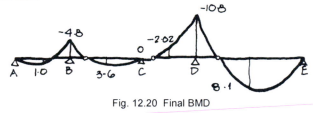

Fig. 12.20 Final BMD

The **SFD** can also be drawn. The shear in each span is the **SFD** for the span as a simply supported beam with an 'adjustment' for the effect of the support moment – this is as shown in **Fig. 12.7.3**.

$$S_{DE} = (3 \times 6.0) \div 2 + 10.8 \div 6.0 = \textbf{10.8kN} \text{ and } S_{ED} = (3 \times 6.0) \div 2 - 10.8 \div 6.0 = \textbf{7.2kN}$$

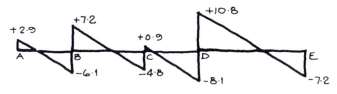

Fig. 12.21 Final SFD

A simple approach to calculations 345

The neutral axis is shown at a depth of **d/2**. In the technical literature there is a lot of detail about the depth of the neutral axis and the shape of the stress distribution in the concrete, but for the simple approach, the details given in **Fig. 12.32** are sufficient. If the distance from the bottom of the beam to the centre of the reinforcement is known (chosen), it is usually from about **40mm** to **70mm**, then the lever arm dimension can be calculated.

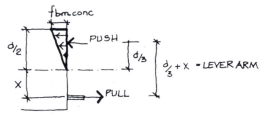

Fig. 12.33 Concrete beam lever arm

Using the information from these two diagrams it is possible to calculate the force in the rebar.

Example 12.14   Calculate the force in the reinforcement due to the bending moment in the beam of **Example 12.12**. Assume the cover = 40mm

M = 18kN.m ;   lever arm = d/3 + x = 300/3 + (150 − 40) = 210mm   so

Force in reinforcement = 18 E6 ÷ 210 = 86 E3 N

Stress in reinforcement = $f_{bm.st\text{-}act}$ ÷ A_{st} where **A_{st} = Area of the reinforcement**

Having calculated the actual stresses in the structure they have to be checked against the allowable stresses for the material to ensure the chosen section is adequate. Before these are given it should be clear which method of design is being used. In **Section 6.1** three approaches are explained and are illustrated in **Figs. 6.19, 20** and **21**. Until the late 1970s virtually all calculations were carried out using **permissible stress design**, since then it has been generally superseded by **limit state design**. Limit state design multiplies the loads by factors, typically **1.5**, and divides the ultimate stress by factors, typically **1.3**[1]. The factors are given in technical codes. For the simple approach outlined in this chapter it is better to ignore the limit state partial factors and work with the unfactored loads and the permissible stresses. **The most important point to remember is to state clearly in the calculations which approach is being used.** In limit ltate terminology calculations using the unfactored loads is called the **serviceability limit state** or **SLS** for short.

Material	Grade	Tensile stress	Comp. stress	Shear stress
Structural steel	Mild steel	165	155	120
	High tensile	230	215	160
Concrete		-	7	0.4 – max 4
Reinforcement	Mild steel	140	140	140
	High tensile	260	260	260
Timber	Average	6	6	0.7

Table 12.6 Permissible stresses in N/mm^2

Using these stresses it is possible to check whether a structural member is adequate. In reinforced concrete beams it is usual to check that the concrete is adequate, and then size the reinforcement from the force, thus obtaining the cross-sectional area required. If the compressive or shear stresses are exceeded in a concrete element it is possible to give additional strength by adding compression or shear reinforcement.

The stresses given in **Table 12.6** are based on 'usual' grades of the material; it is possible to encounter material with both higher and lower usable stresses. Generally 'mild steel' is used for structural steelwork and 'high tensile' steel for reinforcement. Compressive stresses have to be reduced, often considerably, when elements are slender, see **Section 12.8**.

12.8 Triangulated structures

Structures made from beams and columns are probably the structural form used most commonly in buildings but, especially for roof structures, trusses are often used. Some typical trusses are shown in **Fig. 7.34**. Trusses are usually supported like simply supported beams or cantilevers and the truss geometry itself is usually a sequence of triangles. The structural elements of the truss, for calculation purposes, are considered to be pinned to each other so that the elements only have axial forces. All this means that trusses are almost always **statically determinate** so the forces can be found from the equilibrium statements given on page **342**.

In the past, graphical methods were popular for finding forces in trusses but nowadays hand calculations either find the forces from considering joint equilibrium or the equilibrium at a cut, see **Fig. 7.36**. Both require the concept of **resolution of forces** (or its equivalent the **force triangle**). This concept is shown in **Fig. 7.10**. The basis for all these calculations are the 'well known' trigonometrical relationships for a right-angled triangle between the hypotenuse and the sine and cosine of the angle θ.

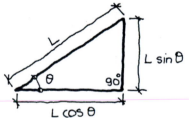

Fig. 12.34 Trigonometrical relationships for a right-angled triangle

Using these relationships it is possible to resolve a diagonal force into **vertical** and **horizontal components** which is equivalent to drawing a **triangle of forces**.

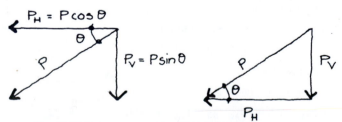

Fig. 12.35 Force components and triangle of forces

This idea can be 'turned around' to find two forces that resist a third force.

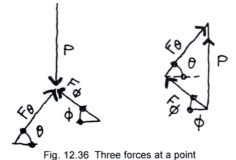

Fig. 12.36 Three forces at a point

A separate triangle of forces can be drawn for each 'resisting' force F_θ and F_φ.

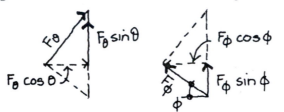

Fig. 12.37 Force triangles for F_θ and F_φ

From **Fig. 12.37** the horizontal and vertical equilibrium conditions can be written as:

$$F_\theta \cos \theta = F_\varphi \cos \varphi \qquad \text{and} \qquad F_\theta \sin \theta + F_\varphi \sin \varphi = P$$

Example 12.15   Calculate the forces F_1 and F_2 for the arrangement shown in the figure.

For horizontal equilibrium: $F_1 \cos 30° = F_2 \cos 45°$ so

$0.866\,F_1 = 0.707\,F_2$ giving $F_2 = 1.225\,F_1$

For vertical equilibrium: $F_1 \sin 30° + F_2 \sin 45° = 10\text{kN}$

so $0.5\,F_1 + 0.707\,F_2 = 10\text{kN}$: substituting $F_2 = 1.225\,F_2$ gives

$F_1 = 7.32\text{kN}$ and $F_2 = 8.97\text{kN}$

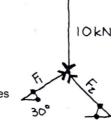

This example shows how forces in two members meeting at a joint can be found from joint equilibrium.

Example 12.16   Calculate the forces in the truss shown in the figure from joint equilibrium.

Find reactions R_A and R_C (as for beam – page 338)

$13.66 \times R_A = 10 \times 5.0$ so $R_A = 3.66\text{kN}$

$13.66 \times R_C = 10 \times 8.66$ so $R_A = 6.34\text{kN}$

Equilibrium at joint A

Vertical: $F_{AB} \sin 30° = 3.66$ so $F_{AB} = 7.32\text{kN}$

Horizontal: $F_{AB} \cos 30° = F_{AC}$ so $F_{AC} = 6.34\text{kN}$

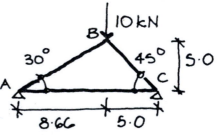

Equilibrium at joint C

Vertical: $F_{CB} \sin 45° = 6.34$ so $F_{CB} = 8.97$kN

Horizontal: $F_{CB} \cos 45° = F_{CA}$ so $F_{CA} = 6.34$kN

Equilibrium at joint B – as Example 12.15

As the forces have been calculated at the joints it is now possible to draw a diagram showing the forces in the truss members. Compression is shown as positive and tension is shown as negative.

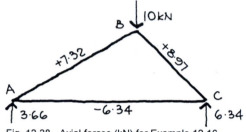

Fig. 12.38   Axial forces (kN) for Example 12.16

To find the forces from the equilibrium of a slice the **BMD** and **SFD**, calculated as though the truss is a beam, are used.

Example 12.17   Calculate the forces in elements **AB** and **AC** of the truss used in **Example 12.16** by considering the equilibrium of the truss cut, for example at 4.33m from joint **A**.

Draw the BMD and SFD as though the truss was a beam. Note: the reactions R_A and R_B calculated previously are used.

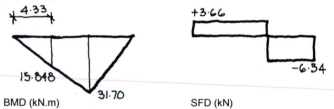

To find the forces the equilibrium at the cut is examined.

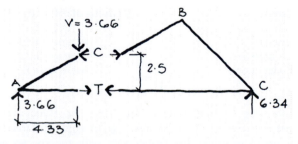

The vertical force **V = 3.66kN**, and the horizontal forces **C** and **T** are found from:

C = T = Moment ÷ Lever arm = 15.848 ÷ 2.5 = **6.34kN**

The force in **AC** is given directly from **T**: $F_{AC} = T = 6.34\text{kN}$ (tension)

The force in **AB** is given by the force triangle so:

$F_{AB} = C \div \cos 30° = V \div \sin 30° = 7.32\text{kN}$ (compression)

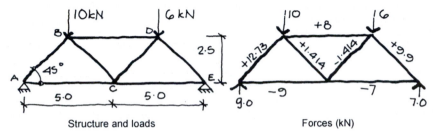

For the simple approach the equilibrium at a cut is often quicker. The maximum bending moment and shear force are calculated from which the maximum top, bottom and diagonal member forces are rapidly calculated.

Exercise 12.9   Verify the forces shown for the truss in **Fig. 12.39**. Hint: calculate the reactions then find the forces in the members at the supports. Then proceed to joints where there are only two unknown forces.

Structure and loads   Forces (kN)

Fig. 12.39 Truss and forces for Exercise 12.9

The results should also be checked by slicing the truss at several positions and following the procedure of **Example 12.17**.

12.9 Deflection and stiffness

It is an everyday experience to find materials that are hard, such as stone, concrete or soft, such as rubber, plastic, and that 'thin' things are easier to bend or stretch than 'thick' ones. But for calculations these experiences have to be quantified, for the material and for the element.

As the **Engineer's theory**, see page **65**, is being used the material is assumed to be linear elastic which means that the stiffness of the material can be characterised by a number. This number is called the **modulus of elasticity**, or **E**, and has the dimensions of force per area; usually **N/mm^2** is used. Stiffer materials have higher values for **E**; see page **119**.

Material	Modulus of elasticity – N/mm^2
Steel	210 E3
Concrete	Approx. 14 E3
Timber – softwood	Average 9 E3
Timber – hardwood	Average 14 E3

Table 12.7 Values of modulus of elasticity

As can be seen the only definite value is for steel. The value for concrete is approximate because it is dependent on the mix, type of aggregate, amount of water, age, and other factors. The values for timber vary with the species and because timber is a natural material, each piece is slightly different. This shows that any calculations for structural movement due to load can only be approximate.

To relate the values of **E** to loads, another definition has to be introduced, that of **strain**. If two short columns of the same length and cross-section are made of different material but carry equal loads, the column with a material of lower **E** will compress more.

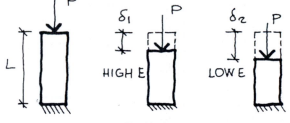

Fig. 12.40

The column with the lower **E** will compress more but how can they be compared numerically? The answer is to compare the strains. **Strain**, usually written **ε**, is defined as **the ratio of the deflection to the original length**. In this case the ratio of $\delta_1 : L$ will be smaller than $\delta_2 : L$ because the **E** is higher. Now **Hooke's Law**, see page **7**, can be stated in terms of **stress, f, strain, ε,** and the **modulus of elasticity, E,** as:

Stress = Modulus of elasticity times **strain**   or $f = E \times \varepsilon$

Stiffness of a structural element has a particular meaning in calculation and is defined by the relationship:

Force = Stiffness times **deflection**   or $P = K \times \delta$

With these definitions it is now possible, by simple algebra, to find expressions for the axial stiffness and deflection of a column. This is done as follows:

Stress = Force divided by **Area**   and   **Strain = Deflection** divided by **Length**

or $\qquad f = \dfrac{P}{A}$ $\qquad$ and $\qquad$ $\varepsilon = \dfrac{\delta}{L}$

which, substituting for stress and strain in Hooke's Law, gives

$$\frac{P}{A} = E \times \frac{\delta}{L} \qquad \text{rearranging gives} \qquad P = \left(\frac{EA}{L}\right) \times \delta = K \times \delta$$

where **K** is the **stiffness** of the column with units of force per length – **kN/m**. This expression can also be arranged to give the deflection:

$$\delta = \frac{PL}{EA} \qquad \text{and curvature} \quad K = \frac{EA}{L}$$

Example 12.18   Calculate the axial deflection and the stiffness of the column shown for values of E of **60 E3** and **5 E3 N/mm^2**.

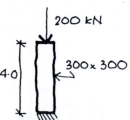

E		Calculation	Result
60E3	δ	$(200E3 \times 4E3) \div (60E3 \times 300^2)$	0. 15mm
	K	$(60E6 \times 0.3^2) \div 4$	1.35 E6 kN/m
5E3	δ	$(200E3 \times 4E3) \div (5E3 \times 300^2)$	1.78mm
	K	$(5E6 \times 0.3^2) \div 4$	112 E3 kN/m

Note: The calculations for δ are in **N** and **mm** but for **K** they are in **kN** and **m**.

To understand numerically how the bending of a beam is related to a vertical deflection, a rather artificial situation, from a practical point of view, is examined. A beam composed of two equal flanges, each with area **A** and a distance **d** apart, is bent by a moment **M**.

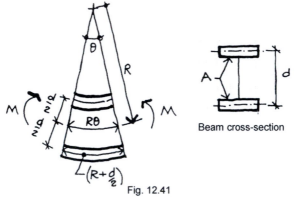

Beam cross-section

Fig. 12.41

Looking at a small slice of the beam it is assumed that it is bent into a circular shape by **M**, and the radius of the neutral axis is **R**. The length of the neutral axis, which does not change length due to bending is **Rθ** – see **Fig. 3.36**, but the length of the bottom flange has increased to **(R + d/2)θ**. As the unbent length was **Rθ**, the **strain** in the flange can be found as follows:

$$\varepsilon = \frac{(R + d/2)\theta - R\theta}{R\theta} = \frac{d}{2} \times \frac{1}{R} = \frac{d}{2} \times K$$

The strain is as before, the extension divided by the original length, this time of the flange. The reciprocal of the radius **R** is **K** (the Greek letter kappa) and is the **curvature** of the beam at the slice. Now the stress in the flange can be found from Hooke's Law as:

$$f = E \times K \times \frac{d}{2}$$

As the moment **M** is the force in the flange times the lever arm **d**, the moment can be written in terms of **E, A, d** and **K**, as

$$M = f \times A \times d = E \times K \times \left(A \times \frac{d^2}{2} \right) = E \times I \times K$$

Now the moment on the slice is given in terms of the **modulus of elasticity**, the **curvature** and the **moment of inertia, I**. This new term **moment of inertia** is borrowed from dynamics and is the part inside the brackets. It should really be called, and sometimes is, the **second moment of area** as it is the area multiplied twice by the distance to the neutral axis, so, in this case:

$$I = 2 \times A \times \left(\frac{d}{2} \right)^2 = A \times \frac{d^2}{2}$$

Algebraic expressions and actual values for different shapes and standard cross-sections are widely available in technical literature. The above examination not only used an I beam without a web but only looked at a 'slice'. What about a whole beam? If a whole beam had the same moment at every point then the vertical deflection can be found.

Consider a beam of span **L** with equal and opposite moments **M** applied at each end. At every point the bending moment is the same, **M**, so the slice is the whole length of the beam and the beam is bent into a circular arc.

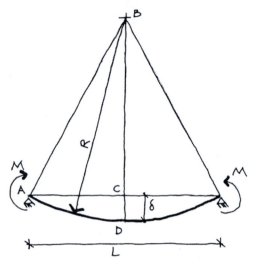

Fig. 12.42

The deflection, δ, can be found from an application of Pythagoras' theorem as:

$$\delta = CD = BD - BC = R - \sqrt{(AB^2 - AC^2)} = R - \sqrt{(R^2 - (L/2)^2)}$$

The radius, **R**, can be found from the moment, span and the moment of inertia of the beam. So for a given beam the deflection can be found.

Example 12.19 Calculate the central deflection for the beam shown. The section is made of steel and the flanges have the same dimensions as an **IPE 180**, see **Fig. 12.31**.

$$I = 91 \times 8 \times \frac{172^2}{2} = 1077\,E4\,mm^4$$

$$M = E \times I \times K = E \times I \times \frac{1}{R}$$

rearranging $R = \dfrac{E \times I}{M}$ so, working in Newtons and millimetres, R is calculated as:

$$R = \frac{210E3 \times 1076E4}{20E6} = 112980\,mm \qquad \therefore \quad \delta = 112980 - \sqrt{(112980^2 - 2000^2)} = 17.7\,mm$$

So the central deflection, for this rather artificial case, can be calculated from an examination that just uses simple geometry. As in most beams the size of the bending moment varies along the beam; the radius **R**, shown in **Fig. 12.41**, will be different for each point. In other words the curvature **K** is not constant, which means Pythagoras' theorem, used for **Fig. 12.42**, will not apply. To find deflections in these cases a more complex analysis is required. Alternatively the algebraic expressions given in technical handbooks can be used.

As a beam with a constant bending moment is unusual in real structures it might seem that this approach is of little use. It does not give the 'correct' deflection for beams loaded differently but it can act as a guide. Supposing, for **Example 12.19** the correct value of I, obtained from tables is **1317 E4 mm⁴**, then the deflection will be reduced in proportion to the increased value for I, that is:

$$\delta = \frac{1077\,E4}{1317\,E4} \times 17.7 = 14.5mm$$

Alternatively the calculations could be re-done with the new value. But how does this value compare with deflections calculated using more complex analysis for loads of different types? Below, a comparison is made between the calculated value and values for three other loadings.

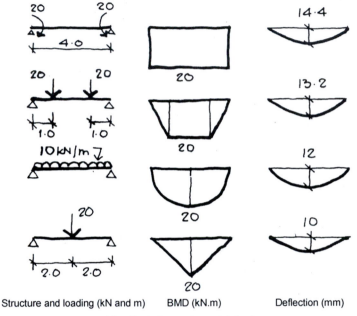

Structure and loading (kN and m)   BMD (kN.m)   Deflection (mm)

Fig. 12.43 Comparison of deflections

Unsurprisingly the nearer the shape of the **BMD** is to a rectangle, the closer the values are. For the central point load, the 'constant moment approach' overestimates the deflection by 44%. Given the fact that at the preliminary stages many other values are approximate, loading, actual material or even the dimensions, this is acceptable for the first stage and provides a guide. Having calculated a deflection does it show that the structure is stiff enough? Guides to acceptable deflections are given in many codes but they are not always clear. As a general guide the following limitations are typical for deflections due to the **live loads**.

Structure	Maximum deflection
Cantilever	Length/180
Beams (with brittle finishes)	Span/360
Beams in general	Span/250
Horizontal per storey	Storey height/300

Table 12.8 Maximum permissible deflections for live loads

As can be seen from the calculations a beam's stiffness is directly related to the value of **EI**, that is, the product of the **modulus of elasticity** with the **moment of inertia**. As it is rarely practical to alter **E**, stiffness is altered by **I**, that is, changing the dimensions of the structural cross-section. In general it is not easy to calculate deflections and this simple approach can only indicate some key values. However these should show whether a chosen structure is sufficiently stiff.

12.10   Slenderness and axial stability

A structure must be sufficiently stiff for the deflections under load to be acceptable, but there is an additional stiffness requirement; parts of the structure that are axially loaded must have sufficient stiffness to prevent buckling-initiated collapse. The ideas of axial stability and slenderness are explained in **Section 6.4** so here it is only necessary to indicate how to calculate the slenderness and how this affects the permissible stress.

As buckling is due to an element bending under an axial load, 'slenderness' is partially dependent on its bending stiffness, that is **E** × **I**. It is also dependent on its **effective length L$_E$**. The effective length is dependent on how the ends of the member are supported; the four classic cases are shown.

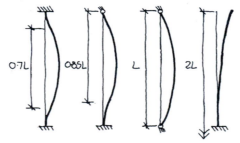

Fig. 12.44 Effective length for different support conditions

These effective lengths are for elements supported 'ideally', that is fully fixed or with perfect pins, which do not occur in real structures. The designer has to decide on what is a reasonable effective length. Whilst resistance to buckling is dependent on the **EI**, slenderness is calculated by dividing the effective length by the **minimum radius of gyration, r$_{min}$**. The radius of gyration is another term borrowed from dynamics. When a mass **m** is rotated at a radius **r** then the moment of inertia is given by mr^2. The moment of inertia **I** was defined on page **358**, so if the mass is considered to be the cross-sectional area **A** then the radius of gyration can be calculated.

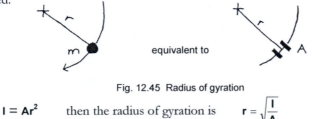

Fig. 12.45 Radius of gyration

As $I = Ar^2$ then the radius of gyration is $r = \sqrt{\dfrac{I}{A}}$

In the mathematical analysis of buckling, the minimum radius of gyration plays a central role in defining slenderness. To avoid the possibility of buckling, the allowable stress in an axially loaded member has to be reduced by a factor that is related to the slenderness of the element. These have been calculated and are available in technical codes. Due to the material, the values of **E**, and the maximum allowable stress, there is some variation in the value of the reduction factor. The typical range for the relationship between this factor and the slenderness is shown in **Fig. 12.46**. These curves are the envelope of values obtained from a number of technical publications. The range is due to modifications introduced to take into account initial defects such as lack of perfect straightness. This is another example of how the basis for numerical calculations is not exact.

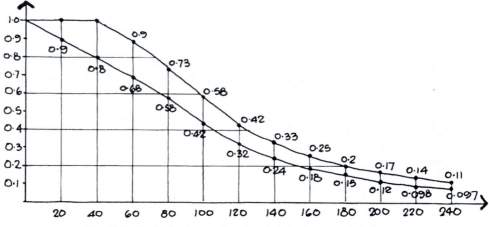

Fig. 12.46 Reduction factors plotted against slenderness ratio L_E/r_{min}

When **r** is found it has to be the **minimum value**, so the minimum value of **I** has to be used.

Example 12.20 Calculate the allowable axial load that a mild steel column, supported as shown, can carry if it is:
1   An IPE 180
2   A circular tube (CHS) of dia. 168.3mm and wall thickness 5mm

Assuming the connection to the concrete foundation is a pin joint and the connection to the concrete super-structure is nearly fixed then:

$L_E = 0.9 \times 4.0 = 3.60m$

Section properties from tables are:

Section	A mm^2	I$_{min}$ mm^4	Calculation	r$_{min}$ mm
IPE 180	23.95 E2	100.9 E4	$\sqrt{(100.9\ E4 \div 23.95\ E2)}$	20.5
168.3 CHS	25.7 E2	856 E4	$\sqrt{(856\ E4 \div 25.7\ E2)}$	58

Calculate the slenderness; find the reduction factor using an average value.

Section	Calculation	L_E/r_{min}	factor	Calculation	f$_{all}$ N/mm^2
IPE 180	3.6 E3 ÷ 20.5	176	0.2	0.2 × 155	31
168.3 CHS	3.6 E3 ÷ 58	62	0.8	0.8 × 155	124

Calculate the allowable axial load, N_{all}, from **A** and f_{all}.

Section	Calculation	N_{all} kN
IPE 180	31 × 23.95 E2 ÷ E3	74.3
168.3 CHS	124 × 25.7 E2 ÷ E3	319

Exercise 12.10   Repeat the calculations of Example 12.20 for the following sections:
1   HEA 120A
2   150 x 100 rectangular tube (RHS) with wall thickness of 5mm

The material is mild steel and the section properties are:

Section	A mm^2	I_{min} mm^4
HEA 120A	25.34 E2	230.9 E4
150 x 100 RHS	23.9 E2	396 E4

Exercise 12.11   Compare capacities of the four sections in terms of the weight of material used. The weights are given in **kg/m**.

IPE 180	168.3 CHS	150 x 100 RHS	HEA 120 A
18.8	20.1	18.7	19.9

Where other parts of structures are in compression, such as the flanges and webs of beams, diagonals of trusses for example, the allowable stress will be reduced if they are slender. And the reduction will be as dramatic as shown in **Fig. 12.46**. Technical literature provides guidance for many situations, but stresses can often be checked approximately by considering the part in compression as an 'axial member'.

12.11   Four examples of simple calculations

To see how the simple approach can give useful information with the minimum of calculation, some examples, all of which have already appeared in the book, are now given. Parts of these real structures are calculated. These are:

- **Simple building,** the wind bracing system section sizes
- **Zarzuela Hippodrome,** the roof structure tie
- **Federal Reserve Bank,** stresses at the base of the end tower
- **Centre Pompidou,** floor truss section sizes and deflection

As exact dimensional information is not available for all these examples, reasonable assumptions are made as necessary.

Example 12.21

A Simple Building – (see Chapter 8)

Calculate the sizes of the elements of the wind-bracing system that resist the longitudinal wind forces.

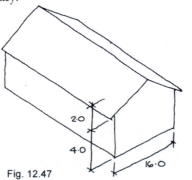

Fig. 12.47

The basic wind speed is assumed to be **50m/s** and the building is situated in the country. The relevant dimensions are shown in **Fig. 12.47**. The bracing structure is shown in **Fig. 12.47**. Only the section sizes of the diagonal members are required as the other members are part of the portal frames.

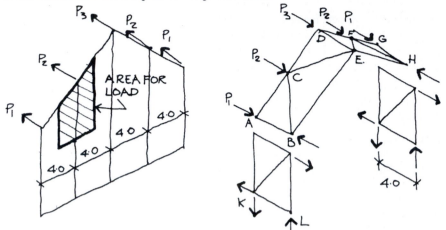

Fig. 12.48 Wind load and bracing structure

The first step is to calculate the wind load.

	Symbol	Calculation	Result
Basic wind speed	V	given	50m/s
Coefficient	S	Table 12.3	0.88
Design wind speed	V_s	0.88 × 50	44m/s
Wind load	q	0.613×44^2 E-3	$1.2kN/m^2$

Then forces, **P_1, P_2** and **P_3** on the bracing structure.

	Symbol	Calculation	Result
Wind load on end walls	$q \times C_p$	1.2 (0.7 - (-0.3))	1.2 kN/m^2
P_1	Area × q	4/2 × 4/2 × 1.2	4.8kN
P_2	=	4 × 5/2 × 1.2	12.0kN
P_3	=	4 × 6/2 × 1.2	14.4kN

For the purposes of the calculation of forces, the truss is assumed to be flat. The forces are found by considering the equilibrium of the joints. 'Vertical' and 'horizontal' are used to distinguish the directions, not the position in the building.

Joint B

Direction	Equilibrium	Force
'Vertical'	24 - 4.8 = F_{BC} sin 45°	F_{BC} = 27.15kN
'Horizontal'	F_{BE} = F_{BC} cos 45°	F_{BE} = 19.20kN

Joint C

Direction	Equilibrium	Force
'Vertical'	27.15 sin 45 ° = 12 + F_{CE} sin 45°	F_{CE} = 10.18kN
'Horizontal'	F_{CD} = (27.15 +10.18) sin 45°	F_{CD} = 26.40kN

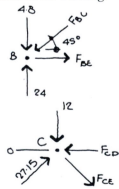

Joint D

Direction	Equilibrium	Force
'Vertical'	Equal to the load	$F_{DE} = 14.40$kN
'Horizontal'	Equal to F_{CD}	$F_{DF} = 26.40$kN

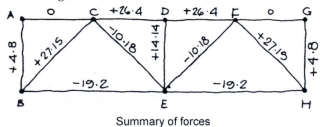

The forces in the horizontal truss that forms part of the wind-bracing are summarised in the diagram.

Summary of forces

Now structural sections can be chosen for the diagonal members, circular hollow sections (**CHS**) are usual, and the actual stress, f_{act}, calculated.

Element	N_{act} kN	CHS	A mm^2	Calculation	f_{act} N/mm^2
AB	4.80	60.3 × 3.2	5.74 E2	4.80 E3 ÷ 5.74 E2	8.4
BC	27.15	114.3 × 3.6	12.50 E2	27.15 E3 ÷ 12.5 E2	21.7
CE	10.18	76.2× 3.2	7.33 E2	10.18 E3 ÷ 7.33 E2	13.9
DE	14.40	60.3 × 4.0	7.07 E2	14.40 E3 ÷ 7.07 E2	20.4

The allowable stresses, f_{all}, is calculated and checked against the actual stresses to make sure that $f_{all} \geq f_{act}$ is true for all elements. As wind is reversible all elements are designed for compression.

Element	L_E mm	r_{min} mm	Slenderness	Coeff.	f_{all} N/mm^2
AB	4.0 E3	20.2	198	0.15	155 × 0.15 = 23.3
BC	5.7 E3	39.2	145	0.3	46.5
CE	5.7 E3	25.8	220	0.12	18.6
DE	4.0 E3	20	200	0.15	23.3

This shows that $f_{all} \geq f_{act}$ is true for all elements. The sizing of the vertical structure is left as an **Exercise**.

Example 12.22 The Zarzuela Hippodrome (see Section 9.3)

Design the tie down for the roof.

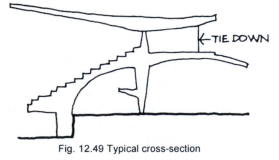

Fig. 12.49 Typical cross-section

The roof structure is considered to be a simply supported beam with two cantilevers. This means that the forces can be calculated from equilibrium as the structure is **statically determinate**. The spacing of the columns and ties is **5.1m**, and the thickness of the shell roof varies from **55mm** to **125mm**, there are no finishes; assume average thickness of **100mm**. Therefore the load will be the self-weight of the concrete roof plus an allowance for snow, assume **0.6m**.

Element	Load	kN/m
Roof	0.1 × 5.1 × 25 =	12.8
Snow	0.6 × 5.1 × 1.0 =	3.1
	Total =	15.9

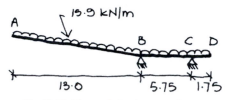

Fig. 12.50 The roof structure as a beam

Calculate the bending moments, shear forces and reactions for loads on each span separately.

Span AB

Force	Calculation	Result
S_{BA}	−15.9 × 13	−206.7kN
M_{BA}	15.9 ×13² ÷ 2	−1343.6kN.m
S_{BC}	1343.6 ÷ 5.25	255.9kN
R_B	206.7 + 255.9	462.6kN
R_C	= −S BC	−255.9kN

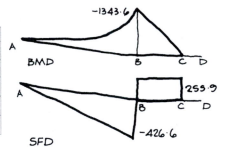

Span BC

Force	Calculation	Result
S_{BC}	15.9 ×5.25 ÷ 2	41.7kN
S_{CB}	−15.9 ×5.25 ÷ 2	−41.7kN
M_{max}	15.9 ×5.25² ÷ 8	54.8kN.m
R_B	= S_{BC}	41.7kN
R_C	= −S_{CB}	41.7kN

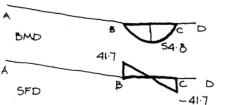

Span CD

Force	Calculation	Result
S_{CD}	15.9 × 1.75	27.8kN
M_{CD}	15.9 ×1.75² ÷ 2	−24.3kN.m
S_{BC}	24.3 ÷ 5.25	−4.6kN
R_B	= S_{BC}	−4.6kN
R_c	27.8 + 4.6	32.4kN

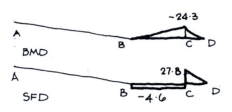

Now the tie down force can be calculated from the sum of the reactions R_c.

Tie down force = N_{act} = Sum of R_c = $-2\,55.9 + 41.7 + 32.4 = -181.8kN$

Note that this force includes the effect of snow on spans **BC** and **CD** which reduces the total force. To take account of the possibility on less snow take a design force of **200kN**. From this, the diameter of a mild steel tie can be calculated.

$$A_{req} = N_{act} \div f_{all} = 200\,E3 \div 155 = 1290mm^2$$

$$\therefore \text{ use 42 dia. tie } (A_{act} = 1385mm^2)$$

Example 12.23 The Federal Reserve Bank (see Section 9.5)

Calculate the stresses at the base of the end towers, for vertical and wind loads.

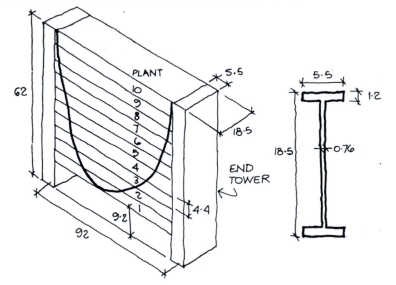

Fig. 12.51 Main dimension of building and tower structure

Calculate a typical floor load using assumed values.

Component	kN/m^2
Self-weight	4.0
Finishes	1.2
Live load	3.0
Partitions	1.5
Total	**9.7**

Calculate the load to the facade per floor, from the floor and the cladding.

Element	Load	kN/m
Floor	9.7 × 18.5 ÷ 2	89.7
Cladding	1.2 × 4.4	5.3
	Total	**95**

Calculate the load to one tower, assume **14** floors (to take into account plant loads and roof) and roof truss weight of **1200kg/m**.

Element	Load	kN
Floors	14 × 95 × 86.5 ÷ 2	57,522
Truss	12 × 92 ÷ 2	552
	Total	58,074

Calculate the typical floor load in the tower.

Component	kN/m^2
Self-weight	5.0
Finishes	3.0
Live load	4.0
Total	12.0

Calculate the load due to the weight of the tower; this is the self-weight, the weight of non-loadbearing walls and the weight of floors.

Element	Load	kN
Self-weight	(2 × 1.2 × 5.5 + 0.76 × (18.5-2×1.2)) × 25 × 62	39,426
Other walls	(18 × 4 × 0.2) × 25 × 62	22,320
Floors 12N°	12 × (5 × 18) × 12.0	12,960
	Total	74,706

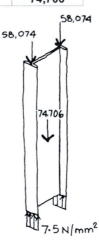

Using the total vertical load on the tower and dividing it by the gross cross-section of the structure, the axial stress is calculated.

Total load = N_{act} = 2 × 58,074 + 74,706 = **190,854kN**

Total area = A_{act} = 2 × 1.2 × 5.5 + 0.76 × (18.5 - 2×1.2) = **25.44 m^2**

Axial stress = f_{ax-act} = 190,854 E3 ÷ 25.44 E6 = **7.5N/mm^2**

To assess the wind load assume the basic wind speed is **50m/s**.

	Symbol	Calculation	Result
Basic wind speed	V	assumed	50m/s
Coefficient	S	Table 12.3	1.04
Design wind speed	V_s	1.04 × 50	52m/s
Wind load	q	0.613 × 52^2 E-3	**1.66kN/m^2**

Calculate the total wind load on the building, ignore the space under the central part and use a total coefficient of **1.0**.

Total load = W_{win} = (92 + 5.5) × 62 × 1.66 = **10,035kN**

The two towers act as cantilevers from the ground, so the cantilever moment for each tower is:

Moment per tower = M_{win} = (10,035 ÷ 2) × 62 ÷ 2 = **155,542kN.m**

The stress due to the wind moment can now be calculated from the push/pull force in the flanges and the area of the flange.

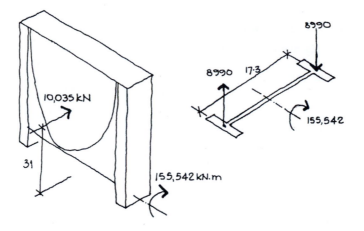

Push = Pull = 155,542 ÷ 17.30 = **8990kN**

and

Flange stress = $f_{bm\text{-}act}$ = 8990 E3 ÷ (5.5 × 1.2) E6 = **1.36N/mm²**

It is now possible to combine the flange stresses at the base of the tower to give the maximum and minimum stress.

Maximum stress = f_{max} = $f_{ax\text{-}act}$ + $f_{bm\text{-}act}$ = 7.5 + 1.36 = **8.86N/mm²**

and

Minimum stress = f_{min} = $f_{ax\text{-}act}$ − $f_{bm\text{-}act}$ = 7.5 − 1.36 = **6.14N/mm²**

This shows that the stresses are acceptable for concrete in compression, see **Table 12.6**, and that there are no tensile stresses at the bottom of the tower.

Exercise   Recalculate the axial forces and stresses ignoring live loads and allowances for finishes and partitions. Check the combined stresses.

Example 12.24 The Pompidou Centre – (also see pages 318-322)

Calculate the forces in the floor structure and size the top and bottom members of the truss. Estimate the central deflection under live and partition loads.

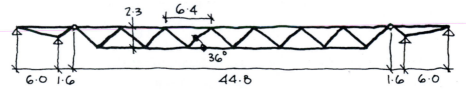

Fig. 12.52 Floor structure of Centre Pompidou

Calculate a typical floor load using published information and assumed values.

Component	kN/m²
110 mm slab	2.8
Finishes	1.2
Live load	5.0
Partitions	1.2
Total	**10.2**

Calculate the load on the truss and add an assumed truss self-weight of **1000kg/m**, the trusses are spaced at **12.9 m**.

Element	Calculation	kN/m
Floor	10.2 × 12.9	131.6
Truss self-weight	assumed	10.0
	Total	**141.6**

Calculate the maximum bending moment and shear force. Calculate the truss forces in the top and bottom members; these are the push/pull forces. The forces in the end diagonal members resist the shear and are calculated using the triangle of forces.

$$\text{Maximum moment} = M = w \times L^2 \div 8 = 141.6 \times 44.8^2 \div 8 = \textbf{35,525kN.m}$$

$$\text{Push force} = \text{pull force} = M \div d = 35,525 \div 2.3 = \textbf{15,445kN}$$

$$\text{Maximum shear force} = S = w \times L \div 2 = 141.6 \times 44.8 \div 2 = \textbf{3171kN}$$

$$\text{Maximum diagonal forces} = S \div \sin 36° = 3171 \div 0.587 = \textbf{5395kN}$$

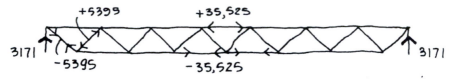

Maximum truss forces

Now it is possible to choose structural elements for the top, bottom and diagonal members and check the actual stresses, f_{act}. Twin circular tubes are used for the top member, and twin circular bars for the bottom member. The diagonal members are single bars and tubes. This is the arrangement used in the actual project.

Element	N_{act} kN	Section	A mm²	Calculation	f_{act} N/mm²
Top	15,445	2 × 457 × 32 CHS	85.4 E3	15.45 E6 ÷ 85.4 E3	181
Bottom	−15,445	2 × 220 dia. bar	76 E3	15.45 E6 ÷ 76 E3	203
Diag. tens	−5395	180 dia. bar	25.5 E3	5.4 E6 ÷ 25.5 E3	212
Diag. comp	5395	406 × 25 CHS	30 E3	5.4 E6 ÷ 30 E 3	180

The allowable stresses, f_{all}, are calculated using high tensile steel.

Element	L_E mm	r_{min} mm	Slenderness	Coeff.	f_{all} N/mm²
Top	6.4 E3	151	42	0.9	194
Bottom	-	-	-	-	215
Diag. T	-	-	-	-	215
Diag. C	3.9 E3	135	29	0.95	204

This shows that $f_{all} \geq f_{act}$ is true for all elements.

The deflection is calculated using the constant moment approach used for the beam on page **359**. The deflection is only for the live load and the partition load so the bending moment, M_{defl}, has to be reduced in proportion to this load to the total load.

$$M_{defl} = (((5.0 + 1.2) \times 12.9) \div 141.6) \times 35,525 = \mathbf{20,066kN.m}$$

Calculate the moment of inertia, **I**, of the truss from the area of the main members, see page **358**. As the areas are not equal this calculation is not quite true, but it is sufficiently accurate for this simple approach. The larger area is used.

$$I = A \times \frac{d^2}{2} = 85.4E3 \times \frac{2300^2}{2} = \mathbf{2.25E11mm^4}$$

Calculate the radius from the moment, moment of inertia and the modulus of elasticity, see page **359**.

$$R = \frac{EI}{M_{defl.}} = \frac{210E3 \times 2.25E11}{20,066E6} = \mathbf{2,354,729mm}$$

Now, using Pythagoras' theorem, see page **359**, the deflection can be calculated.

$$\delta = 2,354,729 - \sqrt{\left(2,354,729^2 - 22,400^2\right)} = \mathbf{106mm}$$

Which is equivalent to the **span ÷ 422**.

12.12   Summary

It has been shown how it is possible to make significant calculations, on two pages or so, using no more than the basic arithmetic operations. Apart from the conceptual understanding and some basic technical data, all that was needed was some simple algebraic manipulations and elementary trigonometry. However, the essential point is the conceptual understanding, which makes sense of the numbers and how they relate. No calculations should be done if the underlying concepts are not understood.

Some new quantities were introduced – strain, moment of inertia, section modulus and radius of gyration. Most of these arose almost naturally, without the need for new concepts. With these it is possible to make links to the relationships that form the basis of the mathematical treatment of structural behaviour.

- **external loads to internal forces or equilibrium**
- **stresses to internal movements (strains)**
- **internal movements to deflections of the structure**

For axially loaded elements, these three relationships have been given as:

- **external loads to internal forces or $P = A \times f$**
- **stresses to strains or $\varepsilon = E \times f$**
- **internal movements to deflections or $\delta = \varepsilon \times L$**

In the case of the beam, the same relationships exist but here the internal force is the moment, **M**, and the internal movement the curvature, **K = 1/R**.

- **external loads to internal forces or $M_x = wL \times x - wL^2/2 \times x - wx \times x/2$ (see page 337)**
- **stresses to strains or $M = E \times I \times K$**
- **deflections to internal movements or $\delta = R - \sqrt{(R^2 - (L/2)^2)}$**

In all mathematical theories, these relationships appear and are related to define various forms of governing equations. Unfortunately these relationships are often 'hidden' in the mathematics, so whilst following any mathematical development it is always worthwhile asking where and how these relationships are appearing.

As can be seen, assumptions were being made continually in the calculations so exact numerical accuracy, with many significant figures, is not required but the numbers must be of the correct magnitude. In some ways numerical calculations are an expression of ignorance in the sense that sizes of structural members are 'unknown' until they are calculated.

Some form of simple calculation should always be done at the outset of a project, not only to test initial ideas but to provide a check on subsequent more detailed calculations. Structural computer programs, especially with graphical output, can be a great help in understanding structural behaviour, and simple models can be checked against initial hand calculations.

With the availability of programs that can accept enormous structural models, there is an unfortunate tendency to put whole buildings into the computer before the basic behaviour is understood – this should always be avoided. Quite often whole building models are unnecessary as adequate analysis can be done with a number of simple smaller models. When complex analysis is required, the results must always be reviewed against the structural behaviour predicted by simplified calculations, and significant differences properly understood.

References – Chapter 12

1   A Beal – **Factors of ignorance?** – The Structural Engineer, Vol. 79/No. 20 16 Oct. 2001 – pp 15-16

CHAPTER 13   *The mathematical basis*

For a complete picture of structural behaviour, as this book wants to give, the use of mathematics for the understanding of structures has to be included. Whilst research into the applications of mathematics for the description of structural behaviour continues, the basis was laid at the beginning of the 19th century which led to three things:

- **methods of carrying out predictive calculations became available**
- **the separation of structural concepts from architectural concepts began**
- **the excessive interest in theory by engineers reduced their design capacity**

This is not to say that there is anything wrong, as such, with the use of mathematics as a tool for predicting structural behaviour, in fact it is essential. The ever increasing use of mathematics as a tool is part of technological advancement. However it should be generally available and not restricted to a small group. The reasons for this are buried deep in societies' view of mathematics in general. As mathematics is a demanding subject there is a predominant idea that only a chosen few are capable of using mathematics for anything; nothing could be less true. In mathematics, as with structural behaviour, it is the concepts that have to be grasped, after which calculations become arithmetic.

To understand the mathematical basis of the behaviour of structures, no new structural concepts are required. But this mathematical world can only be entered through the **differential calculus**. This was developed independently in the 17th century by Isaac Newton and Gottfried Leibniz, and remains the single most important tool for the mathematical description of the physical world.

In this chapter only skeletal structures will be considered but almost all mathematical analysis carried out for building structures uses this idealisation. Only the rudiments of the differential calculus are required for this analysis and they are explained in this chapter. Apart from this, simple algebraic manipulation and the basic arithmetic operations are also used.

13.1   Functions and differentiation

The new mathematics required is to make possible the differentiation of ordinary functions with respect to one of the variables. This may sound technical but a clear physical picture of the process can be had by imagining how it feels to ride a bicycle along a smooth straight but undulating road that runs beside a lake. The journey has a start point, an **origin**, and a **reference axis**, the water level of the lake. As the road undulates the slope, the **gradient**, is changing continuously and how this varies is the information that the process of differentiation provides.

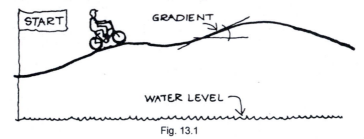

Fig. 13.1

This picture is converted to a mathematical description. The line representing the water level is renamed the **x-axis**. The distance travelled from the start point is called the **x-coordinate** and the height of the road above the water is called the **y-coordinate**. The profile of the road itself is called the **graphical representation** of the **function**. The **gradient of the function**, the slope of the road, is given by how a line drawn tangential to the function meets the x-axis. **Fig. 13.2** shows this.

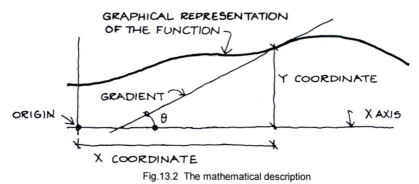

Fig.13.2 The mathematical description

For each point on the function there is an **x** and a **y** coordinate and these are related by the function. This can be written as a mathematical relationship as

$$y = f(x)$$

This means that **y is a function of x**, and for any given value of **x** the function **f** gives the value for **y**. The function could take many forms, like 'add 3', or 'multiply x by 17 and take away 2.5'. In this way the graphical representation of the function, or **graph** for short, can be drawn. Values of **x** are chosen allowing the values of **y** to be calculated from the function. For each value of **x** the 'height' of **y** is drawn from the x-axis; joining the tops of these lines by a smooth line gives the graph of the function.

Example 13.1 Draw the graph of the function **y = 0.25 x²**, a parabolic function.

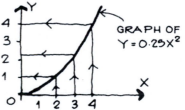

when **x = 2, y** = 0.25 × 2² = **1**.
when **x = 3, y** = 0.25 × 3² = **2.25** etc

374 Building structures

The question is: what is the gradient of the graph of the function for any value of **x**? For a first approximation of the gradient, values near to **x** can be chosen and the straight lines joining the points will give the approximate gradient.

Example 13.2　　Find the approximate gradient of the function **y = 0.25x²**, at **x = 2**, by considering values below of, **x = 1.5** and **1.75** then above of **x = 2.25** and **2.5**. Compare the results and draw diagrams.

For **x = 2, y** = 0.25 × 2² = 1,

using values of **x** less than 2

x = 1.5, **y** = 0.5625
∴ **gradient** = (1 − 0.5625) ÷ (2 − 1.5) = **0.875**
x = 1.75, **y** = 0.7656
∴ **gradient** = (1 − 0.7656) ÷ (2 − 1.75) = **0.9376**

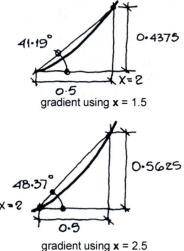
41·19°　　　　　　　0·4375
0·5　　　X = 2
gradient using x = 1.5

using values of **x** more than 2

x = 2.25, **y** = 1.2656
∴ **gradient** = (1.2656 - 1) ÷ (2.25 − 2) = **1.0675**
x = 2.5, **y** = 1.5625
∴ **gradient** = (1.5625 - 1) ÷ (2.5 − 2) = **1.125**

48·37°　　　　　　0·5625
X = 2
0·5
gradient using x = 2.5

the angles of the gradient lines can be calculated from **tan θ = gradient, gradient** = 0.875, θ = **41.19°** and **gradient** = 1.125, θ = **48.37°**

Four approximate values have been obtained and, as can be seen, the nearer the adjacent value chosen is to x = 2, the nearer the gradient seems to be to the correct value. The reader should experiment with other near values.

This method of finding the gradient by using points that are near can give a good approximation but it is time consuming. A mathematically based method is needed. This is done by considering a small interval on the x-axis called 'delta x' and denoted by δ**x**. Suppose the function gives a value **y** for a value **x**, then it will give a value **y + δy** for a value **x + δx**. It should be noted that δ**x** and δ**y** are not necessarily equal.

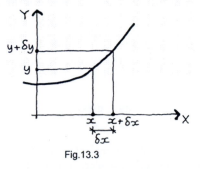

Fig.13.3

Now, by using the function to calculate the values at **x** and **x** + δ**x**, the same geometric triangular construction can be made to find the value of the gradient at **x**.

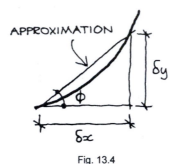

Fig. 13.4

The approximate gradient of the graph of the function at **x** is written as:

$$\text{gradient} = \frac{\delta y}{\delta x} = \tan \phi$$

Example 13.3 For the function $y = x^2$ obtain an expression for δ**y** in terms of **x** and δ**x** and another expression for the gradient.

$$y = f(x) = x^2$$

and
$$(y + \delta y) = f(x + \delta x) = (x + \delta x)^2 = x^2 + (2x\delta x) + \delta x^2$$

and as
$$\delta y = (y + \delta y) - y = f(x + \delta x) - f(x)$$

then the expression for δ**y** is

$$\delta y = (x^2 + (2x\delta x) + \delta x^2) - x^2 = (2x\delta x) + \delta x^2$$

to obtain the expression for the gradient each side is divided by δ**x** giving

$$\frac{\delta y}{\delta x} = \frac{2x\delta x}{\delta x} + \frac{(\delta x)^2}{\delta x} = 2x + \delta x$$

In **Example 13.2** it was shown how, as the interval between **x** and the near point reduces, that is as δ**x** gets smaller and smaller, so the approximation for the gradient becomes more accurate.. In **Example 13.3**, as δ**x** gets smaller, the gradient gets nearer to **2x**.

This approximate gradient at **x** has to be made into the actual gradient at **x**, that is the **differential**. This is done by making δ**x** so small that it is as near to zero as possible without actually being zero and so can be ignored in the part **2x** + δ**x**. This process of δ**x** approaching the limiting value zero is written as:

$$\frac{dy}{dx} = \text{limit}_{\delta x \to 0} \frac{\delta y}{\delta x}$$

The symbol on the left of the equals sign is the differential called 'dee y by dee x'. Now the differential **dy/dx**, of the function $y = f(x) = x^2$ with respect to the **x-axis** can be written:

$$\frac{dy}{dx} = \frac{df(x)}{dx} = 2x$$

This process of obtaining a differential of a function, called **differentiation,** is the basic operation of the differential calculus. It depends on the concept of δ**x**→0. This poses some intellectual problems because how can a number be so small, infinitely small, that is as close to zero as possible but at the same time be a number? When the differential calculus was discovered simultaneously by Leibniz and Newton in the late 17th century, see **page 8**, it was subjected to a devastating critique by Bishop Berkley who noted that *"…if something is neglected, no matter how small, we can no longer claim to have the exact result but only an approximation".*[1] The intellectual problem persisted for nearly 200 years and was only clarified in 1872 by Weierstrass. However. the process of differentiation, using the intellectually suspect infinitesimally small numbers, yielded useful results so research using the new mathematics progressed rapidly.

So far only the function $y = f(x) = x^2$ has been differentiated. Clearly a process is needed to differentiate any function having terms like x^n; this is given by the **general rule for differentiation**:

$$\frac{dy}{dx} = nx^{n-1}$$

This is the **central relationship** used for differentiating functions.

Example 13.4   Differentiate the function $y = x^3 - 0.2x^5$ with respect to x and evaluate the gradient at $x = 1.2$. Draw the graph and the gradient line at $x = 1.2$.

using the general expression for differentiation

$$\frac{dy}{dx} = 3x^{3-1} - 0.2 \times 5x^{5-1} = 3x^2 - x^4$$

and at $x = 1.2$, the gradient is

$$\text{gradient} = \frac{dy}{dx} = 3 \times 1.2^2 - 1.2^4$$

$$= 4.32 - 2.0736 = 2.24$$

and as **gradient = tan θ** then

$\tan \theta = 2.246$ so $\theta = 66°$

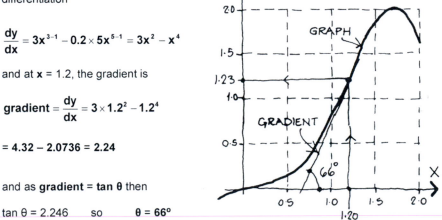

Any function $y = f(x)$ that contains any number of powers of x, that is, x^n, can be differentiated piecewise using the general rule. More complex functions can also be differentiated but as they are not required here these need not be explained. There are two important points to be noted about the expression for the general rule of differentiation which are:

- **it defines a new function, the derived function**
- **it is a differential equation**

Why the process of differentiation defines a new function is shown in **Example 13.4**. Here the derivative, **dy/dx**, was given in terms of **x**; hence it is a function of **x** and can have a graphical representation.

Example 13.5 Draw the graph of the derived function of

$$y = x^3 - 0.2x^5$$

that is

$$\frac{dy}{dx} = 3x^2 - x^4$$

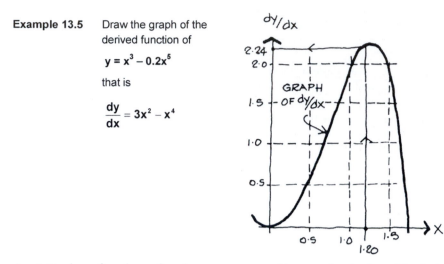

As **dy/dx** is a function of **x**, it seems reasonable to ask whether this derived function can be differentiated, and it can be by using the general rule.

Example 13.5 contd. Differentiate, with respect to **x**, the derived function $\dfrac{dy}{dx} = 3x^2 - x^4$

$$\frac{d}{dx}\left(\frac{dy}{dx}\right) = \frac{d^2y}{dx^2} = 2 \times 3x^{2-1} - 4x^{4-1} = 6x - 4x^3$$

The second derivative, or the derived function of the derived function, is called '**dee two y by dee x squared**'. This process can be continued until there are no more **x**s to be differentiated. And **dy/dx = $3x^2 - x^4$** is a **differential equation** because it contains **dy/dx**, a differential.

Physical phenomena, which include the behaviour of structures, can often be described by differential equations. In the following sections, differential equations are developed that describe the behaviour of a column and of a beam. These equations are developed for the general case and then solutions are sought for particular cases, a cantilever with a uniformly distributed load for example. The solution will be in the form of a function, or functions, and these will represent bending moments, shear forces, displacements and curvatures. So 'solving' the differential equation means finding a function.

Example 13.6 What is the 'solution' to the differential equation **dy/dx = $3x^2 - x^4$**?

from **Example** 13.4 the solution is $y = x^3 - 0.2x^5$

because if it is differentiated it will equal the right-hand of the differential equation.

The answer in **Example 13.6** has been obtained by 'undifferentiating' the differential equation. How can this be done in general, and is it the only 'solution'? To answer this in a general way the process of **integration** must be explained.

13.2 Integration

What is needed is, given derived function **dy/dx = f(x)**, a general rule for finding another function, **y = f(x)**, that gives the derived function when differentiated. The derived function is assumed to be of the type **y = x^n**. This rule can be stated directly, from the general rule for differentiation given on page **377**, as the **general rule for integration**:

$$\int y\,dx = \int x^n dx = \frac{x^{n+1}}{n+1} + C$$

The sign $\int$ means 'the integral of' and the **dx** means that the integration is being carried out with respect to **x**. The letter **C** is the **constant of integration** and is explained later.

Example 13.7   Given the derived function   **dy/dx = 3x^2 – x^4**, find, by using the general rule of integration, a suitable function in the form **y = x^n**

$$\int \left(\frac{dy}{dx}\right) dx = y = \int (3x^2 - x^4)dx = \int 3x^2 dx - \int x^4 dx = \frac{3x^{2+1}}{2+1} - \frac{x^{4+1}}{4+1} + C = x^3 - 0.2x^5 + C$$

The derived function has been integrated piecewise, that is, each part individually. As can be seen the original function, **y = x^3 – 0.2x^5**, has been recovered but with the addition of **C**, the constant of integration. Why has this constant of integration appeared? The reason is that the recovered function is not unique because if there were two functions **y = f$_1$(x) = x^3 – 0.2x^5 + 0.5**, and **y = f$_2$(x) = x^3 – 0.2x^5 – 0.5**, when differentiated, using the general rule, both would give **dy/dx = 3x^2 – x^4**. Here **C** takes the value **+0.5** in **f$_1$(x)** and **–0.5** in **f$_2$(x)**. If the graphs of the two functions are drawn it can be seen that the gradients, which are what the derived functions give, are the same.

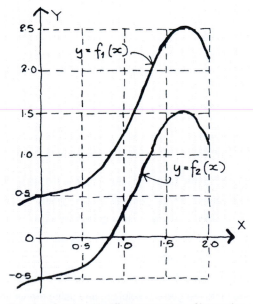

Fig. 13.5 Graphs with different constants of integration

To return to the cycling analogy shown in **Fig. 13.1**; given a profile of a road, the same road can be placed at any height above the level of the water level. The cyclist will experience the same gradients. Therefore to find the unique function, **y = f(x)**, the unique road, one more piece of information is required. This a specific value of **y** for some **x**. So to obtain the graph shown for **Example 13.4**, the values at **x = 0, y = 0**, would be sufficient, in other words **C = 0**.

What has been achieved is the solution of a **first order differential equation** by **direct integration**. A general solution was obtained and, with extra information, a unique solution was obtained. The solutions are in the form of functions. In this example the first order differential equation is **dy/dx = 3x² – x⁴** and the general solution is **y = f(x) = x³ – 0.2x⁵ + C**. As **C** can take any value, there is an infinite number of these equations. With one piece of extra information **C** can be evaluated and a unique solution obtained.

The term **first order** was used to denote that only **dy/dx** was involved. But if the derived equation involves **d²y/dx²**, a **second order differential** equation, can a solution, in the form of **y = f(x)** be obtained by direct integration? It can be, by proceeding as before, but now the integration has to be carried out twice.

Example 13.8   Given the derived function $d^2y/dx^2 = 6x - 4x^3$, find, by using the general rule of integration, a general solution in the form $y = x^n$

First application of the general rule of integration

$$\int \left(\frac{d^2y}{dx^2}\right)dx = \frac{dy}{dx} = \int(6x - 4x^3)dx = \int 6xdx - \int 4x^3dx = \frac{6x^{1+1}}{1+1} - \frac{4x^{3+1}}{3+1} + C = 3x^2 - x^4 + C$$

Second application of the general rule of integration

$$\int \left(\frac{dy}{dx}\right)dx = y = \int(3x^2 - x^4 + C)dx = x^3 - 0.2x^5 + Cx + D$$

So the general solution is: $y = x^3 - 0.2x^3 + Cx + D$

Each time the integration rule is used another constant of integration appears, as it has been used twice in this example there are two, **C** and **D**. But because **C** appeared due to the first application of the integration rule, it is subject to the rule for the second integration. That is **C**, when integrated with respect to **x**, becomes **Cx**. This can be seen formally as:

$$\int Cdx = \int Cx^0dx = \frac{Cx^{0+1}}{0+1} = Cx$$

where the convention **x⁰ = 1**, has been used. Now to obtain a unique solution two additional pieces of information are needed to evaluate **C** and **D**.

Example 13.8 cont. Suppose the additional information is that at **x = 0, y = –0.5**

Then, substituting these values into the general solution gives:

$$-0.5 = 0^3 - 0.2 \times 0^5 + C \times 0 + D = D$$

allowing the constant of integration **D** to be evaluated as **–0.5**

the second piece of information is obtained from:

y = 0 which gives **x = 0.835**

substituting these values into the general solution, and using the value for **D** gives:

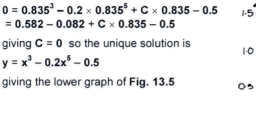

$$0 = 0.835^3 - 0.2 \times 0.835^5 + C \times 0.835 - 0.5$$
$$= 0.582 - 0.082 + C \times 0.835 - 0.5$$

giving **C = 0** so the unique solution is

$$y = x^3 - 0.2x^5 - 0.5$$

giving the lower graph of **Fig. 13.5**

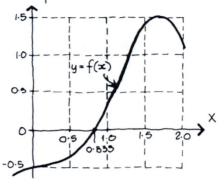

Differential equations of this type of any order can be solved by this method of direct integration. Every time the order of a differential equation increases so the integration has to be carried out one more times, giving more constants of integration. For a fourth order equation, $d^4y/dx^4 = f(x)$, the integration has to be carried out four times, and each time a constant of integration will be needed. So the final function $y = f(x)$, the solution, will need four extra pieces of information for a unique solution. The differential equation of the beam, see **Section 13.4**, is of this type.

With these two mathematical processes, differentiation and integration, and the solution of the consequent differential equations by direct integration, the mathematical world of structures can be entered.

13.3   The axially loaded element

In this section the mathematical description of an axially loaded element is derived. This will be in the form of a second order differential equation. First the structural element has to be considered as an **interval** on the x-axis.

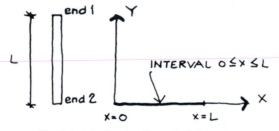

Fig.13.6 Actual and mathematical elements

Now all the required information about the axially loaded element is given in the form of functions of **x**. So the applied load of **p** kN/m becomes **p(x)**, the axial force in the element **N** kN becomes **N(x)** and the axial displacement **u** mm becomes **u(x)**. The functions may have values outside the interval $0 \le x \le L$, but these are of no interest. As far as signs are concerned, values of the functions are considered positive in the direction from **end1**, that is **x = 0**, to **end2**, that is **x = L**. For axial forces this means tensile forces **N** are positive with corresponding positive axial displacements **u**.

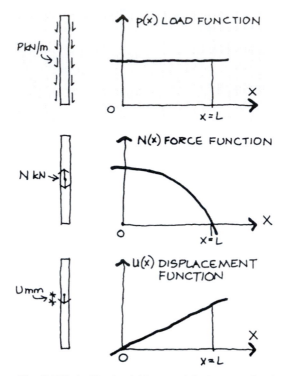

Fig. 13.7 Typical load, axial force and displacement functions

These functions are obtained by solving the governing differential equation of the axially loaded element. This is derived by applying concepts of equilibrium and stress and strain that have already been used to a thin 'slice' of the element. It is assumed that the force applied to the element, **N**, increases across it by δ**N**, but that the load along the element, **p**, is sensibly constant over the thickness of the 'thin' slice δ**x**.

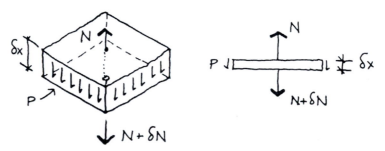

Fig. 13.8 Forces on a slice

For equilibrium of the slice in the axial direction, that is in the direction of the **x** axis:

$$N = p\delta x + (N + \delta N)$$

so cancelling the **N**s, rearranging and dividing by δ**x** and assuming δ**x** and δ**N** → **0** the equilibrium equation can be written as the following **differential** equation:

$$p(x) = -\frac{dN}{dx}$$

In a similar way the **axial displacement** of the slice can be related to the **strain**, that is the displacement divided by the original length, see page **357**:

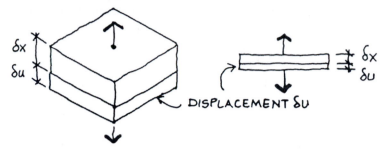

Fig. 13.9 Displacement of a slice

From the definition of strain, and letting δx and $\delta u \rightarrow 0$ the following **differential equation** can be written:

$$\varepsilon = \frac{du}{dx}$$

Using the assumption that the axial stress f_{ax} is constant over the cross-section of area **A**, it can be related to the axial force **N**, see page **66**, as:

$$f_{ax} = \frac{N}{A}$$

Using **Hooke's Law** to relate stress to strain by the modulus of elasticity **E**, see page **357**, then:

$$E = \frac{f_{ax}}{\varepsilon} = \frac{N}{A\varepsilon}$$

To express the relationship between strain ε and internal force **N**, this is rearranged as:

$$N = EA\varepsilon$$

Now three equations have been derived that express the following relationships:

- **external load** to **internal force** or $p(x) = -dN/dx$

- **internal force** to **strain** or $N = EA\varepsilon$

- **strain** to **displacement** or $\varepsilon = du/dx$

These are the same as the relationships listed on page **371**, but now two of the relationships are expressed by differential equations. It is now possible to combine these relationships into one equation as follows:

$$p(x) = -\frac{dN}{dx} = -\frac{d}{dx}(EA\varepsilon) = -\frac{d}{dx}\left(EA\frac{du}{dx}\right) = -EA\frac{d}{dx}\left(\frac{du}{dx}\right) = -EA\frac{d^2u}{dx^2}$$

It is assumed that **E** and **A** are constant throughout the length of the element, so they are not functions of **x**. The complete behaviour of an axially loaded (one-dimensional) element can now be described by the **second order governing differential equation**:

$$\frac{d^2u}{dx^2} = -\frac{p(x)}{EA}$$

This differential equation relates the applied load function **p(x)**, to the axial displacement function **u(x)** of the element. The solution will be in the form of a displacement function **u(x)** that satisfies this equation, this can be obtained by integrating twice with respect to **x**. Proceeding as **Example 13.8**, the solution **u = f(x)** is:

$$u(x) = \int\left(\int \frac{d\,u}{dx^2}dx\right)dx = \int\left(\int \frac{-p(x)}{EA}\,dx\right)dx = -\int\left(\frac{p(x)x}{EA} + C\right)dx = -\frac{p(x)x^2}{2EA} + Cx + D$$

This is the **general solution** for the displacement function **u(x)** in terms of the load function **p(x)**, and the constants of integration **C** and **D**. It should be noted that if the load function varies along the length, see load function of **Exercise 13.1**, then theses terms have to be integrated as part of the solution process For a particular element the constants of integration can be evaluated from given information.

Example 13.9   An element of length **L** is restrained against axial displacement top and bottom and is loaded axially with a constant load **p** kN/m. Find the displacement and force functions **u(x)** and **N(x)**, from the governing differential equation. Draw graphs of these functions.

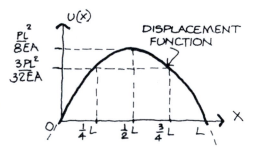

As the load is constant it does not vary with **x** so the displacement function **u** is:

$$u(x) = -\frac{px^2}{2EA} + Cx + D$$

What information is available to allow the evaluation of the constants of integration, **C** and **D**? The support conditions are known giving the following information: at **x = 0**, the axial displacement **u** is **0** and likewise at the other end, that is at **x = L**. First use the information that **u = 0** at **x = 0**. So:

$$u(0) = 0 = -\frac{p \times 0^2}{2EA} + C \times 0 + D \qquad\qquad \text{giving} \qquad D = 0$$

using **u = 0** at **x = L**

$$u(L) = 0 = -\frac{pL^2}{2EA} + CL \qquad\qquad \text{giving} \qquad C = \frac{pL}{2EA}$$

Substituting the values for **C** and **D** into the displacement function the unique solution for this element is obtained, with some algebraic rearrangement, as:

$$u(x) = \frac{p}{2EA}(Lx - x^2) \qquad \text{thus at x = L/2}$$

$$u\left(\frac{L}{2}\right) = \frac{p}{2EA}\left(\frac{L^2}{2} - \frac{L^2}{4}\right) = \frac{1}{4}\left(\frac{pL^2}{2EA}\right)$$

substituting other values of **x** into the displacement function gives the information required to draw the graph of the function **u(x)**, for **0 ≤ x ≤ L**, which has the parabolic shape shown.

To obtain the force function **N(x)**, the equations for **internal force/strain**, **strain/displacement** and the expression for the displacement function are used as follows:

$$N(x) = EA\varepsilon = EA\frac{du}{dx} = EA\frac{d}{dx}\left(\frac{p}{2EA}(Lx - x^2)\right) = \left(\frac{p}{2}\right)\frac{d}{dx}(Lx - x^2) = \frac{pL}{2} - px$$

thus substituting the value **x = L/2** into the force function $N(x) = \dfrac{pL}{2} - px$ gives **N(L/2) = 0**

substituting other values of **x** into the
force function gives the information
required to draw the graph of the
function **N(x)**, for **0 ≤ x ≤ L**, which has the
linear shape shown.

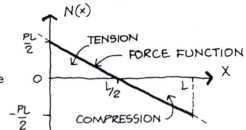

The functions **u(x)** and **N(x)** have values for all values of **x**, but for values outside the interval **0 ≤ x ≤ L** they do not relate to the structural element and so are of no interest. The results of this analysis in the interval **0 ≤ x ≤ L** show that the maximum axial displacement will be at the mid-point, that is **x=L/2**. The top half of the element will be in tension and the bottom half in compression which makes physical sense.

The constants of integration were evaluated using information that depended on the way the element was restrained at its ends. In the example, the condition that the axial displacement was zero, **u = 0**, at each end, **x = 0** and **x = L**, was used. Because these values were at the ends of the element, in effect the boundary of the element with the 'rest of the world', these are often called the **boundary conditions**. As it is usually at the boundary something definite is known, the use of boundary conditions is common for the solution of these differential equations.

Exercise 13.1 An element of length **L** is supported top only, at **x = 0**, and is loaded axially with a linearly varying load (**p** × x/L)kN/m. Show that the displacement and force functions **u(x)** and **N(x)** are as follows:

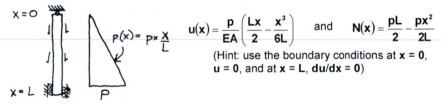

$$u(x) = \frac{p}{EA}\left(\frac{Lx}{2} - \frac{x^3}{6L}\right) \quad \text{and} \quad N(x) = \frac{pL}{2} - \frac{px^2}{2L}$$

(Hint: use the boundary conditions at **x = 0**, **u = 0**, and at **x = L**, **du/dx = 0**)

Draw graphs of these functions and obtain the values shown below.

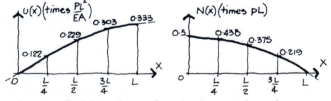

Note: The reader may find it easier to first do the exercise using a constant value for **p** rather than the varying one shown.

13.4 The laterally loaded beam

The process for developing the mathematical description of a laterally loaded beam is the same as that used for the axially loaded element in the previous section. Once again the beam is considered to be an interval $0 \leq x \leq L$ on the x-axis.

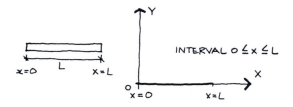

Fig. 13.10 Actual and mathematical beam

As with the axially loaded element, the load on the beam is a function of **x**.

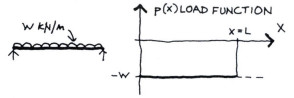

Fig. 13.11 The load function **p(x)**

Unlike the axially loaded element there are two force functions, the shear force function **S(x)** and the bending moment function **M(x)**.

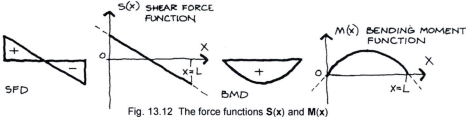

Fig. 13.12 The force functions **S(x)** and **M(x)**

And again there are two displacement functions, the slope function **θ(x)** and the lateral displacement function **u(x)**.

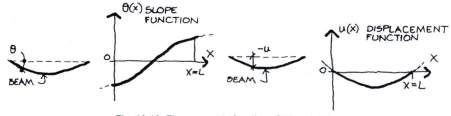

Fig. 13.13 The geometric functions **θ(x)** and **u(x)**

As with the axially loaded element, the equilibrium of a thin slice is examined to establish relationships between the applied load **w**, the shear force **S** and the bending moment **M**. Again the forces are assumed to be increasing along the beam, that is in the **x** direction, whilst the load is sensibly constant along the slice.

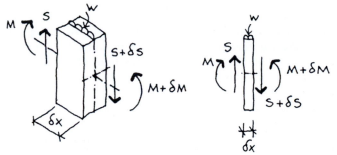

Fig. 13.14 Forces on a slice

As with the axially loaded element, the beam slice has to be in equilibrium in the direction of the shear forces **S** so:

$$S = w\delta x + (S + \delta S)$$

So cancelling the **S**s, rearranging and dividing by δ**x** and assuming δ**x** and δ**S** → **0** the equilibrium equation can be written as the following **differential** equation:

$$w = -\frac{dS}{dx}$$

But the beam slice also has to be in moment equilibrium. So that the load **w** does not enter the equation, moment equilibrium is considered about the centre of the slice, so the shear forces **S** and (**S** + δ**S**) act at distances δ**x/2** from the faces of the slice. The moment equilibrium is given by:

$$M + \left(S \times \frac{\delta x}{2}\right) + \left((S + \delta S) \times \frac{\delta x}{2}\right) = M + \delta M$$

Now cancelling the **M**s, ignoring the product of the 'small' quantities δ**S**×δ**x/2**, rearranging and dividing by δ**x** and assuming δ**x** and δ**M** → **0**, the moment equilibrium equation can be written as the following **differential** equation

$$S = \frac{dM}{dx}$$

Now there are two differential equations, one relating the shear force to the applied load and the other relating the bending moment to the shear force. These can be combined to give a differential equation that relates the bending moment to the applied load as follows:

$$\frac{dS}{dx} = \frac{d}{dx}\left(\frac{dM}{dx}\right) = \frac{d^2M}{dx^2} = -w(x)$$

Here the equilibrium between bending moment **M** and the load function **w(x)** is given by a second order differential equation. The relationship between the displacement of the beam **u(x)** and the slope **θ(x)** is given directly by the fact that the slope is the **gradient** of the graph of the displacement function, see **Section 13.1**.

$$\theta(x) = \frac{du}{dx}$$

The relationship between the bending moment and the deflected shape of the beam is given in terms of **E** the modulus of elasticity, **I** the moment of inertia, and **K** the curvature of the deflected beam.

$$M(x) = E \times I \times K(x)$$

This relationship was derived from the geometry shown in **Fig. 12.41** and work done on page **358**. But there is no relationship between the displacement function **u(x)** and the curvature function **K(x)**. In **Section 12.9** a beam with constant curvature was used but in most beams the curvature will vary along the beam and so will be a function of **x**.

In **Section 13.1** the idea of a function was explained, this is a formal mathematical relationship expressed by **y = f(x)**. 'Pictures' of functions were then drawn using the idea of a graphical representation, see **Example 13.1**. From this the mathematical operation of differentiation was defined by considering the gradient of the graph of the function, that is, the graph became a **geometric object**. In this way the line of the beam that deflects under lateral loading is both a curved geometric object and the graph of the displacement function **u = f(x)**. Not only does this curved geometric object have a slope (gradient) at each point it also has a radius of curvature **R**, and hence the curvature **K = 1/R**.

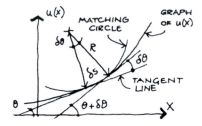

Fig. 13.15 Graph of function u(x) and matching circle

A relationship is required between **u(x)** and **K(x)**, this is derived from geometric considerations. A small part of the graph of the function **u = f(x)** is matched to a circle of radius **R**. This is shown in **Fig. 13.15**. It is assumed that the part of the graph **δs** is so small that it matches exactly the arc of the matching circle of radius **R**. So this gives the relationship:

$$\delta s = R\delta\theta$$

and the curvature is given as:
$$K = \frac{1}{R} = \frac{\delta\theta}{\delta s}$$

as **δs** and **δθ→0** the curvature is given by the differential equation:

$$K = \frac{d\theta}{ds}$$

That is, the curvature is the gradient, the rate of change, of the angle that the tangent line makes with the x-axis with respect to the length of the graph. What is required however, is the curvature in terms of the function **u = f(x)** with respect to **x**. The derivation of this requires more differential calculus and quite a lot of algebraic manipulation. This adds nothing to the understanding of structures and the derivation is widely available in elementary books on the calculus.[2] Therefore the relationship is simply stated as the following rather complicated differential equation:

$$K(x) = \frac{\dfrac{d^2y}{dx^2}}{\left(1 + \left(\dfrac{dy}{dx}\right)^2\right)^{3/2}}$$

Example 13.10   Obtain the expression for the curvature function $K(x)$ for the parabolic function $y = x^2$. Calculate the curvature at $x = 1$. Draw the graph and show the matching circle for $x = 1$.

Using the general rule for differentiation given on page **378**

$$\frac{dy}{dx} = 2x \qquad \text{and} \qquad \frac{d^2y}{dx^2} = 2$$

substituting these values in the general expression for the curvature $K(x)$ gives:

$$K(x) = \frac{\dfrac{d^2y}{dx^2}}{\left(1+\left(\dfrac{dy}{dx}\right)^2\right)^{3/2}} = \frac{2}{\left(1+(2x)^2\right)^{3/2}} = \frac{2}{\left(1+4x^2\right)^{3/2}}$$

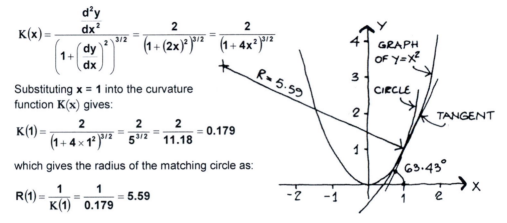

Substituting $x = 1$ into the curvature function $K(x)$ gives:

$$K(1) = \frac{2}{\left(1+4\times 1^2\right)^{3/2}} = \frac{2}{5^{3/2}} = \frac{2}{11.18} = 0.179$$

which gives the radius of the matching circle as:

$$R(1) = \frac{1}{K(1)} = \frac{1}{0.179} = 5.59$$

The position of the centre of the matching circle can obtained from the fact that the radius is at 90° to the tangent line to the graph of $y = f(x)$

The equation for the curvature of a beam was first given by James Bernoulli at the end of the 17th century. Clearly the expression is complicated due to the presence of the differential in the denominator. James' nephew Daniel Bernoulli proposed an important simplification for real beams which was that the differential $(dy/dx)^2$ in the denominator could be neglected without loss of accuracy. This gives the far simpler differential equation for curvature as:

$$K(x) = \frac{d^2y}{dx^2}$$

In the mathematical treatment of beams, the function $u = f(x)$ is the actual geometry of the beam deflected under load. For beams used in real building structures the gives the ratio of deflection to the span of about **300** (see **Table 12.8**). So if a parabola was to represent the geometry of the beam, it would be much 'flatter' than the parabola used in **Example 13.10**.

Example 13.11   A beam spans 6m. Derive a parabolic expression for the deflected shape assuming a central deflection of span/300. Calculate the radius of curvature for mid-span and 1.5m from the centre.

$6 \div 300 = 0.02$ so at $x = 3$, $y = 0.02$ $\therefore 0.02 = C \times 3^2$ so $C = 0.02 \div 9 = 1/450$

$\therefore$ the equation of the deflected beam is $u = \dfrac{x^2}{450}$

giving $\dfrac{du}{dx} = \dfrac{2x}{450}$ and $\dfrac{d^2u}{dx^2} = \dfrac{1}{225}$

The mathematical basis 389

substitution in the expression for curvature at **x = 0** gives

$$K(0) = \frac{\left(\dfrac{1}{225}\right)}{\left(1+(0)^2\right)^{3/2}} = \frac{1}{225} \qquad \text{so} \qquad R = 225m$$

and for **x = 1.5**

$$K(1.5) = \frac{\left(\dfrac{1}{225}\right)}{\left(1+\left(\dfrac{2\times 1.5}{450}\right)^2\right)^{3/2}} = \frac{1}{225.015} \qquad \text{so} \qquad R = 225.015m$$

This example shows that for the deflected shapes of real beam, Daniel Bernoulli's approximation is valid. This allows the mathematical description of the beam to be given in the form of ordinary differential equations.

Now three equations have been derived, similar to those for the axially loaded element, see page **383**, that express the following relationships:

- **external load** to **internal bending moment** or $d^2M/dx^2 = -p\,(x)$

- **bending moment** to **curvature** or $M(x) = E \times I \times K(x)$

- **curvature** to **displacement** or $K(x) = d^2u/dx^2$

Again these are the same relationships listed on page **371**, but two of the relationships are expressed by differential equations. It is possible to combine these relationships into one equation as follows:

$$-p(x) = \frac{d^2M}{dx^2} = \frac{d^2}{dx^2}(E \times I \times K(x)) = \frac{d^2}{dx^2}\left(E \times I \times \frac{d^2u}{dx^2}\right) = EI\frac{d^4u}{dx^4}$$

where it is assumed that **E** and **I** are constant throughout the length of the beam. Now the complete behaviour of a laterally loaded beam is described by the **fourth order governing differential equation**:

$$EI\frac{d^4u}{dx^4} = -p(x)$$

This differential equation relates the applied load function **p(x)**, to the lateral displacement function **u(x)** of the beam. The solution will be in the form of a displacement function **u(x)** that satisfies this equation and can be obtained by integrating it four times with respect to **x**. Basically this is the same as for the axially loaded element shown on page **383**, but as the integration is done **four times** there will be four constants of integration with the attached powers of **x**. As with the axially loaded element, see page **384**, if the load varies along the beam then the integration will have to take account of this, see **Exercise 13.1**. The steps of the integration are as follows:

1st integration

$$EI\int\left(\frac{d^4u}{dx^4}\right)dx = EI\frac{d^3u}{dx^3} = \int -p(x)dx = -p(x)x + A$$

2nd integration

$$EI\int\left(\frac{d^3u}{dx^3}\right)dx = EI\frac{d^2u}{dx^2} = \int(-p(x)x + A)dx = -p(x)\frac{x^2}{2} + Ax + B$$

3rd integration

$$EI\int\left(\frac{d^2u}{dx^2}\right)dx = EI\frac{du}{dx} = \int\left(-p(x)\frac{x^2}{2} + Ax + B\right)dx = -p(x)\frac{x^3}{6} + A\frac{x^2}{2} + Bx + C$$

4th integration

$$EI \int \left(\frac{du}{dx}\right) dx = EIu(x) = \int \left(-p(x)\frac{x^3}{6} + A\frac{x^2}{2} + Bx + C\right).dx = -p(x)\frac{x^4}{24} + A\frac{x^3}{6} + B\frac{x^2}{2} + Cx + D$$

There are now five equations, one algebraic equation and four differential equations. These equations have the following physical meanings:

1. The lateral displacement $u(x)$: $u(x) = \frac{1}{EI}\left(-p(x)\frac{x^4}{24} + A\frac{x^3}{6} + B\frac{x^2}{2} + Cx + D\right)$

2. The slope $\theta(x)$: $\theta(x) = \frac{du}{dx} = \frac{1}{EI}\left(-p(x)\frac{x^3}{6} + A\frac{x^2}{2} + Bx + C\right)$

3. The bending moment $M(x)$: $M(x) = EI\frac{d^2u}{dx^2} = -p(x)\frac{x^2}{2} + Ax + B$

4. The shear force $S(x)$: $S(x) = EI\frac{d^3u}{dx^3} = -p(x)x + A$

5. The lateral load $p(x)$: $p(x) = -EI\frac{d^4u}{dx^4}$

As with the axially loaded element, the constants of integration are evaluated from the boundary conditions. For a laterally loaded beam there are three idealised support conditions and each one defines two boundary conditions, these are:

1 **Pinned support**

the beam is fixed against vertical movement so the vertical displacement is zero:

$$u(x) = \frac{1}{EI}\left(-p(x)\frac{x^4}{24} + A\frac{x^3}{6} + B\frac{x^2}{2} + Cx + D\right) = 0$$

the beam is free to rotate so the bending moment is zero:

$$M(x) = EI\frac{d^2u}{dx^2} = -p(x)\frac{x^2}{2} + Ax + B = 0$$

2 **Fixed support**

the beam is fixed against vertical movement so the vertical displacement is zero:

$$u(x) = \frac{1}{EI}\left(-p(x)\frac{x^4}{24} + A\frac{x^3}{6} + B\frac{x^2}{2} + Cx + D\right) = 0$$

the beam is fixed against rotation so the slope is zero:

$$\theta(x) = EI\frac{du}{dx} = -p(x)\frac{x^3}{6} + A\frac{x^2}{2} + Bx + C = 0$$

3 **Free 'support'**

the beam is free to displace vertically so the shear force is zero:

$$S(x) = EI\frac{d^3u}{dx^3} = -p(x)x + A = 0$$

the beam is free to rotate so the bending moment is zero:

$$M(x) = EI\frac{d^2u}{dx^2} = -p(x)\frac{x^2}{2} + Ax + B = 0$$

So finally, after all this mathematical derivation applying the differential calculus to the concepts of beam behaviour, it is possible to obtain all the information about a laterally loaded beam. This information gives the distribution of the shear forces and bending moments as well as information about the slope of the deflected beam and the lateral displacement. In practical terms the maximum lateral displacement of a beam is required to check that it is within acceptable limits, see **Table 12.8** and occasionally the end rotations of a beam are required.

With this new description of the behaviour of a beam, the '**basic building block**' of structural engineering, the laterally loaded, simply supported beam is now analysed.

Example 13.12   Use the mathematical description of the beam to derive expressions for the shear force, **S(x)**, the bending moment, **M(x)**, the slope, θ(x) and the lateral displacement **u(x)** for a simply supported beam of span **L**, loaded laterally with a constant load of **w** kN/m.

The general expressions given on page **391** are used. For them to apply to the beam shown, the constants of integration, **A**, **B**, **C** and **D** have to be evaluated using the boundary conditions at **x = 0** and **x = L** for a pinned support.

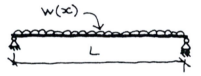

These boundary conditions are shown diagrammatically.

First use the boundary conditions **M(0) = 0** at **x = 0** and **L** to evaluate **A** and **B**.

at x = 0 $M(0) = -w\dfrac{0^2}{2} + A \times 0 + B = 0$ ∴ **B = 0**

at x = L $M(L) = -w\dfrac{L^2}{2} + AL = 0$ ∴ **A = wL/2**

Now use the boundary conditions **u(0) = 0** at **x = 0** and **L** to evaluate **C** and **D**.

at x = 0 $EIu(0) = -w\dfrac{x^4}{24} + A\dfrac{x^3}{6} + B\dfrac{x^2}{2} + Cx + D = -w\dfrac{0^4}{24} + \dfrac{wL}{2} \times 0 + C \times 0 + D = 0$

∴ **D = 0**

at x = L $EIu(L) = -w\dfrac{L^4}{24} + A\dfrac{L^3}{6} + B\dfrac{L^2}{2} + CL + D = -w\dfrac{L^4}{24} + \dfrac{wL}{2}\dfrac{L^3}{6} + CL = 0$

∴ **C = −wL³/24**

Now all the constants of integration have been evaluated using the boundary conditions and are summarised as follows:

A = wL/2   **B = 0**   **C = -wL³/24**   **D = 0**

To obtain the expressions for the various functions for this specific beam the values of the constants, noting that **B** and **D = 0**, are substituted into the expressions as follows:

For the shear force function $S(x)$:

$$S(x) = EI\frac{d^3u}{dx^3} = -wx + A = -wx + \frac{wL}{2}$$

For the bending moment function $M(x)$:

$$M(x) = EI\frac{d^2u}{dx^2} = -w\frac{x^2}{2} + Ax = -w\frac{x^2}{2} + \frac{wL}{2}x$$

The graphs of shear force and bending moment functions are:

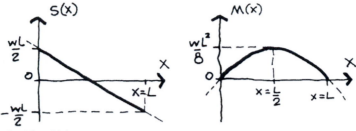

For the slope function $\theta(x)$:

$$\theta(x) = \frac{du}{dx} = -w\frac{x^3}{6EI} + A\frac{x^2}{2EI} + C\frac{1}{EI} = -w\frac{x^3}{6EI} + wL\frac{x^2}{4EI} - wL^3\frac{1}{24EI}$$

For the displacement function $u(x)$:

$$u(x) = \frac{1}{EI}\left(-w\frac{x^4}{24} + A\frac{x^3}{6} + Cx\right) = -w\frac{x^4}{24EI} + wL\frac{x^3}{12EI} - wL^3\frac{x}{24EI}$$

The graphs of slope and displacement functions are:

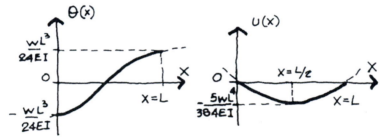

The results for the shear force and bending moment functions were derived, using equilibrium considerations alone, on page **336**, for this beam. A method was given in **Section 12.9** for calculating the deflection of a beam bent to a circular shape, but now it is possible to calculate the deflection for any beam and load function.

Example 13.13   Calculate the central deflection of a simply supported beam spanning 4m loaded laterally by **10kN/m**. The beam is an **IPE 180** so I = **1317 E4** mm⁴ and E = **210 E3** N/mm².

Working in millimetres and Newtons the central deflection is

$$u_{central} = \frac{-5wL^4}{384EI} = \frac{-5 \times 10 \times 4000^4}{384 \times 210E3 \times 1317E4} = \frac{-1.28E16}{1.062E15} = -12mm$$

which is the value given in **Fig. 12.43**.

In **Chapter 12** a not altogether successful attempt, see pages **341-344**, was made to find the shear forces and the bending moments in a beam that had a fixed support at one end and a pinned one at the other end. This type of beam is sometimes called a **propped cantilever**.

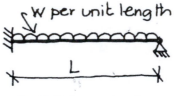

Fig. 13.16 A propped cantilever

The reason that it was 'not altogether successful' was that only the equilibrium conditions could be used and these did not yield enough equations. To overcome this, a 'pin' was 'inserted' in the guessed position of the point of contraflexure. Now, with the geometrical information available, the mathematically 'correct' distribution of shear forces and bending moments can be found by using the right boundary conditions.

Example 13.14   Use the mathematical description of the beam to derive expressions for the shear force, **S(x)**, the bending moment, **M(x)**, the slope, θ(**x**) and the lateral displacement **u(x)** for the 'propped cantilever' shown in **Fig. 13.16**.

As before the constants of integration, **A, B, C** and **D** have to be evaluated using the boundary conditions at **x = 0** and **x = L**.

These boundary conditions are shown diagrammatically.

$u(0)=0$ $u(L)=0$
$\theta(0)=0$ $M(L)=0$

First use the boundary conditions M(L) = 0 at **x = L** to obtain a relationship between **A** and **B**.

$$M(L) = -w\frac{L^2}{2} + AL + B = 0 \qquad \therefore \quad B = w\frac{L^2}{2} - AL$$

Now use the boundary conditions θ(**0**) = 0 at **x = 0** and L to evaluate **C**

$$\theta(0) = \frac{1}{EI}\left(-w\frac{0^3}{6} + A\frac{0^2}{2} + B\times 0 + C\right) = 0 \qquad \therefore \ C = 0$$

Now use the boundary conditions u(**0**) = 0 at **x = 0** to evaluate **D**

$$EIu(0) = -w\frac{0^4}{24} + A\frac{0^3}{6} + B\frac{0^2}{2} + D = 0 \qquad \therefore \ D = 0$$

Now use the boundary conditions u(**L**) = 0 at **x = L** to evaluate **A**

$$EIu(L) = -w\frac{L^4}{24} + A\frac{L^3}{6} + \left(w\frac{L^2}{2} - AL\right)\frac{L^2}{2} = 0 \ \text{ giving } \quad AL^3\left(\frac{1}{2}-\frac{1}{6}\right) = wL^4\left(\frac{1}{4}-\frac{1}{24}\right)$$

which gives $A = \frac{5}{8}wL$ and hence $B = \frac{wL^2}{2} - \left(\frac{5wL}{8}\right)L = -\frac{wL^2}{8}$

Now all the constants of integration have been evaluated using the boundary conditions and are summarised as follows:

$$A = \frac{5}{8}wL \qquad B = -\frac{wL^2}{8} \qquad C = 0 \qquad D = 0$$

394 Building structures

To obtain the expressions for the various functions for this specific beam the values of the constants are substituted into the expressions as follows:

For the shear force function **S(x)**: $S(x) = EI\dfrac{d^3u}{dx^3} = -wx + A = -wx + \dfrac{5wL}{8}$

For the bending moment function **M(x)**:

$$M(x) = EI\frac{d^2u}{dx^2} = -w\frac{x^2}{2} + Ax + B = -w\frac{x^2}{2} + \frac{5wL}{8}x - \frac{wL^2}{8}$$

The graphs of shear force and bending moment functions are:

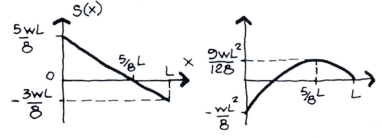

For the slope function **θ(x)**, noting **C and D = 0**:

$$\theta(x) = \frac{du}{dx} = -w\frac{x^3}{6EI} + A\frac{x^2}{2EI} + B\frac{x}{EI} = -w\frac{x^3}{6EI} + \left(\frac{5}{8}wL\right)\frac{x^2}{2EI} + \left(-\frac{wL^2}{8}\right)\frac{x}{EI}$$

For the displacement function **u(x)**, noting **C and D = 0**:

$$u(x) = \frac{1}{EI}\left(-w\frac{x^4}{24} + A\frac{x^3}{6} + B\frac{x^2}{2}\right) = -w\frac{x^4}{24EI} + \left(\frac{5}{8}wL\right)\frac{x^3}{6EI} + \left(-\frac{wL^2}{8}\right)\frac{x^2}{2EI}$$

The graphs of slope and displacement functions are:

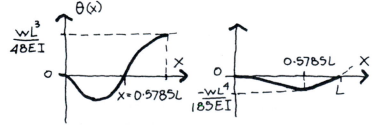

Exercise 13.2   Evaluate the displacement u at **0.5785 L** and plot the functions for slope **θ(x)** and displacement **u(x)** to scale.

With this new analysis it is now possible to calculate the mathematically 'correct' moments at the support and at mid-span shown in **Fig. 12.15**. This is left as an **exercise**.

In **Chapter 12**, beams are loaded with point loads as they often are in real structures. How can these be dealt with using the mathematical approach? The short answer is not very easily. Implicit in the **Fig. 13.1** cycle ride was a smooth and continuous undulating road. There were no gaps in the road – it was continuous, and no steps or similar obstacles – it was smooth. For a point load on a beam to become a mathematical function it will only have a value at a point, the point of load application, and will not exist elsewhere.

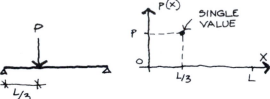

Fig. 13.17 Point load as a function

Without the comforts of continuity and smoothness, the limit process, $\delta x \rightarrow 0$, explained on pages **375-376**, does not work. There are basically two ways to resolve this: firstly, use more complex functions to give the point load function the required properties of continuity and smoothness.[3] Secondly, can be considered to be several beams joining the parts of the original beam between the non-continuous loads. Then considerations of continuity of the beam at the load positions can be used to formulate simultaneous equations. Both these approaches are outside the scope of this brief introduction.

13.5 The general beam element

The treatment of a single beam, with various different boundary conditions, given in the previous section is useful from a practical point of view but limited. Because in skeletal frames the beams are joined to other beams, what is wanted is an analysis that allows for this. The first step is to derive what are known as the **slope deflection equations**. These relate the bending moments and shear forces in a beam to end rotations and displacements. From a historical point of view the mathematical analysis of beams given in the previous system had been given by Navier in his 1826 book and the extension to the slope deflection equations by Clapeyron in 1857. Until the wide availability of programmable computers in the late 1970s, engineers and mathematicians struggled to find methods of general analysis, many of which were based on these equations.

However, before the derivation of these equations it is important to be clear about signs, that is + and − , so far these have been used in a rather casual manner. Signs are important in the derivation of the slope deflection equations so first the signs used for the beam equation are clarified. The idea of positive and negative gradient, slope, must be clear, this is really like going uphill, positive, and downhill, negative, on the **Fig. 13.1** cycle ride from the start point.[*]

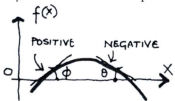

Fig. 13.18 Positive and negative slopes

---

[*] Few cyclists would agree with this.

To see how this applies to the analysis of the simply supported beam given in **Example 13.12**, the results are examined with respect to signs. As has been seen the functions given by the analysis are sequential derived functions, so the derived function of the load function **w(x)** is the shear function **S(x)**. This means the slope of the shear function is constant and negative with a value of **−w**.

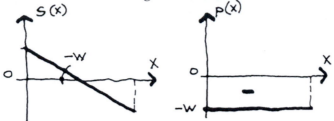

Fig. 13.19 The load function as the derived function of **S(x)**

Similarly the shear force function **S(x)** is the derived function of the bending moment function **M(x)**. So the values of the shear function give the gradient of the bending moment function.

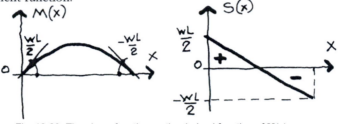

Fig. 13.20 The shear function as the derived function of **M(x)**

This can be continued with the curvature function **K**, (= **M/EI**), which is the derived function of the slope function **θ(x)**.

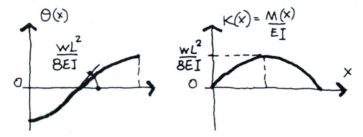

Fig. 13.21 The curvature function as the derived function of θ(**x**)

And finally the slope function θ(**x**) gives the gradient of the displacement function **u(x)** and is the actual slope of the real beam.

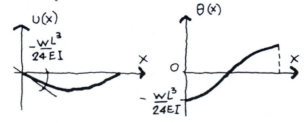

Fig. 13.22 The slope function as the derived function of u(x)

The mathematical basis **397**

The sign convention shown also agrees with that shown in **Figs. 2.24** and **25**. An exception is drawing the positive bending moment above the x-axis. This still means tension on the bottom of the beam but has to be drawn like this to agree with the vertical positive axis.

The **general beam element** does not have a lateral load applied but has displacements and rotations imposed at the ends, these are called **prescribed boundary conditions**. To aid clarity, the rotations and displacements are treated separately and then the results added. First the end rotations:

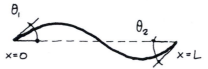

Fig. 13.23 End rotations of the beam element

To obtain a beam of this shape bending moments have to be applied to the ends which cause bending throughout the beam element.

Fig. 13.24 End moments and **BMD**

It should be noted the **BMD** has been drawn not the bending moment function. Associated with this bending moment distribution are end reactions and a constant shear force.

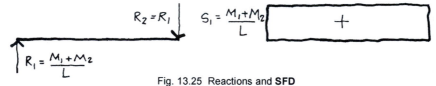

Fig. 13.25 Reactions and **SFD**

The reactions are obtained by considering moment and vertical equilibrium as follows.

Consider moment equilibrium about the right-hand end: $R_1 \times L = M_1 + M_2$ $\therefore$ $R_1 = \dfrac{M_1 + M_2}{L}$

and from vertical equilibrium: $R_1 = -R_2 = -\left(\dfrac{M_1 + M_2}{L}\right)$

The differential equation of the beam is now used to obtain relationships between the end rotations θ_1 and θ_2 and the end moments M_1 and M_2. There is no lateral load and the bending moment function can be written directly from the **BMD** as:

$$M(x) = -M_1 + (R_1 \times x) = -M_1 + \left(\dfrac{M_1 + M_2}{L}\right)x$$

Giving directly the second order differential equation:

$$EI\dfrac{d^2u}{dx^2} = -M_1 + \left(\dfrac{M_1 + M_2}{L}\right)x$$

Now integrating the equation with respect to **x** gives:

$$\int EI\left(\frac{d^2u}{dx^2}\right)dx = EI\frac{du}{dx} + A = -M_1x + \left(\frac{M_1+M_2}{L}\right)\frac{x^2}{2} + A$$

From the prescribed boundary condition $du/dx = \theta_1$ at $x = 0$ the constant of integration **A** can be evaluated as follows:

$$EI\frac{du}{dx} = EI\theta_1 = -M_1 \times 0 + \left(\frac{M_1+M_2}{L}\right)\frac{0^2}{2} + A \qquad \text{giving} \qquad A = EI\theta_1$$

so the differential equation for the slope is: $\qquad EI\frac{du}{dx} = -M_1x + \left(\frac{M_1+M_2}{L}\right)\frac{x^2}{2} + EI\theta_1$

As before the differential equation for the lateral displacement function **u(x)** is obtained by integrating the slope function and this gives:

$$\int EI\left(\frac{du}{dx}\right)dx = EIu(x) + B = -M_1\frac{x^2}{2} + \left(\frac{M_1+M_2}{L}\right)\frac{x^3}{6} + EI\theta_1x + B$$

as at **x = 0, u = 0** then **B = 0**, so the differential equation for the displacement is:

$$EIu(x) = -M_1\frac{x^2}{2} + \left(\frac{M_1+M_2}{L}\right)\frac{x^3}{6} + EI\theta_1x$$

What is required are equations that relate the end moments M_1 and M_2 to the end rotations θ_1 and θ_2. This is done by rewriting the equations for slope and displacement at **x = L**. Using the slope equation and noting that at **x = L, du/dx = θ_2**:

$$EI\theta_2 = -M_1L + \left(\frac{M_1+M_2}{L}\right)\frac{L^2}{2} + EI\theta_1$$

which can be rearranged as

$$M_1 = M_2 + \frac{2EI}{L}(\theta_1 - \theta_2)$$

and using the displacement equation and noting that at **x = L, u = 0**:

$$0 = -M_1\frac{L^2}{2} + \left(\frac{M_1+M_2}{L}\right)\frac{L^3}{6} + EI\theta_1L$$

which dividing by L^2 and multiplying by **6** and rearranging gives:

$$M_2 = 2M_1 - \frac{6EI\theta_1}{L}$$

now this value for M_2 can be substituted into the equation for M_1, giving an expression for M_1 in terms of **E, I, L**, θ_1 and θ_2:

$$M_1 = \left(2M_1 - \frac{6EI\theta_1}{L}\right) + \frac{2EI}{L}(\theta_1 - \theta_2)$$

which can be rearranged to give the first slope deflection equation for rotations:

$$M_1 = \frac{4EI\theta_1}{L} + \frac{2EI\theta_2}{L}$$

substituting this value into the expression for M_2 and rearranging, the second slope deflection equation for rotations is obtained as:

$$M_2 = \frac{4EI\theta_2}{L} + \frac{2EI\theta_1}{L}$$

This gives the first part of the derivation of the slope deflection equations. It should be noted that **E** and **I** have been assumed to be constant throughout the length of the beam which means that the structural material and the cross-section do not vary. Also these equations assume that the end rotations, θ_1 and θ_2 are in the directions shown in **Fig. 13.23**. The reader should carry out all the rearranging of the various equations in detail.

Before moving to the derivation for the equations for an end lateral displacement an example is given.

Example 13.15 Assuming that the prescribed end rotations of a beam element are in the sense shown in **Fig. 13.23** and are both **equal** to θ, derive expressions for the slope function $\theta(x)$ and the lateral displacement function $u(x)$. Draw the graphs of these functions.

Substitute $\theta_1 = \theta_2 = \theta$ into the slope deflection equations to obtain values for M_1 and M_2 in terms of the rotation θ.

$$M_1 = M_2 = \frac{4EI\theta}{L} + \frac{2EI\theta}{L} = \frac{6EI\theta}{L}$$

Substituting these values in the differential equation of the slope function, see page **399**, gives:

$$EI\frac{du}{dx} = -M_1 x + \left(\frac{M_1 + M_2}{L}\right)\frac{x^2}{2} + EI\theta_1 = -\frac{6EI\theta}{L}x + \left(\frac{12EI\theta}{L^2}\right)\frac{x^2}{2} + EI\theta$$

dividing by **EI** and rearranging, the following expression for the slope function is obtained:

$$\frac{du}{dx} = \theta\left(1 - \frac{6}{L}x + \frac{6x^2}{L^2}\right)$$

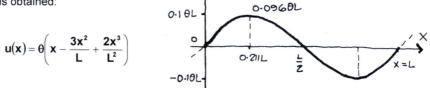

and substituting the values for M_1 and M_2 in the differential equation of the displacement function, see page **399**, gives:

$$EIu(x) = -M_1\frac{x^2}{2} + \left(\frac{M_1 + M_2}{L}\right)\frac{x^3}{6} + EI\theta_1 x = -\frac{6EI\theta}{L}\frac{x^2}{2} + \left(\frac{12EI\theta}{L^2}\right)\frac{x^3}{6} + EI\theta x$$

dividing by **EI** and simplifying and rearranging, the following expression for the displacement function is obtained:

$$u(x) = \theta\left(x - \frac{3x^2}{L} + \frac{2x^3}{L^2}\right)$$

Note: The vertical scales used in the graphs are NOT the same as the horizontal ones.

Now the other part of the slope deflection equation can be derived, that is, the effect of a prescribed displacement, in a similar way.

400 Building structures

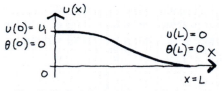

Fig. 13.26 End displacement of the beam element

The bending moments and the end reactions take exactly the same form as those for the end rotations.

Fig. 13.27 End moments and reactions

The second order differential equation relating the curvature to the bending moment function is exactly as before, see page **399**.

$$EI\frac{d^2u}{dx^2} = -M_1 + \left(\frac{M_1 + M_2}{L}\right)x$$

And again the equation for the slope is of the same form as that given on page **399**.

$$EI\frac{du}{dx} = -M_1x + \left(\frac{M_1 + M_2}{L}\right)\frac{x^2}{2} + A \quad \text{as at } x = 0, du/dx = 0 \quad \text{then} \quad A = 0$$

The equation for the lateral displacement also has the same form, see page **399**, except **A = 0**, so:

$$EIu(x) = -M_1\frac{x^2}{2} + \left(\frac{M_1 + M_2}{L}\right)\frac{x^3}{6} + B \quad \text{at } x = 0, u = u_1 \text{ so } B = EIu_1$$

As before, what is required are expressions that relate the end moments **M₁** and **M₂** to the prescribed displacement **u₁**, this is done by using the other boundary conditions. At **x = L, du/dx = 0**, gives:

$$0 = -M_1L + \left(\frac{M_1 + M_2}{L}\right)\frac{L^2}{2} = -M_1L + \frac{M_1L}{2} + \frac{M_2L}{2} \quad \text{giving } M_1 = M_2 = M$$

and at **x = L, u = 0** giving

$$0 = -M_1\frac{L^2}{2} + \left(\frac{M_1 + M_2}{L}\right)\frac{L^3}{6} + EIu_1 = -M\frac{L^2}{2} + \left(\frac{2M}{L}\right)\frac{L^3}{6} + EIu_1 = \left(-3M + 2M + \frac{6EIu_1}{L^2}\right)\frac{L^2}{6}$$

which gives, after some cancelling and rearranging the other part of the slope deflection equation as:

$$M_1 = \frac{6EIu_1}{L^2} = M_2$$

Before assembling the complete slope deflection equations, the slope and displacement functions for a prescribed end displacement are derived in the following example:

Example 13.16 Assuming that at **x = 0** the lateral displacement is **u₁**, derive expressions for the slope function **θ(x)** and the lateral displacement function **u(x)**. Draw the graphs of these functions.

Substitute the values for M_1 and M_2 given by the slope deflection equation into the equation of the slope function to obtain the slope in terms of the displacement u_1.

$$EI\frac{du}{dx} = -M_1 x + \left(\frac{M_1 + M_2}{L}\right)\frac{x^2}{2} = -\left(\frac{6EIu_1}{L^2}\right)x + \left(\frac{6EIu_1 + 6EIu_1}{L^3}\right)\frac{x^2}{2}$$

Dividing by **EI** and rearranging this gives:

$$\frac{du}{dx} = \left(\frac{6u_1}{L^2}\right)\left(\frac{x^2}{L} - x\right)$$

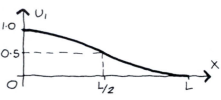

Now substitute the values for M_1 and M_2 given by the slope deflection equation into the equation of the displacement function to obtain the displacement in terms of u_1.

$$EIu(x) = -M_1\frac{x^2}{2} + \left(\frac{M_1 + M_2}{L}\right)\frac{x^3}{6} + EIu_1 = -\left(\frac{6EIu_1}{L^2}\right)\left(\frac{x^2}{2}\right) + \left(\frac{6EIu_1 + 6EIu_1}{L^3}\right)\left(\frac{x^3}{6}\right) + EIu_1$$

dividing by **EI** and rearranging, the following expression for the displacement function is obtained:

$$u(x) = \left(\frac{6u_1}{L^2}\right)\left(-\frac{x^2}{2} + \frac{x^3}{3L}\right) + u_1$$

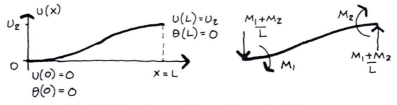

If there is a prescribed displacement at **x = L**, that is **u(L) = u₂** then the boundary conditions and forces are as shown in **Fig.13 .28**.

Fig. 13.28 Boundary conditions and forces for u(L) = u₂

As all the forces are opposite to the case for the prescribed boundary condition **u(0) = u₁** then the slope deflection equation for this prescribed displacement can be written immediately, by inserting a minus sign, as follows:

$$M_2 = -\frac{6EIu_2}{L^2} = M_1$$

Now a diagram can be drawn for a beam element with all the prescribed boundary conditions occurring simultaneously.

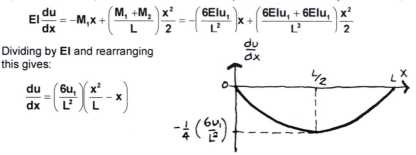

Fig. 13.29 Prescribed boundary conditions for the general beam element

402 Building structures

Now the partial slope deflection equations, given on pages **399, 401** and **402**, can be added together to give the complete equations as follows:

$$M_1 = \frac{4EI\theta_1}{L} + \frac{2EI\theta_2}{L} + \frac{6EIu_1}{L^2} - \frac{6EIu_2}{L^2}$$

and

$$M_2 = \frac{4EI\theta_2}{L} + \frac{2EI\theta_1}{L} + \frac{6EIu_1}{L^2} - \frac{6EIu_2}{L^2}$$

and the end forces S_1 and S_2 are given directly from $\pm(M_1 + M_2)/L$ as

$$S_1 = \frac{6EI(\theta_1 + \theta_2)}{L^2} + \frac{12EI(u_1 - u_2)}{L^3} = -S_2$$

On page **357** stiffness was defined by the relation:

Force = Stiffness × **Deflection**

The slope deflection equations give exactly this relationship. M_1, M_2, S_1 and S_2 are **forces** applied to the end of the beam element, the rotations θ_1 and θ_2 and the displacements u_1 and u_2 are **deflections**. Terms like **4EI/L** and **6EI/L²** are the **stiffness** and are sometimes called **stiffness coefficients**.

The slope deflection equations were first written by Clapeyron in 1857, in 1914 A Bendixen presented the 'slope deflection method', in 1922 KA Čališev used them to present an approximate method. In 1930 Hardy Cross presented the method of **moment distribution** which again uses the slope deflection equations. His method became the most widely used for structural analysis before programmable computers became available. Yet again these equations were used to develop computer programs for structural analysis. The basis for this is explained in the next section.

13.6 Joint stiffness

The slope deflection equations are not much good on their own as real beams rarely have prescribed boundary conditions. The value of the equations is that, having described the structural behaviour of a **general beam element**, in terms of end rotations and displacements, frames can be analysed as assemblies of elements.

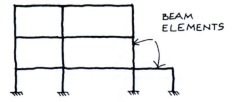

Fig.13.30 Frame as an assembly of beam elements

The method of analysis is to derive equations for the joints that relate the forces on the joint to the displacement of the joint. This is done through the stiffness coefficients of the elements that meet at a joint to give the **joint stiffness**. Consider a simple structure of two vertical axially loaded elements loaded where they are joined.

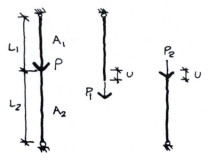

Fig. 13.31 Axial elements

The vertical displacement at the joint is **u**, so the upper member has to stretch by **u** and the lower member has to compress by **u**. So the force in each member is calculated for the displacement **u** from the stiffness, see page **357** for axial stiffness.

For the upper member $u = \dfrac{P_1 L_1}{EA_1}$ and for the lower member $u = \dfrac{P_2 L_2}{EA_2}$

So $P_1 = \left(\dfrac{EA_1}{L_1}\right) u$ and $P_2 = \left(\dfrac{EA_2}{L_2}\right) u$

Giving $P = P_1 + P_2 = \left(\dfrac{EA_1}{L_1} + \dfrac{EA_2}{L_2}\right) u$ and the stiffness of the joint is $k_{joint} = \left(\dfrac{EA_1}{L_1} + \dfrac{EA_2}{L_2}\right)$

Now consider another simple structure consisting of two vertical and two horizontal beam elements meeting at a joint. The remote ends of all the elements are totally fixed.

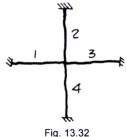

Fig. 13.32

The joint can now move in three ways, it can displace vertically u_V, horizontally u_H and it can rotate by θ.

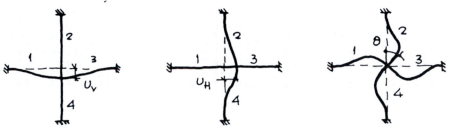

Fig. 13.33 Joint movements

And associated with these movements are three joint forces, a vertical force P_V, a horizontal force P_H and a moment M.

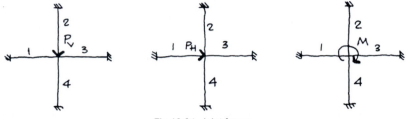

Fig.13.34 Joint forces

The joint stiffness k_{JOINT}, that links the movements to the forces, now consists of three parts; a vertical stiffness k_V, a horizontal stiffness k_H and a rotational stiffness k_θ. The equilibrium of the joint, vertical, horizontal and rotational, is given by three equations:

$$P_V = k_V \times u_V \qquad P_H = k_H \times u_H \qquad M = k_\theta \times \theta$$

Assume, for simplicity, that all the elements have the same length, cross-section and are made of the same material. The joint equilibrium equations now have the following form:

$$P_V = (k_{1\text{- LATERAL}} + k_{2\text{- AXIAL}} + k_{3\text{- LATERAL}} + k_{4\text{- AXIAL}}) \times u_V$$

$$P_H = (k_{1\text{- AXIAL}} + k_{2\text{- LATERAL}} + k_{3\text{- AXIAL}} + k_{4\text{- LATERAL}}) \times u_H$$

$$M = (k_{1\text{- ROTATIONAL}} + k_{2\text{- ROTATIONAL}} + k_{3\text{- ROTATIONAL}} + k_{4\text{- ROTATIONAL}}) \times \theta$$

Then using the axial stiffness and the slope deflection equations the three equilibrium equations can be written using the stiffness coefficients as follows

$$P_V = \left(\left(\frac{12EI}{L^3}\right)_1 + \left(\frac{EA}{L}\right)_2 + \left(\frac{12EI}{L^3}\right)_3 + \left(\frac{EA}{L}\right)_4\right) \times u_V$$

$$P_H = \left(\left(\frac{EA}{L}\right)_1 + \left(\frac{12EI}{L^3}\right)_2 + \left(\frac{EA}{L}\right)_3 + \left(\frac{12EI}{L^3}\right)_4\right) \times u_H$$

$$M = \left(\left(\frac{4EI}{L}\right)_1 + \left(\frac{4EI}{L}\right)_2 + \left(\frac{4EI}{L}\right)_3 + \left(\frac{4EI}{L}\right)_4\right) \times \theta$$

Example 13.17 Calculate the stiffness coefficients for the structures shown. Calculate the vertical displacement u_V and the rotation θ for the loads shown. Calculate the bending moments in member **3** and draw the **BMD**. For all the members $A = 0.09m^2$, $I = 6.75E\text{-}4m^4$ and $E = 1E6\ kN/m^2$

Directly from the above equations

$$k_V = \left(\left(\frac{12EI}{L^3}\right)_1 + \left(\frac{EA}{L}\right)_2 + \left(\frac{12EI}{L^3}\right)_3 + \left(\frac{EA}{L}\right)_4\right)$$

and as $EI = 675kN/m^2$ and $EA = 90000kN$

$$k_V = \left(\left(\frac{12 \times 675}{4^3}\right)_1 + \left(\frac{90000}{4}\right)_2 + (= 1)_3 + (= 2)_4\right)$$

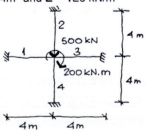

giving:

$k_V = ((127)_1 + (22500)_2 + (127)_3 + (22500)_4)) = 45\ 254\text{kN/m}$ and $k_H = k_V = 45\ 254\text{kN/m}$

$$k_\theta = \left(\left(\frac{4EI}{L} \right)_1 + \left(\frac{4EI}{L} \right)_2 + \left(\frac{4EI}{L} \right)_3 + \left(\frac{4EI}{L} \right)_4 \right) = \left(\left(\frac{4 \times 675}{4} \right)_1 + (= 1)_2 + (= 1)_3 + (= 1)_4 \right)$$

giving $k_\theta = ((675)_1 + (675)_2 + (675)_3 + (675)_4)) = 2700\text{kN.m/radian}$

substituting these values into the equilibrium equations gives

$P_V = 500 = 45\ 254 \times u_V$ so $u_V = 500 \div 45\ 254 = 0.011\ m \equiv 11mm$

$P_H = 0 = 45\ 254 \times u_H$ so $u_H = 0$ and

$M = 200 = 2700 \times \theta$ so $\theta = 200 \div 2700 = 0.074\ \text{radians} \equiv 4.24°$

To obtain the bending moments in beam element **3**, the values for u_V and θ are entered into the slope deflection equations.

$$M_1 = \frac{4EI\theta}{L} + \frac{6EIu_V}{L^2} = \frac{4 \times 675 \times 0.074}{4} + \frac{6 \times 675 \times 0.011}{4^2} = 49.95 + 2.78 = 52.73\text{kN.m}$$

$$M_2 = \frac{2EI\theta}{L} + \frac{6EIu_V}{L^2} = \frac{2 \times 675 \times 0.074}{4} + \frac{6 \times 675 \times 0.011}{4^2} = 24.98 + 2.78 = 27.767\text{kN.m}$$

BMD for beam element 3

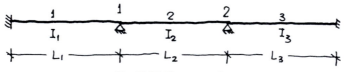

-27.76

52.73

Exercise 13.3 Calculate the axial forces, bending moments and shear forces in all the beam elements for the structures shown in **Example 13.17**. Draw the **AFD**, **BMD** and **SFD** for all the beam elements.

The structure shown in **Fig. 13.32** has only one joint that is able to have displacements, so the three equilibrium equations given on page **405** could be solved directly, as was shown in **Example 13.17**. But real structures tend to have far more than one joint that can have displacements. To see what happens when more than one joint can have displacements, consider a three-span beam with the extreme ends completely fixed in position.

Fig. 13.35 Three-span beam

Here each beam element has a different span and moment of inertia. The only possible joint deformations are rotations at joints **1** and **2**, θ_1 and θ_2. At these joints there will be moments M_1 and M_2.

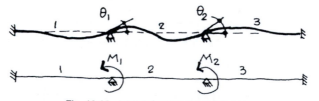

Fig. 13.36 Joint deformations and forces

Using the slope deflection equations, the equilibrium equations can be written for each joint. At joint **1** the total moment, M_1 is the sum of the end moments of beam elements **1** and **2**, so:

M_1 = m_2 (of beam element 1) + m_1 (of beam element 2)   giving:

$$M_1 = \left(\frac{4EI_1\theta_1}{L_1}\right)_{beam1} + \left(\frac{4EI_2\theta_1}{L_2} + \frac{2EI_2\theta_2}{L_2}\right)_{beam2}$$

And similarly, M_2 is the sum of the end moments of beam elements **2** and **3**, so:

M_2 = m_2 (of beam element 2) + m_1 (of beam element 3)   giving:

$$M_2 = \left(\frac{4EI_2\theta_2}{L_2} + \frac{2EI_2\theta_1}{L_2}\right)_{beam2} + \left(\frac{4EI_3\theta_2}{L_3}\right)_{beam3}$$

Now the two equations are linked as θ_1 and θ_2 appear in both. So the actual value of θ_1 and θ_2 must satisfy each equation at the same time, that is simultaneously, so there are **two simultaneous equations**. Each time there is a joint in a structure, if it is not restrained in any way, it will be able to have the three movements shown in **Fig.13.33**. Also at the joint will be the three forces shown in **Fig.13.34**. The equilibrium equations at each joint will give a set of **simultaneous equations** in terms of the joint forces, the joint movements and the stiffness coefficients. Usually the joint forces are known from the loading on the structure and the stiffness coefficients are known from the geometry and material of the structure, so the unknowns are the joint deformations. What has been achieved is to turn the 'problem' of structural analysis into the 'problem' of solving a set of simultaneous equations.

13.7 The stiffness method

The stiffness method, as it is generally called, is now the predominant method of structural analysis and uses the equilibrium relationship already given as:

Force = Stiffness × Deflection

Using the concept of stiffness coefficients, the structural analysis of any structure is turned into a set of simultaneous equations which are based on the known loads and structural properties. The solution of these equations gives the values of the deformations at the joints. From these values it is then possible to calculate the forces, axial and shear forces and bending moments, in the individual elements. Thus all the required information about the structural behaviour is obtained.

The fact that structural behaviour could be described by a set of simultaneous equations has been known at least since the end of the 19th century. The difficulty facing the analyst was their solution. With hand methods of calculation it is extremely difficult to solve more than very few equations, six would be quite a lot. Throughout the 20th century engineers and mathematicians battled, with limited success, to find methods to do this. However, with the arrival of the programmable computer, programs could be written to solve large numbers of simultaneous equations. With current computers thousands of simultaneous equations can be solved which permits the numerical analysis of huge structures. This penultimate section shows how these equations are obtained and organised.

To set up and solve the simultaneous equations, a high level of organisation is needed, this has two parts. The first is to rationalise the symbols used for a beam element. Firstly, a joint axes system is chosen.

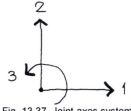

Fig. 13.37 Joint axes system

Thus the horizontal direction has suffix **1**, the vertical **2** and rotations **3**. Now all deformations at a joint are called **u**, with the joint number and a suffix, so **u2₂** is the vertical displacement at joint number **2**.

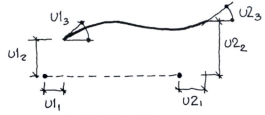

Fig. 13.38 Joint displacements **u**

And all forces at a joint are called **p**, with the joint number and a suffix, so **p1₃** is the moment at joint number **1**.

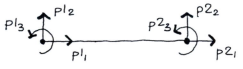

Fig. 13.39 Joint forces **p**

Using these new 'organised names' for M_1 and M_2 in the equilibrium equations given on page **407** for the three-span beam are rewritten as:

$$p1_3 = \frac{4EI_1 u1_3}{L_1} + \frac{4EI_2 u1_3}{L_2} + \frac{2EI_2 u2_3}{L_2} \quad \text{and} \quad p2_3 = \frac{4EI_2 u2_3}{L_2} + \frac{2EI_2 u1_3}{L_2} + \frac{4EI_3 u2_3}{L_3}$$

The second part of the organisation of the equations is to write them in **matrix form**. Matrices and matrix algebra are described in many books[4] but little of that is needed here. Essentially a matrix is a mathematical object that has lists of numbers, or other mathematical 'things', inside square brackets. The two equations above can be written in matrix form as follows:

$$\begin{bmatrix} p1_3 \\ p2_3 \end{bmatrix} = \begin{bmatrix} 4EI_1/L_1 + 4EI_2/L_2 & 2EI_2/L_2 \\ 2EI_2/L_2 & 4EI_2/L_2 + 4EI_3/L_3 \end{bmatrix} \begin{bmatrix} u1_3 \\ u2_3 \end{bmatrix}$$

On the left-hand side of the equals sign is a vertical list of the forces, the **force matrix p**. On the right-hand side there are two matrices. One has two rows each of two elements, the stiffness coefficients, and is the **stiffness matrix K**. The other has a vertical list of the displacements, the **displacement matrix u**. Now the two equations can be written as a **matrix equation**.

$$[p] = [K][u]$$

On the right-hand side of the matrix equation, two matrices, **K** and **u**, are multiplied together. The rule for matrix multiplication is that a row of the first matrix multiplies a column of the second matrix by multiplying the individual elements and adding them together. So for two matrices **A** and **B**, each with three rows and three columns, multiplication gives:

$$
\begin{bmatrix} a_{11} & a_{12} & a_{13} \\ a_{21} & a_{22} & a_{23} \\ a_{31} & a_{32} & a_{33} \end{bmatrix} \times \begin{bmatrix} b_{11} & b_{12} & b_{13} \\ b_{21} & b_{22} & b_{23} \\ b_{31} & b_{32} & b_{33} \end{bmatrix} = \begin{bmatrix} (a \times b)_{11} & (a \times b)_{12} & (a \times b)_{13} \\ (a \times b)_{21} & (a_{21} \times b_{12} + a_{22} \times b_{22} + a_{23} \times b_{32})_{22} & (a \times b)_{23} \\ (a \times b)_{31} & (a \times b)_{32} & (a \times b)_{33} \end{bmatrix}
$$

Here only the $(a \times b)_{22}$ element is shown in detail. As the matrix **u** only has one column, the multiplication of **K** and **u** results in a new matrix of only one column.

$$
\begin{bmatrix} 4EI_1/L_1 + 4EI_2/L_2 & 2EI_2/L_2 \\ 2EI_2/L_2 & 4EI_2/L_2 + 4EI_3/L_3 \end{bmatrix} \times \begin{bmatrix} u1_3 \\ u2_3 \end{bmatrix} = \begin{bmatrix} (4EI_1/L_1 + 4EI_2/L_2) \times u1_3 + (2EI_2/L_2) \times u2_3 \\ (2EI_2/L_2) \times u1_3 + (4EI_2/L_2 + 4EI_3/L_3) \times u2_3 \end{bmatrix}
$$

The result of the matrix multiplication is a matrix of one column with two elements. These elements are the expressions of the right-hand side of the two equilibrium equations given on page **408**. To save the constant writing of elements like $4EI_1/L_1 + 4EI_2/L_2$ the matrix equation can be rewritten as:

$$
\begin{bmatrix} p1_3 \\ p2_3 \end{bmatrix} = \begin{bmatrix} k_{11} & k_{12} \\ k_{21} & k_{22} \end{bmatrix} \begin{bmatrix} u1_3 \\ u2_3 \end{bmatrix}
$$

Using this matrix way of writing equations, it is now possible to write all the equations for the beam element using the new organised notation of **u**, **p** as

$$
\begin{bmatrix} p1_1 \\ p1_2 \\ p1_3 \\ \cdots \\ p2_1 \\ p2_2 \\ p2_3 \end{bmatrix} = \begin{bmatrix} EA/L & \circ & \circ & \vdots & -EA/L & \circ & \circ \\ \circ & 12EI/L^3 & 6EI/L^2 & \vdots & \circ & -12EI/L^3 & 6EI/L^2 \\ \circ & 6EI/L^2 & 4EI/L & \vdots & \circ & -6EI/L^2 & 2EI/L \\ \cdots & \cdots & \cdots & \vdots & \cdots & \cdots & \cdots \\ -EA/L & \circ & \circ & \vdots & EA/L & \circ & \circ \\ \circ & -12EI/L^3 & -6EI/L^2 & \vdots & \circ & 12EI/L^3 & -6EI/L^2 \\ \circ & 6EI/L^2 & 2EI/L & \vdots & \circ & -6EI/L^2 & 4EI/L \end{bmatrix} \begin{bmatrix} u1_1 \\ u1_2 \\ u1_3 \\ \cdots \\ u2_1 \\ u2_2 \\ u2_3 \end{bmatrix}
$$

The dotted lines show how the matrices can be divided into sub-matrices so this equation can now be written in an even more compact form as:

$$
\begin{bmatrix} P_1 \\ \cdots \\ P_2 \end{bmatrix} = \begin{bmatrix} K_{11} & \vdots & K_{12} \\ \cdots & \vdots & \cdots \\ K_{21} & \vdots & K_{22} \end{bmatrix} \begin{bmatrix} U_1 \\ \cdots \\ U_2 \end{bmatrix}
$$

Where **P₁** represents all the forces at **end 1**, **U₁** all the displacements at **end 1** and **K₁₁** the sub-matrix of stiffness coefficients that give **forces at end 1** due to **displacements at end 1**, and similarly for **end 2**. As can be seen from **Fig. 13.38** the general beam element is not joined to the 'rest of the world'. This is like the beam equation before it had any boundary conditions, see **Section 13.4**. Now suppose that the beam element is completely supported at **end 1**, and unsupported at **end 2**, in other words a cantilever. Furthermore let there be a downwards load of *P* at **end 2**.

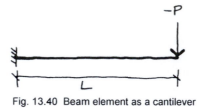

Fig. 13.40 Beam element as a cantilever

Now all the joint loads, except for $p2_2$, are zero as are all the displacements at **end 1**. And because there are no axial forces, the axial displacement $u2_1$ is also zero. This means there now only two unknowns, the displacements $u2_2$ and $u2_3$. This makes the equilibrium matrix equation look quite different:

$$
\begin{bmatrix} \circ \\ \circ \\ \circ \\ \cdots \\ -P \\ \circ \end{bmatrix} =
\begin{bmatrix}
\circ & \circ & \circ & \vdots & \circ & \circ & \circ \\
\circ & \circ & \circ & \vdots & \circ & \circ & \circ \\
\circ & \circ & \circ & \vdots & \circ & \circ & \circ \\
\cdots & \cdots & \cdots & \vdots & \cdots & \cdots & \cdots \\
\circ & \circ & \circ & \vdots & \circ & \circ & \circ \\
\circ & \circ & \circ & \vdots & \circ & 12EI/L^3 & -6EI/L^2 \\
\circ & \circ & \circ & \vdots & \circ & -6EI/L^2 & 4EI/L
\end{bmatrix}
\begin{bmatrix} \circ \\ \circ \\ \circ \\ \cdots \\ \circ \\ u2_2 \\ u2_3 \end{bmatrix}
$$

Where a stiffness coefficient, k_{11} for example, is multiplied by zero it is ineffective so it has been set to zero in the stiffness matrix. For this particular beam element the stiffness matrix has been **reduced** from 6 columns and 6 rows to 2 columns and 2 rows. In 'matrix language' the **6×6** matrix is reduced to a **2×2** matrix. So for the cantilever with a point load the equations are:

$$
\begin{bmatrix} -P \\ \circ \end{bmatrix} =
\begin{bmatrix} 12EI/L^3 & -6EI/L^2 \\ -6EI/L^2 & 4EI/L \end{bmatrix}
\begin{bmatrix} u2_2 \\ u2_3 \end{bmatrix}
$$

Example 13.18   For the cantilever shown, with $I = 3m^4$ and $E = $ 1E6 kN/m^2, write the equilibrium equations in matrix form.

−100 kN

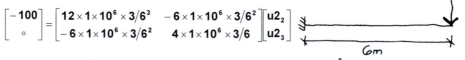

6m

$$
\begin{bmatrix} -100 \\ \circ \end{bmatrix} =
\begin{bmatrix} 12 \times 1 \times 10^6 \times 3/6^3 & -6 \times 1 \times 10^6 \times 3/6^2 \\ -6 \times 1 \times 10^6 \times 3/6^2 & 4 \times 1 \times 10^6 \times 3/6 \end{bmatrix}
\begin{bmatrix} u2_2 \\ u2_3 \end{bmatrix}
$$

evaluating the stiffness coefficients, and putting a factor of 1×10^6 outside the stiffness matrix, the equilibrium equations in matrix form are:

$$
\begin{bmatrix} -100 \\ \circ \end{bmatrix} = 1 \times 10^6
\begin{bmatrix} 0.167 & -0.5 \\ -0.5 & 2 \end{bmatrix}
\begin{bmatrix} u2_2 \\ u2_3 \end{bmatrix}
$$

Putting the equilibrium equations into matrix form, as in the example, does not provide the 'answer' because what are required are the values of the displacements $u2_2$ and $u2_3$, in other words the solution to the two simultaneous equations. This is done by using the **inverse matrix** of **K**, which is the matrix **K^{-1}**. To explain this a small amount of matrix algebra is required. For an ordinary algebraic equation like **y = 4x** for any value of **y** the unknown **x** is found by dividing each side of the equation by **4**. That is, multiplying each side by the inverse of **4** which is **¼**. So:

$$\frac{1}{4} \times \mathbf{y} = (\mathbf{4})^{-1} \times \mathbf{y} = \left(\frac{1}{4}\right) \times (\mathbf{4}) \times \mathbf{x} = (\mathbf{4})^{-1} \times (\mathbf{4}) \times \mathbf{x} = \mathbf{1} \times \mathbf{x} = \mathbf{x}$$

This lengthy derivation for the solution of the simple equation has been done to show the similarities between ordinary algebra and matrix algebra. Matrix algebra is very, but not completely, similar to ordinary algebra, so, using a similar derivation, the solution to the matrix equation [p] = [K][u] can be written as:

$$[\mathbf{K}]^{-1}[\mathbf{p}] = [\mathbf{K}]^{-1}[\mathbf{K}][\mathbf{u}] = [\mathbf{I}][\mathbf{u}] = [\mathbf{u}]$$

Here the matrix [I] is the **unit matrix** and functions in matrix multiplication as the number **1** does in ordinary multiplication, that is, it does not change the matrix it multiplies. The unit matrix has **1** for the diagonal elements and **0** elsewhere so:

$$\begin{bmatrix} 1 & 0 \\ 0 & 1 \end{bmatrix} \times \begin{bmatrix} a_{11} & a_{12} \\ a_{21} & a_{22} \end{bmatrix} = \begin{bmatrix} 1 \times a_{11} + 0 \times a_{21} & 1 \times a_{12} + 0 \times a_{22} \\ 0 \times a_{11} + 1 \times a_{21} & 0 \times a_{12} + 0 \times a_{22} \end{bmatrix} = \begin{bmatrix} a_{11} & a_{12} \\ a_{21} & a_{22} \end{bmatrix}$$

Or as matrix algebra: $[\mathbf{I}][\mathbf{A}] = [\mathbf{A}]$

So if $[\mathbf{K}]^{-1}[\mathbf{K}] = [\mathbf{I}]$ then $[\mathbf{K}]^{-1}$ is the inverse matrix of $[\mathbf{K}]$

So all that is required for any $[\mathbf{K}]$ is its inverse $[\mathbf{K}]^{-1}$, unfortunately this is not a simple matter. Methods for finding inverse matrices were devised a long time ago but the actual computation by hand calculations, except for quite small matrices, is almost impossible. The computer has changed all this. Now computers automatically assemble the matrices and then find their inverse. So the problem of inverting matrices, providing a computer is available, is a thing of the past. To see how it all works, but without explaining how they were obtained,[5] inverse matrices are used here.

Example 13.19   For the cantilever in **Example 13.18** using the given inverse matrix $\mathbf{K}^{-1}$ calculate the unknown displacements and draw a diagram of the cantilever showing the deflected shape.

The inverse matrix is given as $[\mathbf{K}]^{-1} = \dfrac{1}{10^6}\begin{bmatrix} 24 & 6 \\ 6 & 2 \end{bmatrix}$

As $[\mathbf{u}] = [\mathbf{K}]^{-1}[\mathbf{p}]$ then $\begin{bmatrix} u2_2 \\ u2_3 \end{bmatrix} = \dfrac{1}{10^6}\begin{bmatrix} 24 & 6 \\ 6 & 2 \end{bmatrix}\begin{bmatrix} -100 \\ 0 \end{bmatrix} = \dfrac{1}{10^6}\begin{bmatrix} -2400 \\ -600 \end{bmatrix}$

Giving the vertical displacement

$u2_2 = -2\,400 \div 10^6$ m $\equiv -2.4$ mm

and the rotation

$u2_3 = -600 \div 10^6$ radians $\equiv -0.034°$

$u2_2 = -2.4\,\text{mm}$

$u2_3 = -0.034°$

Exercise 13.4   Carry out the matrix multiplication for $\mathbf{K}^{-1} \times \mathbf{K}$ to get the unit matrix I.

Exercise 13.5   Enter the values for $u2_2$ and $u2_3$ obtained in **Example 13.19** into the slope deflection equations to obtain the bending moments and shear forces in the cantilever. Draw the **BMD** and the **SFD**.

To end this section a slightly more complicated structure, a two-span 'beam', is examined. The procedure follows that used for the single beam.

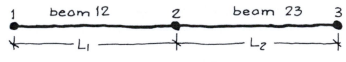

Fig. 13.41 General two-span 'beam'

Now the equilibrium matrix equation can be written in partition form, using sub-matrices as

$$
\begin{bmatrix} P_1 \\ \cdots \\ P_2 \\ \cdots \\ P_3 \end{bmatrix} = \begin{bmatrix} K_{11} & \vdots & K_{12} & \vdots & K_{13} \\ \cdots & \cdots & \cdots & \cdots & \cdots \\ K_{21} & \vdots & K_{22} & \vdots & K_{23} \\ \cdots & \cdots & \cdots & \cdots & \cdots \\ K_{31} & \vdots & K_{32} & \vdots & K_{33} \end{bmatrix} \begin{bmatrix} U_1 \\ \cdots \\ U_2 \\ \cdots \\ U_3 \end{bmatrix}
$$

The meaning of the sub-matrices is as before. The elements of the column matrices are sets of three forces and displacements at each joint. So for example P_1 is the sub-matrix of the forces $p1_1$, $p1_2$ and $p1_3$ at joint **1**, and U_3 is the sub-matrix of the displacements $u3_1$, $u3_2$ and $u3_3$ at joint **3**. The sub-matrices of the stiffness matrix are not quite so straightforward. The sub-matrices K_{11}, K_{12} and K_{21} are as before, see page **410**, but K_{22} now has to include the effect of both **beam 12** AND **beam 23**. This is because the force required to displace joint **2** is related to the stiffness of ALL the beam elements that are connected to the joint, see **Figs. 13.32 to 34**. By the same logic because **'end2'** of **beam 23** is NOT joined by the beam to joint **1** the sub-matrix K_{13} will be zero, as will K_{31}. The equilibrium matrix equation is now be written in detail:

$$
\begin{bmatrix} p1_1 \\ p1_2 \\ p1_3 \\ \cdots \\ p2_1 \\ p2_2 \\ p2_3 \\ \cdots \\ p3_1 \\ p3_2 \\ p3_3 \end{bmatrix} =
\begin{bmatrix}
\frac{EA_1}{L_1} & 0 & 0 & \vdots & -\frac{EA_1}{L_1} & 0 & 0 & \vdots & 0 & 0 & 0 \\[4pt]
0 & \frac{12EI_1}{L_1^3} & \frac{6EI_1}{L_1^2} & \vdots & 0 & -\frac{12EI_1}{L_1^3} & \frac{6EI_1}{L_1^2} & \vdots & 0 & 0 & 0 \\[4pt]
0 & \frac{6EI_1}{L_1^2} & \frac{4EI_1}{L_1} & \vdots & 0 & -\frac{6EI_1}{L_1^2} & \frac{2EI_1}{L_1} & \vdots & 0 & 0 & 0 \\[2pt]
\cdots & \cdots & \cdots & \vdots & \cdots & \cdots & \cdots & \vdots & \cdots & \cdots & \cdots \\[2pt]
-\frac{EA_1}{L_1} & 0 & 0 & \vdots & \frac{EA_1}{L_1}+\frac{EA_2}{L_2} & 0 & 0 & \vdots & -\frac{EA_2}{L_2} & 0 & 0 \\[4pt]
0 & -\frac{12EI_1}{L_1^3} & \frac{6EI_1}{L_1^2} & \vdots & 0 & \frac{12EI_1}{L_1^3}+\frac{12EI_2}{L_2^3} & -\frac{6EI_1}{L_1^2}+\frac{6EI_2}{L_2^2} & \vdots & 0 & -\frac{12EI_2}{L_2^3} & \frac{6EI_2}{L_2^2} \\[4pt]
0 & \frac{6EI_1}{L_1^2} & \frac{2EI_1}{L_1} & \vdots & 0 & -\frac{6EI_1}{L_1^2}+\frac{6EI_2}{L_2^2} & \frac{4EI_1}{L_1}+\frac{4EI_2}{L_2} & \vdots & 0 & -\frac{6EI_2}{L_2^2} & \frac{2EI_2}{L_2} \\[2pt]
\cdots & \cdots & \cdots & \vdots & \cdots & \cdots & \cdots & \vdots & \cdots & \cdots & \cdots \\[2pt]
0 & 0 & 0 & \vdots & -\frac{EA_2}{L_2} & 0 & 0 & \vdots & \frac{EA_2}{L_2} & 0 & 0 \\[4pt]
0 & 0 & 0 & \vdots & 0 & -\frac{12EI_2}{L_2^3} & -\frac{6EI_2}{L_2^2} & \vdots & 0 & \frac{12EI_2}{L_2^3} & -\frac{6EI_2}{L_2^2} \\[4pt]
0 & 0 & 0 & \vdots & 0 & \frac{6EI_2}{L_2^2} & \frac{2EI_2}{L_2} & \vdots & 0 & -\frac{6EI_2}{L_2^2} & \frac{4EI_2}{L_2}
\end{bmatrix}
\begin{bmatrix} u1_1 \\ u1_2 \\ u1_3 \\ \cdots \\ u2_1 \\ u2_2 \\ u2_3 \\ \cdots \\ u3_1 \\ u3_2 \\ u3_3 \end{bmatrix}
$$

As with the single beam element these two beam elements are not joined to the 'rest of the world', so they need supports, boundary conditions. Suppose at joints **1** and **2** the elements are pinned and there is a downward load of **P** at joint **3**.

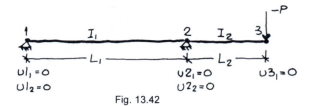

Fig. 13.42

Now five of the displacements are zero so the matrices are reduced in size by five to give:

$$\begin{bmatrix} p1_3 \\ p2_3 \\ p3_2 \\ p3_3 \end{bmatrix} = \begin{bmatrix} 0 \\ 0 \\ -P \\ 0 \end{bmatrix} = \begin{bmatrix} 4EI_1/L_1 & 2EI_1/L_1 & 0 & 0 \\ 2EI_1/L_1 & 4EI_1/L_1 + 4EI_2/L_2 & -6EI_2/L_2^2 & 2EI_2/L_2 \\ 0 & -6EI_2/L_2^2 & 12EI_2/L_2^3 & -6EI_2/L_2^2 \\ 0 & 2EI_2/L_2 & -6EI_2/L_2^2 & 4EI_2/L_2 \end{bmatrix} \begin{bmatrix} u1_3 \\ u2_3 \\ u3_2 \\ u3_3 \end{bmatrix}$$

Exercise 13.6   Carry out the matrix multiplication in the detail for the above equation to get the four slope deflection equations. (Hint: take great care with signs etc.)

Example 13.20   For the two-span beam shown, with $I = 3m^4$ and $E = 1E6\ kN/m^2$, write the equilibrium equations in matrix form. Using the given inverse matrix K^{-1} calculate the unknown displacements and draw a diagram showing them.

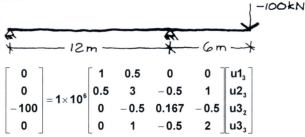

$$\begin{bmatrix} 0 \\ 0 \\ -100 \\ 0 \end{bmatrix} = 1 \times 10^6 \begin{bmatrix} 1 & 0.5 & 0 & 0 \\ 0.5 & 3 & -0.5 & 1 \\ 0 & -0.5 & 0.167 & -0.5 \\ 0 & 1 & -0.5 & 2 \end{bmatrix} \begin{bmatrix} u1_3 \\ u2_3 \\ u3_2 \\ u3_3 \end{bmatrix}$$

the inverse matrix K^{-1} is 'given' as:

$$[K]^{-1} = \frac{1}{10^6} \begin{bmatrix} 1.33 & -0.67 & -4 & -0.67 \\ -0.67 & 1.33 & 8 & 1.33 \\ -4 & 8 & 72 & 14 \\ -0.67 & 1.33 & 14 & 3.33 \end{bmatrix}$$

so now the unknown displacements are evaluated as:

$$\begin{bmatrix} u1_3 \\ u2_3 \\ u3_2 \\ u3_3 \end{bmatrix} = \frac{1}{10^6} \begin{bmatrix} 1.33 & -0.67 & -4 & -0.67 \\ -0.67 & 1.33 & 8 & 1.33 \\ -4 & 8 & 72 & 14 \\ -0.67 & 1.33 & 14 & 3.33 \end{bmatrix} \begin{bmatrix} 0 \\ 0 \\ -100 \\ 0 \end{bmatrix} = \frac{1}{10^6} \begin{bmatrix} 400 \\ -800 \\ -7200 \\ -1400 \end{bmatrix}$$

Giving the vertical displacement at joint 3 as $u3_2 = -7200 \div 10^6\ m \equiv -7.2mm$

and the rotations at the joints 1, 2 and 3 as $u1_3 = -400 \div 10^6$ radians $\equiv -0.024°$

$u2_3 = -800 \div 10^6$ radians $\equiv -0.046°$ and $u3_3 = -1400 \div 10^6$ radians $\equiv -0.08°$

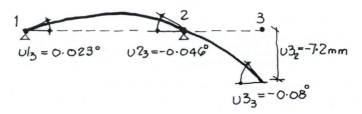

$U1_3 = 0.023°$ $U2_3 = -0.046°$ $U3_z = -7.2mm$

$U3_3 = -0.08°$

Exercise 13.7   Carry out the matrix multiplication for $\mathbf{K}^{-1} \times \mathbf{K}$ to get the unit matrix $\mathbf{I}$.
(Note: A more accurate result will be obtained by using the values as fractions rather than decimals.)

Exercise 13.8   Enter the values for the displacements obtained in **Example 13.20** into the slope deflection equations to obtain the bending moments and shear forces in the beams. Draw the **BMD** and the **SFD**.

The procedure for the stiffness method, for any given structure, can now be summarised as follows:

- **Calculate the stiffness matrices of the individual elements**

- **Assemble the structure stiffness matrix using the individual matrices**

- **Reduce the overall matrices by introducing the support conditions**

- **Obtain the inverse $\mathbf{K}^{-1}$ of the structure stiffness matrix**

- **Calculate the unknown joint displacements**

- **Use the calculated displacements to evaluate the forces in the beam elements**

Nowadays this analysis is almost always carried out by a computer. The structure geometry and loading are entered as data and the computer, by setting up and solving the matrix equation, calculates and outputs the displacements and member forces.

13.8 Summary

The inclusion of this chapter in what is, in many ways, an elementary book may seem strange. So why is it here? Reading and understanding this chapter will demand a considerable effort on the part of most readers and it is not necessary for getting the all-important conceptual understanding of structural behaviour. It is included however for several reasons, which are:

- **It allows the dedicated reader to move into the mathematical world of engineering**

- **It shows how the mathematical approach has become fundamental for the analysis of structures**

- **It illustrates why a split occurred between engineers and architects**

- **It shows how the mathematical approach uses the basic structural concepts**

- **It gives a deeper understanding of structural behaviour**

Only the outline of the mathematical approach is given here, whole books, even libraries, are dedicated to this subject. What is presented shows the essential points which are:

- **Derivation of governing differential equations**

- **Obtaining solutions to these equations where possible**

- **Developing programmable routines to deal with a variety of similar structures**

As complications are introduced such as two-dimensional elements, three-dimensional structures, the effect of buckling, dynamic loads, tapered elements, non-linear materials or large displacements, the mathematical description can become extremely complex. But when dealing with these complexities it is essential that the concepts are always clear.

References – Chapter 13

1   PJ Davis & R Hersh – **The mathematical experience** – Penguin Books 1983 – ISBN 0-14-02-2456-4
     p 244
2   AJ Sherlock et al - **Calculus** – Arnold 1982 – ISBN 0-7131-3446-1 – p 482-483
3   JT Oden & EA Ripperger – **Mechanics of elastic structures** – Hemisphere Pub. Co. 1967 – ISBN 0-07-
     047507-5 – p 171
4   FGJ Norton – **Advanced mathematics** – Pan Books 1982 – ISBN 0-330-29429-6, Ch. 19
5   ibid.

FURTHER READING

Buildings may seem innocently simple objects but they are often socially, culturally, aesthetically and technically complex, and this has generated a vast number of books, indeed there are specialist libraries devoted to them. Below is a selection of books covering various aspects of building design and construction. These will allow the reader to expand on the knowledge obtained from this book. Most of the books listed have been written with the general reader in mind and so avoid difficult technicalities, but some make technical demands which dedicated readers of the current book should be equipped to meet. Unfortunately some of the books listed are not currently in print but the effort of locating a copy should be rewarded.

The books are listed in author alphabetical order.

S Brand – **How buildings learn** – Viking 1994 – ISBN 0 670 83515 3

Written by the author of the 1960s alternative living bible the *"The Whole Earth Catalog"*, the book looks critically at how buildings are altered over time. Not written by a building professional, it is full of acute observations not 'professionally' prejudiced.

EJ O'Brien & AS Dixon – **Reinforced & Prestressed Concrete Design – The Complete Process** – Longman 1995 – ISBN 0-470-23365-6 (out of print)

This is a text book intended for engineering students and practitioners. It is recommended to those, for its clarity and explanation of structural design as a process, who want to understand structural engineering in some depth.

L Hellman – **Architecture A to Z – A rough guide** – Wiley – Academy

An irreverent cartoon history of architecture, to the point and often hilarious.

J Heyman – **The science of structural engineering** – Imperial College Press 1999 – ISBN 1-86094-189-3

An accessible non-mathematical outline to what tends to be a rather specialist subject.

A Holgate – **The art in structural design** – OUP 1986 – ISBN 0 19 356 177 6

An unusual book written by an engineering lecturer, it deals with many subjects not usually given much coverage. These include the 'engineer-architect relationship', the 'design process' and the 'generation of trial solutions'. The author is quite happy to give refreshingly forthright opinions.

HS Howard – **Structure an architect's approach** – McGraw Hill 1966 (out of print)

Sadly long out of print, the book opens with *"This book attempts to answer the question: 'What should an architect know about structure?'"*. Seven existing buildings are described in detail and simple calculations, in the spirit of **Chapter 12**, are included. These are carried out using Imperial units.

D Johnson – **Advanced structural mechanics** – Collins 1986 – ISBN 0-00-383165-5

A relatively accessible book with good illustrations and numerical examples on the more difficult aspects of structural theory. The non-technically trained reader may need some mathematical 'reinforcement'. One for those who enjoyed **Chapter 13**.

RJ Mainstone – **Developments in structural form** – Architectural Press 2001 – ISBN 0-750-6545-11 14 00 65032

This book deals, in a basically non-technical manner, with a large range of building structures. The basic structural actions are described and are illustrated by numerous examples from all periods. The author is an experienced engineer and a renowned authority on the history of engineering. A must.

A Orton – **The way we build now** – Chapman Hall 1988 – ISBN 0 419 15780 8

A unique book divided into basically two parts. The first part deals in depth with the technical aspects of buildings and includes a long section on structures. The second part of the book, the unique part, gives technical details, with drawings and photographs, of over seventy 20th century projects.

SN Pollalis – **What is a bridge?** – MIT Press 1999 – ISBN 0-262-16174-5

Describes in detail all the aspects of the design and construction of Santiago Calatrava's not universally admired bridge at Seville in Spain. The clear text is accompanied by numerical details and beautiful drawings. A rare opportunity to see how engineering is done.

B Risebero – **The story of Western architecure** – MIT Press 1985 – ISBN 0-262-68095-5 (out of print)

A masterly survey that explains how social, political and economic forces shape architecture. Copiously illustrated by the author's brilliantly clear drawings.

D Seward – **Understanding structures** – Macmillan 1994 – ISBN 0-333-54199-5

Intended as a text book it deals with structural concepts and calculations in a simple, clear and methodical way. Numerical calculations accompany the whole text. Can be seen as an extension of **Chapter 12**.

S Williams – **Hongkong Bank – The building of Norman Foster's masterpeice** – Jonathan Cape 1989 – ISBN 0-224-02490-6 (out of print)

A fascinating 'no holds barred' account of the design and building of what has become an icon of 20th century architecture. Light on hard technical detail but the reader will be able to 'read between the lines'.

INDEX

Note: In cases of frequently repeated words like force, load, etc the index lists the most important entries.